Crescents

Junior Cycle English for Second and Third Year

Philip Campion

Declan O'Neill

Karol Sadleir

The Educational Company of Ireland

First published 2015
The Educational Company of Ireland
Ballymount Road
Walkinstown
Dublin 12
www.edco.ie

A member of the Smurfit Kappa Group plc

ISBN 978-1-84536-354-3

Editors: Una Murray and Sarah Butler
Design and Layout: Identikit Design Consultants
Cover Design: Ann Marie Burke
Illustrators: Beatrice Bencivenni, Mike Phillips, Q2A Media Services Pvt. Ltd.

The paper used in this book comes from Managed Forests in Northern Europe For every tree felled, at least one new tree is planted

Photograph Acknowledgements
Alamy, Corbis, Getty Images, iStock, Rex Features, Shutterstock, Topfoto, Easkey Britton by Gerry Mooney, reproduced by kind permission of the *Sunday Independent*, Easkey Britton © Swilly, 'Lahinch' © Laura Hutton/Inpho, 'Whales' © John Cleary reprinted with permission, 'Jennifer Howitt Browing' © Andrew Crowley, 'Gary Soto' © Carolyn Soto, The Original Vampire Diaries – Dracula's Castle © Owen Sherwood, *Son of Rambow* film poster used with permission of StudioCanal, additional *Son of Rambow* material reprinted courtesy of Hammer & Tongs, and Maggie Ferreira, *The Shadow of a Gunman* © Jackie Jasperson, *The Shadow of a Gunman* © Richard Campbell, *Noughts & Crosses* photo by Keith Pattison © RSC, 'Benandonner' © James Battersby reprinted by permission www.jamesbattersby.co.uk, Of Mice and Men © Peter Coombs/Steppenwolf Theatre Company, Dorian Lockett photographed by Eric Chazankin reprinted by permission of the photographer and Cinnabar Theater in Petaluma, California, 'Rob the Squirrel' © Paul Williams, ISPCA website reprinted with permission, Blood Ivory © Asher Jay, Noticenature.ie, 'Monty the Penguin' © John Lewis, *Woman's Way* Front Cover Issue 11, March 24, 2015 used with permission, SafeFood.ie website reprinted by permission, Vendetta © Catherine Doyle 2015 reproduced with permission of Chicken House Ltd. All rights reserved, NASA.

All logos used by permission, all rights reserved.

Web references in this book are intended as a guide for teachers. At the time of going to press, all web addresses were active and contained information relevant to the topics in this book. However, The Educational Company of Ireland and the authors do not accept responsibility for the views or information contained on these websites. Content and addresses may change beyond our control and pupils should be supervised when investigating websites.

08A18

Contents

Digital Resources (available at www.edcodigital.ie)

Introduction

Crescents is first and foremost full of rich and interesting texts, the heart of good classroom experience.

The total *Crescents* package consists of this student textbook, a student Portfolio, a bank of digital resources (available on edcoDigital), a free *How to Create an e-Portfolio* e-book, a *Son of Rambow DVD* and a Teacher's Resource Book and CD.

As the new Specification states, thinking and learning in English begins in the oral domain. Therefore new and original resources are needed. *Crescents* is new and offers teachers a complete planning tool as they face into the new Junior Cert. It actively integrates the 39 learning outcomes of the Specification for Junior Cycle English under the three strands, oral language, reading and writing.

The opening page of each unit clearly states the aims and objectives of the unit in learner-friendly language and also lists the texts and extracts dealt with in that unit.

Crescents material reflects differentiation and is suitable for use by students of all abilities, with opportunities for the teacher to gauge which tasks to set on a whole class basis or on a more differentiated basis. The tasks are designed for paired and individual response, are interactive and aim to facilitate deep learning.

Crescents is organised into 16 carefully planned units that continually address the 39 learning outcomes. Many of the units explore a theme. For instance, Unit 1 contains a suite of non-literary texts exploring the theme of Ordinary Heroes; Unit 3 gives the student an exciting experience of the world of Gothic literature; while Unit 10, with its focus on media and message, is themed around care for animals.

Crescents contains a mixture of new texts, prescribed texts and well-loved favourites. There is a good balance of Irish and international authors. An extensive set of interesting and unusual poems offers a wide choice to teachers and students. Mini-anthologies of three poets aim to help students to understand the life of the poet through the poems.

The oral, writing and further creative activities in *Crescents* have inbuilt peer- and self-assessment opportunities as well as frequent opportunities for both formative and summative assessment.

The first exercises are always in oral form in order to engage learners and stimulate thinking. There is always an option of asking students to record their thoughts on these tasks. These are followed by deeper reading and exploration which lead to writing responses and very creative further activities.

Students have the opportunity to store a collection of their best responses and projects in the student Portfolio book that accompanies the textbook.

We believe that Second and Third Year learners who use *Crescents* should enjoy learning in and through English. We have set out to support learners to develop as skilled communicators, as listeners, speakers, readers and writers. *Crescents* will help students to grow personally through exploring and using language. Further, *Crescents* is designed to develop learners to appreciate and understand the content and structure of language.

The following elements are key to our approach:

····⟩ The three strands – **oral language**, **reading** and **writing** – are integrated throughout

····⟩ The key skills are embedded in the teaching approaches and student activities

····⟩ Guided by the learning outcomes, teachers and students are given clear guidance for each unit of work

····⟩ The learning outcomes are realised through engaging, differentiated and rich assessment tasks

····⟩ We provide rich texts in varied unit styles

····⟩ We emphasise the primacy of oral language as the basis for thinking and writing

····⟩ We offer structured group and pair work throughout

····⟩ e-Portfolio activities and other digital resources accompany each unit to enhance the students' learning experience

····⟩ We provide a scaffolded approach to writing as a process, with models of writing supplied

····⟩ We encourage peer learning; students become assessors of their own and others' work

····⟩ We provide opportunities for teachers to reflect on knowledge and skills acquired by the students.

We, the authors, thank Aisling Brennan who created the original Space Exploration unit for *Crescents*. We are equally grateful to Alicia McGivern for creating the highly informative unit on *Son of Rambow*. Special thanks also to Nick Goldsmith, Garth Jennings and David OReilly for their generous contributions to the *Son of Rambow* unit.

    We hope that learners will not only develop skills but will continually come back to them and improve them. After all, the learning outcomes are not an end in themselves; rather they represent a rich and varied growth path.

Philip Campion
Declan O'Neill
Karol Sadleir

Audio material, student Portfolio/e-Portfolio activities and digital resources are referenced throughout the textbook using the following icons:

 Audio: recordings of poems, extracts etc. (available on the teacher's CD)

 Audio: exclusive interviews with journalists, authors and actors (available at **www.edcodigital.ie**)

 Templates and tables in the student Portfolio connect to exploration and creative activities in the textbook

 e-Portfolio activity for each unit, with step-by-step guidelines available in your *How to Create an e-Portfolio* e-book on how to create and use e-Portfolio systems and how to build digital artefeacts

 Digital presentations in the classroom to support learning and encourage student engagement

 Animated tutorials based on grammar topics and other useful information, with follow-up worksheets in the Teacher's Resource Book

Teachers can access the exclusive interviews, the free *How to Create an e-Portfolio e-book*, the PowerPoints and animations online at **www.edcodigital.ie**.

Ordinary Heroes

In this unit you will:

····▸ experience non-fiction texts about people and animals who are regarded as heroes

····▸ read a range of different writing from newspaper and online reports, to war stories and biography

····▸ examine how different types of hero can appeal to different people

····▸ prepare and deliver an oral presentation on your hero.

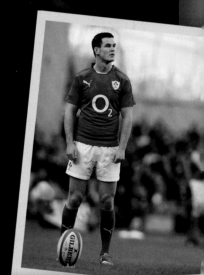

You will encounter the following texts:

- An article on Easkey Britton from the *Sunday Independent*

- Two reports on animals from *The Kerryman* and *TheJournal.ie*

- A newspaper report from *The Telegraph* on the Paralympian Jennifer Howitt Browning

- An extract from *Small Wars Permitting* by Christina Lamb

- An audio interview with a former Irish army Captain on life in war-torn countries

- An extract from *Marley and Me* by John Grogan

- An extract from *The Test* by Brian O'Driscoll

Sunday Independent

Easkey: surf's new role model

The five-time Irish surf champion Easkey Britton seems to have been born for the sport, writes Sophie White, and now she's busy coaching a new generation of enthusiasts, especially girls, in a sport that remains male-dominated.

'Somehow your body stays in one piece, but it's like being in a bomb explosion. You hear this roar behind you and then it all starts to get dark . . . If you stay conscious, you're OK.'

Easkey Britton is the five-time Irish national surf champion, a PhD student, big-wave rider, journalist, artist and marine conservationist. She knows a little something about balance. Easkey is the daughter of Ireland's 'first family' of surfing. Together with her sister Becky-Finn, she grew up balanced on a surf board, more often than not riding the very wave that she is named after.

For the Brittons, surfing is very much a family affair. Becky-Finn recalls with a laugh

that growing up in their house, everything from mealtimes to bedtime was arranged to accommodate the surf. Dad, the surfer and artist Barry Britton, would bring the girls surfing before and after school. 'We'd get out of the uniform and into the wetsuit in the time it took to get from school to the beach or I'd arrive into school and my hair would still be wet and I'd be a bit late with a note saying I had been at the dentist!'

Even at this young age, however, Easkey appreciated the need for balance in her life. She credits her parents for keeping her focused and encouraging her academic interests as well as her surfing.

'I did well in school, I think because I had my passion and energy focused in something else that was healthy and that gave me a good grounding.'

At the age of 16, Easkey had the opportunity to travel to Tahiti and ride the fearsome Teahupoo wave.

There was much debate in the family about whether she could go, which is unsurprising as Teahupoo translates as 'place of skulls' and has claimed the lives of five surfers. In the end, she did go and credits the trip as a real turning point in her career. It was the first time Easkey had surfed with other girls her age who shared her drive and enthusiasm.

It also gave her her first taste of big-wave riding.

The surf scene in Ireland is growing more focused on riding the awesome giants found at places like Mullaghmore and the Cliffs of Moher.

In order to surf these waves, the surfers team up with jet-ski drivers who can tow the surfer onto the wave.

This allows surfers to surf waves that were previously inaccessible or impossible to catch with just paddle power. It has also made surfing these spots safer (Easkey is active in the Irish Tow Surf Rescue Club).

Tow-in surfing is a team sport and with the expertise of her cousin Neil on the jet-ski, Easkey became the first woman to tow-surf the famous Aileen's Wave at the Cliffs of Moher at just 21 years of age.

Teahupoo wave, Tahiti

Aileen's wave, Cliffs of Moher

In videos of her surfing, Easkey looks incredibly vulnerable as she speeds down the faces of these giants.

'When you're on the wave I don't think you breathe, you're just thinking let me make it,' as indeed her family are probably thinking back on shore.

It does sound like being 'a bit nuts' may be a requirement for this way of life. The build-up to a big wave sounds excruciating. There are sleepless nights before the big day. Usually launching the jet-skis can take quite a while and once the teams are out past the surf they will sit and observe conditions for quite a while before any attempt is made to catch a wave.

The wait can be nerve-wracking and then making the decision to go for it even harder – 'it's really tough because, of course, every fibre of your being is usually screaming "what are you doing?" So you have to have that thing in your mind that you can just switch off and focus,' she says.

Focus is definitely not something Easkey Britton is lacking. This year, her surfing provided therapy during the stressful final year of her PhD in marine science, and although she took a step back from competition she found time to focus more on coaching. The surf world is still very male-dominated – 'you only have to look at the world surf tour and see what the guys get as prize money and see the girls getting about half that. The woman's world number one, Melanie Redman, couldn't get any sponsorship because of her age,' she says.

Easkey enjoys having more time to mentor the new generation of surfers, especially the younger girls entering a male-dominated sport.

After her enormous success in the last few years on both the national and international surf scene, Easkey was not wary of stepping back.

'Surfing is just a way of being . . . competition for me has always been about testing yourself and meeting other people. I've never been one to have a game plan . . . I'll just wait for the next big swell and take it from there.'

Oral exploration

1 How did Easkey get her name?

2 Why does she love surfing?

3 Apart from being a surfing champion, what else has Easkey achieved?

4 How does she show that her interest in surfing helped her to do well in school?

5 Why was there such concern in her family when she wanted to surf the Teahupoo wave in Tahiti?

6 Why does Easkey think that surfing is male-dominated and what is she doing to change this? Does it make her heroic in any way?

Read, write, explore

1 The reporter says, 'Easkey Britton seems to have been born for the sport'. Why does the writer think that this is true?

2 'When you're on the wave I don't think you breathe, you're just thinking let me make it.' Easkey describes the experience on the big waves as being both scary and exciting. Write out some of the phrases or sentences she uses. Use them to write a short account of a surfing experience.

3 With your partner, write down some facts about the character and life of Easkey and then write a short character profile of her. Here are some headings you might use:

⋯⊱ Age   ⋯⊱ Education   ⋯⊱ Family background

⋯⊱ Personal strengths   ⋯⊱ Achievements   ⋯⊱ Ambitions

Exploring the Beaufort scale

Easkey gives a very vivid description of her experience out on the ocean as she rides the big waves.

> Somehow your body stays in one piece, but it's like being in a bomb explosion. You hear this roar behind you and then it all starts to get dark . . . If you stay conscious, you're OK.

Before going out to sea, surfers should consult the Irish National Meteorological Service (Met Éireann) to find out wind speeds and the general state of the weather in order to ensure their safety. If the weather is really bad, it would be too dangerous to surf.

Storms in Lahinch, County Clare. © Laura Hutton/Inpho

Weather is measured using many different methods. The Beaufort scale is one of them. It is a way of accurately describing wind forces and the weather conditions they cause – from the very calm to the very stormy. It was created by an Irishman, Francis Beaufort, who was born in Navan, County Meath, in 1774. It is now used in the weather forecasts to warn sailors and travellers of dangers that might arise.

The Beaufort scale

Force	Conditions	Wind Speed (mph)	Effects on Land	Effects on sea
0	Calm	Under 1	Calm; smoke rises vertically	Sea like a mirror
1	Light Air	1-3	Smoke drift indicates wind direction; weather vanes do not move	Ripples only
2	Light Breeze	4-7	Wind felt on face; leaves rustle; vanes begin to move	Small wavelets
3	Gentle Breeze	8-12	Leaves, small twigs in constant motion; light flags extended	Large wavelets; crests begin to break
4	Moderate Breeze	13-18	Dust, leaves and loose paper raised off ground; small branches move	Small waves; some 'white horses'
5	Fresh Breeze	19-24	Small trees begin to sway	Moderate waves; many 'white horses'
6	Strong Breeze	25-31	Large branches of trees in motion; whistling sound in wires can be heard	Large waves; probably some spray
7	Near Gale	32-38	Whole trees moving; resistance felt when walking against wind	Mounting sea; foam
8	Gale	39-46	Twigs and small branches broken off trees	Moderately high waves
9	Strong Gale	47-54	Slight structural damage; slates blown from roofs	High waves; dense foam; visibility affected
10	Storm	55-63	Seldom experienced on land; trees broken; structural damage occurs	Very high waves; visibility impaired; sea surface looks white
11	Violent Storm	64-72	Very rarely experienced on land; usually with widespread damage	Exceptionally high waves; poor visibility
12	Hurricane	73 or higher	Violence and destruction	14-metre-high waves; air filled with foam and spray; visibility bad

Test your reading of the Beaufort scale

Watch the weather forecast on TV tonight and pay attention to what the presenter says about the wind. Then do the exercises on the Beaufort scale below.

Note: Beaufort number is now referred to as 'Force'. So Beaufort 1 = Force 1, Beaufort 2 = Force 2, and so on.

1 What sea conditions would you expect at sea when the wind is Force 2?

2 How would trees behave in a Force 7 wind?

3 If the wind speed is 20.8–24.4 m/s, what is that speed in miles per hour?

4 What conditions at sea would you expect to see in such a wind?

5 What advice would you give to someone travelling by car in your local area in a wind that is Force 10?

6 As the wind speed increases, which seems more terrifying – being in a boat or being on land? Explain your choice.

Create

Prepare and deliver a short oral communication on a hobby or an activity that interests you. Perhaps it is reading, singing, listening to music or playing a sport.

Use some of the following questions as prompts to help you to structure your presentation:

1 What is my hobby? Give a very brief description.

2 How/when did it start?

3 Is there any hero who inspires your interest?

4 Why?

5 What other people share your interest or hobby?

6 Why would you recommend your hobby to other students in your class?

Two rescue reports

Save the whales and dolphins!

A pilot whale

Background

Pilot whales, like the killer whale, are members of the dolphin family, and share the characteristic intelligence of the bottlenose dolphin. They are extremely large, second only to the killer whale in size. Pilot whales share a strong social bond and often congregate in groups of over a hundred.

You will now read two reports from different media sources on the rescue of whales and dolphins in County Kerry.

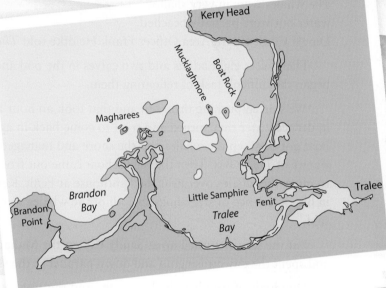

Tralee Bay

Before you read

Are you more concerned about the welfare of wild animals than that of domesticated animals?

Report 1

The Kerryman

Rescuers save the whales

The story of the rescue of a pod of pilot whales in Tralee Bay last week generated huge publicity nationally and beyond these shores.

The drama began on Wednesday when a young local woman spotted the whales in shallow water at Derrymore, near Tralee, and raised the alarm. Valentia Coast Guard then tasked the Dingle Coast Guard unit who sent five members to the location.

▶ **Animation**

Verbs and nouns

Have you ever noticed how the same word, for example, *spot,* can function as a verb or adjective in one form, *spotted*, and as a noun in another form, *spot*? As you read the first report make a note of any verb that can function as a noun in another form.

'I contacted the Whale and Dolphin Group and also Kevin Flannery of Dingle Oceanworld. There were wildlife rangers at the scene and also Paddy Fenton, the County Veterinary Officer. It appears that one or two of the adult whales were sick or injured and had almost stranded themselves on the beach and had been followed by the rest. The whales were in very shallow water but were partially beached,' Dingle Coast Guard Area Officer Frank Heidtke told *The Kerryman*.

There were eight adults and two calves in the pod and rescue workers and volunteers began the difficult task of refloating them.

'We started pushing them out and that took an hour and a half. But when the whales were in deeper water they turned and tried to come back in again. The Fenit RNLI inshore rescue boat got between the whales and the shore and managed to shepherd them into the deeper waters of Tralee Bay. Then the big lifeboat came out from Fenit and the two boats managed to move the whales over near the lighthouse at Fenit. Kevin Flannery said it was the first time in his experience of strandings that all of the whales were successfully refloated,' Mr Heidtke said.

But the whales turned up at Sandy Bay on the Maharees peninsula the following morning and spent the day cruising up and down parallel to the shore.

Hundreds of people visited the scene and the area experienced some serious traffic congestion.

Members of the National Park and Wildlife Service (NPWS), Kerry County Council, the Irish Whale and Dolphin Group (IWDG) and Gardaí were on duty at the scene.

'We're expecting them to come ashore again and if we can isolate the one the others are following then we can put it down. If we do that the rest will be refloated and we expect them to return to deeper waters. I will give the sick whale a lethal injection but if that doesn't work we may have to shoot it,' Paddy Fenton told *The Kerryman*.

The possibility of having to shoot the whale in front of hundreds of people on a public beach was an option that did not appeal to the authorities.

As the day wore on Dr Simon Berrow of the IWDG briefed the crowd on these options and explained what steps were going to be taken.

'This is a difficult situation for the whales but it's a privilege for you because these creatures are rarely found close to land. They are members of the dolphin family and can be quite aggressive. They even bully the sperm whales which are ten times their size,' he said.

Then he and a number of wildlife rangers went outside the whales in a dinghy and tried to push them ashore but it didn't work.

There was no trace of the pod in Tralee Bay on Friday, which came as a relief to all involved. However, the whales were back in Sandy Bay on Saturday evening but disappeared again over the weekend.

Report 2

Fishermen rescue massive family of 70 dolphins beached in west Kerry

A common dolphin

The incident has been described as 'highly unusual' by a local expert.

A group of Kerry fishermen have been praised for rescuing as many as 70 dolphins from a beach yesterday.

The beaching, described as 'highly unusual', was spotted when three lobster pot fishermen were heading out to sea at 7am in Smerwick Harbour.

The fishermen, along with director of Dingle Oceanworld Aquarium Kevin Flannery, worked for hours to move the animals to safety.

'We removed the calves first,' Flannery told *TheJournal.ie*. 'There was about fifteen of them, I've never seen so many in a pod before.'

'My figuring was that the calves that were fully ashore had gotten stuck there while chasing mackerel. Their screeching attracted the older dolphins, who were caught in shallow water, who in turn got stuck as well.

'Using the fishermens' boats, we transported the younger dolphins out to sea, and then encouraged and herded the older ones out of the harbour.'

He said that the fishermen deserve 'enormous praise', as all three gave up a day's work to carry out the rescue.

Flannery added that beachings like this, although rare, have occurred in other countries.

Oral exploration

Discuss the following with your group or partner:

Report 1

1 Decide on three important facts about the rescue of the whales.

2 What problems did the rescuers encounter?

3 Name two people involved in the rescue. What did they do?

4 How did the rescuers propose to deal with the sick whales?

5 What is your opinion of their policy? Think of both sides of the argument.

Report 2

1 Why had the dolphin calves beached?

2 Why did the older dolphins follow the calves?

3 How did the fishermen deal with the situation?

4 Why did the fishermen deserve praise? Do you consider them to be heroes?

Comparing reports

Make a judgement of both reports under the following headings and decide which is the better report.

Portfolio 1A

- **Use of facts:** Which report makes better use of facts to inform the reader?
- **Use of quotations:** Which article makes better use of quotations? Write out the quotations that you think were interesting and informative.
- **Drama:** Which report is more dramatic?
- **Informative:** Which report did you learn most from?

Create

Work in groups. Imagine that you and your group are the online reporters for the local paper in Tralee and are responsible for the Twitter feed for the newspaper. You have just heard about the events in the bay. Work with a partner to order the sequence of events and then rewrite the events of the report as a series of tweets. Use the Twitter page in your Portfolio.

Portfolio 1B

Overcoming disaster

Background

Here is a newspaper report on the Paralympian gold medallist Jennifer Howitt Browning. Jennifer had a serious fall in her local park when she was nine years old and lost the use of her legs.

Before you read

What is the worst possible thing that could happen to you today? Describe it to your partner. Describe how you might cope with the situation.

The Telegraph

'Let's keep the Paralympic legacy going and change lives'

© *Andrew Crowley*

When Jennifer Howitt Browning was nine years old she broke her back in a fall at a summer camp in San Francisco. The blonde youngster, known as Jen, whose world centred on playing football, didn't smile for a year. 'My main thought as I sat in my wheelchair was, "Poor me",' Jen, now thirty, admits.

A year later her father, David Howitt, took her to a basketball group for children with disabilities and after twelve months of saying 'no' to playing, she gave it a try. 'It was a Eureka moment,' she smiles as her face lights up.

'But it wasn't until 2000 when I went to see the film *Billy Elliot*, about a boy who wanted to be a ballet dancer, that I could express how it made me feel. Just before the film ends Billy auditions for a ballet school and an examiner asks how dancing makes him feel.

'He said, "Like a bird, and so free." It was exactly what playing basketball did for me. It made me believe I could still do what I wanted to, and anything else with my life.'

She went on to win a gold medal at the Paralympics in Athens in 2004 with the United States basketball team, and coached the British women's Paralympic basketball team (they came seventh).

* * * *

The Paralympics showed the world what can be done, and helping to motivate and empower those with similar injuries to herself is, Jen says, 'closest to my heart'.

'There is always a sense of loss after an accident and I want to help people find the catalyst that moves them on.

'After a spinal injury it is natural to grieve for the life you have lost. But it is a different form of grief to losing a member of your family. This, at some level, stays with you.'

'The important thing with a disability is to think about life in a different way, otherwise the grief becomes a deadweight. Sport did that for me and I wouldn't change what happened when I was nine. All the amazing things I've done have been because of my accident.'

* * * *

Jen became team captain and later joined the US team. 'Winning gold in 2004 in Athens was amazing. Dad's prime aim after the accident was to find something to make it all right for me, and when he saw me after the medal ceremony he said, "I am so proud of you." He, mum and I then lost it and cried our hearts out. It was one of the best moments of my life.

'The subsequent two months were amazing, too. Not only had I won a gold medal but I fell in love with Mike [Browning] and won a Rhodes scholarship to Oxford University to do a masters in international development.'

Mike, an English engineer, and Jen met in Australia where she studied for a year as part of her degree in international politics. That summer he came to visit her in the States, and they married in 2009.

They now live near Bristol where he runs his own bicycle shop.

Oral exploration

1 What was Jen's first reaction to her disability?

2 How did her father help her to make progress?

3 Describe the effect of the film *Billy Elliot* on Jen.

4 Describe the success that Jen has enjoyed as a Paralympian.

5 What did you learn about Jen from reading this article?

6 Would you consider her to have been heroic in her response to her difficulty?

Read, write, explore

1 Look at the photograph of Jen at the start of the article. What does this photo tell you about her success in life and about her personal happiness?

2 Discuss with your partner what you learned about coping with disability and the importance of support. Write down the advice you would give to people who are tasked with helping others to cope with unexpected life-changing experiences like Jen's.

3 Write what you imagine Jen's diary might say over the course of her life so far. Write four entries in your Portfolio. Here are some suggested moments:

Portfolio 1C

- She has been told she will never walk again.
- She sees the film *Billy Elliot*.
- She wins Olympic Gold as her parents look on.
- She meets Mike Browning, her future husband.

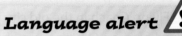
Language alert

When? The uses of the past and present tense

Here is another quote from the original article.

> My dad understood how much I needed sport in my life, but when he told me he had found a basketball club for children with disabilities I replied, 'I don't want to hang out with other people in wheelchairs.' It took a year before I tried it, but I was hooked the moment I held the ball. I joined the club and the individuals there became my second family. Travelling round the country playing matches built up my confidence.

There are twelve examples of past-tense verbs in this paragraph. The past tense is used to show that the actions occurred at a definite time before the present.

1 Underline in blue the past-tense verbs in this extract.

There is one use of the present tense, in a negative sentence. Underline it in red.

Why is that single verb in the present tense? Select an answer:
(a) The reporter actually should have used all past-tense verbs.
(b) Jen is telling the reporter exactly what she said to her father at the time.
(c) All quotes must be in the present tense.
(d) The present tense is best for expressing anger.

In pairs compare your answers.

Rule: To make the past tense in English the rule is that you add 'ed' or 'd' or change 'y' to 'ied'. For example, join/joined and try/tried.

2 Form the past-tense of each of the following:
···⟩ blend, commence, conquer, cry, hate, join, lie, mutter, need, phone, seem, waste

3 Some of the past-tense verbs in the Jennifer Howitt paragraph above do not follow this rule. They are called irregular verbs, for example, build/built.

4 List the six other irregular past-tense verbs used in the paragraph quoted above.

5 What is the present tense of the following ten past-tense forms of irregular verbs?
···⟩ bent, broadcast, froze, hung, led, lent, meant, rang, rose, swam

War reporting

Christina Lamb

Background

Christina Lamb always wanted to write and decided to become a journalist to have some adventures and make some money. She says, 'I was twenty-one when I set off to live in the frontier town of Peshawar to report on the war in Afghanistan, and I had absolutely no idea what foreign correspondents needed – or did for that matter. I could hardly carry my suitcase, which contained lots of novels including a dog-eared copy of Rudyard Kipling's *Kim*, a supply of wine gums, a bottle of Chanel perfume, Mahler's Fifth, and a pink felt rabbit. I will never forget getting off the Flying Coach in the old city just as the sun was setting, struggling with this oversized case, and being surrounded by rickshaws honking and people trying to sell me things, and realising I didn't have a clue where I was going to stay.'

In the following extract Lamb describes her experience of patrolling with British troops in Helmand province, Afghanistan. American and British forces invaded Afghanistan in response to the attacks on the Twin Towers in New York on 11 September 2001. The Taliban (an Afghani-armed group) opposed their invasion.

Before you read

If you haven't experienced war at first hand, try to describe the images of war or violence that you have seen on TV. What makes them distressing?

Extract from

Small Wars Permitting

We sat on a raised bank at the edge of the field under a mulberry tree along with a few other men, one of whom seemed to be glaring at us from under his sparkly prayer cap. 'We are British not Americans,' explained the major through an interpreter. 'We come at the invitation of your government as friends and brothers to help you and find out what you need.'

An old man with a white beard said the other elders were at the mosque for prayers. (Later we would realise it was not prayer time.) He said the village had no problems and suggested we come back for tea two days later on Thursday at 10 a.m. when everyone would be around. As we took our leave, he pointed in the opposite direction to the way we had come. 'If you go that way there is a bridge,' he said.

Afghans are the most hospitable people on earth, offering everything when they have nothing. I was thinking it was unlike them not to offer tea to visitors, but Major Blair seemed happy. 'I think that went well – they seemed quite friendly,' he said to me as we walked away.

Almost immediately a burst of gunfire rang out from the ridge to the left where the FSG[1] was deployed. 'We've had a contact,' crackled the message over the radio.

They had spotted a gathering of twelve to fourteen men dressed in black and armed. Two of the support group's vehicles had peeled off to try to intercept them, but as they did so RPGs[2] started to rain in on the support base – followed by small-arms fire.

For a moment we stood staring up at the ridge listening to the gunfire and explosions. Then we started walking again through a field, looking for the bridge.

Within seconds we heard the staccato crack of Kalashnikovs.

* * * *

As I looked up, a rocket-propelled grenade flew over our heads about ten feet above, bursting in the field near a group of paras[3] who had made the sprint in better time.

I struggled back to my knees in time to see the first mortar round land exactly where we had been only half a minute earlier. The troops returned fire. A prolonged burst of rapid machine-gun and rifle fire. Then, using white phosphorus grenades as cover, they moved left to take up firing positions behind the ridge.

Again we were diving to the ground to avoid incoming fire, but this time it was to our left flank[4] as well as the original direction. Feeling very exposed, we returned fire and ran back to a ridge along the field at right angles to our position.

Once again we took incoming fire, this time from behind us. Their mortars were mercifully slow at retargeting and they fell where we had just left.

All around me was shouting and screaming. The two platoons had been scattered by the ferocity of the ambush. In the deep ditches their radios were not working. The soldiers were releasing canisters of red or green smoke to show each other their positions, even though this would reveal them to the Taliban too.

The firing came back again and again, wave after wave of it, with hardly any break between. The eight-foot-deep irrigation ditches which criss-crossed the fields had turned into trenches. In and out of them we climbed, slipping and falling in the muddy water as the paras tried to regroup, yelling instructions I did not understand like 'Go firm!' which means stay still.

'When we shout "rapid fire!", run,' yelled Corporal Matt D'Arcy as we crouched in yet another ditch. 'Rapid fire!' he screamed and ears ringing amid a clatter of heavy fire that I could not identify as ours or theirs, I forced myself to climb out of the trench.

*   *   *   *

I thought about my husband Paulo and our six-year-old son Lourenço back home in East Sheen, south-west London; of the World Cup birthday party Lourenço was due to have on Sunday afternoon; and how stupid it would be to die in this Helmand field from a Taliban bullet.

In my belt purse were some of Lourenço's toy cars and pens he had given me for the 'poor children of Afghanistan'. I had taken them to the village but never got a chance to give them out. I had to survive and the image of my son's face kept me running and jumping into yet another trench.

[1] **FSG:** Fire Support Group; [2] **RPGs:** rocket-propelled grenades; [3] **paras:** paratroopers; [4] **flank:** side.

Oral exploration

1 How do you know from paragraph one that the soldiers are not very welcome?

2 Major Blair says, 'I think that went well'. How is he proven wrong?

3 Do you consider Lamb to be calm under fire? Discuss why or why not. Is she brave? Could she be considered a hero?

4 How did thoughts of her family at home help her to deal with the situation of war?

Read, write, explore

1 Christina Lamb soon becomes suspicious of the Afghanis that she has met. Describe the signs that warn her that she and the British soldiers may be in danger. What do we learn from this about her skills as a reporter?

2 Descriptive language

Read again the three paragraphs beginning, 'All around me was shouting and screaming'.

(a) From the *first* paragraph pick out one sentence that gives you a strong sense of the battle. Write down a reason as to why it does its job well.

(b) The following sentences and phrases are taken from the *second* paragraph. They convey a sense of how chaotic battle is.

'The firing came back again and again, wave after wave of it, with hardly any break between.'

How does the writer make this description dramatic?

'. . . ditches which criss-crossed the fields had turned into trenches.'

How is this sentence suggestive of the First World War?

'In and out of them we climbed, slipping and falling in the muddy water . . .'

Write out the words that suggest movement and say how they help you to picture the chaos of the situation.

(c) Describe how Lamb brings the battle to life in the *third* paragraph. Mention the use of **dialogue**, a **strong image** and **strong verbs**.

Crescents interview

1 Listen to the *Crescents* interview with Dr Tom Clonan, a former army Captain. Note his comments on the following:

- His experiences of army life
- His experiences of war zones
- His comments on the extract

2 What similarities/differences are there between the experiences of Christina Lamb and Captain Clonan?

Create

Prepare and deliver orally a report for radio news. Work with a partner.

⋯⟩ Watch a bulletin of news about a troubled area of the world. Look up images that show life in this place. Find reports about the situation. Take down notes, facts and figures.

⋯⟩ Decide on your joint opinion as to what should be done to help solve the problem.

⋯⟩ Now assemble and deliver your own first-hand report based on what you have learned.

⋯⟩ The communication should be about two minutes.

The perfect dog

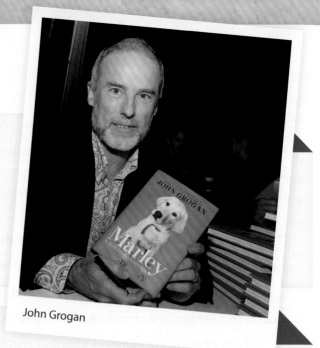

John Grogan

Background

John Grogan is an award-winning journalist who lives in Pennsylvania in the United States with his wife Jenny and their three children. In this biographical extract, Grogan recalls getting his first dog and how he grew to love him.

Before you read

What is your favourite animal? Talk about the two or three things about the animal that make you like it.

Extract from

MARLEY AND ME

In the summer of 1967, when I was ten years old, my father caved in to my persistent pleas and took me to get my own dog. Together we drove in the family station wagon far into the Michigan countryside to a farm run by a rough-hewn woman and her ancient mother. The farm produced just one commodity – dogs. Dogs of every imaginable size and shape and age and temperament. They had only two things in common: each was a mongrel of unknown and indistinct ancestry, and each was free to a good home. We were at a mutt ranch.

'Now, take your time, son,' Dad said. 'Your decision today is going to be with you for many years to come.'

I quickly decided the older dogs were somebody else's charity case. I immediately raced to the puppy cage. 'You want to pick one that's not timid,' my father coached. 'Try rattling the cage and see which ones aren't afraid.'

I grabbed the chain-link gate and yanked on it with a loud clang. The dozen or so puppies reeled backward, collapsing on top of one another in a squiggling heap of fur. Just one remained. He was gold with a white blaze on his chest, and he charged the gate, yapping fearlessly. He jumped up and excitedly licked my fingers through the fencing. It was love at first sight.

I brought him home in a cardboard box and named him Shaun. He was one of those dogs that give dogs a good name. He effortlessly mastered every command I taught him and was naturally well behaved. I could drop a crust on the floor and he would not touch it until I gave the okay. He came when I called him and stayed when I told him to. We could let him out alone at night, knowing he would be back after making his rounds.

Not that we often did, but we could leave him alone in the house for hours, confident he wouldn't have an accident or disturb a thing. He raced cars without chasing them and walked beside me without a leash. He could dive to the bottom of our lake and emerge with rocks so big they sometimes got stuck in his jaws. He loved nothing more than riding in the car and would sit quietly in the backseat beside me on family road trips, content to spend hours gazing out the window at the passing world. Perhaps best of all, I trained him to pull me through the neighbourhood dog-sled-style as I sat on my bicycle, making me the hands-down envy of my friends. Never once did he lead me into hazard.

He was with me when I smoked my first cigarette (and my last) and when I kissed my first girl. He was right there beside me in the front seat when I snuck out my older brother's Corvair for my first joyride.

Shaun was spirited but controlled, affectionate but calm. He even had the dignified good manners to back himself modestly into the bushes before squatting to do his duty, only his head peering out. Thanks to this tidy habit, our lawn was safe for bare feet.

Relatives would visit for the weekend and return home determined to buy a dog of their own, so impressed were they with Shaun – or 'Saint Shaun,' as I came to call him. It was a family joke, the saint business, but one we could almost believe. Born with the curse of uncertain lineage, he was one of the tens of thousands of unwanted dogs in America. Yet by some stroke of almost providential good fortune, he became wanted. He came into my life and I into his – and in the process, he gave me the childhood every kid deserves.

The love affair lasted fourteen years, and by the time he died I was no longer the little boy who had brought him home on that summer day. I was a man, out of college and working across the state in my first real job. Saint Shaun had stayed behind when I moved on. It was where he belonged. My parents, by then retired, called to break the news to me. My mother would later tell me, 'In fifty years of marriage I've only seen your father cry twice. The first time was when we lost Mary Ann' – my sister, who was stillborn. 'The second time was the day Shaun died.'

Saint Shaun of my childhood. He was a perfect dog. At least that's how I will always remember him. It was Shaun who set the standard by which I would judge all other dogs to come.

Oral exploration

1 How did the writer persuade his father to get him a dog?

2 Why did he call the place where he got the dog 'a mutt ranch'?

3 He describes the woman who owns the ranch as 'rough-hewn'. What do you think she looks like?

4 Think about the author's name and the name he gave to his new dog. Can you see a connection? What is it?

5 Describe what happened when the writer grew up and went to college. How did his father react to Shaun's death? Might he be crying about more than just Shaun's passing?

Read, write, explore

1 Describe the dog farm and its owners. Tell your partner if such a dog farm would be permitted in the Ireland of today. What objections might people have to a 'dog farm'?

2 Describe how Shaun persuaded the writer that he was the dog he should choose. What aspects of the dog's character are shown in paragraph four, 'I grabbed the chain-link gate . . . '?

3 How is Shaun's special appeal to the writer shown in paragraph five? On your own, write out the five most important things that Shaun did to impress his owner. Now show your partner the five things you have chosen and agree on a common list. What does the list tell you about the dog's nature? Write a six-line account of Shaun's character.

PowerPoint – Features of writing

All of the writers that we have read about so far demonstrate a confidence in their writing, but they were not born writers. Writing is a skill that they developed over time. Look at the PowerPoint presentation to learn a quick and easy way to improve your own writing skills.

Saying goodbye

Brian O'Driscoll

Background

Brian O'Driscoll is one of Ireland's most well known and celebrated sporting heroes. He played national and international rubgy until his retirement in 2014. This is an extract from his autobiography, *The Test*. Here we meet him at home on the day he will play his last professional rugby match for Leinster.

Before you read

Describe how you felt at a time when you had to say goodbye to someone or something. Tell your partner how you felt.

Extract from

THE TEST

The day begins like any other. I'm awoken by the sound of chat coming from across the landing, just a mumble at first but then rising in pitch to a full-blown call to action.

Get up, get up, wherever you are. I want my bottle!

I check the time on my phone. It reads 7.02 am, but it's three minutes ahead, the leeway I give myself after a lifetime of trying never to be late.

Beside me, my wife Amy is still sleepy after working into the early hours of the morning. No point in two of us not getting any more shut-eye: I throw back the covers and answer the call.

The nursery door is open, and as I peek around the corner, Sadie, aged fifteen months, is standing up at the near end of her cot, the soother still in her mouth.

'Hello!' I say.

She smiles, pleased to see me. She spits out the soother because she knows it stays in the cot, alongside Audrey the rabbit and Merle the bear.

Gently, I pull her out of her sleeping-bag and she points as she does every morning, to the creature stencilled in green on the opposite wall.

'Will we give Ernie a kiss?'

I hold her up. She plants a smacker on the owl, perched on his tree, who watches over her.

It's breakfast time on the morning of my final day as a rugby player.

I turn on the coffee machine and make Sadie's bottle – five ounces, enough to keep her happy for now, with room left for the main course of Weetabix and Readybrek mixed with fruit puree.

When I was a boy, my parents drilled good manners into me. Now, as a father myself, I find myself almost wrestling the food back from my little one if I don't hear the magic word, or challenging some of the kids who come up to me on the street . . .

'Give us a picture!'

'Sign this!'

'Selfie!'

It's the bee in my bonnet.

'I'll give you another go. Now try asking nicely . . . '

In the kitchen, I hand Sadie her bottle.

'Ta-ta,' she says.

That's my girl.

We hang out for a couple of hours, just the two of us, while Amy sleeps. I pick up my iPad, type 'nursery rhyme songs' into Google as she lies on my chest and before each one ends I know what's coming up next . . .

'Baa Baa Black Sheep', 'Happy Birthday', 'Row Row Row Your Boat', 'Old MacDonald'. . .

On my phone there are emails from the night before. Near the top of my inbox is one sent by Johnny Sexton at 20:55.

He has never mailed me before, but I've been expecting it. A few days have passed since he called me from Paris, the place he calls home now, the city where we played our last game together, in the Six Nations a couple of months ago. He was looking for my email address. 'And I don't want the one for BOD Inc,' he said. 'I don't want your mum or your sister reading it first, like it's fan mail.'

Me and Sexto, we shared some special times. Like everyone at Leinster, I was desperately disappointed to see him leave, but I completely understood his decision.

We had shouting matches on the training field in our day, but they were always about what was better for us as a group of players. You need that in a team, sometimes. He wore his heart on his sleeve and the fierce competitive streak burning inside him sometimes boiled over.

There were times when I smiled and tried to reason with him: 'Johnny, you don't always have to have the last word!'

But it was hard to penetrate the wall of certainty he built around himself, the conviction that he had to be right, all the time: 'Says you!'

Now, as I read his email, I feel moved by the generous sentiments.

And I wish he was here, still wearing the Leinster number 10 jersey, alongside me in our backline. One last time.

Oral exploration

1 'The day begins like any other.' How does Brian O'Driscoll's day begin?

2 In what way is this day different for him?

3 Show how O'Driscoll seems to be a fairly normal dad.

4 How does he entertain his daughter Sadie?

5 Why does he miss Johnny Sexton on this day?

Read, write, explore

1 Brian O'Driscoll is better known as a player of rugby than as a father. Pick out sentences and phrases from his interaction with Sadie that show his tenderness as a father.

2 Which seems more important to O'Driscoll, the last rugby match that he is about to play or the time he has with his daughter?

3 From your reading of this, what values does he hold as important in his life?

4 Describe Johnny Sexton's attitude to O'Driscoll from what you read about his email.

5 Write the email that Sexton might have written to his friend on his retirement.

6 What do you learn about Sexton's character from what O'Driscoll writes?

7 How do you know that O'Driscoll respects Sexton?

8 In what sense can Sexton be described as Brian O'Driscoll's hero?

Oral presentation

Create an oral presentation on your hero. You may choose one of the authors or characters featured in this unit or you might choose one of your own.

You can focus on some of the following:

- Describe the important quality for which your hero stands out.
- Describe a difficult event or challenge your hero overcame.
- Include a quote by or about your hero.
- Use interesting images that convey personality and heroic qualities to the audience.
- Use interesting words and phrases that will grab the attention of your audience.

Plan your two-minute presentation. Aim to have about six slides. Use the presentation template in your Portfolio.

Portfolio 1D

 Animation – Advice on giving a presentation

Create – My hero flyer

Imagine that a national day of celebration has been organised in honour of your favourite hero. This hero can be a historical figure, a modern-day personality, a fictional character or the person that you chose for your oral presentation above. You have been asked by the organising committee to create a flyer using online software to advertise the details and outline the events of the day. When you have created your flyer, show it to the class and then upload it to your e-Portfolio.

Note for Teachers: You will find step-by-step guidelines for this activity in your *How to Create an e-Portfolio* e-book. Log on to www.edcodigital.ie to access the e-book.

Poetry to Remember

In this unit you will:

- read interesting and unusual poems
- read poems out loud
- think and talk about your reactions to the poems
- learn about the poetic techniques that poets use to impress you
- think about poems and their themes
- practise writing your responses to poems.

You will encounter work by the following:

- Gary Soto
- Dorothy Parker
- Liz Lochhead
- W. B. Yeats
- Eric Finney
- James Kirkup
- Michael Rosen
- Julie O'Callaghan
- Li-Young Lee
- Czesław Miłosz
- Richard Wilbur
- Fleur Adcock
- Billy Collins
- Patrick Kavanagh
- Siegfried Sassoon
- Peggy Seeger and Ewan MacColl

Poetry to remember

Portfolio 2A

Before you launch into the unit, think about any poems or poets you have read or come across before now. Jot down some thoughts in your Portfolio.

Different ages, different feelings

Gary Soto (1952–) was raised in Fresno, California. His parents were Mexican-American and working class. At a young age, he worked in the fields of the San Joaquin Valley. He became interested in poetry during his high school years. He lives in Northern California.

Gary Soto

Before you read

How do you react to having your picture taken by your parents or a relative? Describe the best and the worst picture taken of you.

Ode to Family Photographs

This is the pond, and these are my feet.
This is the rooster, and this is more of my feet.

Mama was never good at pictures.

This is a statue of a famous general who lost an arm,
And this is me with my head cut off.

This is a trash can chained to a gate,
This is my father with his eyes half-closed.

This is a photograph of my sister
And a giraffe looking over her shoulder.

This is our car's front bumper.
This is a bird with a pretzel in its beak.
This is my brother Pedro standing on one leg on a rock,
With a smear of chocolate on his face.

Mama sneezed when she looked
Behind the camera: the snapshots are blurry,
The angles dizzy as a spin on a merry-go-round.

But we had fun when Mama picked up the camera.
How can I tell?
Each of us is laughing hard.
Can you see? I have candy in my mouth.

Gary Soto

Mood

Like us, poems have **moods**! When we talk about a poem's mood, we mean the general way it makes us feel. Moods can be described in many different ways. A poem's mood can, for example, be *joyful*, *solemn*, *playful*, *depressing* or *uplifting*. Often we find that a poem has one general mood, *sad* or *happy*, but we try to use more exact words to give the individual flavour of each poem's mood.

Oral exploration

1. Read the poem out loud, placing emphasis each time on the words 'This is'. Do you agree that the phrase 'This is' is typical of the way people talk about their pictures?

2. Point out some of the activities that the family were engaged in as the photos were being taken.

3. 'Mama was never good at pictures'. Which three or four pictures described in the poem show that Mama was really bad at taking photos?

4. Describe Mama's personality based on the non-family photos mentioned. Point to the relevant lines.

Read, write, explore

1. Describe the mood of this poem as you see it. Where is the mood most obviously reflected? Write out the lines.

2. An 'ode' is defined as 'a poem of praise and emotional enthusiasm'. In your opinion, does this description fit Gary Soto's 'Ode to Family Photographs'? Explain why or why not.

3. In pairs, create a PowerPoint presentation which illustrates this poem. Set up and take the photos as described in the poem. Add in the relevant lines beside each photo.

Create

1. Choose a picture from your photo album that you feel captures a moment in time. It could be a happy or a sad moment. In your Portfolio, describe who is in the picture, when and where it was taken, why it was taken, how it captures the moment in time and how you feel looking back on it.

2. Follow Soto's method and write a poem or ode for a set of snaps that depict your own family in a quirky way.

Portfolio 2B

Dorothy Parker (1893–1967) was an American poet, short story writer, critic and satirist.

Dorothy Parker

Before you read

Have you ever been out of sorts yourself?
What feelings did you have at the time?
What words did you use to express your feelings?

Symptom Recital

I do not like my state of mind;
I'm bitter, querulous, unkind.
I hate my legs, I hate my hands,
I do not yearn for lovelier lands.
I dread the dawn's recurrent light;
I hate to go to bed at night.
I snoot at simple, earnest folk.
I cannot take the simplest joke.
I find no peace in paint or type.
My world is but a lot of tripe.
I'm disillusioned, empty-breasted.
For what I think, I'd be arrested.
I am not sick, I am not well.
My quondam[1] dreams are shot to hell.
My soul is crushed, my spirit sore;
I do not like me any more.
I cavil,[2] quarrel, grumble, grouse.
I ponder on the narrow house.
I shudder at the thought of men.
I'm due to fall in love again.

Dorothy Parker

[1] **quondam:** former;
[2] **cavil:** object unnecessarily.

Oral exploration

1 Take turns reading the poem to the student beside you. One reads slowly, the other more quickly. Discuss and decide which pace better suits the content of the poem.

2 Close the book. From memory each student tries to write down as many lines, ideas and words as they can remember. Afterwards, work together to recreate as much of the poem as possible. Then compare this with the original.

3 What words would you use to describe the mood of the poem? Listen to the audio version of the poem. Pick out some lines where the mood is strongest. Do the last two lines change your impression of the poet's mood? Do those lines surprise you?

Read, write, explore

1 Every second line rhymes with the one before it. Check this out.
Why does the poet use so many double rhymes (also called *rhyming couplets*)? Write the poet a note telling her how you enjoyed this technique.

2 Which couplet do you think best sums up the poet's feeling of misery? Say why you chose this couplet.

3 Look up the meaning of both 'symptom' and 'recital' in a dictionary. Do you think that they work together to convey the meaning of the poem? Say why.

4 The poet uses plenty of repetition and a lot of alliteration. Listen to the poem and write down some. Say what effect they have on you as you hear them.

Examples of repetition	Examples of alliteration

Create

1 Imagine that the poet was your friend and asked for advice about managing the way she feels. Be her counsellor! Either write out or record the advice you would give to her in order to improve her mood.

2 How do you feel about homework? Use the poem as a model to write your own poem.

3 You meet the poet again but this time she has found Mr Right and is head-over-heels in love. What 'Symptom Recital' might she write now? Try to write it for her (10 lines at least). Record it and play it to your group.

Portfolio 2C

Liz Lochhead (1947–) was born in Motherwell, Lanarkshire, Scotland. She has had a varied career as teacher, playwright, broadcaster and poet. She has said, however, that 'when somebody asks me what I do, I usually say writer. The most precious thing to me is to be a poet. If I were a playwright, I'd like to be a poet in the theatre'. In January 2011, Lochhead was named as the second Scots Makar (or national poet).

Liz Lochhead

Before you read

Have you ever lost touch with a friend? Recall what happened and why.

The Choosing

We were first equal Mary and I
with the same coloured ribbons in
　　mouse-coloured hair
and with equal shyness
we curtseyed to the lady councillor
for copies of Collins' Children's Classics.
First equal, equally proud.

Best friends too Mary and I
a common bond in being cleverest (equal)
in our small school's small class.
I remember the competition for top desk
or to read aloud the lesson
at school service.
And my terrible fear
of her superiority at sums.

I remember the housing scheme
where we both stayed.
The same house, different homes,
where the choices were made.

I don't know exactly why they moved,
but anyway they went.
Something about a three-apartment
and a cheaper rent.

But from the top deck of the high-school bus
I'd glimpse among the others on the corner
Mary's father, muffled, contrasting strangely
with the elegant greyhounds by his side.
He didn't believe in high school education,
especially for girls,
or in forking out for uniforms.

Ten years later on a Saturday —
I am coming from the library —
sitting near me on the bus,
Mary
with a husband who is tall,
curly haired, has eyes
for no one else but Mary.
Her arms are round the full-shaped vase
that is her body.
Oh, you can see where the attraction lies
in Mary's life —
not that I envy her, really.

And I am coming from the library
with my arms full of books.
I think of the prizes that were ours for the taking
and wonder when the choices got made
we don't remember making.

Liz Lochhead

Oral exploration

Listen carefully to the audio of the poem and jot down answers to the
following questions after talking about them.

1 What was a common trait shared by the speaker and her best friend when they
   were children?

2 What sort of place did the two friends come from?

3 How often is the word 'equal' used? Why?

4 Mention at least one major difference between them as young women.

Read, write, explore

1 Do you think the speaker missed the friendship as she grew up? Quote to support
   your opinion.

2 How do the images 'vase' and 'library' reveal the different paths (destinies) that
   awaited the two friends after childhood?

3 What tone or attitude do you sense from the phrase 'not that I envy her, really'? Explain.

4 The poet selects adjectives well, e.g. 'elegant greyhounds', 'terrible fear', 'full-shaped
   vase' and 'mouse-coloured hair'. Which adjective is the most revealing and why?

5 Do you think that a younger reader and an older reader would respond differently
   to this poem? Read the poem to an adult. Watch their reaction. Ask them what
   memories it brings up.

Create

Imagine that the speaker drops a book and Mary picks it up for her when they get off
the bus. Write the conversation with a partner. Act your conversation out to the class.

Hint: Would there be awkwardness, surprise or delight? Maybe one of them would
pretend not to recognise the other.

After you have done this task, on one side of a page make a note of all the things that
were said, and on the other side all the things that you thought, but didn't or couldn't
say. These are your internal thoughts. Be honest. What do you notice?

Two short poems by W. B. Yeats

William Butler Yeats (1865–1939) is remembered as Ireland's 'national poet' and was one of the great figures of English language and literature in the twentieth century. He was awarded the Nobel Prize for Literature. For nearly all of his life, Yeats loved a woman called Maud Gonne. He could never persuade her to marry him, despite proposing many times. The two poems included below, 'He Wishes for the Cloths of Heaven' and 'When You Are Old', were handwritten by him into a little book and presented to Maud as a sign of his love.

W. B. Yeats

He Wishes for the Cloths of Heaven

Had I the heaven's embroidered cloths,
Enwrought[1] with golden and silver light,
The blue and the dim and the dark cloths
Of night and light and the half-light,

I would spread the cloths under your feet:
But I, being poor, have only my dreams;
I have spread my dreams under your feet;
Tread softly because you tread on my dreams.

W. B. Yeats

[1] **Enwrought:** decorated or embroidered

Oral exploration

1 Read the poem aloud once. Decide whether the poem should be read fast or slow. Listen to the audio version of the poem and compare your thoughts.

2 How does the young lover show his love in lines 1–6? Pick out words and images that tell you this. Which is your favourite image? Explain your choice.

3 Do you feel sorry for the young lover? Do you expect him to win the heart of his love? What lines tell you this?

Read, write, explore

1 The speaker uses a lot of repetition in the poem. Jot down the three examples that you think are important. How do they help create the mood? In your opinion, what is that mood?

2 Imagine that someone who loved you wrote this poem for you. How would you respond to the poet? Write a short reply.

3 Think about what you see as the theme of the poem. Look at the images in the poem. Which ones express that theme best?

4 Do you like this poem? Why? Why not?

When You Are Old

When you are old and grey and full of sleep,
And nodding by the fire, take down this book,
And slowly read, and dream of the soft look
Your eyes had once, and of their shadows deep;

How many loved your moments of glad grace,
And loved your beauty with love false or true,
But one man loved the pilgrim soul in you,
And loved the sorrows of your changing face;

And bending down beside the glowing bars,
Murmur, a little sadly, how Love fled
And paced upon the mountains overhead
And hid his face amid a crowd of stars.

W. B. Yeats

How poets use *assonance*

Assonance is when the same vowel sounds are purposely used to create a sound pattern.

Assonance is another word for the poem's vowel music. Listen to the repeating 'o' and 'ee' (including 'ea', 'ey' and 'ei') sounds in:

'And slowly read, and dream of the soft look
Your eyes had once, and of their shadows deep;'

Here Yeats is using **assonance** to slow down the line speed to create a mood of regret and nostalgia.

Oral exploration

1 Read the poem aloud and pay attention to the rhythm. Try to make it fit with the subject matter, old age. Now listen to the audio version and note the rhythm.

2 Choose four or six lines from the poem that most appealed to you.
What appealed to you (e.g. mood, imagery, assonance, general feeling)?
Tell your partner why.

3 Discuss how a young Maud Gonne might have responded. 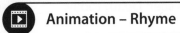 **Animation – Rhyme**

Read, write, explore

1 What aspects of growing old does Yeats capture in the poem? Write them down and the lines that suggest them.

2 Decide what you think is Yeats's attitude towards Maud in old age. Where is this most obvious? Write the lines and say why.

Create – A choral reading

Spend a little time rehearsing a class or group reading of these two poems by Yeats. Provide a very short introduction to each of them. Record the reading as you perform for another class group.

Mysteries

Eric Finney is a British poet.

Before you read

Discuss with a partner, what you know about 'The Grim Reaper'. Imagine the Grim Reaper met you and tried to set up an appointment for you. What would you say to him to put him off?

A Final Appointment

Enter the servant Abdul
His face ashy grey,
Fear in his eyes —
He has seen Death today.

Begs release of his master,
Plans instant flight:
'I must be far from
This city tonight!'

'Why?' asks the Sultan,
A man kind and clever,
'You have said many times
You would serve me for ever.'

'Master, I love you,
That much you must know,
But down in the city
A half hour ago

Death himself was out walking,
Reached cold hands to me:
The threat was quite plain
For the whole world to see.

I must leave Death behind!
To Baghdad I'll take flight.
Master, give me a horse —
I can be there tonight!'

So Abdul escapes,
Fear driving him on,
And very soon after
His servant has gone

The Sultan himself
Walks out in the city,
Walks among the cripples
And beggars with pity;

Like Abdul, meets Death
As he walks in that place,
Peers into the folds of his cloak
For his face;

Sees it not; hears a voice
That is cold, clear and dry:
'Look not for my face —
See that and you die.'

But the Sultan speaks boldly
Asking Death, 'For what cause
Did you threaten this morning
To make Abdul yours?'

Death replied, 'To your servant
I issued no threat.
Indeed sir, I knew that
His time was not yet.

This morning your servant
Had nothing to fear;
I was taken aback
To see the man here;

Gave a start of surprise
Knowing well that I had
An appointment with Abdul
Tonight in Baghdad.'

Eric Finney

Oral exploration

1 Does this poem end with a twist? Explain.

2 A student said of this poem, 'It's terrible! Everyone is so nice in the poem and yet Abdul gets it in the end!' What do you think of the characters in the poem?

3 Death seems quite nice as he talks to others in the poem. How does the poet show his character? Is this a more effective characterisation of death than showing him as a scary monster?

4 Look at the setting of the poem. Pick out words and phrases that show what life was like in the city where Abdul lived. Describe what life must have been like.

Read, write, explore

1 What would you suggest is the theme of this little poem? What is the poet telling us about our relationship with death? Think about poor Abdul's attempt to escape.

2 Now having decided that you know what the theme is, work with your partner and think of a better title for this poem. Try out a few before making a final decision.

3 What is the general mood of the poem? Does it reflect poor Abdul's terrible situation or does it make light of it? Write your answer in your journal.

Create – Virtual art exhibition

Imagine that your class has been asked to put together a virtual art exhibition in your school based around images of 'Death/The Grim Reaper'.

You have been asked to look for famous visual representations of death, and to discuss the artist that created them, the era, details from the paintings and why you chose them.

You can use PowerPoint/Prezi or your own preferred program to present the information.

Note for Teachers: You will find step-by-step guidelines for this activity in your *How to Create an e-Portfolio* e-book. Log on to www.edcodigital.ie to access the e-book, as well as a sample PowerPoint presentation for this activity.

 PowerPoint

James Kirkup

James Kirkup (1918–2009) was a prolific English poet, translator and travel writer. He wrote over 30 books, including autobiographies, novels and plays.

Before you read

Are you afraid of the dark? Recall one time when you panicked in the dark. Think about what it felt like.

The House at Night

Some stealthy spider is weaving round my bed
and mice are nibbling the curtains overhead.
Weird footsteps make the floorboards crack,
the staircase creaks, chill draughts thrill down my back
from some forgotten window out of sight —
    this is the house at night.

There's a whispering on the landing
where a creepy tropic plant is standing,
and the coatrack in the hall
lets fall a scarf — a long, soft fall:
a snake's loose coils that rapidly grow tight —
    this is the house at night.

From the distant kitchen come the notes
of dripping taps, plink-plonking secret codes
I cannot get the meaning of: a sudden
icy shudder — the refrigerator groans — a hidden
oven, cooling, ticks in rustling ember-light —
    this is the house at night.

— But even stranger is my own tense breathing
as I lie here speechless looking at the ceiling
that seems to swim all round like falling snow.
I can hear my eyelids batting gently, slow —
then quick as heartbeats as I freeze with fright
at something in the mirror shining bright —
has someone left the telly on all night?
No, thank heaven, it's all right,
it's only the moon's pale, spooky light
touching my tangled sheets with chalky white —
yes, this is the house at night.

James Kirkup

Oral exploration

1 There are lots of sound effect words (onomatopoeia) in the first three stanzas. Read the poem aloud, and then listen to the audio version. Agree on the onomatopoeic words and write them down in your journal. Talk about the effect they have on you as you read.

2 As you listen to the poem, what images best capture the mood? Now put a name to the general mood.

3 If you were to make a little film of this poem, what colour lighting would you use, what noises would you add to create the atmosphere, what sound effects would you generate? Link your choices to words and phrases used in the poem.

Read, write, explore

1 Check on how the poet uses *rhyme* in the poem. Does it help to reinforce the scary atmosphere? Write about some of the rhymes and their effect on you?

2 Read the last stanza again. Write down three ways in which it is different from the first three stanzas. Is it scarier? Say why.

3 Write down four dramatic images (word pictures) from stanza four that you consider to be well written and very effective. Say why they are effective.

Create

Imagine you have been asked to illustrate this poem for a poetry book aimed at students between ten and thirteen years of age. Write each stanza out in your copy and illustrate the poem to the best of your ability.

Food! We love it!

Michael Rosen (1946–) is an English children's novelist and poet, and has written over 140 books. He was the fifth British Children's Laureate from June 2007 to June 2009. Rosen was one of the first poets to bring poetry into the classroom through school visits throughout the United Kingdom and further afield.

Michael Rosen

Before you read

OMG! Have you ever felt embarrassed by something your father/guardian said or did? Recall one incident!

HOT FOOD

We sit down to eat
and the potato's a bit hot
so I only put a little on my fork
and I blow
whooph whooph
until it's cool
just cool
then into the mouth
nice.
And there's my brother
he's doing the same
whooph whooph
into the mouth
nice.

There's my mum
she's doing the same
whooph whooph
into the mouth
nice.

But my dad.
My dad.
What does he do?
He stuffs a great big chunk of potato
into his mouth.
Then
that really does it.
His eyes pop out
he flaps his hands
he blows, he puffs, he yells
he bobs his head up and down
he spits bits of potato
all over his plate
and he turns to us and he says,
"Watch out everybody—
the potato's very hot."

Michael Rosen

Oral exploration

1   Work in groups of four. Each of you tries to say the sounds 'whooph whooph' to your group. Each member of the group tries to spell the sounds you have actually made. Write them down and compare. No right or wrong! The group must agree on the actual pronunciation of 'whooph whooph' in order to prepare for a group reading.

2   Work in pairs. Try to say and then try to write down the sound (or noise) you might make in each of the following situations:

   ● You turn on the shower, it's freezing
   ● In bare feet, you stub your toe
   ● You bite your tongue
   ● You have seen the person you really, really fancy.

   Try to put some of the sounds into a loose poem modelled on the one by Michael Rosen.

3   Do a group reading of 'Hot Food'. Work in groups of four.
   One member of the group speaks the lines of one of the first three characters (the narrator, brother and mother) using a quiet and restrained tone. Then the full group dramatises the father, by exaggerating the verbs (e.g. *pop*, *flaps*, *blows*, *puffs*, *yells*) in particular.

Create – Blogging

Michael Rosen writes a regular blog on his website. Often his blogs are funny. Here is one on 'Exams'.

Read it and then draft a blog entry (max. 200 words) on one of the following topics – 'Fast Food', 'Family Outings', 'An Embarrassing Moment' or any other topic that you think is important at the moment.

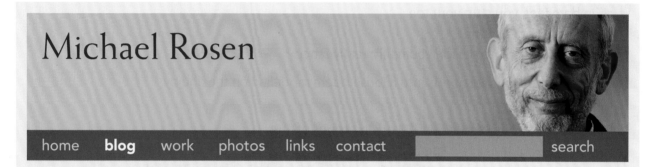

home **blog** work photos links contact [   ] search

Wednesday, 22 October 2014

Exams

A lot of time is being wasted in schools trying to teach a whole lot of unnecessary stuff. The point of schools is to pass exams. Exams are tests in who can write fast. Or put another way, exams find out who can write slowly. That's what they're for. So, instead of wasting loads of time muddling this up with writing answers to questions that no one cares about, school can concentrate on the business of learning to write fast. And of course, it's not just about writing fast. It's about writing fast for over an hour. In hard exams it can be for two hours. And when I say 'writing' this has to be writing by hand. This is really important. I'm out and about in the real world, and all the successful people I meet spend several hours every day writing fast by hand. So my school of the future will be full of children writing fast by hand. And, here's the innovation: they won't be thinking at the same time. To be really fast, they'll be copying. In front of them will be iPads or laptops, with a lot of writing up on screen. It can be anything, ads for soft drinks, poems that celebrate a well-known fast food, instructions for self-assembly wardrobes...and the children will be copying these. Teachers – or teaching assistants, or assistants to teaching assistants can come round and if a child is slowing down, they can give them a little nudge to remind them to speed up.

Then at the end of the year, when the child's fate is to be decided, the big exam will discover who can really write fast, who can write not-so-fast, who writes slowly and who writes really, really slowly.

Michael Rosen

(293 words)

Julie O'Callaghan (1954–) was born in Chicago. She has lived in Ireland since 1974 and is a member of the Irish academy of arts, Aosdána.

Julie O'Callaghan

Before you read

Have you ever been in a situation where you felt others were judging you? Did you react by shutting up, or did you stand up and let them know how you felt? Imagine one such past situation; what would you say now?

Note: A Federal Case is a case of really serious crime.

Federal Case

Wow, I said I'd love a Big Mac
with piles of mush spurting out the sides.
So what? Is it such a Federal Case?
Maybe it's a mortal sin cuz
I've got a yen for some junk food.
You'd have thought I'd cursed his mother
or told him I hated his guts
the way he looked at me
like I was a gun-lobby supporter.
Holy cow, it isn't the end of the world
if some processed, bleached, portion-controlled,
regulated bun and a little cereal-filled meat,
cheese and slop goes plonk into my stomach!
I've gone out with this guy
only five times and already he's getting
like a Nazi over what I want to eat.

Julie O'Callaghan

Oral exploration

1 The speaker in this poem is very annoyed. Explain to your partner why she is so annoyed.

2 Why might her boyfriend not approve of her choice of food? Is he right? Do a little research online about McDonald's food. Decide who is in the right, the speaker or her boyfriend. Have a stand-up vote in class on whether the boyfriend is right or wrong.

3 Try to describe the poet's tone as she makes her complaint about her boyfriend's attitude to her eating a Big Mac. Try out different tones as you read the poem to your partner. See which reading best gets the right tone.

4 Read the final three lines of the poem again. Look up the word 'Nazi' in the dictionary. Decide with your partner whether her response is over the top or fair.

5 Look at the tone used. Decide whether the poet is altogether serious in what she says in the poem.

Create

Write a complaint about a product, a service or a school situation you found yourself in that made you mad. See the following example of a letter of complaint.

Dear Ms Brett,

I am a second year student in Class 2 Gold and on behalf of my classmates I want to bring to your notice something that is happening every day in the Lunch Hall and it's not fair to let it continue.

The situation is this. Every fortnight, my class does 'Clean Up' after lunch. We don't mind it and helping the good state of the school. It should take about ten minutes to finish it. However, a group of sixth years leave a terrible mess that it is taking us fifteen minutes to clean and makes us late for afternoon assembly. Some sixth years even laugh at us having to do the work. We have asked the supervising teacher to talk to them but they don't pay any attention to her at all.

As you are the Principal, we in Class 2 Gold ask you to get involved and give the sixth years a good talking to. Students from the other second year classes will back up what we say, as they get the same treatment.

We know and trust that you will take this situation seriously and we look forward to the problem being solved soon.

Yours sincerely,

Leja Kaminskas

(Class representative, Class 2 Gold)

Use the template in your Portfolio to sketch out your thoughts, note some points and draft your letter of complaint.

Portfolio 2D

Li-Young Lee (1957–) was born in Jakarta, Indonesia, to Chinese parents. His father had been a personal physician to Mao Zedong while in China, and moved his family to Indonesia. In 1959, the Lee family fled the country to escape anti-Chinese sentiment. After five years of travelling through Hong Kong, Macau and Japan, they finally settled in the United States in 1964.

Li-Young Lee

Before you read

Think about your favourite food. Tell the student beside you (or the whole class) the aspects of this food that make it your particular favourite, such as taste, colour and smell.

From Blossoms

From blossoms comes
this brown paper bag of peaches
we bought from the boy
at the bend in the road where we turned toward
signs painted *Peaches*.

From laden boughs, from hands,
from sweet fellowship in the bins,
comes nectar at the roadside, succulent
peaches we devour, dusty skin and all,
comes the familiar dust of summer, dust we eat.

O, to take what we love inside,
to carry within us an orchard, to eat,
not only the skin, but the shade,
not only the sugar, but the days, to hold
the fruit in our hands, adore it, then bite into
the round jubilance of peach.

There are days we live
as if death were nowhere
in the background; from joy
to joy to joy, from wing to wing,
from blossom to blossom to
impossible blossom, to sweet impossible blossom.

Li-Young Lee

What is *metaphor*?

Poets and other writers like to compare one thing with another so that we can imagine both things better.

In Shakespeare's *Romeo and Juliet*, when Romeo first catches sight of Juliet, he is captivated by her loveliness and says, 'Juliet is the sun'. Romeo does not mean this literally. He is using a metaphor to say something about the bright, warm and unique quality of Juliet's beauty.

So also, when the poet Li-Young Lee calls peaches 'nectar at the roadside', he is using the comparison to tell us that peaches are as appealing as honey.

Oral exploration

1 The poet is celebrating peaches! Decide on the number of things he likes about this fruit by writing down words or phrases that he uses to describe them and his experience of them.

2 Look again at stanza two. Trace the peach's journey from the 'boughs' to the poet eating the peach.

3 Read stanza three out loud to your partner or to the group. Decide on the words that best express the poet's tone as he describes his love of peaches.

4 What is the poet's mood in the final stanza? Read it and listen to the repetitions. Do the repetitions suggest what the mood might be? Now, say what you think the mood is.

Read, write, explore

1 One reader of this poem said it was like a prayer or a hymn to the peach. Which stanza expresses best the emotion of the prayer or the hymn? Write down phrases and words that suggest this feeling. Say why they remind you of the language of prayer or hymn.

Hint: Think of repetition.

2 Try to explain what the poet means when he says, 'There are days we live/as if death were nowhere/in the background.' Try to explain what he means by this. You may have to think about the concerns of older people to answer this one.

3 The poem ends with four references to 'blossom'. How has the meaning of blossom changed from its first mention in line 1 to the four mentions in the last stanza?

Hint: Think about tone and metaphor.

4 Go online and choose images that might represent your experience of a fruit (or any food) that you love. Create a collage of words and images. Give the collage a title.

Create

You know the food that makes your mouth water. Write a hymn in praise of the physical aspects of your favourite food. Use stanza three as a model to celebrate:

···❯ its colour   ···❯ its smell
···❯ its taste   ···❯ its touch

Begin each sentence with, 'I love...' or 'O, to...'

Refer to the template in your Portfolio.

Portfolio 2E

Getting on with life

Czesław Miłosz (1911–2004) was born in Szetejnie, Lithuania (then under the domination of the Russian tsarist government). In 1980, Miłosz was awarded the Nobel Prize for Literature.

Czesław Miłosz

Before you read

Think about the ordinary things in your daily life that give you happiness. Talk about one of them with your partner. Say why it makes you happy.

GIFT

A day so happy.
Fog lifted early. I worked in the garden.
Hummingbirds were stopping over the honeysuckle flowers.
There was no thing on earth I wanted to possess.
I knew no one worth my envying him.
Whatever evil I had suffered, I forgot.
To think that once I was the same man did not embarrass me.

In my body I felt no pain.
When straightening up, I saw blue sea and sails.

Czesław Miłosz

Oral exploration

1 Before you listen to a reading of this poem read it to yourself and then with your partner. Discuss whether the reading should be fast or slow. Give a reason for your choice.

2 Is the speaker in the poem a young or an older person? Discuss using evidence from the poem.

3 Besides the things that he sees about him, what other things go to make the speaker happy? Do you think that these things are important in a person's life? Why?

Read, write, explore

1 In your opinion, what is the theme of this poem? What lines suggest the theme to you? Explain why.

2 What images appeal to you? How do they help you to get the poem's theme?

3 Read aloud line four again. Think about why the poet said 'no thing' in that line, instead of 'nothing'? Suggest a reason as to why he wrote it this way.

Richard Wilbur (1921–) was born in New York City. His first poem was published in *John Martin's Magazine* when he was eight years old. He studied at Amherst College before serving in the United States army during World War II. He has written numerous children's books and has won the Pulitzer Prize for poetry twice.

Richard Wilbur

Before you read

Think about a time when you experienced something beautiful in the natural world for the first time. Recall the experience. Tell some of the details to your group or partner.

A Summer Morning

Her young employers, having got in late
From seeing friends in town
And scraped the right front fender on the gate,
Will not, the cook expects, be coming down.

She makes a quiet breakfast for herself.
The coffee-pot is bright,
The jelly where it should be on the shelf.
She breaks an egg into the morning light,

Then, with the bread-knife lifted, stands and hears
The sweet efficient sounds
Of thrush and catbird, and the snip of shears
Where, in the terraced backward of the grounds,

A gardener works before the heat of day.
He straightens for a view
Of the big house ascending stony-gray
Out of his beds mosaic with the dew.

His young employers having got in late,
He and the cook alone
Receive the morning on their old estate,
Possessing what the owners can but own.

Richard Wilbur

Oral exploration

1 Listen to a reading of the poem. The first stanza tells us that the cook will have some free time. Explain how we know this from stanza one.

2 Try to explain to your partner or group what the poet might mean by the image, 'She breaks an egg into the morning light'. Consider the colour of the egg yolk as you think of your answer.

3 Read stanzas two, three and four out loud. Consider how the mood of these stanzas will affect your pace of reading. Describe the mood and say how the rhyme and alliterations (pick some out) help to create the mood.

4 What things do the cook and the gardener notice during this peaceful morning scene? What senses are used by each as they survey the scene? Give examples.

Read, write, explore

1 Write down two or three images that help you to picture the morning scene. Say how each one is effective in communicating a picture of the peaceful scene. Use quotations.

2 Read the final stanza. The poet draws a distinction between the cook and the gardener on the one hand, and the sleeping owners of the house on the other. Write down the difference in simple language.

3 Reflect further – concentrate first on the word 'possessing'. Then think of the meaning of 'own'. Check out possible meanings in the dictionary. What difference between 'possess' and 'own' is the poet trying to suggest?

4 What is the theme or main idea that ends the poem? How does the final stanza sum up the poem's theme? Write out the theme in a short paragraph with a quote or two.

Create – Dictionary work

The words 'own' and 'possess' are called **synonyms** because they share a very similar but subtly different meaning.

Find synonyms for the following three words – *chatter, miserable, angry* – from the list below:

walk – (*verb*) saunter	**mum** – (_____) _____
amusing – (*adjective*) _____	**complain** – (_____) _____
talk – (_____) _____	**rabbit** – (_____) _____
sad – (_____) _____	**ill** – (_____) _____
annoyed – (_____) _____	

Now find synonyms for the remaining words. Remember to label the words as nouns, adjectives or verbs, as appropriate.

Fleur Adcock (1934–) was born in New Zealand. She has spent much of her adult life in England, first as a librarian in London and later as a freelance poet, writer and critic. She has received many literary awards for her poetry, which deals with everyday happenings, but often with a darker twist, as seen in the poem you are about to read.

Fleur Adcock

Before you read

Can you remember when you were five?
What did you think about?

For a Five-Year-Old

A snail is climbing up the window-sill
into your room, after a night of rain.
You call me in to see, and I explain
that it would be unkind to leave it there:
it might crawl to the floor; we must take care
that no one squashes it. You understand,
and carry it outside, with careful hand,
to eat a daffodil.

I see, then, that a kind of faith prevails:
your gentleness is moulded still by words
from me, who have trapped mice and shot wild birds,
from me, who drowned your kittens, who betrayed
your closest relatives, and who purveyed
the harshest kind of truth to many another.
But that is how things are: I am your mother,
and we are kind to snails.

Fleur Adcock

1 Decide with your group the theme or main idea that the poet is writing about.

Hint: You will find its strongest expression in stanza two.

2 The mother seems to feel guilt about herself in stanza two. Why is that? What would you say to her to lessen the feeling of guilt?

Read, write, explore

1 'The mother is not a hypocrite.' Write down and explain your view on this statement.

2 What is the tone of the last sentence, 'I am your mother, and we are kind to snails'?

3 One reader suggested that the child's 'gentleness' is just a passing phase and that he or she will end up doing cruel things like the mother. What is your view on this?

Create

There are two stanzas in the poem. Read the first one again and stop. Imagine another stanza two where the poet chooses to keep with the tone and loving mood of the first. Write out some things she might say to herself and her child.

Billy Collins (1941–) was born in New York City. He is a popular, bestselling poet in America. He writes poems that are very witty, but also poems that are tender and moving.

Billy Collins

Before you read

What sounds get on your nerves? Have you ever been 'driven mad' by a nagging noise? How did it feel and what did you do about it?

Another Reason Why I Don't Keep a Gun in the House

The neighbours' dog will not stop barking.
He is barking the same high, rhythmic bark
that he barks every time they leave the house.
They must switch him on on their way out.

The neighbours' dog will not stop barking.
I close all the windows in the house
and put on a Beethoven symphony full blast
but I can still hear him muffled under the music,
barking, barking, barking,

and now I can see him sitting in the orchestra,
his head raised confidently as if Beethoven
had included a part for a barking dog.

When the record finally ends he is still barking,
sitting there in the oboe section barking,
his eyes fixed on the conductor who is
entreating him with his baton

while the other musicians listen in respectful
silence to the famous barking dog solo,
that endless coda[1] that first established
Beethoven as an innovative genius.

Billy Collins

[1] **Coda:** piece of music at the end of a longer piece.

Oral exploration

1 In stanza one, what aspects of the dog's barking really get on the poet's nerves?

2 How does he first try to deal with the noise?

3 In stanza three the poet begins to imagine the dog as part of the orchestra. What does this tell you about his state of mind?

4 In the last two stanzas when the record ends, the poet creates a picture of the dog giving a 'barking dog solo'. Has the poet got used to the barking or is he seeing the funny side of things?

5 Is the poet very easily annoyed, in your opinion, or has he a justifiable reason for his annoyance?

Read, write, explore

1 Look again at the title of the poem. Suggest some other reasons the poet could have for not keeping a gun in his house.

   Hint: Think of his personality as revealed in this poem.

2 If he had a gun, what might he do? Go through his options. Be imaginative.

3 What do you find humorous in this poem? Say why.

Create

Work as a group on the notion of Pets' Rights.

   You have been asked to write a list of basic rights (minimum five) that all pets should have. Write the list. The first one is done for you.

> ### All pets should have the right to:
> Be treated with kindness

Patrick Kavanagh (1904–1967) was born in in the village of Inniskeen in County Monaghan. His father was a shoemaker and had a small farm. At the age of thirteen, Kavanagh became an apprentice shoemaker. He gave it up fifteen months later, admitting that he didn't make one wearable pair of boots. For the next twenty years, Kavanagh worked on the family farm before moving to Dublin in 1939. He became a major Irish poet and was an influence on Seamus Heaney, whose poetry you will read in your Case Study on Heaney.

Patrick Kavanagh

Before you read

Imagine that the world and everything in it were about to disappear tomorrow. However, you have the opportunity to keep the one person or object that you value most. Say why that person or object means so much to you.

In Memory of My Mother

I do not think of you lying in the wet clay
Of a Monaghan graveyard; I see
You walking down a lane among the poplars
On your way to the station, or happily

Going to second Mass on a summer Sunday –
You meet me and you say:
'Don't forget to see about the cattle –'
Among your earthiest words the angels stray.

And I think of you walking along a headland
Of green oats in June,
So full of repose, so rich with life –
And I see us meeting at the end of a town

On a fair day by accident, after
The bargains are all made and we can walk
Together through the shops and stalls and markets
Free in the oriental streets of thought.

O you are not lying in the wet clay,
For it is harvest evening now and we
Are piling up the ricks against the moonlight
And you smile up at us – eternally.

Patrick Kavanagh

Oral exploration

1 How would you rate this poem on a scale of 1–5? (5 equals really love it.)

Poll the class. What is the result? Note the various reasons.

2 The poet obviously loved his mother. Discuss and decide on the one aspect of her character that he liked most.

Read, write, explore

1 This is a poem where Kavanagh mostly celebrates the living memory of his mother. Yet he mentions the 'wet clay' twice in the poem. Why, in your opinion, does he mention this at the start and at the end of the poem?

2 Kavanagh often wrote from his rich experience of the Irish countryside. Write down two or three images that show how this poem reflects his rural experience. Which is your favourite image? Explain why.

3 The poet knows that his mother is gone and yet she is intensely present to him in memory. What do you think he means by the image at the end of the poem, 'And you smile up at us – eternally'.

4 '… we can walk/Together through the shops and stalls and markets/Free in the oriental streets of thought'.

What does the metaphor of 'the oriental streets of thought' tell you about the relationship Kavanagh had with his mother?

Create

'The oriental streets of thought' – impressionistic writing of your memories and feelings

Sometimes we remember things that happen to us, not in full sentences, but in powerful images expressed in single words or phrases.

Choose a time when you were very happy and try to write about it, recording only the important details, images and feelings.

Don't worry about how your writing looks on the page. Just write down the stream of your thoughts as they occur to you. Read what you have written to your class or group.

Siegfried Sassoon (1886–1967) was born in Kent, England. He was educated at Marlborough, and Clare College, Cambridge. He volunteered for war service in 1914. As the war progressed, and as the number of casualties mounted, the young soldiers became very disillusioned with the war. This poem by Sassoon expresses their anger and cynicism towards the generals responsible for conducting it. Although wounded twice, he survived the war and lived until 1967.

Siegfried Sassoon

Before you read

Have you ever felt very cross or angry when you have seen someone treated unfairly? Reflect on the feeling. Did you do anything about the situation?

Base Details

If I were fierce, and bald, and short of breath,
I'd live with scarlet Majors at the Base,
And speed glum heroes up the line to death.
You'd see me with my puffy petulant face,
Guzzling and gulping in the best hotel,
Reading the Roll of Honour. 'Poor young chap,'
I'd say – 'I used to know his father well.
Yes, we've lost heavily in this last scrap.'
And when the war is done and youth stone dead,
I'd toddle safely home and die – in bed.

Siegfried Sassoon

Onomatopoeia

Poets, indeed all writers, use the device of onomatopoeia or sound words when they want to add drama or energy to a description. We use them all the time as a short cut to imitate sounds and actions, e.g. 'thump', 'buzz', 'clang'.

Oral exploration

1 Read the poem aloud and discuss the attitude of the speaker, 'I', in the poem. Then, read the poem again and talk about the tone you might use to communicate the speaker's feeling toward the 'Majors at the Base'. Try out different tones. Name the best tone.

2 Look online for videos of the action and conditions in the trenches of World War I. Do you think that the Majors understood these conditions? Pick out evidence from the poem.

3 The ordinary soldiers get little mention in the poem. Find the references to them. What do the references tell about them?

Read, write, explore

1 The poet uses very strong images to describe the physical aspects of the Majors (lines 1–3). Use them to write a description of the Majors. In your writing keep some of the poem's critical, satirical tone.

2 How does the alliteration and onomatopoeia help to communicate how horrible the Majors look and sound?

3 The poet uses the word 'scarlet' when describing the Majors. They did wear scarlet on their lapels but try to see the word as a metaphor. If so what might the word mean?

4 How does the final line help to contrast the war's outcome for the Majors with its outcome for the ordinary soldiers? Is it a good image? Say why.

Create

Write a letter to the 'Scarlet Majors' in which you oppose going to war and suggest that taking part in peace talks is a much better option. With the person beside you, think about some reasons. Then draft the letter in your Portfolio.

Portfolio 2F

Be sure to state your case clearly and to make one or two good arguments.

Preparing an oral presentation

The ballad – 'The Springhill Mining Disaster' by Seeger/MacColl

In the 1950s, the town of Springhill, Nova Scotia was devastated by two of the worst mining disasters in Canadian history. An explosion in 1956 killed thirty-nine miners, and another seventy-four died in the collapse of 1958. Despite much hardship, the people of Springhill have shown a will to survive that is tougher than coal.

This ballad refers to the 'bump' (underground earthquake) which occurred on 23 October 1958. It was the most severe underground earthquake in North American mining history. Miners were trapped underground and many died. The ballad celebrates their bravery and criticises the dangers of mining.

There are numerous online clips, which give graphic footage of the disaster. There are also several online recordings of the ballad. Read the ballad before doing any research.

The Springhill Mining Disaster

In the town of Springhill, Nova Scotia
Down in the dark of the Cumberland Mine
There's blood on the coal and the miners lie
In the roads that never saw sun nor sky,
In the roads that never saw sun nor sky.

In the town of Springhill, you don't sleep easy
Often the earth will tremble and roll
When the earth is restless, miners die;
Bone and blood is the price of coal,
Bone and blood is the price of coal.

Down at the coal face, miners working
Rattle of the belt and the cutter's blade.
Rumble of the rock and the walls closed round
The living and the dead men two miles down,
The living and the dead men two miles down.

Twelve men lay two miles from the pitshaft
Twelve men lay in the dark and sang
Long hot days in the miners tomb
It was three feet high and a hundred long,
It was three feet high and a hundred long.

Three days passed and the lamps gave out
Our foreman rose on his elbow and said
We're out of light and water and bread
So we'll live on song and hope instead,
So we'll live on song and hope instead.

Listen for the shouts of the barefaced miners
Listen thru the rubble for a rescue team,
Six hundred feet of coal and slag,
Hope imprisoned in a three foot seam,
Hope imprisoned in a three foot seam.

Eight days passed and some were rescued
Leaving the dead to lie alone
Thru all their lives they dug their grave
Two miles of earth for a marking stone,
Two miles of earth for a marking stone.

© Peggy Seeger and Ewan MacColl

Exploring the ballad – Leading to an oral presentation

1 What are the main facts that you learn about the 1958 mining disaster? Collect all the facts about the miners and the mine in the Facts Collection Sheet in your Portfolio.

Portfolio 2G

2 The spirit of the miners is praised in this ballad. What features of their character most impress you?

3 How does the use of repetition of words and phrases help to portray the disaster?

4 Try to work out with your partner the meaning of the following lines:

'Thru all their lives they dug their grave
Two miles of earth for a marking stone'

5 How does the ballad writer give us a sense of time passing during the rescue? How does this make the ballad more dramatic?

6 As preparation for your oral presentation, work out a timeline of the rescue using information from the ballad.

Oral presentation in groups of three (3–4 minutes)

Using the ballad text, online resources and recordings of the ballad, prepare a three-minute oral presentation on any aspect of the ballad or the disaster itself.

Here are some suggestions:

1 Do a live news report with images describing events as they happen.

2 Present a PowerPoint (or use another resource) to give information about the disaster.

3 Do interviews with one or two people, such as a miner, a miner's wife or a resident of Springhill.

4 Perform the ballad (spoken) with pictures and an introduction.

5 Make a brief scientific report on what actually happened and the consequences.

The Gothic Experience

In this unit you will:

‣ understand the conventions of Gothic literature

‣ write your own Gothic short story.

You will encounter the following texts:

● *Dracula* by Bram Stoker – 1897

● *Frankenstein* by Mary Shelley – 1818

● *Wuthering Heights* by Emily Brontë – 1847

● 'The Listeners' by Walter de la Mare – 1912

● 'The Wolves of Cernogratz' by Hector Hugh Munro/Saki – 1913

● 'Escape to Nowhere'
by Kate O'Connor (Junior Cycle student) – 2014

The Gothic experience

Before you launch into this unit, take time to reflect on what you think is meant by the word 'Gothic'? Note your thoughts in your Portfolio. This will help you to write your own Gothic story at the end of the unit.

Portfolio 3A

Gothic images

Oral exploration

····▶ In pairs, talk and think about the following images with the person beside you. Write down at least eight descriptive words, phrases and whole sentences that come to mind. Choose the best five and swap them with the pair beside you.

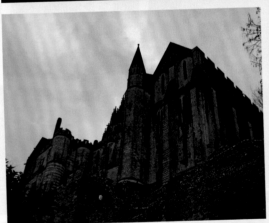

····▶ Use a dictionary or thesaurus to find dramatic synonyms (words that have a similar meaning) for the words you have chosen, e.g. *scary – terrifying, eerie – weird*.

Portfolio 3B

····▶ Use the Gothic dictionary sheet in your Portfolio to collect all the words which will help you to describe your Gothic experience.

····▶ Choose your three favourite words and share them with the class. Note any additional ones from your classmates and add them to your list.

····▶ Refer and add to your Gothic dictionary as you work through this unit.

Origins of Gothic stories and the Gothic style

Before you read the Gothic stories in this unit, read the following to find out where people's interest in the dark and scary Gothic experience first came from.

Gothic stories and poems were inspired by people's experience of Gothic buildings and architecture. Gothic architecture itself is characterised by pointed arches, gargoyles, tall spires, high vaulted ceilings and shadowy passageways.

Gothic literature began to be written in the 18th century, as a response to the fact that science and philosophy appeared to be able to explain all of human nature and the world. Gothic writing suggested that there is a darker, mysterious, more disturbing reality hiding in the shadows of our civilised world. The style of architecture gave Gothic writers the perfect settings for their dark, troubling creations such as Dracula or the monster in *Frankenstein*.

Remember, Gothic writers aim to scare us by exploring the darkness inside us and the things we fear, such as graveyards at night, terrible secrets of the past, nightmares and spooky empty houses. Gothic literature tells stories that are loaded with ghosts, monsters, storms, strange characters and inexplicable events. They are set in the past, sometimes in distant lands like Transylvania (home to Dracula) or lesser known parts of Europe. The action often happens in settings like the ones we have already looked at.

Gargoyle

Notre Dame Cathedral, Paris

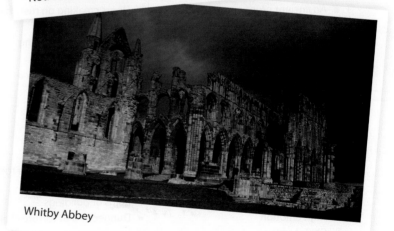

Whitby Abbey

Create

Find out what you can about Whitby Abbey and its associations with *Dracula*. Create a poster for the local tourist board to attract tourists to the area for Halloween.

Portfolio 3C

The conventions of Gothic writing

Gothic narratives use similar methods to create the atmosphere, mood and setting. Together, these methods are known as **conventions**. Other genres, or types of stories, such as romance, horror and detective stories, also have their own conventions.

Look at the list of conventions given below (common settings, themes, character types of Gothic writing). Arrange the Gothic elements into an appropriate category. We have given you two categories already. For example, *howling winds* and *thunder and lightning* are Gothic examples of Weather Conditions.

You can create your own categories or ask your teacher to help you to come up with some. Use the Gothic conventions chart in your Portfolio to complete this task.

Portfolio 3D

Setting
- A castle
- Wild landscapes

Gothic
Conventions

Weather Conditions
- Howling winds
- Thunder and lightning

- An ancient prophecy
- Thunder and lightning
- Omens, portents, visions
- Pouring rain
- Snow blizzard
- Howling winds
- Hysteria
- Eerie sounds
- Tombs
- Ancient mansions
- Supernatural or inexplicable events
- Sighs, moans
- High emotion
- Chains rattling
- Blood-curdling screams
- Fear
- Women in distress
- Gusts of wind blowing out lights
- A castle
- Doors suddenly slamming shut
- Wild landscapes
- Baying wolves
- Grey clouds
- Crazed laughter

- Doors creaking on rusty hinges
- Unreturned love
- Footsteps approaching
- Mysterious creatures
- Women entranced by a powerful male
- Tension
- Lights in abandoned buildings/rooms
- Ghosts
- Characters trapped in a room
- Graveyards
- Ruins of buildings
- Dungeons and torture chambers
- Lovers parted
- Family secrets
- Midnight
- Crumbling castles
- Vampires
- Ancestral curses
- Dimly lit gloomy settings
- Enigmatic figures with supernatural powers
- Hidden rooms
- Spirits
- Strangers

- Witchcraft
- Remote or exotic locations
- Dark towers
- Secret passages and pathways
- Dream and nightmares
- Damsels in distress
- Monsters
- The witching hour/twilight
- Papers discovered from the past
- Doubles and *Doppelgänger*
- Unnatural acts of nature
- The use of 'Magic Numbers' such as 3, 7, 13
- Demonic pacts
- Monsters coming to life
- Murder
- Chanting
- Madness
- Demons
- Blood-red moon
- Total eclipse of the sun
- Ancient scrolls
- Diabolic possession
- Suspense

Gothic stories

Now that you have a sense of the elements of Gothic literature, you need to start thinking about your own Gothic story. To spark your imagination let's read some extracts from classic and more recent Gothic writing. We will start with Bram Stoker, the author of *Dracula*, published in 1897.

Bram Stoker

Dracula by Bram Stoker

Bram Stoker (1847–1912) wrote one of the best-selling novels of all time. He was born in Clontarf in Dublin and was bedridden for most of his childhood.

© Dover Publications

Before you read

In groups, look at the cover of the book. Describe the appearance of the castle and its setting.

- What country do you think it is?
- What era?
- Who do you think lives there?
- Would you be tempted to spend a night in the castle? Why or why not?
- If you could bring one person with you, who would it be and why?

Listen, write, explore

Listen to the following extract from the novel, *Dracula*. While listening, pay particular attention to the **setting**, the **character description** and how the writer **creates tension**. The extract describes the unsuspecting Jonathan Harker's first encounter with Count Dracula in his castle in Transylvania.

Things to look out for		
• Feelings	• Interesting descriptive words or phrases	• Picture of character
• Setting		• Character description
• Sounds	• Literary devices	• Unusual occurrences
	• Light and dark imagery	• Narrator

Extract from
Dracula

In this extract from *Dracula*, Jonathan Harker, a young solicitor from London, has arrived at Count Dracula's castle, high in the Carpathian Mountains in Transylvania. Jonathan is recording his experiences in his journal.

1 I stood in silence where I was, for I did not know what to do. Of bell or knocker there was no sign; through these frowning walls and dark window openings it was not likely that my voice could penetrate. The time I waited seemed endless, and I felt doubts and fears crowding upon me. What sort of place had I come to, and among what kind of people? What sort of grim adventure was it on which I had embarked? Was this a customary incident in the life of a solicitor's clerk sent out to explain the purchase of a London estate to a foreigner? Solicitor's clerk! Mina would not like that. Solicitor—for just before leaving London I got word that my examination was successful; and I am now a full-blown solicitor! I began to rub my eyes and pinch myself to see if I were awake. It all seemed like a horrible nightmare to me, and I expected that I should suddenly awake, and find myself at home, with the dawn struggling in through the windows, as I had now and again felt in the morning after a day of overwork. But my flesh answered the pinching test, and my eyes were not to be deceived. I was indeed awake and among the Carpathians.[1] All I could do now was to be patient, and to wait the coming of the morning.

2 Just as I had come to this conclusion I heard a heavy step approaching behind the great door, and saw through the chinks the gleam of a coming light. Then there was

the sound of rattling chains and the clanking of massive bolts drawn back. A key was turned with the loud grating noise of long disuse, and the great door swung back.

3 Within, stood a tall old man, clean shaven save for a long white moustache, and clad in black from head to foot, without a single speck of colour about him anywhere. He held in his hand an antique silver lamp, in which the flame burned without a chimney or globe of any kind, throwing long quivering shadows as it flickered in the draught of the open door. The old man motioned me in with his right hand with a courtly gesture, saying in excellent English, but with a strange intonation:—

4 'Welcome to my house! Enter freely and of your own will!' He made no motion of stepping to meet me, but stood like a statue, as though his gesture of welcome had fixed him into stone. The instant, however, that I had stepped over the threshold, he moved impulsively forward, and holding out his hand grasped mine with a strength which made me wince, an effect which was not lessened by the fact that it seemed cold as ice—more like the hand of a dead than a living man. Again he said:—

5 'Welcome to my house. Come freely. Go safely; and leave something of the happiness you bring!' The strength of the handshake was so much akin to that which I had noticed in the driver, whose face I had not seen, that for a moment I doubted if it were not the same person to whom I was speaking; so to make sure, I said interrogatively:—

6 'Count Dracula?' He bowed in a courtly way as he replied:— 'I am Dracula; and I bid you welcome, Mr Harker, to my house. Come in; the night air is chill, and you must need to eat and rest.' As he was speaking, he put the lamp on a bracket on the wall, and stepping out, took my luggage; he had carried it in before I could forestall him. I protested, but he insisted:—

7 'Nay, sir, you are my guest. It is late, and my people are not available. Let me see to your comfort myself.' He insisted on carrying my traps[2] along the passage, and then up a great winding stair, and along another great passage, on whose stone floor our steps rang heavily. At the end of this he threw open a heavy door, and I rejoiced to see within a well-lit room in which a table was spread for supper, and on whose mighty hearth a great fire of logs, freshly replenished, flamed and flared.

[1] **Carpathians:** mountains; [2] **traps:** luggage.

Oral exploration

1 Discuss with your partner what you both learn about Dracula from the way the narrator describes how he looks and acts. Jot down some agreed points and share them with the class.

2 What first impressions of Dracula's character do you both get from the way he greets Harker and the things he says to him? Note three agreed points and share them with the class.

3 'Dracula is extraordinary!' With your partner decide on three ways in which Dracula appears very different from the ordinary host welcoming a guest.

Read, write, explore

1 Read paragraph one again. What were Jonathan's main fears as he waited to meet Count Dracula?

2 In paragraph two, the writer uses many onomatopoeic words (words that sound like their meaning, such as 'oink'). Why, in your opinion, does he use them? What effect do they have on you, the reader? Write down other sound words that could be used in this paragraph.

3 Paragraph three creates an eerie Gothic experience for the reader. Write out the words or phrases that help to create a sense of threat. Try to describe the nature of the threat.

4 How does the writer use the setting of the great castle to create a mysterious Gothic feel?

5 List three or more phrases that you consider 'archaic' or 'old-fashioned', i.e. no longer used in the same manner.

Create – A Gothic transformation

Work with a partner to transform a character.

Imagine that a celebrity that you know was to change, over a period of time, into a strange Gothic character resembling Dracula. Before you launch into your own one, look at the example outlined in the PowerPoint. Think about how the celebrity changes into a Gothic-type character.

[ ] PowerPoint

Now over to you. Choose one of the celebrity characters from the PowerPoint for a Gothic transformation.

1 Write a short introduction/profile for one of the celebrity characters shown. Don't forget to include the following:

- Appearance – such as hair colour, unusual dress or other outstanding features.
- Personality – such as friendly, funny or helpful.

2 Imagine that this character began to change into a Gothic-type character like Dracula.

- Discuss and write a description or profile of the character, showing how he or she has changed.
- How might the way they usually speak or the things they usually say alter?

⋯⋗ Use the transformation chart in your Portfolio to record your findings.

Portfolio 3E

Punctuation

1 Choose a sentence from the extract where commas are well used to construct a clear list or series of details.

2 What effect do the question marks have in paragraph one?

3 How does the author's use of dashes help the reader's understanding?

4 Collect your answers from the class and create an answer to the following question.

Question on *Dracula*

Question

How does Bram Stoker use imagery (similes) and punctuation (dashes, exclamations, speech marks) to give drama and atmosphere to the action that happens in paragraphs four and five? Make notes.

Compare your notes with the following sample answer.

Sample answer

The scene is an eerie one. Dracula is welcoming a visitor; this is scary enough but the writer highlights the welcomes with exclamation marks (!) to give some shock value at the start.

Dracula's strangeness is further highlighted when the writer uses the simile, 'stood like a statue'. The cold, stony images are repeated with another simile, 'cold as ice'. The scariness of the situation is heightened by the use of the dash (—) 'cold as ice — more like the hand of a dead than a living man'. The dash here represents a pause to give Harker and the reader time to take in the scariness.

In paragraph five, the dialogue (within the speech marks) further adds to the drama of the situation. Dracula welcomes Harker, but seems to threaten him subtly as well when he orders him to 'Come freely. Go safely.' Finally the writer adds to the mystery when Dracula says, 'and leave something of the happiness you bring!' He seems friendly but the exclamation mark (!) may suggest otherwise.

A Gothic Poem

'The Listeners' by Walter de la Mare

Walter de la Mare (1873–1956) was an English poet, short story writer and novelist. He is probably best remembered for his works for children and for his poem 'The Listeners'. His ashes are buried in the crypt of St Paul's Cathedral, where he had once been a choirboy.

Walter de la Mare

Before you read

Listen to a reading of the poem. Write down two things that you liked about the reading and one aspect that you were not so keen on. Make a list of these as a class on the board; these will inform your own reading of the poem.

Note any difficult terms/vocabulary and look them up before you continue.

THE LISTENERS

'Is there anybody there?' said the Traveller,
Knocking on the moonlit door;
And his horse in the silence champed the grass
Of the forest's ferny floor;
And a bird flew up out of the turret,
Above the Traveller's head:
And he smote upon the door again a second time;
'Is there anybody there?' he said.
But no one descended to the Traveller;
No head from the leaf-fringed sill
Leaned over and looked into his grey eyes,
Where he stood perplexed and still.
But only a host of phantom listeners
That dwelt in the lone house then
Stood listening in the quiet of the moonlight
To that voice from the world of men:
Stood thronging the faint moonbeams
    on the dark stair,
That goes down to the empty hall,
Hearkening in an air stirred and shaken
By the lonely Traveller's call.

And he felt in his heart their strangeness,
Their stillness answering his cry,
While his horse moved, cropping the dark turf,
'Neath the starred and leafy sky;
For he suddenly smote on the door, even
Louder, and lifted his head:--
'Tell them I came, and no one answered,
That I kept my word,' he said.
Never the least stir made the listeners,
Though every word he spake
Fell echoing through the shadowiness
    of the still house
From the one man left awake:
Ay, they heard his foot upon the stirrup,
And the sound of iron on stone,
And how the silence surged softly backward,
When the plunging hoofs were gone.

Walter de la Mare

Oral exploration

1 Pick out some descriptions of the silence in the house. Say how they help you to imagine the scene.

2 There is much alliteration (a number of words, having the same first consonant sound occur close together such as *Simple, Simon said*) in the poem. Say some of them and write them down. Can you suggest how they help the rhythm and the mood of the poem?

3 Looking at your table of 'Gothic elements' in your Portfolio, decide in pairs which ones you would use to describe the following: atmosphere, setting and emotions. Where in the poem do these elements occur? Give exact lines.

Read, write, explore

1 Imagine you saw the Traveller leave the castle door and could ask him five questions in order to find out why he is knocking on the door of this empty castle. What questions would you put to him?

2 Solve the mystery. Invent a plot using **The Big Wish** (see page 77 of this unit). This poem is effective more for what it leaves out than for what it puts in: things we can guess but can never know. Using the answers to the questions you asked above, jot down in point form the whole story of the Traveller from the time he left the house long ago, until his return.

3 Imagine that you were the Traveller and after your second knock, the door creaked and opened itself. Then imagine that you went in. Describe what happened next!

Portfolio 3F

Create

The poem is very brief, but we are told quite a lot. Work in pairs to discuss and then write down the main images you would use from the poem in order to make it into a short comic strip. Use the story board sequence in your Portfolio to help you.

Portfolio 3G

A Gothic novel

Wuthering Heights by Emily Brontë

Emily Brontë (1818–1848) was born in Thornton, Yorkshire, England. She lived a quiet life there with her clergyman father; brother, Branwell Brontë; and two sisters, Charlotte and Anne. The sisters enjoyed writing poetry and novels, which they published under pseudonyms. Emily wrote *Wuthering Heights* in 1847—her only published novel—under the pseudonym of 'Ellis Bell'. She died in Haworth, Yorkshire in 1848.

Emily Brontë

Extract from

Wuthering Heights

It is winter and it is snowing hard. Mr Lockwood, the narrator, is forced to spend the night in Wuthering Heights high on the Yorkshire moors. The owner of Wuthering Heights is a man called Heathcliff who continuously mourns the loss of his one true love Catherine Earnshaw who married his rival, Edgar Linton, and died twenty years before. Heathcliff cannot get over Cathy, his one and only early teen dream-love. He longs to join her in the spirit world.

The extract you are about to read finds Mr Lockwood spending the night in Cathy's childhood room, unknown to Heathcliff. Sleeping in Cathy's childhood bed, he has a terrible nightmare where he is visited by the ghost of Cathy who wants to come back to life. As you would expect, Lockwood is terrified!

1   This time, I remembered I was lying in the oak closet,[1] and I heard distinctly the gusty wind, and the driving of the snow; I heard, also, the fir bough repeat its teasing sound, and ascribed it to the right cause: but it annoyed me so much, that I resolved to silence it, if possible; and, I thought, I rose and endeavoured to unhasp[2] the casement.[3] The hook was soldered into the staple: a circumstance observed by me when awake, but forgotten. 'I must stop it, nevertheless!' I muttered, knocking my knuckles through the glass, and stretching an arm out to seize the importunate[4] branch; instead of which, my fingers closed on the fingers of a little, ice-cold hand! The intense horror of nightmare came over me: I tried to draw back my arm, but the hand clung to it, and a most melancholy voice sobbed, 'Let me in—let me in!'

2   'Who are you?' I asked, struggling, meanwhile, to disengage myself. 'Catherine Linton,' it replied, shiveringly (why did I think of *Linton*? I had read *Earnshaw* twenty times for Linton)—

'I'm come home: I'd lost my way on the moor!' As it spoke, I discerned, obscurely, a child's face looking through the window. Terror made me cruel; and, finding it useless to attempt shaking the creature off, I pulled its wrist on to the broken pane, and rubbed it to and fro till the blood ran down and soaked the bedclothes: still it wailed, 'Let me in!' and maintained its tenacious grip, almost maddening me with fear. 'How can I!' I said at length. 'Let *me* go, if you want me to let you in!'

The fingers relaxed, I snatched mine through the hole, hurriedly piled the books up in a pyramid against it, and stopped my ears to exclude the lamentable prayer. I seemed to keep them closed above a quarter of an hour; yet, the instant I listened again, there was the doleful cry moaning on! 'Begone!' I shouted. 'I'll never let you in, not if you beg for twenty years.'

3 'It is twenty years,' mourned the voice: 'twenty years. I've been a waif[5] for twenty years!' Thereat[6] began a feeble scratching outside, and the pile of books moved as if thrust forward. I tried to jump up; but could not stir a limb; and so yelled aloud, in a frenzy of fright. To my confusion, I discovered the yell was not ideal: hasty footsteps approached my chamber door; somebody pushed it open, with a vigorous hand, and a light glimmered through the squares at the top of the bed. I sat shuddering yet, and wiping the perspiration from my forehead: the intruder appeared to hesitate, and muttered to himself.

4 At last, he said, in a half-whisper, plainly not expecting an answer, 'Is anyone here?' I considered it best to confess my presence; for I knew Heathcliff's accents, and feared he might search further, if I kept quiet. With this intention, I turned and opened the panels. I shall not soon forget the effect my action produced.

5 Heathcliff stood near the entrance, in his shirt and trousers; with a candle dripping over his fingers, and his face as white as the wall behind him. The first creak of the oak startled him like an electric shock: the light leaped from his hold to a distance of some feet, and his agitation was so extreme, that he could hardly pick it up.

'It is only your guest, sir,' I called out, desirous to spare him the humiliation of exposing his cowardice further. 'I had the misfortune to scream in my sleep, owing to a frightful nightmare. I'm sorry I disturbed you.'

[1] **closet:** a small room; [2] **unhasp:** loosen the hasp of. A hasp is a clasp for a door, lid, etc.; [3] **casement:** a window sash opening on hinges that are generally attached to the upright side of its frame; [4] **importunate:** troublesome; annoying; [5] **waif:** a person, especially a child, who is homeless, friendless or neglected; [6] **thereat:** after that.

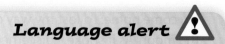

Imagery

Just like poets, fiction writers use images (called imagery) to bring a scene to life in your imagination. Images can create an atmosphere that stays in your mind long after the story is ended.

Look at this image from the extract:

'my fingers closed on the fingers of a little, ice-cold hand!'

•••➤ Say how this image captures Lockwood's surprise and terror. What is the effect of the repetition?

•••➤ What is the effect of the adjectives?

•••➤ Would you call it a Gothic image? Why? Why not?

Oral exploration

1 Discuss Lockwood's dream and say what aspects of it are typical of a bad nightmare.

2 How does the writer make the ghost of the little girl Cathy so scary to Lockwood? Mention three things.

3 'The first creak of the oak startled him like an electric shock: the light leaped from his hold to a distance of some feet, and his agitation was so extreme, that he could hardly pick it up.'

Comment on the writer's use of strong images to paint a vivid word picture of the scene in the quotation above.

4 Why, in your opinion, is Heathcliff so scared by this event? What had he imagined might happen as the oak door opened?

5 Pick out three agreed Gothic elements that you find in this extract. Link the elements to specific phrases or sentences.

Parts of the sentence
(Subject – Verb – Object – Adverbial)

Each sentence you say or write has a shape given by the parts that make it up. Each part helps you to express a particular meaning to help you make good sense.

The following sentences are created from the events in the passage above. They follow a simple shape: subject, verb, object and adverbial. Most sentences are more complicated but these sentences are made simple to help you to understand how the basic shape works.

Subject	Verb	Object	Adverbial
Lockwood	knocked	his knuckles	through the glass
Lockwood	rubbed	the hand	on the broken glass
Terror	made	Lockwood	cruel
Heathcliff	dropped	the candle	in fright

The **subject** is usually found at the start of the sentence. When you write a sentence the subject will tell your reader who (or what) the sentence is going to be about.	The **verb** tells your reader what the subject does, what action he/she takes, how he/she feels and what he/she thinks.	The **object** is affected by the subject. A verb does an action (knock, rub, made, drop). The object is what the verb acts on (knuckles, hand, Lockwood, candle). The verb tells your reader what that action is.	The **adverbial** (or adverbial phrase) is the key to knowing when, where or how the action of the verb happens. The adverbial makes the verb tell how it happens. Sometimes, the adverbial phrase is placed at the beginning for emphasis, as in two of the examples below.

Write out these sentences. Work with a partner to label the different sentence parts – *Subject*, *Verb*, *Object* and *Adverbial*. **Note:** Not all sentences contain all of these sentence parts.

1 Lockwood screamed out loud.
2 Cathy implored Lockwood to let her in.
3 Heathcliff loved Cathy in her absence.
4 The snow fell continuously on the window sill.
5 At that moment, Heathcliff knew the truth.
6 For a long time, Lockwood thought about that night.

Here are some sentences of similar structure. See how you might change the order of the parts in order to create a *more dramatic effect*. **The first one is done for you.**

1 Heathcliff called Cathy's name despairingly. *Despairingly, Heathcliff called Cathy's name.*
2 Lockwood was terrified on seeing the little white hand.
3 The snow fall was relentless as in a nightmare
4 Cathy implored Lockwood with thin wailing cries.
5 Heathcliff was shocked on seeing Lockwood's pale face.

⋯▶ Now find two examples of adverbial sentence openings from the text.
⋯▶ Imagine a tweet or text message that Lockwood might send about that night. You must begin with an adverbial phrase.

Climactic moments

All good stories have at least one crucial and exciting event (the climax) that happens towards the end of the narrative. While every effort should be made throughout a story to create atmosphere, show character and describe happenings, it is particularly important for the climactic scene.

⋯⋯⟩ On your own, think of your favourite film or novel. Describe the climax in a few lines. Swap it with the person beside you and see if they can guess what film or novel it is.

Imagery

Read the first three paragraphs of the *Wuthering Heights* extract again. They represent a moment of climax in the story.

⋯⋯⟩ Watch the animation on strong and weak verbs and then look for strong verb phrases and powerful images that make the experiences dramatic. Write them down.

⋯⋯⟩ Say how your chosen images contribute to the Gothic atmosphere.

The following are some areas that you might consider:

- The description of the weather
- If there is anything particularly shocking about this scene
- Words and phrases that suggest fear or terror
- How the narrator feels.

 Animation – Strong and weak verbs

Create – Audio recording

Imagine that you have been asked to create an audio recording of the extract above from *Wuthering Heights* for a Halloween special radio programme. The producer wants you not only to read it but to act it out, making it as engaging as possible. She/he has asked that you include sound effects and atmosphere. When you are happy with your recording, upload it to your e-Portfolio.

Note for Teachers: You will find step-by-step guidelines for this activity in your *How to Create an e-Portfolio* e-book. Log on to www.edcodigital.ie to access the e-book.

Create your own Gothic story

The final purpose of this unit is to get you ready to write a Gothic short story for your Portfolio.

So start planning now

⋯⋯⟩ Talk through the following steps with a partner or in a small group.

⋯⋯⟩ Jot down ideas as they come to mind and keep your notes as you will need them for writing your first draft.

The elements that go to make up any story

Here is a list of the **elements** that are the basic building blocks for all short stories. Work through these steps with a partner or in a group of three or four. Sketch out your plan in note form in your Portfolio.

Portfolio 3H

Setting makes your story real

⤑ Think of your story's setting very early on. Sketch out in your mind where the main events will happen.

⤑ Consider different historical settings with castles, prisons or secret passageways.

⤑ Consider scary modern settings, for example a deserted city or an experimental medical facility.

⤑ Make sure you clearly imagine the setting as this will help you to create the scary atmosphere.

The character who will keep your reader's interest

⤑ Have an idea of the main character's age, gender and some special features.

⤑ Base your character on a friend or someone you admire from your reading.

⤑ Write out a short description of his/her personality, strengths and weaknesses.

⤑ Remember to consider whether the narration will be in the first or third person. Check the passages in this unit to see who the narrator is in each case.

A situation gets your story started

⤑ Early on in the story put your character in a situation where he/she really wants something. This is known as **The Big Wish**. The wish could be for treasure, power, love, escape or protection. He/she may be:

- sent on a quest for something important (a scroll, a talisman, or a person)
- trying to escape a terrible destiny
- trying to rescue another character
- looking for a solution to a terrible threat.

Complications drive your story

⤑ The hero/heroine wants to succeed quickly in their quest. A good storyteller invents situations that get in the hero's way.

⤑ Start to plot your story by thinking of things, such as chance events or another strong character, that might hinder the hero's progress.

⤑ How the hero reacts to problems can tell us a lot about character.

The final complication – The climax

⤑ The final difficulty for your character could be a problem to solve, an enemy to defeat or a choice to make.

⤑ This will be the climax of the story. It should be full of scary atmosphere and strong descriptions.

The story's end

⤑ The wrapping up of the story.

Now go back over the elements to help you to plan your own short story. By now, you should have the basic outline of your story, the setting and the main character in note form. Keep those notes in your Portfolio.

Another Gothic novel

Now that you have created a rough outline of your story, read the following Gothic story for additional inspiration.

Frankenstein by Mary Shelley

Mary Shelley (1797–1851) was born on 30 August 1797, in London, England. She married poet Percy Bysshe Shelley in 1816. Two years later, she published her most famous novel, *Frankenstein*. Shelley died in 1851, in London, England.

Mary Shelley

Extract from

Frankenstein

Dr Frankenstein is a scientist who dabbles in finding the secret of life. He has just brought to life the corpse that he has assembled in his laboratory. He does not seem pleased with the situation.

1 It was on a dreary night of November that I beheld the accomplishment of my toils. With an anxiety that almost amounted to agony, I collected the instruments of life around me, that I might infuse a spark of being into the lifeless thing that lay at my feet. It was already one in the morning; the rain pattered dismally against the panes, and my candle was nearly burnt out, when, by the glimmer of the half-extinguished light, I saw the dull yellow eye of the creature open; it breathed hard, and a convulsive motion agitated its limbs.

2 How can I describe my emotions at this catastrophe, or how delineate the wretch whom with such infinite pains and care I had endeavoured to form? His limbs were in proportion, and I had selected his features as beautiful. Beautiful! – Great God! His yellow skin scarcely covered the work of muscles and arteries beneath; his hair was of a lustrous black, and flowing; his teeth of a pearly whiteness; but these luxuriances only formed a more horrid contrast with his watery eyes, that seemed almost of the same colour as the dun white sockets in which they were set, his shrivelled complexion and straight black lips.

3 The different accidents of life are not so changeable as the feelings of human nature. I had worked hard for nearly two years, for the sole purpose of infusing life into an inanimate body. For this I had deprived myself of rest and health. I had desired it with an ardour that far exceeded moderation; but now that I had finished, the beauty of the dream vanished, and breathless horror and disgust filled my heart.

4 Unable to endure the aspect of the being I had created, I rushed out of the room, continued a long time traversing my bed chamber, unable to compose my mind to sleep. At length lassitude succeeded to the tumult I had before endured; and I threw myself on the bed in my clothes, endeavouring to seek a few moments of forgetfulness. But it was in vain: I slept, indeed, but I was disturbed by the wildest dreams. I thought I saw Elizabeth, in the bloom of health, walking in the

streets of Ingolstadt. Delighted and surprised, I embraced her; but as I imprinted the first kiss on her lips, they became livid with the hue of death; her features appeared to change, and I thought that I held the corpse of my dead mother in my arms; a shroud enveloped her form, and I saw the grave-worms crawling in the folds of the flannel.

5 I started from my sleep with horror; a cold dew covered my forehead, my teeth chattered, and every limb became convulsed: when, by the dim and yellow light of the moon, as it forced its way through the window shutters, I beheld the wretch — the miserable monster whom I had created. He held up the curtain of the bed and his eyes, if eyes they may be called, were fixed on me. His jaws opened, and he muttered some inarticulate sounds, while a grin wrinkled his cheeks. He might have spoken, but I did not hear; one hand was stretched out, seemingly to detain me, but I escaped, and rushed down stairs. I took refuge in the courtyard belonging to the house which I inhabited; where I remained during the rest of the night, walking up and down in the greatest agitation, listening attentively, catching and fearing each sound as if it were to announce the approach of the demoniacal corpse to which I had so miserably given life.

6 Oh! no mortal could support the horror of that countenance. A mummy again endued with animation could not be so hideous as that wretch. I had gazed on him while unfinished, he was ugly then, but when those muscles and joints were rendered capable of motion, it became a thing such as even Dante could not have conceived.

Gothic vocabulary

···▸ In groups of three, underline one word from each paragraph which you do not understand the meaning of – to a maximum of three.

···▸ Look in the dictionary and note the meanings of these words. Listen to each group as they read out the words they didn't know. When it comes to your turn, read out only the words no one else has called out. You have five minutes to look up the words and five minutes to share meanings.

···▸ Use the Gothic dictionary sheet in your Portfolio.

Oral exploration

Now that you have thought about the elements of your own story plan, talk about the elements of a story as they apply to the *Frankenstein* extract.

···▸ **Setting makes the story real**

  ···▸ Look at the details that describe the setting. Is it night time or day time? What details would you add to make the setting clear to the reader? Write them down and share them.

···▸ **The main character – The narrator**

  ···▸ Try to describe to your partner the qualities of the main character, Dr Frankenstein. Point to phrases in the extract that describe him, but use your own descriptions as well. Do you admire him? Why? Why not?

···▸ **Dr Frankenstein's situation**

  ···▸ From what you read about him, what was the Doctor's **Big Wish** before we meet him in the extract? What did he want to achieve? How did he go about his plan?

···▸ **A major complication**

  ···▸ The Doctor seems to have achieved his **Big Wish**: to give life to a lifeless corpse. Explain why he is so unhappy. Look at the description of the monster to help you to explain the sudden twist in the story. Write down some of his features. Draw him if you wish.

···▸ **Speculate – The final complication (climax)**

  ···▸ Try to imagine how the story of Dr Frankenstein might end. Remember it's a Gothic tale so someone will end up miserable. Write notes to describe the climax of the story as you might invent it. Share your version with the class.

···▸ **Speculate – The end**

  ···▸ What happens to the Doctor and the monster in the final scene?

Read, write, explore

1 What sort of an atmosphere is created in the first paragraph? How does the writer achieve this?

2 Read the description of Frankenstein's monster carefully. How do we know that he is not fully human?

3 How does the writer capture the fear of the monster's creator? Use reference to the extract in your answer.

4 Using the 'Gothic Conventions' grid, find at least three Gothic features that you think would apply to this extract.

5 Who is narrating the story and what is the effect of this style of narration on you, the reader?

6 The monster has no name in the novel. Yet we mistakenly call the monster 'Frankenstein' after its creator. Why do you think this happens? Is it a good name?

Writing skills

Planning your Gothic story

Create your setting

Use the following questions to help you to think about the setting where the most important events of your story will happen. Make notes in your Portfolio.

Portfolio 31

1 Where in the world will you start the story? Practise describing the scene. Try things out – write, draw and judge later.

2 What places will your main character visit? Describe one threatening place.

3 When will important things happen? Describe a stormy night-time scene with a pale clouded moon. Describe an eerie night scene in an old building.

4 Now, write a description of the main setting.

A full Gothic short story

'The Wolves of Cernogratz'
by Hector Hugh Munro (Saki)

Hector Hugh Munro (1870–1916) is better known by his pen name, **Saki**. He was a British writer of witty and sometimes macabre Gothic tales. He is considered a master of the short story. As we see from the story 'The Wolves of Cernogratz', he had little time for snobbery, coming from a humble home himself. He died in France fighting in the First World War.

Hector Hugh Munro

The Wolves of Cernogratz

'Are there any old legends attached to the castle?' asked Conrad of his sister. Conrad was a prosperous Hamburg merchant, but he was the one poetically-dispositioned[1] member of an eminently practical family.

The Baroness Gruebel shrugged her plump shoulders.

'There are always legends hanging about these old places. They are not difficult to invent and they cost nothing. In this case there is a story that when any one dies in the castle all the dogs in the village and the wild beasts in the forest howl the night long. It would not be pleasant to listen to, would it?'

'It would be weird and romantic,' said the Hamburg merchant.

'Anyhow, it isn't true,' said the Baroness complacently; 'since we bought the place we have had proof that nothing of the sort happens. When the old mother-in-law died last springtime we all listened, but there was no howling. It is just a story that lends dignity to the place without costing anything.'

'The story is not as you have told it,' said Amalie, the grey old governess. Every one turned and looked at her in astonishment. She was wont to sit silent and prim and faded in her place at table, never speaking unless someone spoke to her, and there were few who troubled themselves to make conversation with her. Today a sudden volubility had descended on her; she continued to talk, rapidly and nervously, looking straight in front of her and seeming to address no one in particular.

'It is not when *any one* dies in the castle that the howling is heard. It was when one of the Cernogratz family died here that the wolves came from far and near and howled at the edge of the forest just before the death hour. There were only a few wolves that had their lairs in this part of the forest, but at such a time the keepers say there would be scores of them, gliding about in the shadows and howling in chorus, and the dogs of the castle and the village and all the farms round would bay and howl in fear and anger at the wolf chorus, and as the soul of the dying one left its body a tree would crash down in the park. That is what happened when a Cernogratz died in his family castle. But for a stranger dying here, of course no wolf would howl and no tree would fall. Oh, no.'

There was a note of defiance, almost of contempt, in her voice as she said the last words. The well-fed, much-too-well-dressed Baroness stared angrily at the dowdy old woman who had come forth from her usual and seemly position of effacement to speak so disrespectfully.

'You seem to know quite a lot about the von Cernogratz legends, Fraulein Schmidt,' she said sharply; 'I did not know that family histories were among the subjects you are supposed to be proficient in.'

The answer to her taunt was even more unexpected and astonishing than the conversational outbreak which had provoked it.

'I am a von Cernogratz myself,' said the old woman, 'that is why I know the family history.'

'You a von Cernogratz? You!' came in an incredulous chorus.

'When we became very poor,' she explained, 'and I had to go out and give teaching lessons, I took another name; I thought it would be more in keeping. But my grandfather spent much of his time as a boy in this castle, and my father used to tell me many stories about it, and, of course, I knew all the family legends and stories. When one has nothing left to one but memories, one guards and dusts them with especial care. I little thought when I took service with you that I should one day come with you to the old home of my family. I could wish it had been anywhere else.'

There was silence when she finished speaking, and then the Baroness turned the conversation to a less embarrassing topic than family histories. But afterwards, when the old governess had slipped away quietly to her duties, there arose a clamour of derision and disbelief.

'It was an impertinence,' snapped out the Baron, his protruding eyes taking on a scandalised expression; 'fancy the woman talking like that at our table. She almost told us we were nobodies, and I don't believe a word of it. She is just Schmidt and nothing more. She has been talking to some of the peasants about the old Cernogratz family, and raked up their history and their stories.'

'She wants to make herself out of some consequence,' said the Baroness; 'she knows she will soon be past work and she wants to appeal to our sympathies. Her grandfather, indeed!'

The Baroness had the usual number of grandfathers, but she never, never boasted about them.

'I dare say her grandfather was a pantry boy or something of the sort in the castle,' sniggered the Baron; 'that part of the story may be true.'

The merchant from Hamburg said nothing; he had seen tears in the old woman's eyes when she spoke of guarding her memories — or, being of an imaginative disposition, he thought he had.

'I shall give her notice to go as soon as the New Year festivities are over,' said the Baroness; 'till then I shall be too busy to manage without her.'

But she had to manage without her all the same, for in the cold biting weather after Christmas, the old governess fell ill and kept to her room.

'It is most provoking,' said the Baroness, as her guests sat round the fire on one of the last evenings of the dying year; 'all the time that she has been with us I cannot remember that she was ever seriously ill, too ill to go about and do her work, I mean. And now, when I have the house full, and she could be useful in so many ways, she goes and breaks down. One is sorry for her, of course, she looks so withered and shrunken, but it is intensely annoying all the same.'

'Most annoying,' agreed the banker's wife, sympathetically; 'it is the intense cold, I expect, it breaks the old people up. It has been unusually cold this year.'

'The frost is the sharpest that has been known in December for many years,' said the Baron.

'And, of course, she is quite old,' said the Baroness; 'I wish I had given her notice some weeks ago, then she would have left before this happened to her. Why, Wappi, what is the matter with you?'

The small, woolly lapdog had leapt suddenly down from its cushion and crept shivering under the sofa. At the same moment an outburst of angry barking came from the dogs in the castle-yard, and other dogs could be heard yapping and barking in the distance.

'What is disturbing the animals?' asked the Baron.

And then the humans, listening intently, heard the sound that had roused the dogs to their demonstrations of fear and rage; heard a long-drawn whining howl, rising and falling, seeming at one moment leagues away, at others sweeping across the snow until it appeared to come from the foot of the castle walls. All the starved, cold misery of a frozen world, all the relentless hunger-fury of the wild, blended with other forlorn and haunting melodies to which one could give no name, seemed concentrated in that wailing cry.

'Wolves!' cried the Baron.

Their music broke forth in one raging burst, seeming to come from everywhere.

'Hundreds of wolves,' said the Hamburg merchant, who was a man of strong imagination.

Moved by some impulse which she could not have explained, the Baroness left her guests and made her way to the narrow, cheerless room where the old governess lay watching the hours of the dying year slip by. In spite of the biting cold of the winter night, the window stood open. With a scandalised exclamation on her lips, the Baroness rushed forward to close it.

'Leave it open,' said the old woman in a voice that for all its weakness carried an air of command such as the Baroness had never heard before from her lips.

'But you will die of cold!' she expostulated.

'I am dying in any case,' said the voice, 'and I want to hear their music. They have come from far and wide to sing the death-music of my family. It is beautiful that they have come; I am the last von Cernogratz that will die in our old castle, and they have come to sing to me. Hark, how loud they are calling!'

The cry of the wolves rose on the still winter air and floated round the castle walls in long-drawn piercing wails; the old woman lay back on her couch with a look of long-delayed happiness on her face.

'Go away,' she said to the Baroness; 'I am not lonely any more. I am one of a great old family . . . '

'I think she is dying,' said the Baroness when she had rejoined her guests; 'I suppose we must send for a doctor. And that terrible howling! Not for much money would I have such death-music.'

'That music is not to be bought for any amount of money,' said Conrad.

'Hark! What is that other sound?' asked the Baron, as a noise of splitting and crashing was heard.

It was a tree falling in the park.

There was a moment of constrained silence, and then the banker's wife spoke.

'It is the intense cold that is splitting the trees. It is also the cold that has brought the wolves out in such numbers. It is many years since we have had such a cold winter.'

The Baroness eagerly agreed that the cold was responsible for these things. It was the cold of the open window, too, which caused the heart failure that made the doctor's ministrations unnecessary for the old Fraulein. But the notice in the newspapers looked very well—

'On December 29th, at Schloss Cernogratz, Amalie von Cernogratz, for
many years the valued friend of Baron and Baroness Gruebel.'

¹ **poetically-dispositioned:** poetically-minded.

What is *tone*?

Julie: 'Miss, I heard you. Would you relax?'

Teacher: 'I don't like the way you are speaking to me, Julie. Please change your tone.'

- ⟶ When the teacher uses the word 'tone' here, she is mainly referring to Julie's attitude as reflected in her voice.
- ⟶ **Tone** is another word for attitude (the way a person feels about something). It can be many things, such as gentle, pessimistic, bitter, loving, cold, optimistic, aggressive, enthusiastic or dismissive.
- ⟶ When a poet, or any writer, writes about something they feel strongly about, their tone is an important element in how we interpret what is being said.

Oral exploration

1. What impression do you get of the Baron and the Baroness from the way they treat Fraulein Schmidt when she first tells them that she is one of the noble von Cernogratz family?

2. Read the following few lines of the Baron to your partner in the tone you think is appropriate.

   'It was an impertinence,' snapped out the Baron, his protruding eyes taking on a scandalised expression; 'fancy the woman talking like that at our table. She almost told us we were nobodies, and I don't believe a word of it. She is just Schmidt and nothing more. She has been talking to some of the peasants about the old Cernogratz family, and raked up their history and their stories.'

   Then ask your partner to read it to you.

   What words would you use to describe the Baron's tone as he speaks about the old lady's claim to be a von Cernogratz? Is there more than one tone?
   What words or phrases used by the narrator most clearly reflect the tone or tones?

3. Discuss the Baroness's attitude to the old lady when she becomes ill. Find quotes that show her attitude clearly and read them out loud.

4. Do you consider Frau Schmidt ungrateful to the Baron and Baroness? Examine the things she says to them.

Read, write, explore

1 The story becomes more Gothic as it progresses. When did the first hint of a Gothic atmosphere strike you as you read it? Consult the table to check the signs. Write down words and phrases as evidence.

2 There is an obvious Gothic atmosphere when the old lady is lying on her bed with the windows open. Write a paragraph on how the writer uses the Gothic techniques to create the atmosphere of expectation.

3 The final scene where the wolves arrive is a great ending to the story. Do you agree with this assessment of the ending? Say why.

4 Comment on how appropriate the setting of this story is. Does it contribute to the Gothic atmosphere at the story's conclusion? How? How not?

Writing skills

Your Gothic short story

1 **Redraft**

Redraft your description of your story's setting. Look at the adjectives and verbs you have used. Are they strong enough? Do they catch the Gothic atmosphere? Remember that Gothic uses exaggeration.

2 **Write**

Write a short description of your hero or main character. Start to get a clear idea of who he or she is.

3 **Describe**

Describe your main character's **Big Wish**.

4 **Plan**

Plan at least one *complication* that will hinder the achievement of **The Big Wish**.

Write your *first full draft*. You will have time to edit and correct it over the next few days.

Portfolio 3J

A modern Gothic tale

'Escape to Nowhere' by Kate O'Connor

You are going to read a Gothic story written by a student, Kate O'Connor, when she was in Second Year.

Read it and use the comments to the side of the story to help you think about how the story produces its dramatic effect. Use the table in your Portfolio (3D) to identify the Gothic elements in the story.

Escape to Nowhere

1 It was her birthday again. Aisha half-opened her eyes, dragging a hand limply across her forehead in an effort to shield them from the morning sunlight. It was unusually quiet, but the thought that she must leave this place drifted through her groggy mind as she squinted and gradually adjusted her eyes to this glaring light. She felt a little cold and over-sleeping just made her more tired as her heavy eyelids drooped. A parchingly dry throat from long unattended thirst made her sit up and frown. Here she was, eighteen years old, well, sort of, and again she was about to make her escape for the umpteenth time… With a supreme effort she slid the lid off her stone tomb with a low grinding sound like the growl of a lioness.

> The main character, Aisha, introduced like a normal girl.

> The setting surprises us, as we see that Aisha is in a tomb. Gothic mystery is created.

2 Hoping to make an impression, she brushed age-long dust from her loosely wrapped, mouldering bandages, some tearing lightly under her attentive touch. It had been a while, to say the least, but now she was restless to wake and start her adventure. First, she set herself a mental reminder to fix the jagged cracks that had appeared in her sarcophagus, the cause of the insufferable brightness. The clean, fresh air made her cough, almost choke, in fact, used as she was to the musty, dusty-tasting tomb.

Further information on the main character. Aisha is a mummy and she is described well. She has a purpose: adventure.

3 She stretched her stiff limbs and swung her legs sideways, toes brushing the cold stone floor. Heaving herself out of the tomb, she shuffled across the floor, dragging wisps of bandages behind her with as much grace as she could muster for a privileged princess. She looked around admiring her section of the extravagantly carved mausoleum. She traced the intricate designs on her sarcophagus with pleasure, each curve perfect, each character beautiful – hieroglyphics to die for, she thought! She wondered who had created them for her. What boy, she wondered, had grieved for her so deeply?

Her situation is introduced: she is a princess, obviously rich and privileged. Eerie Gothic details are given.

4 But first she had to leave this place, this oppressive family pyramid where her father groaned constantly and where her mother whimpered and gibbered in ineffectual complaint. It was final; she must escape this oppressive place; get away from her parents and find and finally fall in love with the one who grieved so deeply for her. Yawning, revealing the black, mouldy hollows in her face, she pushed aside the tomb door with ease, stepping lightly outside, gathering her bandages.

Aisha's Big Wish is introduced: she wants to find love.

5 But there was something different this time… it wasn't like last time at all; last time when she had woken she ascended some craggy, stone steps to a vast shadowy desert plain dimly lit by a ghostly moon. She had wandered around for a while eating the last of her shrivelled fruit and then she hurried back to the safety of her tomb.

Flashback gives information on Aisha's long past.

6 This time, she stepped straight onto a strange, glossy surface. She was indoors, surrounded by walls hung with pretty pictures of her ancient world. She wrinkled her nose. How long had she been asleep? She bent down and inspected the strange floor carefully. There was nobody about, she decided, and she needed to find her lover.

Aisha's situation is developed.

7 She limped along the floor, through galleries of colourful pictures of tombs and then pictures of her mother and father and even one that looked like her when she was a child. She was so entranced that she did not notice voices nearby or approaching footsteps until they were mere cubits away.

8 She had been daydreaming over a golden sword, protected by some kind of solid, see through seal. She wanted her imagined lover to come to life **there and then**, and to bring her to life **there and then** and allow her to escape. If escape was impossible, then he must cross the ages and come back with her to the depths of the pyramid tomb to be hers forever. She turned sharply and darted behind

Aisha's Big Wish is further described. She becomes desperate, threatening.

a shadowy sarcophagus. The voices of living boys and girls laughed together and she froze as they approached. She didn't know what they were saying but they sounded so happy.

9 Then she saw him, this perfect boy, the love of her life, her ancient worn out life. He was on a school tour from Ireland with strange plant emblems on his tee shirt. She thought he looked so happy, so handsome. He was sixteen or seventeen she guessed. He was dressed in a strange way, so unlike the boys of ancient Egypt: he wore jeans and a tee shirt. If she had known the word 'cool' she would have said it. But there was a problem. He was holding hands with a girl who called him Donncha. 'Come on Sinead,' he said to her, 'let's see what's in this gaff,' said Donncha. Jealousy surged in Aisha's dusty breast as she rushed to search for the papyrus display.

> Leading us into the story's climax as Aisha sees Donncha. He is described. Her response to him is described. Passion!

10 Time was running out. If she was to capture Donncha then she must get to the papyrus display and speak the spell that would make him hers forever. The magic would work and he would age in an instant, collapsing to a wizened effigy of lost youth and beauty as she herself was. Then she could lead him back to the sarcophagus for her crazed and dusty nuptials.

> Tension rises as Aisha hatches her awful plan to capture and destroy Donncha. A dark and Gothic moment! The climax of the story.

11 But this is a Gothic story with a happy ending. The group of Irish school children were beginning to enter the papyrus room as Aisha had begun to utter the spell, 'Tooalla, tooalla, duenne.' But she stopped, unable to fight their living waves of laughter and happiness.

12 She cringed as their footsteps seemed right beside her. Suddenly, one boomed in her ear, making her jump. Without looking, in panic, she scrambled to her feet and sprinted away, through the empty darkened rooms. Voices cried out behind her but faded away and no footsteps pursued her. Her heart, such as it was, leapt and she grinned her horrible hollow grin as she rounded a corner and found her tomb. Slamming the door behind her, she climbed into her sarcophagus and pulled the cracked lid over her, her breaths still coming in gasps, her heart, such as it was, racing. Forcing herself to eventually calm down, she crossed her hands over her chest and closed her eyes for another thousand years. There was no escape. Love must wait, she mused, as she drifted back to sleep.

> The Conclusion: Aisha's cunning plan fails as she returns to her tomb.

Kate's preparation

···▷ Kate wrote this story over four days. She wrote some brief outline notes first, followed by a first draft which she showed to her teacher. Then she wrote the final draft which is printed here.

···▷ Below is Kate's brief outline.

I spent four days preparing. The homework was given on a Friday so I had the weekend and Monday to write it and finalise it before the English class on Tuesday.

On Friday, I decided what I'd write my story about and made a note of any words or phrases I wanted to include such as 'dusty-tasting' and 'mouldering bandages'. Of course, other words came to me over the weekend. I wanted a word for an ancient tomb and found just the right one, 'sarcophagus'.

The next stage was writing a draft. I write drafts repeatedly for all the essays and stories I write because it helps me refine what I want to and make it sound as good as possible. Sometimes, you can write a few drafts of a story and give it different endings each time to choose what direction you want it to go in.

As Gothic was new to me I wrote a few drafts over the weekend. Each time I wrote a draft, my story developed that bit more or some new aspect was added to it. I wrote my final draft on Monday. I looked over my favourite draft and chopped and added in pieces from the other drafts so I could make it sound the way I wanted it to. I tried to imagine the teacher marking it too.

The time given to write a story should be used to the fullest extent possible to allow yourself to come up with new ideas and be inspired by things like books or movies for even one word which could change your story. In this case I was also inspired by reading some of the original Dracula story by Bram Stoker.

I got my idea for the plot from a school trip I went on, to see an exhibition on Tutankhamun, the young Egyptian king. I found it really spooky and interesting to see all the artefacts and read about the mysterious ruler. It gave me a setting and situation that I could imagine for Aisha.

Kate

Crescents interview

Now listen to the interview with Kate as she discusses where she got her initial ideas from.

Write your Gothic story

Use the short story rubric in the Portfolio to help you to identify the areas that need more work. This can be done by your parents, your friend, the teacher, or indeed you could have a go yourself. Take comments on board. Be prepared to rewrite some parts of your story in the light of comments.

Portfolio 3J

Write your Gothic short story in your Portfolio.

Then hand the story in to your teacher and move on!

Portfolio 3K

Film in Focus:
Son of Rambow

In this unit you will:

···▸ explore the themes, characters and setting of one of the prescribed films

···▸ understand how it tells the story through different aspects of the film production process

···▸ appreciate the work of different crew members

···▸ use the information in this unit to analyse and discuss any film.

You will encounter the following:

● References to the film

● Extracts from the film script

● Behind-the-scenes interviews with the director and producer

● *Crescents* interview with Irish TV actress Niamh Daly

Exploring film

At the end of this unit you will be asked to make a short presentation on a favourite scene from *Son of Rambow* or a film of your choice, using the information you have learned.

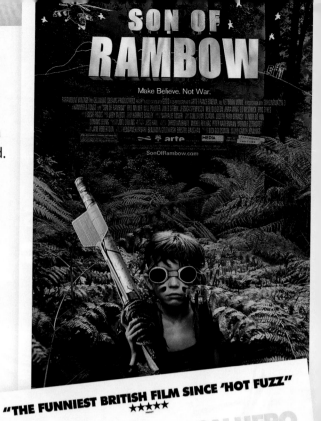

Before viewing

The film poster

1 Before a film is released, posters and trailers are issued to grab your attention and to create interest. In pairs, look at the two *Son of Rambow* posters and pick out the following elements:

- A key image
- The title
- The cast
- Information about the plot/genre (type of film)
- A tag line

2 Which poster do you think is more interesting? Take a vote on the class's favourite. Look at the posters and find the tag lines and the critics' comments.

After viewing

Once you have watched the film, work through the following questions with a partner.

Oral exploration

1 Did you like the film? Look at the posters again and at your Portfolio notes. Do you agree with the critics' comments and/or the tag line? Write your own comment on the film.

2 Read the synopsis of the film and fill in the gaps with the words below.

> Will Proudfoot is the eldest son of a Plymouth Brethren family. The Brethren's _____ moral _____ means that Will has never been _____ to mix with other people, listen to music or _____ TV. That is until he finds himself caught up in the _____ world of Lee Carter, the school _____. Carter exposes Will to a _____ copy of *Rambo: First Blood* and from that _____, Will's mind is blown wide open and he's easily convinced to be the _____ in Lee Carter's _____ home movie.

- *diabolical*
- *pirate*
- *stuntman*
- *moment*
- *allowed*
- *watch*
- *code*
- *terror*
- *extraordinary*
- *strict*

3 Find the three adjectives in the list. Using a dictionary or thesaurus, find synonyms for these three adjectives and use them to write a new synopsis for the film.

Making the film

The story

Three-act structure

There are many different stages involved in making a film. It is a long process from getting a story from an original idea to the completed film you see on screen. Like most stories, popular mainstream films have a **beginning**, a **middle** and an **end**. This is also referred to as a basic **three-act structure**.

Act One: The set-up	**Act Two: The confrontation**	**Act Three: The resolution**
The main characters and setting are introduced, along with the main plot: a problem to be solved.	Obstacles get in the way; something happens to change the direction of the lead character.	The conclusion; all loose ends are tied up. The character defeats the problem, learns to live with the problem, or the problem defeats the character.

Oral exploration

1 Look at the photos from different films. Work with a partner to identify the **three-act structure** in these films. Use the chart in your Portfolio.

Portfolio 4A

2 Compare your chart with the rest of the group.

3 Now discuss the story of *Son of Rambow*. Does it follow a three-act structure? As a group, agree and write a synopsis of each act.

Turning points

As each act unfolds there is usually a major **turning point** which changes the way the action is going.

1 Can you identify these turning points in *Son of Rambow*?

2 Present your three-act synopsis and turning points to the rest of the class. Have you all identified the same turning points? Discuss and decide.

The idea

Here is an account of how the writer/director Garth Jennings came up with the idea for *Son of Rambow*.

The idea for *Son of Rambow* came from a strong desire to tell a story that would capture a specific time in my life: being eleven years old and making home movies with my friends. I made my first home movie after seeing a video copy of *First Blood* (the first *Rambo* movie). My friends and I were so blown away by the film that we just had to make our own version using my father's gigantic video camera.

Trying to capture the impact movies like *First Blood* had on me was difficult to translate into a screenplay but when I moved my story to my next-door neighbours – a Plymouth Brethren family – it all started to fall into place. A boy who had never, ever been allowed to see a film (due to the moral code of the Brethren) would surely have his mind blown if the first film he ever saw was *First Blood*!

There are many facts that have been twisted, exaggerated, skipped over and edited from my childhood but the intention was never to tell a story of how things really were, but how I feel when I look back and remember those extraordinary times and wonderful friendships.

Interview extract courtesy of Garth Jennings.

Read, write, explore

1 What was Garth Jennings' main idea for the film?

2 Can you find the two different points that helped shape his idea?

3 What was his intention in telling the story?

4 Does the director achieve what he set out to do?

The screenplay

Getting the ideas down!

Once Garth Jennings had come up with the idea, it had to be developed into a **screenplay**. This is then worked into a shooting script for production. Read the extract from the shooting script below, then answer the questions in pairs.

> A **screenplay** is the name given to a written work by screenwriters for a television programme or film.

(Film Chapter 1)

FADE IN: MOVIE SCREEN:
We are in the audience looking up at the movie RAMBO: FIRST BLOOD. Stallone leaps out of the bushes and holds Brain Dennehy at knife point. The audience gasp.

RAMBO
Don't push it. Don't push it or I'll give you a war you won't believe...

INT. CINEMA. – DAY
We turn around to see a teenager with a huge, primitive video camera making a pirate copy of the film. This is LEE CARTER, a tough looking 13 year old smoking a cigarette. A man's voice explains:

ADULT WILL (V.O.)
Back in 1982 you were allowed to smoke in cinemas as long as you sat on the right hand side of the auditorium. Lee Carter always sat on the left. Mainly because there was more empty space to make pirate copies of the latest blockbusters, but it was also to further irritate the ushers who were too scared of him to do anything about it.

A gangly teenage usher stands nervously in the wings with his torch.

EXT. CINEMA. – DAY
The film is over. The audience leave. CARTER is chased out by an angry cinema manager. The manager clouts the pathetic USHER and shouts after CARTER.

© Extract reprinted courtesy of Hammer & Tongs

> **Interesting fact**
> Originally there was going to be a voiceover (V.O.) throughout the film. Do you think it was the right decision to remove it?

Oral exploration

1 Name the characters in this scene.

2 List the locations used for this scene.

3 Watch the scene in the film and compare. Are they the same? What, if anything, is different? Why, do you think, has it been changed?

4 Find out the meanings of: Fade in, INT., V.O. and EXT. Write these words and explanations in your film vocabulary sheet in your Portfolio.

Portfolio 4B

5 In groups of three, read the extract again aloud, taking different roles:
(a) Rambo (b) Direction (c) V.O.

Film production

As a novel tells its story through words, a film tells its story through the images you see and the sounds you hear on screen. These images and sounds give the viewer information that makes meaning.

How are the images created?

A film-maker creates images using the different elements of film. The main elements of film are:

- **Sound** (sound from the action or added sound effects and music)
- **Mise-en-scène** (everything that makes up the scene – costumes, props, lighting, body language, etc.)
- **Editing** (how it's all put together)
- **Camera** (creates different types of shot)
- **Lighting** (lights the scene)

A producer oversees each project from the beginning to the end. They may also be involved in the marketing and distribution processes. **Producers** work closely with the directors and other production staff on a shoot.

In film-making, the director doesn't do all the work. Making a film is a collaborative process that requires a lot of skilled people who make up the crew.

Watch the credits for *Son of Rambow* or search online. Find out who is responsible for each of the elements in this film.

© Maggie Ferreira

Look at the photo from the set. Can you name each member of the crew in the photo?

Share your findings with the group and in your Portfolio, complete the end credits roll for *Son of Rambow*.

Portfolio 4C

Shooting *Son of Rambow*

Like any film, *Son of Rambow* contains many different kinds of shot, depending on where the camera is positioned. Here are some examples of shot types:

© Maggie Ferreira

Medium shot
- Contains the character(s) from just below the waist up
- Enables us to see the characters' facial expressions.

Long shot
- Shows the entire person
- Enables the viewer to see the characters in relation to their surroundings.

Close-up
- Contains a character's face
- Enables the viewer to see how the character is feeling and empathise with him/her.

The angles of the camera are also very important. There can be a **high-** or a **low-** angle camera shot.

High-angle
- Camera is above the character looking down
- Can make characters look vulnerable and weak
- Good angle to represent an adult looking at a child (an adult's point of view)

Low-angle
- Camera is placed below the character's eyes looking up
- Makes the character look dominant, powerful and aggressive
- Can make the viewer feel vulnerable and feel empathy towards the character whose point of view we are being shown

Camera movement

Key scene: Chapter 7 (Flying Dog)

> 'For the flying dog scene we had a huge crane, which we positioned in front of the school building. Suspended from the crane on an intricate wire system was the flying dog model, and below that was Bill Milner.'
>
> **Nick Goldsmith, Producer**

Watch the flying dog scene. Focus on how the camera moves and follows the action.

The camera doesn't stay stationary all the time and will move to follow the action.

- **Pan** (camera turns sideways)
- **Track/dolly** (camera is placed on a track to follow the action)
- **Zoom** (the camera lens moves in or out)

Can you find examples of these shots in the flying dog scene?

Create

In groups, choose one scene from the film. Discuss together how you think the scene was created using the different elements of film. Each person chooses a **crew** role and presents a scene to the class.

In focus: The characters

Key scene: Chapter 2 (Torture)

> 'We saw hundreds of actors for the lead roles, but when Bill and Will walked in we instantly knew that they were right for the roles'.
>
> **Nick Goldsmith, Producer**

1 Watch the chapter where Will and Lee first meet. How do the boys differ from each other? What do they have in common? In your Portfolio list any words that describe Will and Lee.

Portfolio 4D

2 After the goldfish bowl incident, the geography teacher describes the two boys as 'a couple of miscreants'. Find out what the word 'miscreant' means. Do you agree?

3 How do you think different people in the film view each boy? In groups, choose one person each from the list below and write up a number of sentences giving your opinion of each boy.

Geography teacher:	'Lee is very disruptive. He's . . . '
Will's mum:	
Lee's brother:	
Classmate:	
Lee:	'Will is . . . '
Will:	'Lee is . . . '
Didier:	

4 Now combine the opinions. Which opinion is closest to the real character? Write a complete description of each boy using the different points of view.

In focus: Will

'This was a visual way to get to know a kid who says nothing and knows no one…
the toilet is a place of sanctuary too!'

Garth Jennings, Director

INT. TOILET CUBICLE:
WILL draws the last character on a glorious Bayeux Tapestry-style
montage that covers the inside of the cubicle. For a moment the
montage moves and makes noises. WILL smiles.

© Extract reprinted courtesy of Hammer & Tongs

Oral exploration

1 How would you describe Will at the start of the film? Brainstorm a list of adjectives
and match them with evidence from the film.

2 Watch the scene extract where we see Will in the toilet for the first time. Read the
screenplay extract and director Garth Jennings' intention for this.

3 Role Play: In pairs, take the roles of Garth/Will.

Garth: What do you want Will to do in this scene? How will you direct him?

Will: How will you appear in this scene? What do you want to show the audience? How
are you feeling at this point in the story? Use some of the adjectives you have listed.

4 Discuss: How closely does the scene resemble the screenplay and Garth's intention?

Theme: Sanctuary

What's the connection between A and B below for Will?

A

Sanctuary: an area around the altar of a church for the clergy and choir

Sanctuary: a shelter from danger or hardship

Sanctuary: a consecrated place where sacred objects are kept

B

Read, write, explore

1 Read what Garth says about the toilet being a place of sanctuary. What do you think he means? Which of the dictionary definitions of sanctuary is most appropriate in this case?

2 Why does Will seek sanctuary? From what or whom? Draw a picture of Will's different sanctuaries and match with the most suitable dictionary definition. Explain your choice in each case.

3 Is there somewhere you have a sanctuary?

Whose locker is it?

1 Will's locker is full of things that reflect his personality. List three of the props.

2 On the film set, who decided what to put in the locker? Refer back to the end credits activity on page 98.

3 If someone opened your locker could they tell it was yours? Choose one prop that reveals your personality; place it in a box with props from everyone else. Pick a prop and guess whose it is.

4 If you were in charge of Lee's locker, what would you include in it?

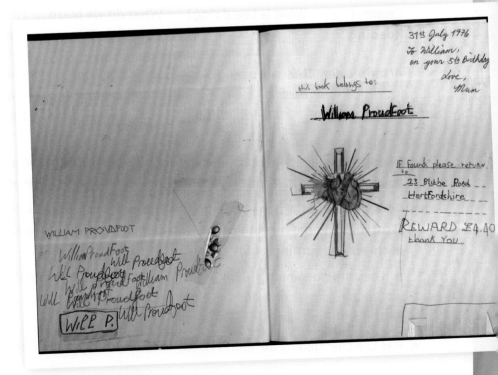

Courtesy of David OReilly

In focus: Lee

Read the quote above. Pick out
the different ways he describes
Lee. How many can you find?
Which of the descriptions best
describes him in your opinion?

Character development

In a film, as the plot unfolds,
the main characters will usually
change too in what is known as a
character arc. Usually, by the end
of the film, the main character
will be different or they will have
learnt something.

1   Consider Lee at different points in the film. Play the DVD
menu and record in your Portfolio the chapter headings. Recall what Lee
does in each chapter and discuss what we learn about him from these
scenes. The first one is started for you.

Portfolio 4E

Chapter heading	What is Lee doing?	What do we learn about him?	How does the film show this?
At the movies	*Lee is recording the film*	*Lee is rebellious, tough, creative*	*Feet on seat. Close-up of face, showing expression…*

2   Choose your favourite Lee scene and watch it again. Using the elements of film that
you have learned, describe how the scene depicts Lee's character (column four).

3   Consider Lee at the beginning, middle and end. Take a look back at your **three-act
structure** and the **turning points** you identified. Match up Lee's behaviour with
each **act** and **turning point**. Describe:

- Lee at the beginning
- Lee at turning point one
- Lee at the middle
- Lee at turning point two
- Lee at the end

4   Has Lee changed by the end? Has he learnt anything, in your opinion?

Key scenes: Lee

The key scenes for Lee's character are Chapter 1 (At the Movies), Chapter 3 (Rambo), Chapter 5 (Screen Tests) and Chapter 10 (The Final Shoot). Watch each of these scenes closely.

1 Why are these scenes significant?

2 Watch Chapter 3 again. Imagine that you are writing Will's diary – how would he describe Lee after that day?

Create

New boy in class!

Imagine that Lee has been expelled and has been accepted into your school. Write a diary account of the first day he arrives in your class. Remember to use some of the ideas you have worked on already.

Language alert

> **Key Scene 5**
> And, cut. Skill. Skills on toast.

1 Who says this? What does it mean? What would you say instead of this?

> **Key Scene 8**
> WILL
> The film is going to be skill with him in it. Come on!
>
> CARTER
> Skill? Look, it doesn't sound right when you say things like me.

© Extracts reprinted courtesy of Hammer & Tongs

2 Who is Will talking about? What does Lee Carter mean? Do you agree with him?

Animation – Idioms

Idioms are word combinations which have a particular meaning that is different from the literal meaning of each word on its own. For example, 'raining cats and dogs' or 'skills on toast'. Watch the animation on idioms to learn more about these weird and wacky word combinations!

Are you talking to me?

What do you think influences the way Lee and Will speak? Think about the oral language that you use. Do you have favourite expressions? Do you use different language in different situations? Over a day, record yourself in three different conversations, for example with a parent, teacher or friend. Transcribe one minute of each conversation and answer these questions.

1 Can you describe your accent? Who/what has influenced it?
2 Which words do you use most often?
3 Do you use different words and language with different people?
4 Compare with your group – what are the most common slang words you use?

In focus: Me

1 How do you think the different people in your life see you? Ask two different people for their opinions, combine with your own and write a description of yourself.
2 Do you have an online self? Is it different from or similar to the description you wrote above?

Setting: Home

Key scene: Chapter 3 (Rambo)

Will: 'So this is your home?' Lee: 'Yep this is it. Home Sweet Home.' (Chapter 3)

1 Will and Lee's homes are very different in the film. Do you agree with Lee's words? Imagine the production decisions in creating the look of each home. Complete the production notes in your Portfolio.

Portfolio 4F

Production notes: Lee's house

Overall appearance
Props
Rooms
Lighting
Colour

Production notes: Will's house

Overall appearance
Props
Rooms
Lighting
Colour

2 A production company is looking for a typical teenager's room for a TV advert. Take a photo of your room (or draw a detailed plan), upload it or print it out and write an accompanying description including the elements above. Why should they choose your room, or why not?

Themes

Breaking the rules

Key scenes: Chapter 2 (Torture) and Chapter 4 (Helping a Friend)

> LEE
> I don't mind taking the
> blame for this if you like.

Both Lee and Will break different sets of rules.

1 In groups complete the rules for each setting below.

2 Add the action that causes the rules to be broken in each case.

3 Then discuss and add a consequence for breaking each of the actions.

Church rules	School rules	Will's home rules	Nursing home rules
Consequence	**Consequence**	**Consequence**	**Consequence**

4 There are spoken rules. Are there unspoken rules in the film too? Explain.

5 Consider the rules you must keep. Are there consequences if you break them? Have you experienced this? Write an account of this.

'My Best Day of All Time' – Will

Watch Chapter 5 again. Start from where Will goes to the shoe-mender's up to his rescue from the lake.

1 Will describes this as his best day of all time. What are the events that make up the day? In groups, come up with a running order of events as they occurred.

2 Here is an example of the actual storyboard from *Son of Rambow*. Create a similar storyboard for the main events of Will's best day ever.

3 What ingredients would make up your best day? Make a list of ingredients and how much you will need of each, for example, a handful of friends. Add directions such as 'pour a cup of sunshine'. Then create your recipe for your best day of all time.

© Storyboard extract courtesy of Garth Jennings

Theme of friendship

**Key scenes: Chapter 6
(Blood Brothers) and
Chapter 12 (Special Feature)**

> 'Will and Lee are lonely souls at the start of this story but they forge a friendship through the making of their own film.'
>
> **Garth Jennings, Director**

1 What, according to Garth, is the key to Will and Lee's friendship?

2 Working in groups, agree on three qualities of a good friendship. Think also about a friendship that is undesirable. You can make your desirable qualities negative, for example reliable/unreliable. As a class, rank the qualities according to their importance.

Portfolio 4G

3 From the start to the end, Will and Lee's friendship changes a lot. Look back at your chapter headings (Portfolio 4E) and see if you can recall the different events concerning their friendship and the qualities demonstrated by each boy. Then fill in the following in your Portfolio.

Portfolio 4H

Incident	What happens (concerning their friendship)	Which desirable or undesirable quality is demonstrated?
Meeting outside Principal's office	*Lee fools Will into giving him his watch*	*cheating, sly*
Lee's house, filming		

4 Work with a partner and choose one of the incidents. One of you should narrate the incident from Lee's point of view while the other should narrate it from Will's point of view.

5 Complete a diary entry based on one of the chosen incidents. Think about how your character (Will or Lee) felt and thought about the incident rather than just what happened.

Portfolio 4I

Friendship and betrayal

Key scene: Chapter 10 (Final Shoot)

> CARTER
> What would you know about promises, blood brother.
>
> WILL
> You drew first blood.

© Extract reprinted courtesy of Hammer & Tongs

Read the quotes above.

1 What do Lee and Will mean?

2 In this scene, both boys feel betrayed. Who do you think is most guilty, Will or Lee or both?

3 Divide the group into **Team Will** and **Team Lee**. Each side defends itself against the accusation of betrayal. Share arguments with the whole class and take a vote. What is the class's decision?

Didier – friend or foe?

Key scenes: Chapter 2 (Torture) and Chapter 11 (Au revoir)

1 Is Didier a friend or a foe? Watch the two scenes and note how the director presents Didier's character.

Evidence from scene	What film techniques are used?	What do we learn about Didier?
Gets off bus last	*Close-up*	

Portfolio 4J

2 Write a character study of Didier, from arrival at school to departure. Remember to include evidence from the text to back up your points.

3 Read the quote below from Garth Jennings. Do you agree?

> 'But it's just a movie and it's really about friendship. School is important but great friends are gold.'
>
> **Garth Jennings, Director**

Location, location, location

Key scene: Chapter 8 (The Wolf)

Location

Disused power plant at Richborough, near Sandwich, Kent, England. Abandoned mid 1990s. Now demolished.

1. When is the above location used in the film?

2. Can you recall all the different locations that are used?

3. In *Son of Rambow*, each school location serves a different purpose for the story. Look at the grid below and find the ten verbs, adjectives and nouns. Then match the appropriate words to the locations. Some may apply to a few locations. Compare with your partner.

Classroom	Yard	Sixth-form common room	Toilets	Corridor

punishment	*learning*	*outsider*	*exclude*	*plotting*
nervous	*boredom*	*cool*	*hidden*	*repetition*
waiting	*artistic*	*troublesome*	*teacher*	*dreaming*
creativity	*fit in*	*oblivious*	*groups*	*forbidden*
unbothered	*bullying*	*friends*	*fun*	*secret*
unsure	*relationships*	*dancing*	*showing off*	*daring*

4. Choose from these words to write a *Son of Rambow* haiku (a three-line poem with seventeen syllables).

5. Now think of your own school as a film set. Which locations will you choose? Over your lunch break, work with a partner and scout for locations. Take some images and write detailed descriptions.

🖥 PowerPoint – The history of film

Setting: The 1980s

Before you read

What do you know about the 1980s in Ireland and England? What were the top technology toys? What TV programmes were popular? What music was in the charts? Collect your information in the class.

The Cure

Son of Rambow is set in 1980s England. This was the era of Margaret Thatcher's government, and the miners' strike. Up-and-coming bands included Duran Duran, Depeche Mode, The Cure, Siouxsie and the Banshees. 1980s fashion featured big shoulders, big hair, stonewashed jeans, dramatic colours and make-up. People were getting VCR players at home, and could record on TV using large VHS tapes. Home video cameras were also becoming common, but, unlike today's digital technology, were large and cumbersome. Editing of tapes was done manually, just like we see in the film. One the most popular films of the early 1980s was *First Blood* starring Sylvester Stallone as a Vietnam veteran. Director Garth Jennings recalls the impact of seeing the film for the first time and he wanted to convey this in *Son of Rambow*.

Read, write, explore

1 Compare and contrast the 1980s described above with Ireland now. What are the main differences and similarities?

2 Interview a family member or friend who recalls the 1980s. Ask them about recording TV programmes or using a video camera. Before you launch into this task you must prepare. Here are some pointers:

   (a) Draw up a list of instructions on how the task was performed in the 1980s.
   (b) Then draw up a list of instructions to explain how to do this **today**.

   Compare the two interviews.

3 Write a similar text for Ireland of 2000s.

The soundtrack

Key scene: Chapter 8 (The Wolf)

> 'Garth and I were discussing the soundtrack probably even before the script was written. There were certain songs that we all grew up with, and instantly created an image for the time.'
>
> **Nick Goldsmith, Producer**

Music in film is called the **soundtrack**. What songs can you remember from the film? Research on the internet and make a list of all the songs used in *Son of Rambow*.

Portfolio 4K

1 Working in groups, brainstorm the songs that you have grown up with. Compile a group soundtrack and present it to the class.

2 Add your group selection to a whole-class soundtrack. Examine the soundtracks chosen. What impression of your era are they suggesting?

3 Imagine that it is your graduation from school. Agree as a class on four songs from this list that you think would reflect your time in school.

Signs and signifiers

In a poem, a poet will create images with similes and metaphors. In a film, there are visual and aural **signs** on which the audience will place meaning. These are known as **signifiers**.

If you are watching a film, what meaning do you put on the following: A full moon? A phone ringing? A knife on the floor? Heavy footsteps?

In *Son of Rambow*, the **watch** takes on different meanings throughout the film. What do you think it means?

Think of any other objects that recur throughout this film or a film of your choice, and consider their importance.

Sweding a film

Lee and Will's film is a 'sweded' version of the original film, *Rambo*.

> To '**swede**' a film is to make your own version of it.

In groups, think of a film that you would like to swede. Then choose one scene for your 'sweded' film, and produce one of the following:

- Story
- Storyboard
- Detail of each person's role
- Shot list
- Soundtrack list
- Rationale for choosing this film to swede

Present your 'sweded' scene to the class.

Behind the scenes

Read what director and writer Garth Jennings has to say about the making of *Son of Rambow*.

On making *Son of Rambow*:

As a film-maker *Son of Rambow* was an adventure from start to finish. It took years to get the story right, five or six months to find the lead actors and raising money is never easy! But for me, it was a dream job. It turned out just how I wanted it to. To see an audience laugh and be moved by the things that move me is the greatest reward of my career. Highlights of making the movie include finding our lead actors and certainly filming anything with Will and Bill was a joy. On our second day of the shoot, we shot the end of the movie – Will (Lee Carter) crying while watching the final film. I was sat next to Will and talked him through what I wanted him to feel and he just did it. It was remarkable. Those tears and sniffs – all natural. I was so caught by surprise I was crying too! Every day on set was a blast… There were of course difficult scenes…

On the success of the film, from first showing to DVD release:

The first showing at Sundance [a film festival] was the first ever public screening. We had only finished the film five days before and no one other than us had seen it! I was so nervous. It started well but there is a moment about ten minutes in when Lee Carter throws a tennis ball at Will's head and the crowd really responded. I suddenly realised that it was playing like it should and we were going to be okay. But nothing prepared me for the floating-on-air feeling of the response at the end. Although the film did not get a great release in the rest of the world, people continue to discover it and be delighted by it.

On directing the young actors:

Our main aim was to protect Will and Bill from becoming self-conscious so we got rid of all video playback on set. This meant that they never saw themselves until the movie was finished (after Sundance). Other than that, I had no specific approach. They were both the loveliest and most talented kids you could hope to meet. Most of the stunts were performed by real stuntmen (like diving in a river or falling out of a car).

On film-making as a collaborative job:

My job was writer and director but Nick and I are the head of a team so we work on the whole thing together.

Nick Goldsmith and Garth Jennings

On the importance of planning the shoot:

Very, very important! Kids are not allowed to work long hours on set so we had to be very quick and know exactly what we wanted. For this and many other reasons, I spent three months storyboarding the entire movie. Apart from the first five minutes, the storyboards are exactly like the finished movie.

On the long shot of Will's family through the hatch at the start and finish:

There just happened to be a hatch in the wall and I liked it as a way to make one long shot to introduce Will's home. I use the same kind of shot at the end of the story so you get the feeling of things coming full circle.

On the soundtrack:

I had chosen almost all of the songs before we started shooting. Some were too expensive but we got everything we wanted in the end. I knew I was going to use 'Peek-A-Boo' by Siouxsie and the Banshees for the sixth-form common room scene and shot it to this track.

On the portrayal of school:

When I look back on my own schooldays I remember how easy it was for some kids to fall behind or be left out simply because they did not tick all the right boxes academically or socially. My best friend at school was a boy called Mark Wilson. He was the inspiration for Lee Carter. I've never met a more loyal, tough and lovely kid. But the teachers had him pegged as trouble (which he sometimes was) and never took the time to give him a boost. He later found that support in the army and then with his own family. Mark's brilliance could not be measured on a school chart so I think he got a raw deal. Maybe that's why he gave them hell in return! But it's just a movie and it's really about friendship. School is important but great friends are gold.

On going to film school and advising young film-makers:

I never went to film school. I just went to art school and made loads of short films. I graduated with a first in graphic design from St Martin's School of Art but I had only made short films and animated films. Advice? That's tricky. It's different for everyone. I would definitely say finish what you start – only then can you really learn from what you've done. If you want to direct films then you just have to know that there is a huge gap between where you are now and where you want to be. The only way to close that gap is to keep trying, don't give up and know that it takes a long time.

Read, write, explore

1 Pick out five phrases that tell you something about the process of film-making.
2 Pick out five phrases that tell you something about Garth Jennings as a director.
3 Who was Garth's inspiration for Lee Carter?
4 Pick out one piece of Garth's advice for young film-makers.
5 Find out about the other members of the production team for *Son of Rambow*.

'I made all of the drawings you see Will Proudfoot doing in the film, all the strange props, flipbooks, paper craft objects and so on. I also created the dream sequence, the crayon-style fireworks, and some other scenes of integrated live-action and animation.'

David OReilly

David OReilly

Did you know?

David OReilly, artist and film-maker (1985–), was born in Kilkenny and attended Kilkenny College. He is based in Los Angeles, and has won many awards for his work.

'I think the best feeling was when it [the film] was a success at home in the United Kingdom. Seeing a massive billboard poster of the film was really exciting, and when it was received well in the cinema it made it all worthwhile. I think one of the best things for me was hearing that some kids were having *Son of Rambow* themed parties, which meant that it had a life outside of the actual cinema.'

Nick Goldsmith, Producer

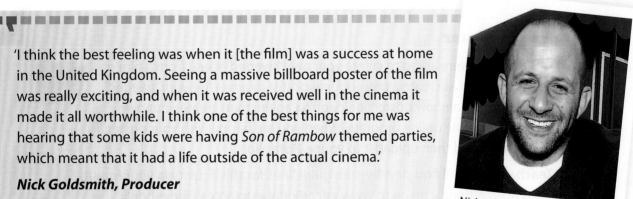

Nick Goldsmith

Working in film

Would you like to work in film? Would you like to go behind or in front of the camera? Consider the positive and negative aspects of both.

Crescents interview

Now listen to an interview with Irish actress Niamh Daly. Niamh has worked in television on many different popular programmes, such as *Fair City* and *Coronation Street*. In the interview, Niamh talks about her work as an actress and what it is like to be on the other side of the camera. As you listen, make notes on the following points:

···⟩ Starting a career as an actor
···⟩ Differences between acting for TV and film
···⟩ Working with other actors on projects
···⟩ The development of characters

My favourite scene

Based on everything that you have learned from this unit, complete the following task.

In groups, make a presentation to the class on a favourite scene from *Son of Rambow* or from a film of your choice. Include in your piece, an element from each of the different stages of the film production process. For example:

- **Pre-production** (screenplay, location scouting, set design and storyboarding)
- **Production** (different shot types and directing actors)
- **Post-production** (soundtrack, adding special effects and animations)
- **Marketing** (posters and taglines)

Explain what this scene tells you about the plot, the characters, the production and why you have chosen it. Make notes in your Portfolio.

Portfolio 4L

Create – Film poster

Earlier in this unit, you were asked to create your own 'sweded' scene from a film of your choice. Now you must create a promotional poster to advertise your 'sweded' film. Look at the *Son of Rambow* posters on page 94 again, then create your own film poster using a suitable online program. When you are happy with your poster, present it to the class and then upload it to your e-Portfolio.

Note for Teachers: You will find step-by-step guidelines for this activity in your *How to Create an e-Portfolio* e-book. Log on to www.edcodigital.ie to access the e-book.

Drama Extracts

In this unit you will:

···▷ read drama extracts from four different dramatists

···▷ explore interesting situations and moments of conflict through drama

···▷ enjoy worlds that are familiar but also worlds that are strange

···▷ explore the world of the theatre from the costumes to stage directions.

You will encounter extracts from the following dramas:

- *Odd Socks* by James Butler
- *The Shadow of a Gunman* by Seán O'Casey
- *Noughts & Crosses* adapted from Malorie Blackman's novel by Dominic Cooke
- *Heartbreak House* by George Bernard Shaw
- *Crescents* interview with an actor

Odd Socks by James Butler

James Butler

James Butler (1955–) is from County Kilkenny, but has been living in Dublin since 1974. This piece is an excerpt from *Odd Socks*, which developed out of workshops with teenagers attending Stage 51 drama school in Knocklyon, Dublin.

Background

This play explores the notion of being yourself. Emma, Rachel and Orla are friends. Orla is going to a different school from the others. Rachel is planning her birthday invite list as the scene unfolds.

Before you read

Have you ever been in a situation when you had to stand up to someone else? How did you manage?

 PowerPoint – Setting the stage

Extract from

Odd Socks

[Orla *stands looking out towards the audience.* Rachel *and* Emma *are making a list.*]

Orla   [*To audience*] Teachers! They do my head in. Miss O'Dea stops me the other morning and points at my hair band.

'Orla Macguire! Since when are we allowed wear hair bands in this school?'

'Hair bands? There's no rule, Miss to say we can't wear hair bands.'

'That thing on your hair is so silvery it's . . . it's like a tiara . . . and we can't have pupils distracting one another with that sort of nonsense.'

'It's just a hair band, Miss.'

'Well I don't like it and as far as I know they are not allowed in this school.'

'They are allowed, Miss. I'm sure of it.'

'Orla Maguire! I don't think I approve of this attitude of yours. In fact your whole class seems to be infected with the same way of behaving. I asked that girl that sits next to you . . . that Jessica what's her name . . .'

'Jessica Farrelly, Miss.'

'Yes! That's the girl. I asked her to please remove those awful dangly earrings she insists on trying to wear and she was downright cheeky to me . . . and I won't even mention the amount of times I have spoken to the class about that lurid nail varnish everyone seems to want to decorate themselves with.'

'We're allowed wear hair bands, Miss.'

'I don't think you are.'

'There's nothing about hair bands in the school journal, Miss.'

'Oh! So now you're an expert on school journals . . . I don't like this questioning attitude, Orla. I understand it . . . but I don't like it.'

[Orla *lets out a groan*]

Teachers! They're all the time telling us to be different, to think for ourselves . . . and then they make us all look the same, walk the same, talk the same. Sheep! That's what they want us to be. Pure white sheep!

Oh yeah . . . , and then Miss O'Dea looks down at my socks.

'Are you wearing odd colour socks?'

'My socks, Miss?'

'Yes! Is one of those socks navy and the other one black. I don't have my glasses but I do believe there's something distinctly odd about those socks you're wearing.'

'We are allowed wear either colour, Miss.'

'I know the rules in relation to the colour of our school socks but I hope we never arrive at a day when you can sport one of each colour.'

And then she walks off leaving me with my mouth hanging open.

[*To the two girls*] Can you believe it! She accused me of wearing odd coloured socks.

Can you believe it? . . . Hey! Are you two listening to me at all . . .?

Rachel	For God's sake, Orla! Give it a rest. You're always going on about that school of yours. Why don't you come back to our school if it's bothering you that much?
Orla	You know very well why I can't do that.
Rachel	Okay. But we're trying to do something important here.
Orla	What are ye doing?

Emma	Rachel is making out her list for who to invite to her birthday party.
Orla	When is it on?
Emma	Next Friday.
Orla	I am . . . invited . . . I hope.
Rachel	Yeah! But just make sure you don't spend your time going on about something . . .
Orla	What do you mean?
Rachel	I don't know. Just don't be going on about things like you want to change the world.
Emma	Yeah! And no moaning.
Orla	I don't moan.
Emma	And what was that long speech you just made?
Orla	Hey! I wasn't moaning. I was just saying how teachers do my head in.
Rachel	Yeah! Well they do our heads in too, Orla but you don't hear us going on and on about it.
Orla	Okay! Not another word from me about school . . . So? What are *we* doing for your birthday Rachel?
Rachel	I'm having a party in my house . . .
Emma	And most of us are sleeping over. You will be allowed sleep over, Orla. Will you?
Orla	Why wouldn't I be?
Emma	Your mother, Orla. We all know what your mother is like because you moan about her so much.
Orla	I don't moan about my mother.
Emma	Okay. Whatever!
Rachel	And we're going to have a few sneaky drinks. So make sure to bring something.
Orla	You're going to be drinking?
Emma	Just vodka and 7-Up . . .
Orla	But your mother will be there, Rachel . . . won't she?
Rachel	She'll be there at the start of it but we won't drink anything until she goes off to bed . . . and she'll go early cos she's got a whole load of *Criminal Minds* just waiting to be watched.
Emma	But the real criminal minds . . .
Rachel	[*Laughing as the two of them high five*] Yeah!

Orla	I won't be drinking.
Emma	Why not?
Orla	Because I promised my mother I wouldn't drink until I'm eighteen.
	[Rachel *and* Emma *exchange a look.*]
Rachel	Oh my God! You promised your mother.
Emma	Oh my God! That is just so old fashioned, Orla. Like promising God you won't lie when you're seven.
Orla	Oh look! Don't go on about it. Anyway I don't like the taste of it.
Emma	You don't like the taste of it? Nobody likes the taste of it. That's why we add 7-Up to it.
Orla	Well I'm just telling you now so you know. Okay?
Rachel	Well you'd better not be going on about it at the time . . . or you'll piss everyone off.
Orla	I'm not that stupid. Here! Show me who else is going to be there.
	[*She goes to take the list but* Rachel *pulls it away from her.*]
	What? I'm not on it! . . . Is that it? . . .
Rachel	Of course you're on it.
Orla	Well then why won't you let me see the list?
Emma	Oh show it to her, Rachel. She's going to find out sooner or later anyway.
	[Rachel *turns the list round for* Orla *to read.* Orla *glances at the list then she gazes in shock at* Rachel.]
Orla	You're inviting her! . . .
Rachel	Yeah! She's in my class. She's on my hockey team.
Emma	She's friends with us now, Orla.
Orla	You can't invite her! . . . not after everything that's happened.
Emma	It's Rachel's party, Orla.
Rachel	Yeah! That's right. It's my party.
Orla	But . . . But . . . But she's the reason I had to leave the school. You know that. Everyone knows that.
Emma	She's different now, Orla. She's changed. Now she's . . . she's fun!
Orla	She's not different. I only saw her yesterday and you should have seen the look she gave me.
Rachel	That's all in your imagination, Orla. She has changed. She's really nice to us now. Isn't she, Emma?
Emma	Yeah.

Orla	But you know what she did . . . you saw the texts she sent me . . . you read what she did on Facebook . . . you read what she wrote in the toilets . . . and you saw what she did to me in the science room. You both saw that . . . you were there . . .
Emma	It's Rachel's party, Orla . . . and she's inviting you . . . even though . . .
Orla	What? Even though . . . even though . . . what?!
Rachel	Even though lots of our friends don't really like you, Orla.
Orla	Who doesn't like me? I never heard anything like that before.
Emma	Look, Orla. This whole thing is typical. You get invited to probably the best party of the year . . . but there's a problem straight away because you're not going to be drinking. You're going to be standing there . . . standing there like a sore thumb. That's why you got picked on in school . . . because you always want to be different to everyone else . . . and it's happening in your new school now . . . you said it yourself . . . teachers are starting to pick on you.
Rachel	Look, Orla . . . all she's saying is that you need to blend in more with everyone else . . . don't be trying to be the odd one out all the time . . . cos you'll only start getting attention you mightn't want to get.
	[Orla *gets to her feet*.]
Orla	If . . . [*groans*] I can't even say her name, can I . . . If she's going to the party then I can't go . . . okay?
	And if you really wanted me there you wouldn't have invited her in the first place. Would you?
	[*She looks at her two friends who exchange a glance and shrug*.]
	Okay. Fine. I'm just sorry I thought you were still my friends . . . but obviously I was mistaken.
	[*She goes over to sit beside* Grace *and* Cormac.]

Oral exploration

Discuss the following with your partner and agree on a response.

1 Why is Orla in conflict with her teacher at the start of the extract?

2 Is the teacher very clear about the rule on hair bands?

3 Do you think the teacher treats Orla fairly? Why?

4 Why did Orla change schools?

5 Do you think that Rachel and Emma are good friends to Orla?

6 Do you think that Orla is right to demand that Rachel not invite the other girl? Why?

Read, write, explore

From your reading of the scene, what kind of character is Orla? Consider the following when writing your answers.

1 What first impressions do you get from her argument with the teacher?

2 What do you learn about her in her discussion with her friends over drinking?

3 What do you learn from her attitude to the party invitation issue?

4 What flaws or faults do you think she has?

5 What admirable qualities does she possess?

6 The theme of this extract is **conforming to the expectations of others**.

Teacher says to Orla: 'I don't like this questioning attitude.'

Emma says to Orla: 'You always want to be different to everyone else . . . '

Rachel says to Orla: ' . . . all we're saying is you need to blend in more with everyone else . . . '

From the above quotes we learn how the other characters feel about the theme of conformity. Based on your reading of the extract, write a short argument on whether you think that Orla should change her attitudes or not.

Conflict and dramatic tension

In this extract **dramatic tension** occurs when Orla and her two friends disagree strongly and that disagreement leads to an argument and bad feelings. As an audience we watch to see how the conflict will play out, who will win the argument and how the characters feel afterwards.

Act it out!

In groups of three, select a part of the extract where the dramatist builds up and then creates a moment of tension between the characters. Be clear where your selection starts and ends. Discuss how the tension is shown. Make some notes describing the feelings of the characters. Refer to your Portfolio.

Portfolio 5A

Divide the roles between the three of you. Practise once and be sure to try to capture the character's feelings and attitude as you say the lines. Then act it out with another group as the audience.

Create

1 Write a funny or serious poem about a boy or girl who refuses to 'blend in'.

2 It is Saturday night and Orla is at home. Rachel, feeling guilty, texts and asks her to come to the party and have some fun. Write out the text conversation that they have. It can end whatever way you decide.

Portfolio 5B

The Shadow of a Gunman
by Seán O'Casey

Seán O'Casey

Seán O'Casey (1880–1964) was born on 30 March 1880, in Dublin. He became involved in the Irish nationalist cause and joined the Irish Citizen Army in 1914. After the Easter Rising (1916), he dedicated himself to writing plays. His first play to be accepted was *The Shadow of a Gunman* in 1923. In 1926 he finished *The Plough and the Stars,* about the Easter Rising in Dublin. His plays caused controversy as they tried to tell a different version of Ireland's turbulent history from the Rising to the end of the civil war. He died in 1964, in Torquay, England.

Background

In this extract, set in a Dublin tenement during the Irish War of Independence, we meet Donal Davoren and Minnie Powell. Donal is a poet who is staying in the tenement flat of his friend (Seamus Shields). Minnie is a local girl, uneducated and poor, who like many others in the tenement believes that Donal is a Republican gunman and therefore a hero in her eyes. This is Minnie's first meeting with Donal. She really fancies him and he buys into her mistaken belief that he is a heroic gunman in order to impress her.

Before you read

What's the best chat-up line that you know?

Extract from

The Shadow of a Gunman

Act 1

Minnie	Are you in, Mr Shields?
Davoren	[*Rapidly*] No, he's not, Minnie; he's just gone out – if you run out quickly you're sure to catch him.
Minnie	Oh, it's all right, Mr Davoren, you'll do just as well; I just come in for a drop o' milk for a cup o' tea; I shouldn't be troublin' you this way, but I'm sure you don't mind.

Davoren	[*Dubiously*] No trouble in the world; delighted, I'm sure. [*Giving her the milk*] There, will you have enough?
Minnie	Plenty, lashins, thanks. Do you be all alone all the day, Mr Davoren?
Davoren	No, indeed; I wish to God I was.
Minnie	It's not good for you then. I don't know how you like to be by yourself – I couldn't stick it for long.
Davoren	[*Wearily*] No?
Minnie	No, indeed; [*With rapture*] there's nothin' I'm more fond of than a Hooley. I was at one last Sunday – I danced rings round me! Tommy Owens was there – you know Tommy Owens, don't you?
Davoren	I can't say I do.
Minnie	D'ye not? The little fellow that lives with his mother in the two-pair back – [*Ecstatically*] he's a gorgeous melodeon player!
Davoren	A gifted son of Orpheus, eh?
Minnie	[*Who never heard of Orpheus*] You've said it, Mr Davoren: the son of poor oul' Battie Owens, a weeshy, dawny, bit of a man that was never sober an' was always talkin' politics. Poor man, it killed him in the long run.
Davoren	A man should always be drunk, Minnie, when he talks politics – it's the only way in which to make them important.
Minnie	Tommy takes after the oul' fellow, too; he'd talk from morning till night when he has a few jars in him. [*Suddenly; for like all her class,* Minnie *is not able to converse very long on the one subject, and her thoughts spring from one thing to another*] Poetry is a grand thing, Mr Davoren, I'd love to be able to write a poem – a lovely poem on Ireland an' the men o' '98.
Davoren	Oh, we've had enough of poems, Minnie, about '98, and of Ireland, too.
Minnie	Oh, there's a thing for a Republican to say! But I know what you mean: it's time to give up the writing an' take to the gun. [*Her roving eye catches sight of the flowers in the vase.*] What's Mr Shields doin' with the oul' weeds?
Davoren	Those aren't Shields', they're mine. Wild flowers is a kindlier name for them, Minnie, than weeds. These are wild violets, this is an *Arum maculatum*, or Wake Robin, and these are Celandines, a very beautiful flower related to the buttercups. [*He quotes.*]

> One day, when Morn's half-open'd eyes
> Were bright with Spring sunshine –
> My hand was clasp'd in yours, dear love,
> And yours was clasp'd in mine –
> We bow'd as worshippers before
> The Golden Celandine.

Minnie	Oh, aren't they lovely, an' isn't the poem lovely, too! I wonder, now, who she was.
Davoren	[*Puzzled*] She, who?

Minnie	Why, the . . . [*Roguishly*] Oh, be the way you don't know.
Davoren	Know? I'm sure I don't know.
Minnie	It doesn't matter, anyhow – that's your own business; I suppose I don't know her.
Davoren	Know her – know whom?
Minnie	[*Shyly*] Her whose hand was clasped in yours, an' yours was clasped in hers.
Davoren	Oh, that – that was simply a poem I quoted about the Celandine, that might apply to any girl – to you, for instance.
Minnie	[*Greatly relieved, coming over and sitting beside* Davoren] But you have a sweetheart, all the same, Mr Davoren, haven't you?
Davoren	I? No, not one, Minnie.
Minnie	Oh, now, you can tell that to someone else; aren't you a poet an' aren't all the girls fond o' poets?
Davoren	That may be, but all the poets aren't fond of girls.
Minnie	They are in the story-books, ay, and fond of more than one, too. [*With a questioning look*] Are you fond of them, Mr Davoren?
Davoren	Of course I like girls, Minnie, especially girls who can add to their charms by the way in which they dress, like you, for instance.
Minnie	Oh, now, you're on for coddin' me, Mr Davoren.
Davoren	No, really, Minnie, I'm not; you are a very charming little girl indeed.
Minnie	Then if I'm a charmin' little girl, you ought to be able to write a poem about me.
Davoren	[*Who has become susceptible to the attractiveness of* Minnie, *catching her hand*] And so I will, so I will, Minnie; I have written them about girls not half so pretty as yourself.
Minnie	Ah, I knew you had one, I knew you had one now.
Davoren	Nonsense. Every girl a poet writes about isn't his sweetheart; Annie Laurie wasn't the sweetheart of Bobbie Burns.
Minnie	You needn't tell me she wasn't; 'An' for bonnie Annie Laurie I'd lay me down an' die'. No man ud lay down an' die for any but a sweetheart, not even for a wife.
Davoren	No man, Minnie, willingly dies for anything.
Minnie	Except for his country, like Robert Emmet.
Davoren	Even he would have lived on if he could; he died not to deliver Ireland. The British Government killed him to save the British nation.
Minnie	You're only jokin' now; you'd die for your country.
Davoren	I don't know so much about that
Minnie	You would, you would, you would – I know, what you are.
Davoren	What am I?

Minnie	[*In a whisper*] A gunman on the run!
Davoren	[*Too pleased to deny it*] Maybe I am, and maybe I'm not.
Minnie	Oh, I know, I know, I know. Do you never be afraid?
Davoren	Afraid! Afraid of what?
Minnie	Why, the ambushes of course; *I'm* all of a tremble when I hear a shot go off, an' what must it be like in the middle of the firin'?
Davoren	[*Delighted at* Minnie's *obvious admiration; leaning back in his chair, and lighting a cigarette with placid affectation*] I'll admit one does be a little nervous at first, but a fellow gets used to it after a bit, till, at last, a gunman throws a bomb as carelessly as a schoolboy throws a snowball.
Minnie	[*Fervently*] I wish it was all over, all the same. (*Suddenly, with a tremor in her voice*) You'll take care of yourself, won't you, won't you, Donal – I mean, Mr Davoren?
Davoren	[*Earnestly*] Call me Donal, Minnie; we're friends, great friends now – [*Putting his arm around her*] go on, Minnie, call me Donal, let me hear you say Donal.

Oral exploration

Discuss the following with your partner and agree on a response.

1 What is Minnie's real motive in coming to Donal's door asking for a 'drop o' milk'?

2 Minnie tries to chat up Donal; 'Do you be alone all the day . . . ?' What does Donal's response tell you about him?

3 Why does Minnie express a sudden interest in being able to write a poem?

4 Donal recites a poem to Minnie. How does she misunderstand it?

5 At what point after this does Donal begin to take advantage of Minnie romantically?

6 Minnie suggests to Donal that he is a Republican gunman. Why, do you think, does he not come clean with her?

Read, write, explore

The characters

1 Minnie is described as follows: 'like all her class, Minnie is not able to converse very long on the one subject'. Do you agree with this estimation of Minnie? Give reasons for your view.

2 In your opinion, is Minnie easily led by Donal? Give reasons for your answer.

3 Say how Donal uses his poetry to attract Minnie's admiration. Is this a fair thing to do? Say why or why not.

4 What is your opinion of Donal, based on his last speech in the extract?

5 Look at the language of the extract. Minnie has the impression that Donal is an educated poet. Write out two things he says that would give her that impression.

6 Minnie herself is less educated. How is this shown? How does this put her at a disadvantage and lead her to expect more than Donal intends?

7 If you met Minnie after this scene, what advice would you give her about poetry and about Donal?

Costume and gesture

Actors use **gestures** (actions) and body movements to tell you what their character is feeling. These can signal their reactions or intentions as well.

The **costume or clothes** that characters wear on stage can give us much information to understand the play better. For example, the costumes can tell us when the play is set, or where it is set.

Costume and gestures help us, the audience, to get involved in the drama and can reveal clues about the characters' attitudes and feelings.

Examine these two images of Donal and Minnie taken from different productions of *The Shadow of a Gunman*.

•••⁞ Write down a piece of dialogue from the extract that would go with each image. Why do you think it suits the image?

•••⁞ Minnie has obviously dressed herself up for her first meeting with Donal. Which image shows this best? Which one best expresses her vulnerable character? Pick out some details.

•••⁞ In each image, Donal is signalling his feelings by his gestures and his facial expression. Describe his feelings and intentions towards Minnie in both images.

Create

1 You have been asked to design the room for this scene. In your Portfolio, create the set. The sketch should label the various props, furniture and lighting. Say why you chose them.

Portfolio 5C

2 In your Portfolio you will see two circles. In the inner circle write words that you would use to describe the room in which the action happens – we will call this their inner world. In the outer circle describe your impression of the world outside the room, what's happening in Ireland around this time. Use hints from the extract to help you.

Portfolio 5D

Noughts & Crosses by Malorie Blackman

Malorie Blackman (1962–) was born in London, England. She has written over sixty books for children and young adults. Her best-known books for young adults are the multi award-winning *Noughts & Crosses* series which includes *Noughts & Crosses* (2001), *An Eye for an Eye* (2003), *Knife Edge* (2004), *Checkmate* (2005) and *Double Cross* (2008). She was also awarded an OBE (Order of the British Empire) in 2008.

Malorie Blackman

Background

Although most of Blackman's characters are black, until this series she had chosen not to foreground the issue of race or ethnic identity. With *Noughts & Crosses*, Blackman addressed racial issues more overtly, depicting a world in which black people, or 'Crosses', are the ruling elite and white people, or 'Noughts', are confined to minority status, denied legal rights and work in menial jobs. The novels focus on the disapproved love affair between a black girl, Sephy, and a white boy, Callum.

The following is an extract from a drama based on the novel *Noughts & Crosses*. In it we learn that Sephy (a cross) loves Callum (a nought). Their situation is made tense, however, because of their bad experiences in Heathcroft, the school they both attended. Further tension is created because Callum's father is under sentence of death on a false terrorist charge. Sephy's father has an important role in government and has some responsibility in the matter. Callum is finding it very difficult to trust Sephy. However, he has a 'secret'; he really loves her.

> **Note**
>
> 1 Noughts are sometimes insultingly referred to as 'Daggers'. Similarly, Crosses are referred to as 'Blankers'.
>
> 2 Jasmine is Sephy's mother, Minerva her sister.

Before you read

Try to explain to your partner the meaning and importance of people being treated equally.

Extract from

Noughts & Crosses

© Keith Pattison/RSC

Act 2, Scene 11

Sephy	Send our love to Gracey!
	[*He goes.*]
Jasmine	I know it's hard for you, darling, but maybe boarding school will be an adventure.
Sephy	I thought you said you cried yourself to sleep every night you were there.
Jasmine	Well, I was only eight when I started. But at your age, it's different. You'll make friends and I'm sure you'll grow to love it.
Sephy	More to the point, I'll be out of your hair.
Jasmine	You know that's not true, Sephy. I'll miss you terribly.
Sephy	Good thing Dad's not sending your Chardonnay supplier away. Then you'd be in real trouble.
Jasmine	What a lovely family meal! We must do it more often.
	[*Jasmine goes.*]
Minerva	You're not seriously thinking of running off with that Blanker.
Sephy	Just watch me.
Minerva	You haven't got the nerve.

Act 2, Scene 12

[*Sephy's Bedroom*]

[*Night time. The sound of pebbles on a window. Sephy goes to her window.*]

Sephy	[*To audience*]. It must have been two o'clock in the morning. It took a while before I heard the strange tip-tapping at my window. And once I was conscious of it, I realised that it'd been going on for a while. I headed for my balcony window and opened it. Tiny stones lay at my feet.

Callum	[*Offstage*]. Sephy!
Sephy	What? How did you get through security?
Callum	[*Offstage*]. I need to see you.
Sephy	I'll come down. It's safer.
Callum	[*Offstage*]. No. I'll climb up.
Sephy	Hang on, I'll tie some sheets together then.
Callum	[*Offstage*]. No, don't bother.
Sephy	[*Offstage, as* Callum *climbs*]. Be quick. The place is crawling with guards. Watch it . . . Mind the living-room window. No. Get your left hand over the balcony. That's it.
	[Callum *enters through the window*.]
	Did you phone me? I didn't hear your signal.
Callum	I was in the prison with my dad.
	[Callum *and* Sephy *take each other in*.]
Sephy	How's your mum?
Callum	She's at my aunt's house.
	[Sephy *goes to her door and locks it*.]
Sephy	They're sending me away to boarding school. In September. The thirteenth. Unlucky for some.
Callum	Well, that's the end of us, I suppose.
Sephy	It doesn't have to be.
Callum	Come off it, Sephy.
Sephy	Remember that time on the beach? The night before you started at Heathcroft? You talked about us going away together. Escaping. Remember?
	[*Pause.*]
	Well, how about it? I've got plenty of money. And we can both work. We could move right away from here. Maybe rent a place up north somewhere. Maybe in the country.
	[*Pause.*]
Callum	Your father must be happy. My dad rots away in prison and, just like that, Kamal Hadley's reputation is restored. Is this the way it's going to be from now on? Whenever a politician is in trouble in the polls, they'll just search out the nearest Nought to put away or string up – or both? Cheaper than starting a war, I suppose.
Sephy	I know your dad didn't kill those people.
Callum	Do you know how long the jury deliberated? One hour. One lousy stinking hour.
	[Sephy *touches* Callum's *cheek*.]

Sephy	I'm so sorry, Callum.
	[Callum *pulls his head away.*]
Callum	I don't want your ruddy pity.
Sephy	Stop it. Please.
Callum	Why should I? Don't you want anyone to know you've got a Blanker in your room?
Sephy	Callum, don't.
Callum	I want to smash you and every other Dagger who crosses my path. I hate you so much it scares me.
Sephy	I know you do. You've hated me ever since you joined Heathcroft and I called you a Blanker.
Callum	And you've hated me for turning my back on you in the dining hall and letting you be beaten up by those girls.
	[*Pause.*]
	Then why is it that I think of you as my best friend?
Sephy	Because you know that's how I think of you. Because I love you. And you love me, I think.
	[*Pause.*]
	Did you hear what I said? I love you.
Callum	Love doesn't exist – friendship doesn't exist between a Nought and a Cross.
Sephy	Then what are you doing in my room?
Callum	I'm damned if I know.
	[Sephy *sits on the bed.* Callum *sits alongside her, but some distance away. They are both very uncomfortable. They look at the floor. Then* Sephy *turns to* Callum *and offers her hand. He turns to her. She starts to lower her hand. He takes it and moves towards her. We hear the gentle sound of waves on the beach. They sit like this for a few moments. Then he kicks off his shoes and lies down on the bed, taking her with him. They hug.*]
	Turn around.
	[Sephy *does so. They spoon together.*]
	Are you okay?
Sephy	Uh-hm.
Callum	I'm not squashing you?
Sephy	Uh-uh.
Callum	You're sure?
Sephy	Callum, shut up.

[Callum *smiles*. Sephy *turns to face him. They kiss*. Sephy *pulls away*.]

Let's just get some sleep – okay?

Callum   Okay.

[*They curl up*.]

Sephy?

Sephy   Mmm.

Callum   Maybe we should go away together.

[Sephy's *nodding off*.]

Sephy   We'll talk about it in the morning.

[*Pause*.]

Callum   I remember years ago when you snuck me my first taste of orange juice. It was icy cold and I'd never tasted anything so sweet and I held each sip in my mouth until it became warm because I couldn't bear to swallow it. I wanted the taste to last for ever, but of course it couldn't.

[*Silence*.]

Sephy, I want to tell you something.

[*Silence*.]

A secret.

[*Silence*.]

Sephy?

[*He realises she's asleep and gives up. They lie still together. The light slowly fades from night to morning as they sleep. Dawn chorus*.]

Act 2, Scene 13

[Sephy's *Bedroom*.]

[*Midday. We hear an offstage knocking at the door*. Sephy *starts to wake up*.]

Sarah   [*Offstage*]. Miss Sephy? It's Sarah and your mother. Are you all right in there?

Jasmine   [*Offstage*]. Persephone, open this door. At once.

[*More knocking*]

Persephone, open the door right this second or I'll get security to break it down.

Sarah   [*Offstage*]. Miss Sephy, are you okay? Please.

Sephy   Just . . . a minute.

[*She shakes* Callum *awake*.]

Callum	What . . . what's the – ?
	[*More knocking.* Sephy *puts her hand over* Callum's *mouth. She points towards the door. He goes to get under the bed.*]
Sephy	[*Whispering*]. Look, why don't I just let them in? I want my mother to know about us. Besides, we haven't done anything wrong.
	[Callum *looks at her.*]
	Bad idea?
Callum	Dur.
	[*He disappears under the bed.* Sephy *goes to put her dressing gown on over her Jackson Spacey dress. More knocking.*]
Sephy	I'm on my way, Sarah. I'm just putting on my dressing gown.
	[*She rushes off to unlock the door and opens it.* Jasmine *rushes past her into the room.* Sarah *follows.* Jasmine *goes to the window and looks out.*]
	What's the matter? Is the house on fire?
Jasmine	D'you know what time it is?
Sephy	So I overslept a few minutes. Big deal.
Sarah	It's almost noon and your door is locked.
Sephy	Maybe I decided to bring a little excitement into your lives.
	[Sephy *notices* Callum's *hand reaching out from under the bed to retrieve his trainers, which are on* Sephy *and* Sarah's *side of the bed. He grabs a trainer and removes it.*]
	I'll be down as soon as I've had my shower. I promise.

Oral exploration

Discuss the following with your partner and agree on a response.

1 Does the world of the extract seem very safe for Callum? Explain.

2 Talk about two important facts that you learn about Callum.

3 How does Sephy feel about Callum?

4 Have they had an easy or a difficult relationship before we meet them in the extract?

5 Does Callum feel angry towards Sephy? Why?

6 How well does she deal with his anger?

Read, write, explore

With a partner, read the following piece of tense dialogue between Sephy and Callum. Note that Callum is very upset at the injustice of his father's trial and sentence. Sephy responds by touching his cheek (gesture) and by speaking to him (dialogue).

Some gestures, such as 'Sephy *touches* Callum's *cheek*,' are provided by the author as **stage directions** to the actors. But others are left up to the actors and directors.

Working with a partner, write in the stage directions you would give to each character in the following extract. How would each move, respond and use gestures to communicate how they feel?

Callum	Do you know how long the jury deliberated? One bloody hour. One lousy stinking hour.
	[**Sephy** *touches* **Callum's** *cheek*.]
Sephy	I'm so sorry Callum.
	[**Callum** *pulls his head way*.]
Callum	I don't want your ruddy pity.
Sephy	Stop it, please.
Callum	Why should I? Don't you want anyone to know you've got a Blanker in your room?
Sephy	Callum, don't.
Callum	I want to smash you and every other Dagger who crosses my path. I hate you so much it scares me.
Sephy	I know you do. You've hated me ever since you joined Heathcroft and I called you a Blanker.
Callum	And you've hated me for turning my back on you in the dining hall and letting you be beaten up by those girls.
	[*Pause*.]
	Then why is it that I think of you as my best friend?

Now act out the passage using your own stage directions.

Dramatic scenarios

A **scenario** is a short outline of a situation or plot. Writers use them to try out interesting dramatic situations or indeed a whole play. If happy with the scenario, the writer goes on to draft and then write the final drama.

Here are some interesting scenarios for you to work on with a partner. Choose your favourite one. First plan what happens and how the scenario ends, then improvise it (for example, make up the dialogue as you go along). Later you should write it out (one page) as a piece of dialogue.

Portfolio 5E

> You are on a shopping trip with your mother. All is going well till you start to object to her buying an item of clothing that she thinks 'will be perfect for you!'

> You are shopping in a big store and on your way out you are stopped by security and they find in your shopping bag a top you innocently forgot to pay for. How do you convince them of your innocence?

> You are a teacher. A parent of a very difficult pupil arrives at the parent/teacher meeting believing his/her child is really an angel. You have to tell her the truth. She is none too pleased. How do you get her onside?

Mood in drama

Mood is the general feeling that a drama produces in you, the audience. Here are some words to describe some different moods that drama can create:

- tension/worry
- humour
- joy
- sadness/sorrow
- romantic feelings
- terror and calm feelings

Reread the drama extract and reflect on three moods it creates in you. From the list above, choose the most appropriate and say where in the extract these moods are created. Compare your moods with your partner's.

Often **music** is played as a background to a film in order to create mood in the audience.

⋯⟩ What is your favourite music from a film?

⋯⟩ What scene does it go with?

⋯⟩ What feelings does it give you?

⋯⟩ What music or song would you play in the background to accompany the scene of Sephy and Callum as they lie together on the bed?

Heartbreak House by George Bernard Shaw

Geoge Bernard Shaw (1856–1950) was born in Dublin in 1856, the third and youngest child of an alcoholic father and an undomestic mother. He developed an interest in literature, music and painting at a very early age, but was never able to go to university. Shaw was a socialist and fought all his life for the interests of the poor and disadvantaged. He will always be remembered for plays such as *Pygmalion*, a play that is best known for its film adaptation, *My Fair Lady*, and *Heartbreak House*. George Bernard Shaw died at the age of ninety-four in Hertfordshire, England.

Geoge Bernard Shaw

Background

This extract from *Heartbreak House* is set in 1913 in an English country house owned by Captain Shotover. He and his guests have just finished a dinner party. Lady Utterword and Mrs Hushabye are the daughters of the Captain. Hector is Mrs Hushabye's husband. They are cultured people who live lives of leisure. Randall (Lady Utterword's brother-in-law), Mazzini Dunn and Boss Mangan, (rich businessmen), are also guests. A noise is heard upstairs. Mazzini goes to investigate and returns having captured a burglar.

Before you read

Look up the meaning of 'farce' in a dictionary and find examples.

Extract from

Heartbreak House

Act 2

Mrs Hushabye	What has happened?
Mazzini	Your housekeeper told me there was somebody upstairs, and gave me a pistol that Mr Hushabye had been practising with. I thought it would frighten him; but it went off at a touch.
The Burglar	Yes, and took the skin off my ear. Precious near[1] took the top off my head. Why don't you have a proper revolver instead of a thing like that, that goes off if you as much as blow on it?
Hector	One of my duelling pistols. Sorry.
Mazzini	He put his hands up and said it was a fair cop.[2]
The Burglar	So it was. Send for the police.
Hector	No, by thunder! It was not a fair cop. We were four to one.
Mrs Hushabye	What will they do to him?
The Burglar	Ten years. Beginning with solitary. Ten years off my life. I shan't serve it all: I'm too old. It will see me out.
Lady Utterword	You should have thought of that before you stole my diamonds.
The Burglar	Well, you've got them back, lady, haven't you? Can you give me back the years of my life you are going to take from me?
Mrs Hushabye	Oh, we can't bury a man alive for ten years for a few diamonds.
The Burglar	Ten little shining diamonds! Ten long black years!
Lady Utterword	Think of what it is for us to be dragged through the horrors of a criminal court, and have all our family affairs in the papers! If you were a native, and Hastings could order you a good beating and send you away,[3] I shouldn't mind; but here in England there is no real protection for any respectable person.

The Burglar	I'm too old to be giv a hiding, lady. Send for the police and have done with it. It's only just and right you should.
Randall	[*Who has relaxed his vigilance on seeing the burglar so pacifically disposed,*[4] *and comes forward swinging the poker between his fingers like a well folded umbrella*]. It is neither just nor right that we should be put to a lot of inconvenience to gratify your moral enthusiasm, my friend. You had better get out, while you have the chance.
The Burglar	[*Inexorably*[5]]. No. I must work my sin off my conscience. This has come as a sort of call to me. Let me spend the rest of my life repenting in a cell. I shall have my reward above.
Mangan	[*Exasperated*]. The very burglars can't behave naturally in this house.
Hector	My good sir, you must work out your salvation at somebody else's expense. Nobody here is going to charge you.
The Burglar	Oh, you won't charge me, won't you?
Hector	No. I'm sorry to be inhospitable; but will you kindly leave the house?
The Burglar	Right. I'll go to the police station and give myself up. [*He turns resolutely to the door: but* Hector *stops him*].
Hector	Oh, no. You mustn't do that.
Randall	[*Speaking together*] No no. Clear out man, can't you; and don't be a fool.
Mrs Hushabye	Don't be so silly. Can't you repent at home?
Lady Utterword	You will have to do as you are told.
The Burglar	It's compounding a felony, you know.
Mrs Hushabye	This is utterly ridiculous. Are we to be forced to prosecute this man when we don't want to?
The Burglar	Am I to be robbed of my salvation to save you the trouble of spending a day at the sessions?[6] Is that justice? Is it right? Is it fair to me?
Mazzini	[*Rising and leaning across the table persuasively as if it were a pulpit desk or a shop counter*]. Come, come! let me show you how you can turn your very crimes to account. Why not set up as a locksmith? You must know more about locks than most honest men?
The Burglar	That's true, sir. But I couldn't set up as a locksmith under twenty pounds.
Randall	Well, you can easily steal twenty pounds. You will find it in the nearest bank.
The Burglar	[*Horrified*]. Oh, what a thing for a gentleman to put into the head of a poor criminal scrambling out of the bottomless pit as it were! Oh, shame on you, sir! Oh, God forgive you! [*He throws himself into the big chair and covers his face as if in prayer*].
Lady Utterword	Really, Randall!

Hector	It seems to me that we shall have to take up a collection for this inopportunely contrite sinner.[7]
Lady Utterword	But twenty pounds is ridiculous.
The Burglar	[*Looking up quickly*]. I shall have to buy a lot of tools, lady.
Lady Utterword	Nonsense: you have your burgling kit.
The Burglar	What's a jimmy and a centre bit and an acetylene welding plant and a bunch of skeleton keys? I shall want a forge, and a smithy, and a shop, and fittings. I can't hardly do it for twenty.
Hector	My worthy friend, we haven't got twenty pounds.
The Burglar	[*Now master of the situation*]. You can raise it among you, can't you?
Mrs Hushabye	Give him a sovereign, Hector, and get rid of him.
Hector	[*Giving him a pound*]. There! Off with you.
The Burglar	[*Rising and taking the money very ungratefully*]. I won't promise nothing. You have more on you than a quid: all the lot of you, I mean.
Lady Utterword	[*Vigorously*]. Oh, let us prosecute him and have done with it. I have a conscience too, I hope; and I do not feel at all sure that we have any right to let him go, especially if he is going to be greedy and impertinent.
The Burglar	[*Quickly*]. All right, lady, all right. I've no wish to be anything but agreeable. Good evening, ladies and gentlemen; and thank you kindly.

[1] **precious near:** almost; [2] **a fair cop:** I deserved to be caught; [3] **away:** a reference to the treatment of Indian wrongdoers by the British ruling class before Indian independence; [4] **pacifically disposed:** quiet; [5] **inexorably:** refusing to be stopped; [6] **at the sessions:** in court; [7] **inopportunely contrite sinner:** inconveniently sorry sinner.

Oral exploration

Discuss the following with your partner and agree on a response.

1 The Burglar: 'Send for the police.' What is unusual about the burglar's attitude to being caught?

2 Hector says, 'No, by thunder! It was not a fair cop. We were four to one.' What does this tell you about his character and what he thinks is important?

3 How does the burglar look for sympathy from Mrs Hushabye?

4 The burglar is quite manipulative. Mention how he uses the feelings of the others to escape the situation.

5 Why does Lady Utterword not want to go to court to prosecute the burglar?

6 What do you think of Mazzini's suggestion that the burglar become a locksmith?

7 Randall suggests that the burglar steal twenty pounds. Describe the burglar's response. Note his gestures.

Paradox

The Burglar	Oh, you won't charge me, won't you?
Hector	No. I'm sorry to be inhospitable; but will you kindly leave the house?

There is something strange and contradictory about this dialogue between the burglar and Hector. The burglar has just stolen the diamonds and Hector is apologising to him for not calling the police!

Another word for this strangeness is a **paradox**.

Here is another example of paradox:

Randall	Well, you can easily steal twenty pounds. You will find it in the nearest bank.
The Burglar	[*Horrified*]. Oh, what a thing for a gentleman to put into the head of a poor criminal scrambling out of the bottomless pit as it were! Oh, shame on you, sir! Oh, God forgive you!

When it is suggested to the burglar that he should steal, he is horrified!

Paradox is a device that lets us laugh at situations that appear normal but are really ridiculous.

Paradoxes can also be of the visual kind. Look at the triangle image. In what way is it a paradox? Discuss.

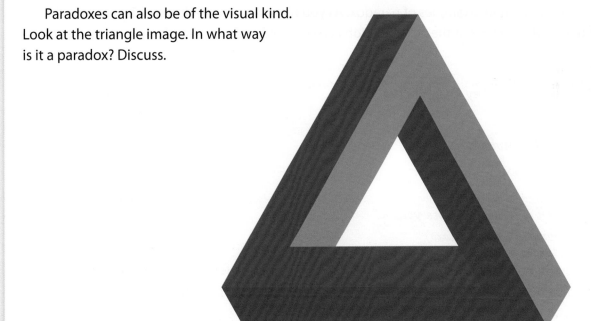

Playing with paradox

'I'm a compulsive liar, I never tell the truth!'

If someone says to you 'I'm a compulsive liar', do you believe them or not? That statement in itself is a paradox, because it is self-contradictory, which is precisely what a paradox is. In the example mentioned, can someone be both a compulsive liar yet tell the truth at the same time?

Another well-known example of a paradox is the 'mighty mouse'. Certainly, 'mighty' and 'mouse' are contradictory ideas. The contradiction can be explained, however, when we understand that the mouse in question might be tiny but his spirit is huge.

Why use paradox? – 'I must be cruel, only to be kind.'

What is the purpose of using a paradoxical statement, instead of just stating your meaning clearly? One reason is that stating your meaning clearly would be boring. It is much more interesting and often funnier for readers to carve out the meaning for themselves. Furthermore, paradoxes are often more memorable and sum up in one statement a very complex idea. So Hamlet, a Shakespearean prince, after telling his mother (whom he loves) a very hurtful truth about her character, then says to her, 'I must be cruel, only to be kind.'

Here are some more examples of paradox. As you read them, write down your explanations of each so that the contradiction can be explained:

You can save money by spending it.

'I can resist everything except temptation.' (Oscar Wilde)

I'm nobody.

The beginning of the end

'Youth is wasted on the young.' (George Bernard Shaw)

A rich man is no richer than a poor man.

Wise fool

Bittersweet

Create

Come up with paradoxical statements of your own.

Farce

The definition of a farce is 'something that the writer intends to be seen as ridiculous, particularly a comedy based on a crazy or unlikely situation'.

We call those situations 'farcical'.

How is the situation in the extract farcical?

Well, a burglar is caught stealing diamonds in a very posh house; he is caught and manages in the end to get the homeowners to pay him to go away!

Read, write, explore

1 What do you think of Mazzini's suggestion that the burglar become a locksmith?

2 With your partner, pick out other farcical or plainly ridiculous statements from the extract. Say why they are farcical.

3 Look at the images from the television shows, **Mr Bean** and **Moone Boy**.
First describe the images in a little detail, focusing on the ridiculous elements.
Then say why the situations are somewhat farcical.

Mr Bean in control on the racetrack!

Martin Moone and his imaginary friend

4 Shaw was a **socialist** all his life and had great sympathy for the poor and the excluded. He believed that the rich should be made to share their wealth with those less well off. How does this extract express these values in a comic way?

Create

With your partner or group, write a short farcical dialogue based on events in school or in your local area. Here are some further suggested situations:

- A builder comes to fix your chimney but ends up demolishing the house!
- Deleted scenes from *Titanic* or another well-known film.
- Two students get each other's exam results in a mix up. One result is brilliant, the other is terrible.
- By some freak chance, your two best friends don't recognise you when you meet them at the bus stop on the first day of school in September.

Portfolio 5F

Create – Radio drama

Choose your favourite extract from the unit and perform it as a radio drama. You will need actors, a producer, a director, a sound engineer and a sound effects creator. Record the drama using software such as Audacity, present it to the class and then upload it to your e-Portfolio.

Note for Teachers: You will find step-by-step guidelines for this activity in your *How to Create an e-Portfolio* e-book. Log on to www.edcodigital.ie to access the e-book.

Crescents interview

Listen to the *Crescents* interview with actor Simon Coury. Simon has acted on stage and screen. In this interview he descibes how he got into acting and how he gets into character. As you listen, make notes on the following:

- How and why he got into acting
- How he gets into character
- The challenges of learning lines.

Irish Tales and Short Stories

In this unit you will:

⋯⋯⇥ learn about the storytelling tradition in Ireland

⋯⋯⇥ read and enjoy classic tales and short stories

⋯⋯⇥ enjoy stories about people ranging from the legendary Finn MacCool to ordinary people and how they deal with the problems they face

⋯⋯⇥ focus on adverbs, idioms and other parts of language

⋯⋯⇥ prepare an oral presentation on the theme of childhood.

You will encounter the following stories:

● 'Finn MacCool and the Giant's Causeway' by a scéalaí

● 'The Tale of the Burial in the Chapel beneath the Waves' by a seanchaí

● 'First Confession' by Frank O'Connor

● 'Christmas Morning' by Frank O'Connor

● 'The Confirmation Suit' by Brendan Behan

The oral tradition of storytelling

The stories in this unit form part of a long tradition of storytelling in Ireland that began with oral storytelling, an art that has lasted for more than a thousand years.

In the past, there were two types of oral storyteller, the **scéalaí**, who told stories of Irish heroes and their high deeds, and the **seanchaí**, whose stories dealt with local folk tales about families, places, fairies, phantoms and ghosts. The first story in the unit is about the deeds of Finn MacCool as told by a scéalaí. This is followed by a seanchaí story called 'The Tale of the Burial in the Chapel beneath the Waves'.

In the time of your great, great grandparents, the nights were long in the winter and homes had nothing in the way of modern entertainments such as radio, television or the Internet. Books were scarce too and so the local storyteller was in high demand to fill the long winter evenings with food for the imagination.

Normally, stories were told at gatherings around the fire in a local person's home. Neighbours would gather and listen as the storyteller embroidered the tale with descriptions and asides. Often the listeners knew the story well but would insist on hearing it again in order to marvel at the skill of the storyteller. The story allowed them to imagine the world of a mythical Ireland with figures like Oisín, Finn MacCool or Queen Maeve engaging in high deeds and great adventures. The world described was fantastic and a million miles away from the poverty experienced by the listeners. When Lady Gregory (a friend of W. B. Yeats) went to collect tales in a Galway workhouse, she was 'moved by the strange contrast between the poverty of the tellers and the splendours of the tales'.

The local seanchaí provided entertainment by telling stories about people and places that his or her audience would recognise. The stories would often consist of an improbable narrative about a local character that would end with a witty punchline.

Neither the scéalaí nor the seanchaí was expected to be personally involved with the characters or to make the story realistic in any way. The more improbable and unexpected the plot, the better it was received.

Queen Maeve's tomb. This enormous cairn on top of Knocknarea in County Sligo is 55 metres in diameter by 10 metres high. Folklore says it was built for the mythical Iron Age Queen Maeve, whose father, the High King of Ireland, gave her Connacht as a gift.

The beginning of short story writing in Ireland

Daniel Corkery (1878–1964), who lived in Cork, was the inspiration to a whole school of Munster short story writers. As a child he would hear the local seanchaí telling tales to a community gathering but he also read literature from other cultures. He was the first Irish writer to develop the art of the modern written short story based on folk experience.

This short story was very different from the tales told in the oral tradition. The written short story expressed the personal concerns of the writer. Events in the story were always credible and the audience was the silent reader enjoying the story in private.

Encouraged by the writings of Corkery, other writers such as Frank O'Connor and Seán Ó Faoláin began writing what would come to be known as the classic Irish short story. These stories did not try to escape the ordinariness of everyday life but showed the humour, the sadness and hopes in the lives of ordinary men, women and children.

The short stories in this unit show the lives of ordinary characters as they deal with everyday human situations like the ones we all must face in our lives. You will now read two stories based on the oral tradition. The first is in the tradition of the scéalaí about the exploits of the great Finn MacCool and the second is a very unnerving tale by a seanchaí.

Seán Ó Faoláin

Stories from the oral tradition

A scéalaí's tale

Before you read

Can you recall any legends or fairy tales where something completely unbelievable happens? Describe the unbelievable event and say if it affected how the story turned out, for example, Rapunzel's long hair.

Finn MacCool and the Giant's Causeway

There was magic in the old times and so it happened that the great Finn MacCool tricked Benandonner, the Red Man of Scotland as I will tell you now.

Now as to the great Finn MacCool, he was born of noble family and during his life grew to be the finest warrior hero in the whole of Ireland as this story will relate. He stood a mighty forty feet tall and I've heard tell that his sword arm was as thick as a bull's neck. Not only that but he could run faster than a wild deer and throw a spear so accurately that it would split a turnip into two halves after travelling three miles.

While he was renowned for his strength he was even more renowned for the quickness of his mind as this tale will show.

But truth to tell, Finn was often gentle in his ways also and nothing pleased him more than to walk the hills of Antrim on windy days with his wife Oonagh. They would marvel at the wild waves crashing on the rocks as they looked across the Sea of Moyle to the hills of the Western Isles of Scotland. It was on one of these walks that they saw the giant shadow and heard the deep roar of the mighty Benandonner, the Red Man of the Western Isles.

Finn, fearing no man, beast or giant, shouted a challenge to the Red Man to come to Antrim for a 'trial of strength' contest to see which of them was the greatest. The Red Man agreed and Finn being a hospitable giant decided to keep his guest's feet from getting wet by building a causeway across the sea to the Western Isles using the great hexagonal stones found on Antrim's shores.

Finn laboured furiously for weeks at this long and difficult task. Working from dawn to dusk, he finally got the causeway built to within a mile of the Red Man's hideout in Fingal's Cave on the island of Staffa.

It was getting late and so he decided to go home for a good night's rest before finishing the work on the following day.

But to her surprise, Oonagh was woken early the following morning by the pounding footsteps of the Red Man approaching like a terrible earthquake. She looked out of the window and on the horizon she saw the massive bulk of this sixty foot giant blocking out the sun. He was huge and fierce and had a massive head crowned with curly red hair and in his right hand he wielded a stone sledge hammer that would reduce a hundred ordinary men to dust in the blink of an eye. And, it was said, he could also throw a deadly spear but in his case it would travel six miles before falling to earth.

Oonagh called Finn but he was exhausted from his heroic labours and completely unfit for a match with the Red Man. She was terrified that if Finn lost the challenge she would be taken off to Scotland as a prisoner and 'spoil of the victor'.

Thinking on her feet, she woke Finn, and together they hatched a clever plan. In a flash he got himself into one of her nightgowns and put a huge bonnet on his head and a big soother in his mouth. He went back to bed and pretended to be fast asleep.

Moments later there was a deafening knock on the front door of Finn's palace and pretending nothing, Oonagh opened the door to the Red Man.

'Where is he hiding, Finn, the miserable coward?' he roared.

Oonagh bade him be quiet, 'Shush now, Benandonner,' she said, pointing to the bedroom door, 'or you'll waken my little baby sleeping quietly there now. Just be patient, you amadán! Finn himself is out for a walk and he will be home to fight with you shortly.'

The Red Man didn't believe her and started to search the palace. When he came to where the disguised Finn was pretending to be asleep, he was shocked and asked Oonagh if this was her child.

'Yes,' she replied, 'That's Finn Óg; sure isn't he the little dote! But don't wake him for he's a terror if he's roused.'

The Red Man looked carefully at the enormous 'baby' and began to shudder at the sight, reckoning that if this hairy monster was Finn's son, then what size of a creature must Finn himself be? He decided he'd seen enough.

Off with him out the door for home. He was last seen hurrying in panic back to the Western Isles of Scotland tearing up Finn's causeway as he went and hurling the stones into the ocean. The only bit of the causeway now remaining is on the north east coast of Antrim, the Giant's Causeway, and to this day you can still go and admire what's left of Finn's heroic handiwork.

Oral exploration

1 How do you know that Finn MacCool is a very strong giant?

2 How is the Red Man shown to be stronger than Finn?

3 Finn and Oonagh are very clever. How is this shown?

4 There is a lot of exaggeration in the story. Pick out the three most outrageous exaggerations in the descriptions of the characters of Finn and the Red Man.

5 Pick out three actions that are exaggerated and say which is the most exaggerated.

6 The story reflects the ancient rivalry between the Scottish and the Irish. How is international rivalry played out between the nations of Europe today? Who are the heroes of today? How are they similar to or different from Finn and the Red Man?

Read, write, explore

1 Imagine the panicked conversation that Oonagh and Finn would have as they realised that Benandonner was coming for him. Look again at the paragraph that begins 'Thinking on her feet'. Write the dialogue. Make sure you include stage directions for your actors (see page 135 in Unit 5, Drama Extracts).

2 The **theme** of any story is the main idea or message that it communicates to you the reader or listener. The following is a list of possible themes that the story on Finn MacCool communicates.

Discuss with a partner why each might or might not be appropriate to the story you have heard. Think carefully.

- Never be hospitable to your enemy
- Never give up
- Brains are better than brawn
- Team work
- Appearances matter

Which one of the above is closest to the message that you take from the story? Which is your second choice? Write down your reasons.

3 Having thought about character, how much do you learn about the characters of Oonagh, Finn and The Red Man? To help you consider this, fill in the following table in your Portfolio using adjectives in the second column and references to the story in the third. The first is done for you.

Portfolio 6A

Character	Adjective	References to the story
Oonagh	Clever	Thinks of a plan to fool The Red Man
Finn		
The Red Man		

Discuss with the class why we need to know so little about the feelings or inner thoughts of the characters in the tale of Finn MacCool and The Red Man.

Create

Invent another story or legend to explain a natural event (a tsunami, an asteroid impact, a volcanic eruption, an earthquake, a comet or an eclipse). You may use characters that you know from legend: Oisín, Finn MacCool, Queen Maeve, etc.

Portfolio 6B

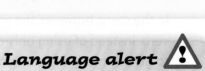

Adverbs and adverbial phrases
Language alert

1 Adverbs

Adverbs tell us more information about the verb in a sentence. They tell us more about when and where things happen. They are often used close to verbs and they give us more information about the verb. Here is an example taken from the tale of Finn MacCool:

> 'Shush now, Benandonner,' she said, pointing to the bedroom door, 'or you'll waken my little baby sleeping **quietly there now**.'

- '**quietly**' is an adverb telling us **how** the baby was sleeping
- '**there**' is an adverb telling us **where** the baby is sleeping
- '**now**' is an adverb telling us **when** he is sleeping

Here is a student's response to the story of 'Finn MacCool and the Giant's Causeway'. The student was asked to use appropriate **adverbs** when writing her response. Some of the adverbs are missing. Fill in the blanks with some or all of the following suggestions.

---

foolishly	almost	only	somewhat
very	stupidly	off	certainly
really	barely	across	cleverly

Finn immediately struck me as being _____ brave but also as being _____ foolish in proudly challenging the great Benandonner to a trial of strength. Firstly, Benandonner was an unknown quantity to Finn.
He had _____ seen him in the distance and had _____ got a notion of his massive strength when he _____ challenged him to a fight.

    Finn comes across as a fairly decent giant but it's his wife Oonagh who is the real star. Finn has _____ got himself into a really bad situation.
Benandonner is _____ twice his size and can well look after himself.
But it's Oonagh who_____ saves Finn's skin with her quick thinking.
The 'Baby' trick is_____ priceless! Benandonner might be strong but he _____ lacks the stuff upstairs and Oonagh uses the trick of dressing Finn as her baby to see 'Benandonner the Dumb'.
Finn wins. Ireland 1: Scotland 0.

Adverbs and adverbial phrases

2 Adverbial phrases

The story of Benandonner and Finn MacCool uses many sentences that contain adverbs. Read the first six paragraphs again and write down any adverbs you find.

In the story, however, the writer uses other effective ways of telling us more about the verb. Instead of using only one word (an adverb) he makes use of an **adverbial phrase** to give us more information about the verb. Here are some examples in bold.

> Not only that but he could run **faster than a wild deer** and throw a spear **so accurately** that it would split a turnip **into two halves after travelling three miles**.
>
> Finn laboured **furiously for weeks** . . .
>
> Working **from dawn to dusk**, he finally got the causeway built **to within a mile** of the Red Man's hideout in Fingal's Cave on the island of Staffa.
>
> Thinking **on her feet**, she woke Finn, and together they hatched a clever plan.
>
> He went **back to bed** and pretended to be **fast asleep**.
>
> **Moments later** there was a deafening knock **on the front door** . . .

Looking at the adverbial phrases in the box above, can you say which phrases tell you:

⋯⋙ **How** the action happened?
⋯⋙ **When** the action happened?
⋯⋙ **Where** the action happened?

See Unit 3, page 75 for further information on adverbs.

Fingal's Cave on the island of Staffa

A seanchai's tale

Look at the title of the following story.
What do you think the story is about?
Now read or listen to the story.

The Tale of the Burial in the Chapel beneath the Waves

In olden times it was known that the ancient burial-ground of the Cantillon family was out on a small island near Ballyheigue in the county of Kerry. This island was situated at no great distance from the shore, but in distant times it was submerged by the Atlantic Ocean as it ate further into the Kerry coastline.

The local fishermen often reported that they saw the ruined walls of an ancient church beneath them in the water, as they sailed over the clear green sea on a sunny afternoon. They called it *Séipéal fo Thoinn*, or the chapel beneath the waves.

However this may be, it is well-known that the Cantillons were, like most other Irish families, strongly attached to their ancient burial-place. This led to the custom, when any of the family died, of the corpse being carried at evening to the strand at Ballyheigue and the coffin left near the water's edge. In the morning it was always found to have disappeared and it was the traditional belief that the ancestors of the deceased had borne it to the family burial ground beneath the waves.

Now, Connor O'Dea, a County Clare man, was related to the Cantillons by marriage. 'Connor of the seven quarters of Breintragh,' as he was commonly called, was known to drink two pints of salt water, for its medicinal qualities, before breakfast. But he would drink double that amount of raw whiskey before nightfall, apparently with little effect on him, though he was often heard then to ramble on about how he never got to attend the Cantillon funerals.

Hailing from a family whose ancestors had their burials at a dolmen near Broadford, he became obsessed with the mystery of the Cantillon sea burials. So, on the death of Florence Cantillon, Connor O'Dea finally decided to satisfy himself about the truth of this story of the old church under the sea: so when he heard the news of old Flory's death, away with him to the church in Ardfert, where Flory was laid out in high style, and a beautiful corpse he made.

That evening the coffin was borne the three miles to the strand at Ballyheigue and left there. Then the mourners departed, one group after another, and at last Connor was left alone. He sat upon a big stone that was sheltered by a projecting rock, and partly hidden from view. There he waited with patience for the appearance of the ghostly undertakers.

The evening came on mild and beautiful. He whistled an old tune which he had heard in his childhood, hoping to keep idle fears out of his head.

It was, in truth, a lovely moonlit night; nothing was to be seen around but the dark rocks, and the white sandy beach, upon which the sea broke with a rough and melancholy murmur. Connor felt rather strange after a while, and almost began to regret his bravado and curiosity. It was such a gloomy sight to see the black coffin resting upon the white strand. His imagination played with the deep moaning of the ocean and soon Connor imagined the sounds as the terrifying wail of the dead man. He soon saw each shadow thrown as a ghost dancing on the shore.

Frozen to the spot, he became weary with watching the narrow house of death but he refused to fall asleep or go home, such was the power of his curiosity.

Long past midnight, when the moon was sinking into the sea, he was startled by the sound of many voices. They gradually became stronger above the heavy and monotonous roll of the sea. He listened, and presently could make out a keen[1] of exquisite sweetness. The notes rose and fell with the rhythm of the waves, which made low murmuring sounds in his ear!

As the keen ended, Connor saw strange and mysterious-looking shapes emerge from the sea, and surround the coffin, which they prepared to launch into the water.

'Oh why again do we march ashore from our sea-hidden island?' whispered a wind-blown shape.

'This comes of marrying with the creatures of earth,' replied a ghostly figure, in a clear, yet hollow tone.

'True,' replied another, with a voice still more fearful, 'our king would never have commanded his gnawing white-toothed waves to devour the rocky roots of the island cemetery, had not his daughter, Durfulla, been buried there by her mortal husband!'

'But time will come,' said a hooded shape, bending over the coffin.

'When human eye—our work shall spy,

And human ear—our keen shall hear.'

'Then,' howled the voice of a chilling phantom, 'our burial of the Cantillons is at an end for ever!'

As this was spoken the coffin was borne from the beach by a retiring wave, and the company of sea spirits prepared to follow it; but at that moment one of them happened to cast her gimlet[2] eye on Connor O'Dea, as fixed with curiosity and as motionless with fear as the stone on which he sat.

'The time is come,' cried the unearthly being, 'the time is come; a human eye looks on the forms of the ocean, a human ear has heard their voices. Farewell to the Cantillons; the sons of the sea are no longer doomed to bury the dust of the earth!'

'Unless,' howled a ghostly voice from among their company, 'unless this witness, Connor O'Dea, for so he is named, shall come with us to the Cantillon sea-tomb there to remain silent forever.'

The company began to move towards Connor but he in terror took to his heels and headed at full speed for home.

So then, one after the other, the ghostly troop turned slowly around, and headed for the ocean vault. Again arose their funeral song; and on the next wave they followed the coffin. The sound of the lamentation died away, and at length nothing was heard but the rush of waters. The coffin and the train of sea people sank over the old churchyard, and never since the funeral of old Flory Cantillon have any of the family been carried to the strand of Ballyheigue, to be conveyed to their rightful burial-place, beneath the waves of the Atlantic.

No more was heard of Connor O'Dea but 'tis said that he lost his mind soon afterwards and is buried deep under the dolmen near Broadford, the last of his family to rest there.

[1] **keen:** a sorrowful song for the dead; [2] **gimlet:** sharp-sighted

Oral exploration

1 This tale would be told by a seanchaí in a darkened room on a winter evening. Which part of the tale would frighten the audience most? Discuss your choices.

2 The seanchaí describes scenes very vividly in order to bring his tale alive in the audience's imagination. Choose two paragraphs where the description is particularly good. Note down your favourite examples of descriptive writing and say why they are effective.

Portfolio 6C

3 Often in a tale like this a character who encounters the spirit world regrets it. Do you think that's true in this tale?

4 Choose one modern story about a boy's or girl's encounter with an alien or spirit world, for example *Twilight* or *Harry Potter*. Does it have any similarities with this story? Say why.

Create

The following are important elements in our enjoyment of this story:

- Eerie setting
- Phantoms
- Human character(s)
- Unsettling events
- Dialogue.

Now is your chance to create a tale (on your own or with a partner) in this tradition that could be told to an audience on a dark winter night. After you have finished, record your story and add sound effects.

Portfolio 6D

Classic Irish short stories

Two short stories by Frank O'Connor

Frank O'Connor (1903–1966) was born in Cork city. He is the author of over a hundred works and is recognised as a master of the Irish short story. This is recognised by the Munster Literature Centre which has run a festival in his honour and to promote the short story since 2000. His memoir, *An Only Child*, published in 1963, also gained widespread acclaim. He grew up in a home with an alcoholic father who mistreated his mother, and this fact comes through in his short story 'Christmas Morning' which you will read in this unit.

Frank O'Connor

First person narrator

This story is told in the **first person**, that is, from the viewpoint of one character. In this case, the young boy, Jackie, tells us what happens. In this way we experience the other characters and events as he sees them, that is, from his **point of view**.

Before you read

Have you ever been in trouble at home or in school? How did you deal with the situation? What did you learn about yourself from the experience?

Background

Children must confess their sins before they can receive First Holy Communion. Children usually make their first Confession at the age of seven. The protagonist in this story has some difficulty getting to grips with the process, and with the Confessional, which is a divided wooden stall within the church where the priest hears confessions.

FIRST CONFESSION

All the trouble began when my grandfather died and my grandmother – my father's mother – came to live with us. Relations in the one house are a strain at the best of times, but, to make matters worse, my grandmother was a real old country woman and quite unsuited to the life in town. She had a fat, wrinkled old face, and, to Mother's great indignation, went round the house in bare feet – the boots had her crippled, she said. For dinner she had a jug of porter and a pot of potatoes with – sometimes – a bit of salt fish, and she poured out the potatoes on the table and ate them slowly, with great enjoyment, using her fingers by way of a fork.

Now, girls are supposed to be fastidious, but I was the one who suffered most from this. Nora, my sister, just sucked up to the old woman for the penny she got every Friday out of the old-age pension, a thing I could not do. I was too honest, that was my trouble; and when I was playing with Bill Connell, the sergeant-major's son, and saw my grandmother steering up the path with the jug of porter sticking out from beneath her shawl I was mortified. I made excuses not to let him come into the house, because I could never be sure what she would be up to when we went in.

When my mother was at work and my grandmother made the dinner I wouldn't touch it. Nora once tried to make me, but I hid under the table from her and took the bread-knife with me for protection. Nora let on to be very indignant (she wasn't, of course, but she knew mother saw through her, so she sided with Gran) and came after me. I lashed out at her with the bread-knife, and after that she left me alone. I stayed there till Mother came in from work, and she made my dinner; but when my Father came in later Nora said in a shocked voice: 'Oh, Dadda, do you know what Jackie did at dinnertime?' Then, of course, it all came out; Father gave me a flaking; Mother interfered, and for days after that he didn't speak to me and Mother barely spoke to Nora. And all because of that old woman! God knows, I was heart-scalded.

Then, to crown my misfortunes, I had to make my first Confession and Communion. It was an old woman called Ryan who prepared us for these. She was about the one age with Gran; she was well-to-do, lived in a big house on Montenotte, wore a black cloak and bonnet, and came every day to the school at three o'clock when we should have been going home, and talked to us of Hell. She may have mentioned the other place as well, but that could only have been by accident, for Hell had the first place in her heart.

She lit a candle, took out a new half-crown,[1] and offered it to the first boy who would hold one finger – only one finger! – in the flame for five minutes by the school clock. Being always very ambitious I was tempted to volunteer, but I thought it might look greedy. Then she asked were we afraid of holding one finger – only one finger! – in a little candle flame for five minutes and not afraid of burning all over in roasting hot furnaces for all eternity. 'All eternity! Just think of that! A whole lifetime goes by and it's nothing, not even a drop in the ocean of your sufferings.' The woman was really interesting about Hell, but my attention was all fixed on the half-crown. At the end of the lesson she put it back in her purse. It was a great disappointment; a religious woman like that, you wouldn't think she'd bother about a thing like a half-crown.

Another day she said she knew a priest who woke one night to find a fellow he didn't recognise leaning over the end of his bed. The priest was a bit frightened – naturally enough – but he asked the fellow what he wanted, and the fellow said in a deep, husky voice that he wanted to go to confession. The priest said it was an awkward time and wouldn't it do in the morning, but the fellow said the last time he went to confession there was one sin he kept back, being ashamed to mention it, and now it was always on his mind. Then the priest knew it was a bad case, because the fellow was after making a bad confession and committing a mortal sin. He got up to dress, and just then the cock crew in the yard outside, and – lo and behold! – when the priest looked round there was no sign of the fellow, only a smell of burning timber, and when the priest looked at his bed didn't he see the print of two hands burned in it? That was because the fellow had made a bad confession. This story made a shocking impression on me.

But the worst of all was when she showed us how to examine our conscience. Did we take the name of the Lord, our God, in vain? Did we honour our father and our mother? (I asked her did this include grandmothers and she said it did.) Did we love our neighbour as ourselves? Did we covet our neighbour's goods? (I thought of the way I felt about the penny that Nora got every Friday.) I decided that, between one thing and another, I must have broken the whole ten commandments, all on account of that old woman, and so far as I could see, so long as she remained in the house I had no hope of ever doing anything else.

I was scared to death of confession. The day the whole class went I let on to have the toothache, hoping my absence wouldn't be noticed; but at three o'clock, just as I was feeling safe, along comes a chap with a message from Mrs Ryan that I was to go to confession myself on Saturday and be at the chapel for Communion with the rest. To make it worse, Mother couldn't come with me and sent Nora instead.

Now, that girl had ways of tormenting me that Mother never knew of. She held my hand as we went down the hill, smiling sadly and saying how sorry she was for me, as if she were bringing me to the hospital for an operation.

'Oh, God help us!' she said. Isn't it a terrible pity you weren't a good boy? Oh, Jackie, my heart bleeds for you! How will you ever think of all your sins? Don't forget you have to tell him about the time you kicked Gran on the shin.'

'Lemme go!' I said, trying to drag myself free of her. I don't want to go to confession at all.'

'But sure, you'll have to go to confession, Jackie,' she replied in the same regretful tone. 'Sure, if you didn't, the parish priest would be up to the house, looking for you. 'Tisn't, God knows, that I'm not sorry for you! Do you remember the time you tried to kill me with the bread-knife under the table? And the language you used to me? I don't know what he'll do with you at all. He might have to send you up to the Bishop.'

I remember thinking bitterly that she didn't know the half of what I had to tell – if I told it. I knew I couldn't tell it, and understood perfectly why the fellow in Mrs Ryan's story made a bad confession; it seemed to me a great shame that people wouldn't stop criticising him. I remember that steep hill down to the church, and the sunlit hillsides beyond the valley of the river, which I saw in the gaps between the houses like Adam's last glimpse of Paradise.

Then, when she had manoeuvred me down the long flight of steps to the chapel yard, Nora suddenly changed her tune. She became the raging malicious devil she really was.

'There you are!' she said with a yelp of triumph, hurling me through the church door. 'And I hope he'll give you the penitential psalms,[2] you dirty little caffler!'[3]

I knew then I was lost, given up to eternal justice. The door with the coloured-glass panels swung shut behind me, the sunlight went out and gave place to deep shadow, and the wind whistled outside so that the silence within seemed to crackle like ice under my feet. Nora sat in front of me by the confession box. There were a couple of old women ahead of her, and then a miserable-looking poor devil came and wedged me in at the other side, so that I couldn't escape even if I had the courage. He joined his hands and rolled his eyes in the direction of the roof, muttering aspirations in an anguished tone, and I wondered had he a grandmother too. Only a grandmother could account for a fellow behaving in that heartbroken way, but he was better off than I, for he at least could go and confess his sins; while I would make a bad confession and then die in the night and be continually coming back and burning people's furniture.

Nora's turn came, and I heard the sound of something slamming, and then her voice as if butter wouldn't melt in her mouth, and then another slam, and out she came. God, the hypocrisy of women! Her eyes were lowered, her head was bowed, and her hands were joined very low down on her stomach, and she walked up the aisle to the side altar looking like a saint. You never saw such an exhibition of devotion; and I remembered the devilish malice with which she had tormented me all the way from our door, and wondered were all religious people like that, really. It was my turn now. With the fear of damnation in my soul I went in, and the confessional door closed of itself behind me.

It was pitch-dark and I couldn't see priest or anything else. Then I really began to be frightened. In the darkness it was a matter between God and me, and He had all the odds. He knew what my intentions were even before I even started; I had no chance. All I had ever been told about confession got mixed up in my mind, and I knelt to one wall and said: 'Bless me, father, for I have sinned; this is my first confession.' I waited for a few minutes but nothing happened, so I tried it on the other wall. Nothing happened there either. He had me spotted all right.

It must have been then that I noticed the shelf at about the one height with my head. It was really a place for grown-up people to rest their elbows, but in my distracted state I thought it was probably the place you were supposed to kneel. Of course, it was on the high side and not very deep, but I was always good at climbing and managed to get up all right. Staying up was the trouble. There was room only for my knees, and nothing you could get a grip on but a sort of wooden moulding a bit above it. I held on to the moulding and repeated the words a little louder, and this time something happened all right. A slide was slammed back; a little light entered the box, and a man's voice said: 'Who's there?'

''Tis me, father,' I said for fear he mightn't see me and go away again. I couldn't see him at all. The place his voice came from was under the moulding, about level with my knees, so I took a good grip of the moulding and swung myself down till I saw the astonished face of a young priest looking up at me. He had to put his head on one side to see me, and I had to put mine on one side to see him, so we were more or less talking to one another upside-down. It struck me as a queer way of hearing confessions, but I didn't feel it my place to criticise.

'Bless me, father, for I have sinned; this is my first confession,' I rattled off all in one breath, and swung myself down the least shade more to make it easier for him.

'What are you doing up there?' he shouted in an angry voice, and the strain the politeness was putting on my hold of the moulding, and the shock of being addressed in such an uncivil tone, were too much for me. I lost my grip, tumbled, and hit the door an unmerciful wallop before I found myself flat on my back in the middle of the aisle. The people who had been waiting stood up with their mouths open. The priest opened the door of the middle box and came out, pushing his biretta back from his forehead; he looked something terrible. Then Nora came scampering down the aisle.

'Oh, you dirty little caffler!' she said. 'I might have known you'd do it! I might have known you'd disgrace me! I can't leave you out of my sight for a minute.'

Before I could even get to my feet to defend myself she bent down and gave me a clip across the ear. This reminded me that I was so stunned I had even forgotten to cry, so that people might think I wasn't hurt at all, when in fact I was probably maimed for life. I gave a roar out of me.

'What's all this about?' the priest hissed, getting angrier than ever and pushing Nora off me. 'How dare you hit the child like that, you little vixen?'

'But I can't do my penance with him, father,' Nora cried, cocking an outraged eye up at him.

'Well, go and do it, or I'll give you some more to do,' he said, giving me a hand up. 'Was it coming to confession you were, my poor man?' he asked me.

''Twas, father,' said I with a sob.

'Oh,' he said respectfully, 'a big hefty fellow like you must have terrible sins. Is this your first?'

''Tis, father,' said I.

'Worse and worse,' he said gloomily. 'The crimes of a lifetime. I don't know will I get rid of you at all today. You'd better wait now till I'm finished with these old ones. You can see by the looks of them they haven't much to tell.'

'I will, father,' I said with something approaching joy.

The relief of it was really enormous. Nora stuck out her tongue at me behind his back, but I couldn't even be bothered retorting. I knew from the very moment that man opened his mouth that he was intelligent above the ordinary. It only stood to reason that a fellow confessing after seven years would have more to tell than people that went every week. It was only what he expected, and the rest was the cackle of old women and girls with their talk of Hell, the Bishop, and the penitential psalms. That was all they knew. I started to make my examination of conscience, and barring the one bad business of my grandmother it didn't seem too bad.

The next time, the priest steered me into the confession box himself and left the shutter back the way I could see him get in and sit down at the further side of the grille from me.

'Well now,' he said, 'what do they call you?'

'Jackie, father,' said I.

'And what's a-trouble to you, Jackie?' he said.

'Father,' I said, feeling I might as well get it over while I had him in good humour, 'I had it all arranged to kill my grandmother.'

He seemed a bit shaken by that, all right, because he said nothing for quite a while.

'My goodness,' he said at last, 'that'd be a shocking thing to do. What put that into your head?'

'Father,' I said, feeling very sorry for myself, 'she's an awful woman.'

'Is she?' he asked. 'What way is she awful?'

'She takes porter, father,' I said, knowing well from the way Mother talked of it that this was a mortal sin, and hoping it would make the priest take a more favourable view of my case.

'Oh, my!' he said, and I could see he was impressed.

'And snuff, father,' said I.

'That's a bad case, sure enough, Jackie,' he said.

'And she goes round in her bare feet, father,' I went on in a rush of self-pity, 'and she knows I don't like her, and she gives pennies to Nora and none to me, and my da sides with her and flakes me, and one night I was so heart-scalded I made up my mind I'd have to kill her.'

'And what would you do with the body?' he asked with great interest.

'I was thinking I could chop that up and carry it away in a barrow I have,' I said.

'Begor, Jackie,' he said, 'do you know, you're a terrible child?'

'I know, father,' I said, for I was just thinking the same thing myself. 'I tried to kill Nora too, with a bread-knife under the table, only I missed her'.

'Is that the little girl that was beating you just now?' he asked.

''Tis, father.'

'Someone will go for her with a bread-knife one day, and he won't miss her,' he said rather cryptically. 'You must have great courage. Between ourselves, there's a lot of people I'd like to do the same to but I'd never have the nerve. Hanging is an awful death.'

'Is it, father?' I asked with the deepest interest – I was always very keen on hanging. 'Did you ever see a fellow hanged?'

'Dozens of them,' he said solemnly. 'And they all died roaring.'

'Jay!' I said.

'Oh, a horrible death!' he said with great satisfaction. 'Lots of the fellows I saw killed their grandmothers too, but they all said "twas never worth it.'

He had me there for a full ten minutes talking, and then walked out the chapel yard with me. I was genuinely sorry to part with him, because he was the most entertaining man I'd ever met in the religious line. Outside, after the shadow of the church, the sunlight was like the roaring of waves on a beach; it dazzled me; and when the frozen silence melted and I heard the screech of trams on the road my heart soared. I knew now I wouldn't die that night and come back, leaving marks on my mother's furniture. It would be a great worry to her and the poor soul had enough.

Nora was sitting on the railing, waiting for me, and she put on a very sour puss when she saw the priest with me. She was mad jealous because a priest had never come out of the church with her.

'Well,' she asked coldly, after he left me, 'what did he give you?'

'Three Hail Marys,' I said.

'Three Hail Marys?' she repeated incredulously. 'You mustn't have told him anything.'

'I told him everything,' I said confidently.

'About Gran and all?'

'About Gran and all.'

(All she wanted was to be able to go home and say I'd made a bad confession.)

'Did you tell him you went for me with the bread-knife?' she asked with a frown.

'I did to be sure.'

'And he only gave you three Hail Marys?'

'That's all.'

She got down from the railing slowly with a baffled air. Clearly, this was beyond her. As we mounted the steps to the main road she looked at me suspiciously.

'What are you sucking?' she asked.

'Bullseyes.'

'Was it the priest gave them to you?'

''Twas.'

'Lord God!' she wailed bitterly, 'some people have all the luck! 'Tis no advantage to anybody trying to be good. I might just as well be a sinner like you.'

---

[1] **half-crown:** a coin worth 30 old pence; [2] **penitential psalms:** a very harsh penance consisting of six psalms; [3] **caffler:** an impish, impertinent boy.

Using 'two', 'too' and 'to'

Two is for the number 2:

- Jackie had **two** parents.

Too is used to mean very or as well:

- I was **too** honest; that was my trouble.
  Lots of the fellows I saw killed their grandmothers **too**.
- I tried to kill Nora **too**, with a bread-knife, under the table, only I missed her.

Use **to** for everything else

1 As part of a verb:
   - I did **to** be sure; I was quite sorry **to** part with him.

2 To indicate direction:
   - Jackie went **to** confession.

Dramatic reversal

Dramatic reversal in a story occurs when the plot line suddenly changes and a character who is expecting events to go in their favour gets a sudden shock when things turn out differently. For example, when Jackie's sister manages to get Jackie into the church she says:

'There you are!' she said with a yelp of triumph, hurling me from her through the church door. 'And I hope he'll give you the penitential psalms, you dirty little caffler!'

However, the opposite happens when the priest gives sweets to Jackie, and his sister is sharply criticised by him:

'What's all this about?' said the priest, getting angrier than ever, and pushing her off me. 'How dare you hit the child like that, you little vixen?'

Oral exploration

1 What things about his grandmother does Jackie not like?

2 What is Jackie's main feeling when he thinks about his grandmother?

3 Jackie's sister has more power than Jackie has in the home. How does she show this in paragraph 3?

4 How does Mrs Ryan try to frighten the children about the flames of Hell?

5 When he examines his conscience, what commandments does Jackie imagine he has broken?

6 When his sister is taking him to make his confession, how does she treat him?

7 What is the priest's first reaction on seeing that Jackie has climbed up onto the shelf in the confessional?

8 After his sister strikes him across the ear, how does Jackie's relationship with the priest develop?

9 What is the response of Jackie's sister to his getting sweets from the priest?

Characters and adjectives

Language alert

In stories, we learn about characters in the following ways:

⟶ by reading how characters think about things and situations

⟶ by seeing how they react to difficult moments in their lives

⟶ by noticing what other characters feel or say about them.

We often use adjectives to describe a character. Here is a list of adjectives that may be used to describe the main characters in the story: Jackie, Jackie's sister and the priest. Match the adjectives to the character and in the third column write a brief reason for your choice of adjective, based on the events in the story. Use the template in your Portfolio to complete the task.

Portfolio 6E

Adjective	Character	Reason

- very innocent
- manipulative
- self-pitying
- impatient

- unsympathetic
- understanding
- jealous

- kind
- nasty
- violent

- immature
- credulous
- imaginative

Read, write, explore

1 Jackie's problem

Jackie's first statement in the story blames all his problems on the fact that his grandmother came to live in his home: 'All the trouble began when my grandfather died, and my grandmother — my father's mother — came to live with us.' Do you agree with his opinion or are there other problems that he has to deal with? What are they?

2 Jackie's sister

Using the adjectives you chose in the exercise on page 164, write a character profile of Jackie's sister and say whether you have any sympathy for her at the end of the story.

Portfolio 6F

3 Jackie's sins

Discuss with a partner and list in order of importance the 'sins' that Jackie must deal with as he approaches his first confession:

- Hating his grandmother
- Jealousy of his sister
- Planning to kill his grandmother
- Wanting to kill his sister
- Anger at his father

Is Jackie a typical seven-year-old? Why? Why not? How is he shown to be very imaginative? Are there any clues to show that he is very clever? After discussing these with a partner, write your response in a paragraph.

4 The priest

Write a paragraph saying whether you agree that the priest is clever in how he solves Jackie's problems for him.

5

We hear the story only from Jackie's point of view. Imagine you were to interview Jackie's sister about her family and how she feels. Use questions such as: You say Jackie is a 'caffler'. How do you justify calling him that?

Create

Reread the story from 'I was scared to death of confession' with a view to creating a **short drama** based on the events in the story. You may choose to fill in some information by having a narrator introduce the drama and the characters. You will need at least four students in your group: Narrator, Jackie, Jackie's sister and the priest.

Christmas Morning

I never really liked my brother, Sonny. From the time he was a baby he was always the mother's pet and always chasing her to tell her what mischief I was up to. Mind you, I was usually up to something. Until I was nine or ten, I was never much good at school, and I really believe it was to spite me that he was so smart at his books. He seemed to know by instinct that this was what Mother had set her heart on, and you might almost say he spelt himself into her favour.

'Mummy,' he'd say, 'will I call Larry in to his t-e-a?' or: 'Mummy, the k-e-t-e-l is boiling,' and, of course, when he was wrong she'd correct him, and next time he'd have it right and there would be no standing him. 'Mummy,' he'd say, 'aren't I a good speller?' Cripes, we could all be good spellers if we went on like that!

Mind you, it wasn't that I was stupid. Far from it. I was just restless and not able to fix my mind for long on any one thing. I'd do the lessons for the year before, or the lessons for the year after: what I couldn't stand were the lessons we were supposed to be doing at the time. In the evenings I used to go out and play with the Doherty gang. Not, again, that I was rough, but I liked the excitement, and for the life of me I couldn't see what attracted Mother about education.

Can't you do your lessons first and play after?' she'd say, getting white with indignation. 'You ought to be ashamed of yourself that your baby brother can read better than you.'

She didn't seem to understand that I wasn't, because there didn't seem to me to be anything particularly praiseworthy about reading, and it struck me as an occupation better suited to a sissy kid like Sonny.

'The dear knows what will become of you,' she'd say. 'If only you'd stick to your books you might be something good like a clerk or an engineer.'

'I'll be a clerk, Mummy,' Sonny would say smugly.

'Who wants to be an old clerk?' I'd say, just to annoy him. 'I'm going to be a soldier.'

'The dear knows, I'm afraid that's all you'll ever be fit for,' she would add with a sigh.

I couldn't help feeling at times that she wasn't all there. As if there was anything better a fellow could be!

Coming on to Christmas, with the days getting shorter and the shopping crowds bigger, I began to think of all the things I might get off Santa Claus. The Dohertys said there was no Santa Claus, only what your father and mother gave you, but the Dohertys were a rough class of children you wouldn't expect Santa to come to anyway.

I was rooting round for whatever information I could pick up about him, but there didn't seem to be much. I was no hand with a pen, but if a letter would do any good I was ready to chance writing to him. I had plenty of initiative and was always writing for free samples and prospectuses.

'Ah, I don't know will he come at all this year,' Mother said with a worried air. 'He has enough to do looking after steady boys who mind their lessons without bothering about the rest.'

'He only comes to good spellers, Mummy,' said Sonny. 'Isn't that right?'

'He comes to any little boy who does his best, whether he's a good speller or not,' Mother said firmly.

Well I did my best. God knows I did! It wasn't my fault if, four days before the holidays, Flogger Dawley gave us sums we couldn't do, and Peter Doherty and myself had to go on the lang.[1] It wasn't for the love of it, for, take it from me, December is no month for mitching, and we spent most of our time sheltering from the rain in a store on the quays. The only mistake we made was imagining we could keep it up till the holidays without being spotted. That showed real lack of foresight.

Of course, Flogger Dawley noticed and sent home word to know what was keeping me. When I came in on the third day the mother gave me a look I'll never forget, and said: 'Your dinner is there.' She was too full to talk. When I tried to explain to her about Flogger Dawley and the sums she brushed it aside and said: 'You have no word.' I saw then it wasn't the langing she minded but the lies, though I still didn't see how you could lang without lying. She didn't speak to me for days. And even then I couldn't make out what she saw in education, or why she wouldn't let me grow up naturally like anyone else.

To make things worse, it stuffed Sonny up more than ever. He had the air of one saying: 'I don't know what they'd do without me in this blooming house.' He stood at the front door, leaning against the jamb with his hands in his trouser pockets, trying to make himself look like Father, and shouted to the other kids so that he could be heard all over the road.

'Larry isn't left go out. He went on the lang with Peter Doherty and me mother isn't talking to him.'

And at night, when we were in bed, he kept it up.

'Santa Claus won't bring you anything this year, aha!'

'Of course he will,' I said.

'How do you know?'

'Why wouldn't he?'

'Because you went on the lang with Doherty. I wouldn't play with them Doherty fellows.'

'You wouldn't be left.'

'I wouldn't play with them. They're no class. They had the bobbies up to the house.'

'And how would Santa know I was on the lang with Peter Doherty?' I growled, losing patience with the little prig.

'Of course he'd know. Mummy would tell him.'

'And how could Mummy tell him and he up at the North Pole? Poor Ireland, she's rearing them yet! 'Tis easy seen you're only an old baby.'

'I'm not a baby, and I can spell better than you, and Santa won't bring you anything.'

'We'll see whether he will or not,' I said sarcastically, doing the old man on him.

But, to tell the God's truth, the old man was only bluff. You could never tell what powers these superhuman chaps would have of knowing what you were up to. And I had a bad conscience about the langing because I'd never before seen the mother like that.

That was the night I decided that the only sensible thing to do was to see Santa myself and explain to him. Being a man, he'd probably understand. In those days I was a good-looking kid and had a way with me when I liked. I had only to smile nicely at one old gent on the North Mall to get a penny from him, and I felt if only I could get Santa by himself I could do the same with him and maybe get something worthwhile from him. I wanted a model railway: I was sick of Ludo and Snakes-and-Ladders.

I started to practise lying awake, counting five hundred and then a thousand, and then trying to hear first eleven, then midnight, from Shandon. I felt sure Santa would be round by midnight, seeing that he'd be coming from the north, and would have the whole of the south side to do afterwards. In some ways I was very farsighted. The only trouble was the things I was farsighted about.

I was so wrapped up in my own calculations that I had little attention to spare for Mother's difficulties. Sonny and I used to go to town with her, and while she was shopping we stood outside a toyshop in the North Main Street, arguing about what we'd like for Christmas.

On Christmas Eve when Father came home from work and gave her the housekeeping money, she stood looking at it doubtfully while her face grew white.

'Well?' he snapped, getting angry. 'What's wrong with that?'

'What's wrong with it?' she muttered. 'On Christmas Eve!'

'Well,' he asked truculently, sticking his hands in his trouser pockets as though to guard what was left, 'do you think I get more because it's Christmas?'

'Lord God,' she muttered distractedly. 'And not a bit of cake in the house, nor a candle, nor anything!'

'All right,' he shouted, beginning to stamp. 'How much will the candle be?'

'Ah, for pity's sake,' she cried, 'will you give me the money and not argue like that before the children? Do you think I'll leave them with nothing on the one day of the year?'

'Bad luck to you and your children!' he snarled. 'Am I to be slaving from one year's end to another for you to be throwing it away on toys? Here,' he added, tossing two half-crowns on the table, 'that's all you're going to get, so make the most of it.'

'I suppose the publicans will get the rest,' she said bitterly.

Later she went into town, but did not bring us with her, and returned with a lot of parcels, including the Christmas candle. We waited for the Father to come home to his tea, but he didn't, so we had our own tea and a slice of Christmas cake each, and then

Mother put Sonny on a chair with the holy-water stoup to sprinkle the candle, and when he lit it she said: 'The light of heaven to our souls.' I could see she was upset because Father wasn't in – it should be the oldest and youngest. When we hung up our stockings at bedtime he was still out.

Then began the hardest couple of hours I ever put in. I was mad with sleep but afraid of losing the model railway, so I lay for a while, making up things to say to Santa when he came. They varied from frivolous to grave, for some old gents like kids to be modest and well spoken, while others prefer them with spirit. When I had rehearsed them all I tried to wake Sonny to keep me company, but that kid slept like the dead.

Eleven struck from Shandon, and soon after I heard the latch, but it was only Father coming home.

'Hello, little girl,' he said, letting on to be surprised at finding Mother waiting for him, and then broke into a self-conscious giggle. 'What have you up so late?'

'Do you want supper?' she asked shortly.

'Ah, no, no,' he replied. 'I had a bit of pig's cheek at Daneen's on my way up.' (Daneen was my uncle.) 'I'm very fond of pig's cheek . . . My goodness, is it that late?' he exclaimed, letting on to be astonished. 'If I knew that I'd have gone to the North Chapel for midnight Mass. I'd like to hear the *Adeste* again. That's a hymn I'm very fond of – a most touching hymn.'

The he began to hum it falsetto.

Adeste fideles
Solus domus dagus.

Father was very fond of Latin hymns, particularly when he had a drop in, but as he had no notion of the words he made them up as he went along, and this always drove Mother mad.

'Ah, you disgust me!' she said in a scalded voice, and closed the room door behind her. Father laughed as if he thought it a great joke; and he struck a match to light his pipe and for a while puffed at it noisily. The light under the door dimmed and went out but he continued to sing emotionally.

Dixie medearo
Tutum tonum tantum
Venite adoremus.

He had it all wrong but the effect was the same on me. To save my life I couldn't keep awake.

Coming on to dawn, I woke with the feeling that something dreadful had happened. The whole house was quiet, and the little bedroom that looked out on the foot and a half of back was pitch-dark. It was only when I glanced at the window that I saw how all the silver had drained out of the sky. I jumped out of bed to feel my stockings, well knowing that the worst had happened. Santa had come while I was asleep, and gone away with an entirely false impression of me, because all he had left me was some sort of book, folded up, a pen and pencil, and a tuppenny bag of sweets. Not even Snakes-and-Ladders! For a while I was too stunned even to think. A fellow who was able to drive over rooftops and climb down chimneys without getting stuck – God, wouldn't you think he'd know better?

Then I began to wonder what that foxy boy, Sonny, had. I went to his side of the bed and felt his stocking. For all his spelling and sucking-up he hadn't done so much better, because, apart from a bag of sweets like mine, all Santa had left him was a popgun, one that fired a cork on a piece of string and which you could get in any huxter's shop for sixpence.

All the same, the fact remained that it was a gun, and a gun was better than a book any day of the week. The Dohertys had a gang, and the gang fought the Strawberry Lane kids who tried to play football on our road. That gun would be very useful to me in many ways, while it would be lost on Sonny who wouldn't be let play with the gang, even if he wanted to.

Then I got the inspiration, as it seemed to me, direct from heaven. Suppose I took the gun and gave Sonny the book! Sonny would never be any good in a gang: he was fond of spelling, and a studious child like him could learn a lot of spellings from a book like mine. As he hadn't seen Santa any more than I had, what he hadn't seen wouldn't grieve him. I was doing no harm to anyone; in fact, if Sonny only knew, I was doing him a good turn which he might have cause to thank me for later. That was one thing I was always keen on; doing good turns. Perhaps this was Santa's intention the whole time and he had merely become confused between us. It was a mistake that might happen to anyone. So I put the book, the pencil, and the pen into Sonny's stocking and the popgun into my own, and returned to bed and slept again. As I say, in those days I had plenty of initiative.

It was Sonny who woke me, shaking me to tell me that Santa had come and left me a gun. I let on to be surprised and rather disappointed in the gun, and to divert his mind from it made him show me his picture book, and cracked it up to the skies.

As I knew, that kid was prepared to believe anything, and nothing would do him then but to take the presents in to show Father and Mother. This was a bad moment for me. After the way she had behaved about the langing, I distrusted Mother, though I had the consolation of believing that the only person who could contradict me was now somewhere up by the North Pole. That gave me a certain confidence, so Sonny and I burst in with our presents, shouting: 'Look what Santa Claus brought!'

Father and Mother woke, and Mother smiled, but only for an instant. As she looked at me her face changed. I knew that look: I knew it only too well. It was the same she had worn the day I came home from langing, when she said I had no word.

'Larry,' she said in a low voice, 'where did you get that gun?'

'Santa left it in my stocking, Mummy,' I said, trying to put on an injured air, though it baffled me how she guessed that he hadn't. 'He did, honest.'

'You stole it from that poor child's stocking while he was asleep,' she said, her voice quivering with indignation. 'Larry, Larry, how could you be so mean?'

'Now, now, now,' Father said deprecatingly, ''tis Christmas morning.'

'Ah,' she said with real passion, 'it's easy it comes to you. Do you think I want my son to grow up a liar and a thief?'

'Ah, what thief, woman?' he said testily. 'Have sense, can't you?' He was cross if you interrupted him in his benevolent moods as if they were of the other sort, and this one was probably exacerbated by a feeling of guilt for his behaviour of the night before. 'Here, Larry,' he said, reaching out for the money on the bedside table, 'here's sixpence for you and one for Sonny. Mind you don't lose it now!'

But I looked at Mother and saw what was in her eyes. I burst out crying, threw the popgun on the floor, and ran bawling out of the house before anyone on the road was awake. I rushed up the lane beside the house and threw myself on the wet grass.

I understood it all, and it was almost more than I could bear; that there was no Santa Claus, as the Dohertys said, only Mother trying to scrape together a few coppers from the housekeeping; that Father was mean and common and a drunkard, and that she had been relying on me to raise her out of the misery of the life she was leading. And I knew that the look in her eyes was the fear that, like my father, I should turn out to be mean and common and a drunkard.

¹ **on the lang:** mitching

Oral exploration

1 'I never really liked my brother'. What specifically did Larry dislike about Sonny?

2 'Mind you, it wasn't that I was stupid.' How does Larry show he is clever at the start of the story?

3 Larry's attitude stirs strong feelings in his mother. What are they?

4 Do you find the father's behaviour amusing? Why? Why not? Discuss reasons for both views.

5 Do you have more sympathy for Larry or his mother at the end of the story?

6 Discuss the New Year's resolution that Larry might make after the events of this story.

7 Now have a whole-class discussion and decide which of the following statements best describes how Larry feels as he's telling the story. Rank them 1–5 (5 = best).

- Larry feels guilty for letting his mother down on two big occasions in the story.
- Larry is so wrapped up in disliking his sibling that he often feels tension towards his mother.
- Larry is jealous of Sonny and all the attention he gets.
- Larry is sorry about the time he spent with Doherty.
- Larry is horrified to learn that there is no Santa Claus.

 PowerPoint – Quiz

Read, write, explore

1 The mother as a parent

The mother continually compares Larry with Sonny. How successful is this tactic in improving Larry's attitude and behaviour throughout the story? Write down your reasons.

2 School life

How is the teacher portrayed in the story? Give details. Does he appear to be a good teacher? Why? Why not? How do we know that Larry fears him?

3 The Doherty gang

What is the appeal of the Doherty gang to Larry? How does Larry show himself to be different from them? Give some details.

4 The father

'Ah, you disgust me!' What is it about the father's behaviour on Christmas Eve that disgusts the mother? Write down some details. What is your opinion of the father's behaviour? Write down your reasons.

5 Santa Claus

What do you find amusing about Larry's take on Santa in the run-up to Christmas morning? Give some amusing details.

6 'I understood it all . . . ' What does Larry realise about Santa Claus, his father and about his mother on that Christmas morning? Does his new knowledge make him happy? Write down your responses.

7 The author

Which character does the author lead you to like, Sonny or Larry? Show some of the ways that the author influences your attitude to each of the brothers.

8 Sonny or Larry?

From the evidence of the story, decide which of her sons, Sonny or Larry, the mother loves more? Note some reasons for your opinion.

Create

Write a letter to the author, Frank O'Connor, in which you comment on the story. Part of the letter should praise him for the story. You should tell him how childhood today is like Larry's in some ways. Part of your letter should also inform the author that childhood has changed in lots of ways.

Portfolio 6G

You can use some of the following sentence suggestions and complete them in the letter.

- Dear Mr O'Connor,
- I enjoyed your story because my brother/sister . . .
- Your story was funny where/when . . .
- Your story taught me an interesting lesson . . .
- I was really surprised by the ending because . . .
- I'd say Larry will improve because . . .

- I actually think Sonny is a user and will turn out . . .
- Nowadays we have technology which . . .
- There's one part of the story which couldn't happen today because . . .

'The Confirmation Suit' by Brendan Behan

Brendan Behan (1923–1964) was born in Dublin. His father was a house painter and the family was steeped in literature and politics. Young Brendan was a rebel and joined the IRA and was trained in bomb-making. At sixteen he was sent to England on a terrorist mission but was arrested and jailed. When released he returned to Ireland but was jailed again for IRA activity. He made good use of his time in prison and developed as a writer. He became a successful playwright and is best known for *The Quare Fellow* and *The Hostage*. His autobiography, *Borstal Boy*, was published in 1958 and gives a brilliant insight into prison life. Behan struggled with alcoholism all his life and it contributed to his early death in Dublin in 1964.

Brendan Behan

Background

'Confirmation' is a Catholic ceremony of faith celebration for older children towards the end of primary school. At the time when this story is set (1930s Ireland), children enjoyed the celebration but also feared the fact that the person who performs the ceremony, the Bishop, might question them about their faith knowledge. To give an incorrect answer to the Bishop was to risk getting into trouble.

Before you read

Think about a time or a situation where an adult has done you a favour or given you something that you did not want and you felt that you had to be grateful. Describe your experience to the class.

The Confirmation Suit

For weeks it was nothing but simony and sacrilege,[1] and the sins crying to heaven for vengeance, the big green Catechism[2] in our hands, walking home along the North Circular Road. And after tea, at the back of the brewery wall, with a butt too to help our wits, what is a pure spirit, and don't kill that, Billser has to get a drag out of it yet, what do I mean by apostate, and hell and heaven and despair and presumption and hope.[3] The big fellows, who were now thirteen and the veterans of last year's Confirmation, frightened us, and said the Bishop would fire us out of the chapel if we didn't answer his questions, and we'd be left wandering around the streets, in a new suit and top-coat with nothing to show for it, all dressed up and nowhere to go. The big people said not to mind them; they were only getting it up for us, jealous because they were over their Confirmation, and could never make it again. At school we were in a special room to ourselves, for the last few days, and went round, a special class of people. There were worrying times too, that the Bishop would light on you, and you wouldn't be able to answer his questions. Or you might hear the women complaining about the price of boys' clothes.

'Twenty-two and sixpence for tweed, I'd expect a share in the shop for that. I've a good mind to let him go in jersey and pants for that.'

'Quite right, ma'am,' says one to another, backing one another up, 'I always say what matter if they are good and pure.' What had that got to do with it, if you had to go into the Chapel in a jersey and pants, and every other kid in a new suit, kid gloves and tan shoes and a *scoil* cap. The Cowan brothers were terrified. They were twins, and twelve years old, and every old one in the street seemed to be wishing a jersey and pants on them, and saying their poor mother couldn't be expected to do for two in the one year, and she ought to go down to Sister Monica and tell her to put one back. If it came to that, the Cowans agreed to fight it out, at the back of the brewery wall; whoever got best, the other would be put back.

I wasn't so worried about this. My old fellow was a tradesman, and made money most of the time. Besides, my grandmother who lived at the top of the next house, was a lady of capernosity[4] and function. She had money and lay in bed all day, drinking porter or malt, and taking pinches of snuff, and talking to the neighbours that would call up to tell her the news of the day. She only left her bed to go down one flight of stairs and visit the lady in the back drawing room, Miss McCann.

Miss McCann worked a sewing-machine, making habits for the dead. Sometimes girls from our quarter got her to make dresses and costumes, but mostly she stuck to the habits. They were a steady line, she said, and you didn't have to be always buying patterns, for the fashions didn't change, not even from summer to winter. They were like a long brown shirt, and a hood attached, that was closed over the person's face before the coffin lid was screwn down. A sort of little banner hung out of one arm, made of the same material, and four silk rosettes in each corner, and in the middle, the letters I.H.S., which mean, Miss McCann said: 'I Have Suffered.'

My grandmother and Miss McCann liked me more than any other kid they knew. I like being liked, and could only admire their taste.

My Aunt Jack, who was my father's aunt as well as mine, sometimes came down from where she lived, up near the Basin, where the water came from before they started getting it from Wicklow. My Aunt Jack said it was much better water, at that. Miss McCann said she ought to be a good judge. For Aunt Jack was funny. She didn't drink porter or malt, or take

snuff and my father said she never thought much about men, either. She was also very strict about washing yourself very often. My grandmother took a bath every year, whether she was dirty or not, but she was in no way bigoted in the washing line in between times.

Aunt Jack made terrible raids on us now and again, to stop snuff and drink, and make my grandmother get up in the morning, and wash herself, and cook meals and take food with them. My grandmother was a gilder by trade, and served her time in one of the best shops in the city, and was getting a man's wages at sixteen. She liked stuff out of the pork butchers, and out of cans, but didn't like boiling potatoes, for she said she was no skivvy, and the chip man was better at it. When she was left alone it was a pleasure to eat with her. She always had cans of lovely things and spicy meat and brawn, and plenty of seasoning, fresh out of the German man's shop up the road. But after a visit from Aunt Jack, she would have to get up and wash for a week, and she would have to go and make stews and boil cabbage and pig's cheeks. Aunt Jack was very much up for sheep's heads too. They were so cheap and nourishing.

But my grandmother only tried it once. She had been a first-class gilder in Eustace Street, but never had anything to do with sheep's heads before. When she took it out of the pot, and laid it on the plate, she and I sat looking at it, in fear and trembling. It was bad enough going into the pot, but with the soup streaming from its eyes, and its big teeth clenched in a very bad temper, it would put the heart crossways in you. My grandmother asked me, in a whisper, if I ever thought sheep could look so vindictive, but that it was more like the head of an old man, and would I for God's sake take it up and throw it out of the window. The sheep kept glaring at us, but I came the far side of it, and rushed over to the window and threw it out in a flash. My grandmother had to drink a Baby Power whiskey, for she wasn't the better of herself.

Afterwards she kept what she called her stock-pot on the gas. A heap of bones and, as she said herself, any old muck that would come in handy, to have boiling there, night and day, on a glimmer.[5] She and I ate happily of cooked ham and California pineapple and sock-eyed salmon, and the pot of good nourishing soup was always on the gas even if Aunt Jack came down the chimney, like the Holy Souls at midnight. My grandmother said she didn't begrudge the money for the gas. Not when she remembered the looks that sheep's head was giving her. And all she had to do with the stock-pot was to throw in another sup of water, now and again, and a handful of old rubbish the pork butcher would send over, in the way of lights or bones. My Aunt Jack thought a lot about barley, too, so we had a package of that lying beside the gas, and threw a sprinkle in any time her foot was heard on the stairs. The stock-pot bubbled away on the gas for years after, and only when my grandmother was dead did someone notice it. They tasted it, and spat it out just as quick, and wondered what it was. Some said it was paste, and more that it was gold size, and there were other people and they maintained that it was glue. They all agreed on one thing, that it was dangerous tack to leave lying around where there might be young children, and in the heel of the reel, it went out the same window as the sheep's head.

Miss McCann told my grandmother not to mind Aunt Jack but to sleep as long as she liked in the morning. They came to an arrangement that Miss McCann would cover the landing and keep an eye out. She would call Aunt Jack in for a minute, and give the signal by banging the grate, letting on to poke the fire, and have a bit of a conversation with Aunt Jack about dresses and costumes, and hats and habits. One of these mornings, and Miss McCann delaying a fighting action, to give my grandmother time to hurl herself out of bed and into her clothes and give her face the rub of a towel, the chat between Miss McCann and Aunt Jack came to my Confirmation suit.

When I made my first Communion, my grandmother dug deep under the mattress, and myself and Aunt Jack were sent round expensive shops, and I came back with a rig that would take the sight of your eye. This time, however, Miss McCann said there wasn't much stirring in the habit line, on account of the mild winter, and she would be delighted to make the suit, if Aunt Jack would get the material. I nearly wept, for terror of what these old women would have me got up in, but I had to let on to be delighted, Miss McCann was so set on it. She asked Aunt Jack did she remember my father's Confirmation suit. *He did*. He said he would never forget it. They sent him out in a velvet suit, of plum colour, with a lace collar. My blood ran cold when he told me.

The stuff they got for my suit was blue serge, and that was not so bad. They got as far as the pants, and that passed off very civil. You can't do much to a boy's pants, one pair is like the next, though I had to ask them not to trouble themselves putting three little buttons on either side of the legs. The waistcoat was all right, and anyway the coat would cover it. But the coat itself, that was where Aughrim was lost.[6]

The lapels were little wee things, like what you'd see in pictures like *Ring* magazine of John L. Sullivan, or Gentleman Jim, and the buttons were the size of saucers, or within the bawl of an ass of it, and I nearly cried when I saw them being put on, and ran down to my mother, and begged her to get me any sort of a suit, even a jersey and pants, than have me set up before the people in this get-up. My mother said it was very kind of Aunt Jack and Miss McCann to go to all this trouble and expense, and I was very ungrateful not to appreciate it. My father said that Miss McCann was such a good tailor that people were dying to get into her creations, and her handiwork was to be found in all the best cemeteries. He laughed himself sick at this, and said if it was good enough for him to be sent down to North William Street in plum-coloured velvet and lace, I needn't be getting the needle over a couple of big buttons and little lapels. He asked me not to forget to get up early the morning of my Confirmation, and him see me, before he went to work: a bit of a laugh started the day well. My mother told him to give over and let me alone, and said she was sure it would be a lovely suit, and that Aunt Jack would never buy poor material, but stuff that would last forever. That nearly finished me altogether, and I ran through the hall up to the corner, fit to cry my eyes out, only I wasn't much of a hand at crying. I went more for cursing, and I cursed all belonging to me, and was hard at it on my father, and wondering why his lace collar hadn't choked him, when I remembered that it was a sin to go on like that, and I going up for Confirmation, and I had to simmer down, and live in fear of the day I'd put on that jacket.

The days passed, and I was fitted and refitted, and every old one in the house came up to look at the suit, and took a pinch of snuff, and a sup out of the jug, and wished me long life and the health to wear and tear it, and they spent that much time viewing it round, back, belly and sides, that Miss McCann hadn't time to make the overcoat, and like an answer to a prayer, I was brought down to Talbot Street, and dressed out in a dinging overcoat, belted, like a grown-up man's. And my shoes and gloves were dear and dandy, and I said to myself that there was no need to let anyone see the suit with its little lapels and big buttons. I could keep the topcoat on all day, in the chapel and going round afterwards.

The night before Confirmation day, Miss McCann handed over the suit to my mother, and kissed me, and said not to bother thanking her. She would do more than that for me, and she and my grandmother cried and had a drink on the strength of my having grown to be a big fellow, in the space of twelve years, which they didn't seem to consider a great deal of time. My father said to my mother, and I getting bathed before the fire, that since I was born Miss McCann thought the world of me. When my mother was in hospital, she took me into her place till my mother came out, and it near broke her heart to give me back.

In the morning I got up, and Mrs Rooney in the next room shouted to my mother that her Liam was still stalling, and not making any move to get out of it, and she thought she was cursed; Christmas or Easter, Communion or Confirmation, it would drive a body into Riddleys, which is the mad part of Grangegorman, and she wondered she wasn't driven out of her mind, and above in the puzzle factory[7] years ago. So she shouted again at Liam to get up and washed and dressed. And my mother shouted at me, though I was already knotting my tie, but you might as well be out of the world as out of fashion, and they kept it up like a pair of mad women, until at last Liam and I were ready and he came in to show my mother his clothes. She hanselled him a tanner[8] which he put in his pocket and Mrs Rooney called me in to show her my clothes. I just stood at her door, and didn't open my coat, but just grabbed the sixpence out of her hand, and ran up the stairs like the hammers of hell. She shouted at me to hold on a minute, she hadn't seen my suit, but I muttered something about it not being lucky to keep a Bishop waiting, and ran on.

The Church was crowded, boys on one side and the girls on the other, and the altar ablaze with lights and flowers, and a throne for the Bishop to sit on when he wasn't confirming. There was a cheering crowd outside, drums rolled, trumpeters from Jim Larkin's band sounded the Salute. The Bishop came in and the doors were shut. In short order I joined the queue to the rails, knelt and was whispered over, and touched on the cheek. I had my overcoat on the whole time, though it was warm, and I was in a lather of sweat waiting for the hymns and the sermon.

The lights grew brighter and I got warmer, and was carried out fainting. But though I didn't mind them loosening my tie, I clenched firmly my overcoat, and nobody saw the jacket with the big buttons and the little lapels. When I went home I got into bed, and my father said I went into sickness just as the Bishop was giving us the pledge.[9] He said this was a master stroke and showed real presence of mind.

Sunday after Sunday, my mother fought over the suit. She said I was liar and a hypocrite, putting it on for a few minutes every week, and running into Miss McCann's and out again, letting her think I wore it every week-end. In a passionate temper my mother said she would show me up, and tell Miss McCann, and up like a shot with her, for my mother was always slim and light on her feet as a feather, and in next door. When she came back she said nothing, but sat at the fire looking into it. I didn't really believe she would tell Miss McCann. And I put on the suit and thought I would go in and tell her I was wearing it this week-night, because I was going to the Queen's with my brothers. I ran next door and upstairs, and every step was more certain and easy that my mother hadn't told her. I ran, shoved in the door, saying: 'Miss Mc., Miss Mc., Rory and Sean and I are going to the Queen's...' She was bent over the sewing-machine and all I could see was the top of her old grey head, and the rest of her shaking with crying, and her arms folded under her head, on a bit of habit where she had been finishing the I.H.S. I ran down the stairs and back into our place, and my mother was sitting at the fire, sad and sorry, but saying nothing.

I needn't have worried about the suit lasting forever. Miss McCann didn't. The next winter was not so mild, and she was whipped before the year was out. At her wake people said how she was in a habit of her own making, and my father said she would look queer in anything else, seeing as she supplied the dead of the whole quarter for forty years, without one complaint from a customer.

At the funeral, I left my topcoat in the carriage and got out and walked in the spills of rain after her coffin. People said I would get my end, but I went on till we reached the graveside, and I stood in my Confirmation suit drenched to the skin. I thought this was the least I could do.

---

[1] **simony, sacrilege:** the practice of buying or selling spiritual benefits, such as pardons, relics etc; the misue of anything regarded as sacred or holy; [2] **Catechism:** a book containing the basic principles of the Catholic religion in the form of questions and answers; [3] **apostate, and hell and heaven and despair and presumption and hope:** children going for Confirmation were expected to learn off definitions of words; [4] **capernosity:** Dublin slang word expressing a combination of 'capability' and 'generosity'; [5] **glimmer:** cooking on a low heat setting; [6] **...where Aughrim was lost:** an idiom or phrase used to describe a disastrous situation; [7] **puzzle factory:** the mental hospital at Grangegorman in Dublin; [8] **tanner:** a coin worth six old pence; [9] **pledge:** promise made at Confirmation not to take alcohol.

Oral exploration

1 Pick out three details that show that many people in the story are poor.

2 How is the lifestyle of the narrator different? Give examples.

3 On balance do you think that the experience of Confirmation was a pleasant or unpleasant experience for the children in the story? Give some details.

4 Miss McCann made habits for the dead. How is this made fun of in the story?

5 What does the boy admire about his grandmother? Mention three things he admires.

6 Why has Miss McCann such strong affection for the narrator?

7 Do you think the mother was right to tell Miss McCann about her son's dishonesty? Why? Why not?

Read, write, explore

1 'I like being liked . . . '

The child narrator says 'I like being liked, and could only admire their taste.'
What does this tell you about the narrator's character? Do other characters in
the story like him? Why? Why not?

2 Grandmother's lifestyle

The grandmother lives a very unhealthy lifestyle. Write some notes from the story
to illustrate this. What advice would you give to the grandmother to help her have
a healthier diet and more active lifestyle? Write it down.

3 The adults – humorous

Which of these adult characters, Aunt Jack, the grandmother, or the boy's father, do
you find most amusing? Write out your reasons.

4 The ending of the story

Why does the mother destroy the relationship between Miss McCann and her son?
Consider the following points as you prepare your answer:

- The mother wishes to cure her son's dishonesty.
- The mother is jealous of Miss McCann's closeness to her son.
- The mother did it out of respect for Miss McCann.

Idioms

Language alert

Playing with language

What is an idiom? We use idioms all the time in our daily speech and writing, for example:
'you're pulling my leg', 'you're having me on' or 'you're winding me up'. As you can see, idioms
use unexpected phrases to convey a message, in this case the same message. Can you say
the message that is common to all these three idioms?

In Ireland idioms are often local or peculiar to a particular place. Do you know any that
are used by people in your local area, town or city?

Below is a list of idioms taken from the story. Match them with the list of more modern
idioms on the right.

Idiom: 'getting it up for us'	getting your back up
Idiom: 'would light on you'	OMG, I nearly died!
Idiom: 'put the heart crossways in you'	at the end of the day
Idiom: 'in the heel of the reel'	playing for time
Idiom: 'fighting a delaying action'	like a bat out of hell
Idiom: 'getting the needle'	the funny farm
Idiom: 'like the hammers of hell'	would come down on top of you
Idiom: 'the puzzle factory'	having us on

Can you think of any other idioms? Describe your journey to school by using as many idioms as
possible within a hundred words! Refer to the animation on idioms on page 105 in Unit 4.

Create

1 Restaurant from hell

Read again the paragraph beginning 'But my grandmother only tried it once.'

Portfolio 6H

> ···} Using the paragraph as a model, write the menu for 'Pu Pu Hot Pot', a very bad restaurant.

> ···} Write a review of the very worst meal you got in that restaurant. The review should cover the cleanliness of the table, the waiter's attitude, the presentation of the food, the quality of cooking and taste of each course. Your final paragraph should be your recommendation to future customers of the restaurant.

> ···} Draw the boy in his suit and use arrows to label the drawing with apt quotes from the story, for example, 'The lapels were wee little things . . . '

2 Virtual literary tour

You have been asked by the Irish Literary Society to create a virtual literary tour using the map of Ireland. They would like you to choose five famous writers or legends and place them in the correct location on the map, creating a fascinating route for potential tourists to follow. Include interesting facts on the writers/legends, as well as useful information on their location.

Animation – Sentences, instructions and phrases

Create the virtual tour using appropriate software, then upload it to your e-Portfolio.

e-Portfolio www@

Note for Teachers: You will find step-by-step guidelines for this activity in your *How to Create an e-Portfolio* e-book. Log on to www.edcodigital.ie to access the e-book.

Oral presentation

The theme of childhood

Childhood – then and now

Each of the short stories in this unit deals with the world of children many years ago. How is their world different from the modern child's world and how is it similar?

You may choose to deal with any of the following aspects as you prepare your presentation:

···} Parents and parenting
···} School and teachers
···} Family life – sibling relationships.

Poetry Case Study

Maya Angelou

In this unit you will:

- enjoy poems by a brave and brilliant poet
- appreciate how a great writer uses poetic technique to great effect
- learn about the evil of racism and the promise of freedom and love
- learn how to prepare for and write a good essay on Maya Angelou.

You will encounter the following poems:

- 'Still I Rise'
- 'Touched by an Angel'
- 'Caged Bird'

An essay or letter on Maya Angelou

After you have enjoyed and studied the poems by Angelou in this short anthology you will be asked to draft and write an essay (two A4 pages) on her poems or write a letter to her, telling her what you think about her poems.

This essay or letter will be the end result of enjoying, learning about, discussing and noting your responses to the poems.

BIOGRAPHY

Maya Angelou

Maya Angelou (1928–2014) was born Marguerite Johnson in St Louis, Missouri in the United States. She had a very difficult early life and was traumatised by abuse. For five years she was silent, but in time she found her voice and that voice has been heard around the world.

At fifteen she started her training to become a dancer and at sixteen became pregnant after a brief romance. She worked many jobs to try to support her family. She was the first female black cable car conductor in America. She went on to become an author, poet, songwriter, playwright, director, performer and singer, as well as a civil rights activist.

She was a close friend and supporter of Martin Luther King, President Bill Clinton and President Barack Obama. Her autobiography, *I Know Why the Caged Bird Sings*, was an international hit.

Before you read

Having read some information on the poet, what do you think a poem with the title 'Still I Rise' might be about?

STILL I RISE

You may write me down in history
With your bitter, twisted lies,
You may tread me in the very dirt
But still, like dust, I'll rise.

Does my sassiness upset you?
Why are you beset with gloom?
'Cause I walk like I've got oil wells
Pumping in my living room.

Just like moons and like suns,
With the certainty of tides,
Just like hopes springing high,
Still I'll rise.

Did you want to see me broken?
Bowed head and lowered eyes?
Shoulders falling down like teardrops,
Weakened by my soulful cries.

Does my haughtiness offend you?
Don't you take it awful hard
'Cause I laugh like I've got gold mines
Diggin' in my own back yard.

You may shoot me with your words,
You may cut me with your eyes,
You may kill me with your hatefulness,
But still, like air, I'll rise.

Does my sexiness upset you?
Does it come as a surprise
That I dance like I've got diamonds
At the meeting of my thighs?

Out of the huts of history's shame
I rise
Up from a past that's rooted in pain
I rise
I'm a black ocean, leaping and wide,
Welling and swelling I bear in the tide.

Leaving behind nights of terror and fear
I rise
Into a daybreak that's wondrously clear
I rise
Bringing the gifts that my ancestors gave,
I am the dream and the hope of the slave.
I rise
I rise
I rise.

Oral exploration

Get into five groups of three or four. Within the group elect one person as timekeeper, one as leader, one as researcher, and one as the recorder. If there are three in your group the leader could keep an eye on the time.

Timekeeper

Ensures that the team sticks to the time allocated by the teacher

Leader

Ensures that everybody has a chance to speak and makes sure that the team stays on task

Researcher

Looks up the meaning/spelling of words in the dictionary and checks out facts on the Internet (if available)

Recorder

Writes down the main ideas that the group comes up with

Use the feedback sheet in your Portfolio to note the answers to the following questions.

Portfolio 7A

Group 1

1 What people do you imagine Maya Angelou is addressing in this poem? Who is 'you'?

2 What attitudes do they hold towards her? Pick out lines that give you clues.

Group 2

3 Read the last section of the poem, beginning 'Out of the huts of history's shame'. How does the last section of the poem help us to understand the theme?

Group 3

4 Maya Angelou seems very confident about herself and who she is. Do you agree? Go through the poem and find examples of this confidence.

Group 4

5 Angelou uses brilliant similes to describe things, for example, ''Cause I walk like I've got oil wells/Pumping in my living room'. What is she trying to convey about herself with this simile?

6 Pick out some other similes (and metaphors) from the poem. What do they tell you about Angelou and how she feels about the things she is describing?

Group 5

7 Read the poem aloud. Then listen to the audio recording. What is the most important message in the poem? What word or words express that message best? Choose three.

Read, write, explore

Having read this poem, write three paragraphs about:

 Portfolio 7B

1 Angelou's personality

····❯ Outline four things that stand out about her life and personality.

2 Her style of writing – provide examples where you can. Comment on at least four of the following:

····❯ Is it hard to understand? Is the language difficult?
····❯ Does it rhyme? Where?
····❯ Does she use repetition? Why? To what effect?
····❯ How does she use imagery – simile and metaphor?
····❯ Are there examples of hyperbole (exaggeration)?
····❯ Are there any rhetorical questions?
····❯ Is there a rhythm?
····❯ What sort of tone does she use?

3 What are the most important things she believes in? Identify two things that seem important to her and provide evidence from the poem.

4 Having read her poem, go online and find a recording or video of the poet reciting her poems. Does the poet look and sound like you expected her to?

PowerPoint – Figuring out figurative language

Writing skills

Preparing for my essay or letter

Write your favourite lines from 'Still I Rise'.

····❯ Write some notes on each line.
····❯ Mention lines that contain good images.
····❯ Mention the feelings that some lines create in you.

Before you read

Think about the poem you have just read. Do you think Angelou has a positive attitude to life? Discuss in class. Now read the following poem.

Touched by an Angel

We, unaccustomed to courage
exiles from delight
live coiled in shells of loneliness
until love leaves its high holy temple
and comes into our sight
to liberate us into life.

Love arrives
and in its train[1] come ecstasies
old memories of pleasure
ancient histories of pain.
Yet if we are bold,
love strikes away the chains of fear
from our souls.

We are weaned[2] from our timidity
in the flush of love's light
we dare be brave.
And suddenly we see
that love costs all we are
and will ever be.
Yet it is only love
which sets us free.

[1] **in its train:** following;
[2] **weaned:** helped to grow out of.

Oral exploration

1 Read the poem together in pairs and mark what you think is the most important line or phrase in it. Try to work out what message the poet is trying to get across to you. Agree on the message and write it down. Share it with the class.

2 Choose any one of the first three lines of the poem and tell your partner which one best expresses the situation of someone without love. Write it down.

3 Look up the word 'liberate' in the dictionary. Discuss what you think Angelou means when she says that love 'comes into our sight/to liberate us into life'. Does she repeat the message elsewhere in the poem? Where? Show your partner.

Read, write, explore

1 What is your favourite image from the poem? Write it down. What does it tell you about the theme or main idea of the poem?

2 Check in the poem for clues as to why Angelou named the poem 'Touched by an Angel'. Do you think it is a good name for the poem? Why? Why not?

3 In the last stanza, Angelou tells us that love will change us. How will it change us? Can you suggest any other ways in which love changes people?

Create – Poetic devices

You have been asked by your primary school principal to teach a lesson on poetic devices to fifth class pupils. You are to use a digital program of your choice to explain the terms alliteration, onomatopoeia and personification. Definitions for the poetic devices will be provided for you, but it is up to you to decide how best to teach them to the class. Create the presentation using appropriate software, then upload it to your e-Portfolio.

Note for Teachers: You will find step-by-step guidelines for this activity in your *How to Create an e-Portfolio* e-book. Log on to www.edcodigital.ie to access the e-book.

Writing skills

Preparing for my essay or letter

Write your favourite lines from 'Touched by an Angel' in your Portfolio.

Portfolio 7C

···⟩ Write some notes on each line.
···⟩ Mention lines that contain good images.
···⟩ Mention the feelings that some lines create in you.

Before you read

Have you ever read about being stuck in a situation (big or small) where it was difficult to escape? How did you feel? How was the situation resolved? How did you feel afterwards?

Caged Bird

The free bird leaps
on the back of the wind
and floats downstream
till the current ends
and dips his wings
in the orange sun rays
and dares to claim the sky.

But a bird that stalks
down his narrow cage
can seldom see through
his bars of rage
his wings are clipped and
his feet are tied
so he opens his throat to sing.

The caged bird sings
with a fearful trill
of the things unknown
but longed for still
and his tune is heard
on the distant hill
for the caged bird
sings of freedom.

The free bird thinks of another breeze
and the trade winds soft through the sighing trees
and the fat worms waiting on a dawn-bright lawn
and he names the sky his own.

But a caged bird stands on the grave of dreams
his shadow shouts on a nightmare scream
his wings are clipped and his feet are tied
so he opens his throat to sing.

The caged bird sings
with a fearful trill
of things unknown
but longed for still
and his tune is heard
on the distant hill
for the caged bird
sings of freedom.

Oral exploration

1 Read to your partner a stanza of the poem that showed the life of the free bird. What did you most like about that stanza?

2 How did you feel about the situation of the caged bird? What lines affected you most? Why?

3 What differences do you notice between the free bird's experience of the world and the experience of the caged bird? Mention two big differences. Make some notes in your Portfolio.

Portfolio 7D

4 Listen again to the reading of this poem. What do you notice about the rhythm in the 'free bird' stanzas and the rhythm in the 'caged bird' stanzas? Is there a difference? What does it mean? Use the template in your Portfolio to jot down your thoughts.

Read, write, explore

1 Pick out strong images used to describe the free bird. Write down what they tell you about its life and experiences. Make notes in your Portfolio.

Portfolio 7E

2 Find the strongest images that tell you about the difficult choice of the caged bird. Write out the images and say whether they promise any hope for the bird.

3 Check again the meaning of *metaphor* (Unit 3, page 45). Imagine that each bird is a metaphor for opposing human experiences. Which bird/metaphor creates the strongest picture in your imagination?

4 Look at the news tonight or check out news websites and record instances of people who have freedom and those whose freedom is threatened or absent. Try to link what you see to one or two images in the poem.

Class discussion

Maya Angelou was passionate about freedom, her own and that of others. Does this poem convince you that freedom is very important? Discuss this question, in pairs first and then as a class.

Drafting my essay or letter on Maya Angelou

Draft your essay or letter in your Portfolio.

Portfolio 7F

In your opinion, is the poetry of Maya Angelou effective at expressing important messages? Write an essay on her themes.

Or

Write a letter to Angelou's family telling them how the poems have affected you personally.

Getting started

What should I write about?

Your essay or letter should concentrate on two or three of the following areas:

1. My favourite Angelou poem – what it means to me. Mention how Angelou's use of language appeals to you.

2. Lines or stanzas that impress me. Show how the poet uses language. Mention the best images, metaphors, etc.

3. A big theme that struck me in at least one of the poems – how does the poem bring the theme to life for me?

4. The things I learned in discussion with my partner or group.

5. The poet's personality – how it comes across to me (refer to tone/images).

6. The effect the poems had on you – things you learned about the world and about yourself.

Remember – get into the habit of using short quotes to support what you say about a poem.

My writing checklist

Read back over your draft essay or letter. Check the content against the following:

Success criteria

My introduction

···ᐅ Did I state the main purpose of my essay?

···ᐅ Did I outline my main argument/opinion?

···ᐅ Did I mention the poems I intend to discuss?

The main body of my essay

···ᐅ Have I a clear, worked out shape for my essay?

···ᐅ Have I used **PEER** to structure my paragraphs:

- **P**oint – should be short – one to two sentences long, emphasising what the focus of your paragraph is

- **E**xample/**E**vidence – follow this with some evidence taken directly from the poems and put it into quotation marks

- **E**xplanation – tell the audience why your point is proven by the evidence you have provided

- **R**efer back to the main point you want to prove – link it all back to the reason you made the point in the first place.

How I use language

···ᐅ Have I thought of the reader?

···ᐅ Have I checked over my spelling and punctuation?

···ᐅ Are my sentences clear?

···ᐅ Does the writing flow?

My conclusion

···ᐅ Have I summarised the main points that I made?

···ᐅ Have I referred back to the reasons why I like this poet?

The basic steps for writing any essay

Prepare any essay or letter by working through these steps.

1 Research

   ⋯> **Check** and **refer to** your **Preparing for my essay** work.

   ⋯> **Homework** – check through it. Reuse any good things you have written.

   ⋯> **Notes** – make sure you go back over and use your best notes and ideas.

   ⋯> **Go online** – research but don't copy from an online source.

2 Plan

   ⋯> **Title** – think about the title of your essay. You can tweak it as you go.

   ⋯> **Plan** – have a plan (a roadmap for your essay).

3 Draft

   ⋯> **First draft** – deal with things you feel are the most important to you. Don't forget to write about the poet's language and imagery.

   ⋯> **Assess your draft** from your reader's point of view. Use the peer-assessment sheet in your Portfolio to help you assess your work. Fix up paragraphing (structure), punctuation, spelling, accuracy of quotations, and add in any good ideas you might have omitted.

Portfolio 7G

Before you write your final draft, refer to the checklist on page 191.

Finish

⋯> **Write your final essay.**

Portfolio 7H

The Novel Experience 1
Of Mice and Men
by John Steinbeck

In this unit you will:

···❯ read about the novelist John Steinbeck

···❯ understand the difficult times he lived and worked in

···❯ learn about the Great Depression

···❯ work through tasks which explore this novel set in America

···❯ study the characters and main events in *Of Mice and Men*

···❯ see the sadness that racism causes

···❯ prepare an essay on an aspect of this or another novel you have read.

Of Mice and Men
by John Steinbeck

Who was John Steinbeck?

1902	Born in Salinas, California in the United States – setting for *Of Mice and Men*
1916	Decided to become a writer at fourteen, having loved reading from an early age
1925	Enrolled at Stanford University California but left without a degree
1929	Struggled to support himself as a journalist and writer during the Great Depression
1937	Had huge success with *Of Mice and Men*
1939	Published his greatest novel, *The Grapes of Wrath*, also about the Great Depression
1940	Won a Pulitzer Prize for *The Grapes of Wrath*
1962	Was awarded Nobel Prize for Literature 'for his realistic and imaginative writings, combining as they do sympathetic humour and keen social perception'
1968	Died in New York City at the age of 66

For more information, watch the short biographical film on Steinbeck on Bio.com's website.

John Steinbeck at the Nobel Prize ceremony

The Great Depression and *Of Mice and Men*

The novel *Of Mice and Men* was written against the background of the Wall Street Crash in October 1929, when share prices suddenly dropped and millions of Americans saw their wealth disappear. Before the Great Crash, a huge number of Americans saw their wealth increase massively during the 1920s which was also called the Roaring Twenties. This increase in wealth encouraged people to buy shares on the stock market.

Week by week, people saw the value of their shares increase and so they bought more and more of them. As the frenzy of share buying increased so did the apparent value of the shares until in late October 1929 doubts began to set in and the value of shares began to tumble. Traders on Wall Street (the place where the shares were bought and sold) began to panic and the value of shares crashed to a fraction of their previous value.

The Great Crash affected everyone, even those who had not bought shares. People ran to their banks to get at their savings, fearing the banks would run out of money. But the banks had also invested in the stock market and had lost billions. Bank customers who rushed to the banks to withdraw their savings found that their money was gone. W. W. Tarpley, a bank officer in Georgia, remembered the mob of people who came to his bank, fearful of losing everything: 'people were losing their homes and some, their savings of a lifetime. The saddest part of it was to see widows who probably had been left a little insurance and had put it all in the bank.'

The Great Crash triggered the Great Depression which lasted over ten years. Millions of people all over America lost not only their money, but also their jobs. Huge numbers of businesses closed because they could not afford to pay their workers. Many lives were drastically changed. Men who had previously expected to have no trouble finding well-paying jobs now had to travel far and wide to find any job they could get (like George and Lennie, the main characters in the novel *Of Mice and Men*).

The effect of the Depression on poor children was particularly severe. It was reported that in the spring of 1933, 20 per cent of the nation's schoolchildren showed evidence of poor nutrition, lack of housing and medical care. School budgets were cut and in some cases schools were shut down by the lack of money to pay teachers. An estimated 200,000 boys left home to wander the streets and beg because of the poor economic condition of their families.

Here is one of the most famous songs about the Great Depression. Based on the title, can you guess what the song lyrics refer to? Read the lyrics. Then search online and listen to a recording of the song.

Brother, Can You Spare a Dime?

They used to tell me I was building a dream
And so I followed the mob,
When there was earth to plow[1] or guns to bear
I was always there, right on the job.

They used to tell me I was building a dream
With peace and glory ahead,
Why should I be standing in line
Just waiting for bread?

Once I built a railroad, I made it run,
Made it race against time.
Once I built a railroad, now it's done.
Brother, can you spare a dime?[2]

Once I built a tower up to the sun
Brick and rivet and lime;
Once I built a tower, now it's done.
Brother, can you spare a dime?

Once in khaki suits,[3] gee, we looked swell
Full of that Yankee Doodly Dum,
Half a million boots went slogging through Hell
And I was the kid with the drum.

Say, don't you remember? They called me 'Al',
It was 'Al' all the time.
Why don't you remember? I'm your pal!
Say buddy, can you spare a dime?

Jay Gorney/E. Y. Harburg (1930)

---

[1] **plow:** American spelling for 'plough'; [2] **dime:** a ten-cent coin; [3] **khaki suits:** many of the men who lost out in the Great Depression had once been soldiers who fought for their country (United States) during World War I (1914–1918).

Read, write, explore

1 What things has the singer done or achieved in his past life? Write out the lines that tell you each job he did. Describe each job, briefly. Talk about them with your partner.

2 What impact has the Great Depression had on the singer? Give a detail.

3 What is the tone of the singer in the last verse? Is he bitter at what has happened in his life? Say how he feels about his situation.

4 In verse 2, the singer says, 'They used to tell me I was building a dream'. Can you say what he means by 'I was building a dream'? Does the singer have any dream now? Why? Why not?

5 Why is the singer asking for only a dime? In your opinion, does he expect to get one?

6 Read the introduction to the Great Depression again. Can you suggest how this song tells the story of a generation in America from the rich 1920s to the Great Depression of the 1930s?

7 Write a letter on behalf of this man to the bank that lost his money.

Photos of the Great Depression

Before you start reading the novel, examine and talk about these images that show the effects of the Great Depression in America during the 1930s.

A mother during the Great Depression

A queue of unemployed, hungry men in a breadline

Children of the unemployed being fed in a soup kitchen

Businesses shut down – 25% of workers were unemployed

Casual migrant workers (transients) who just want to stay in one place, work, and settle down

Working the fields

Children of the Great Depression

Oral exploration

1 In pairs or small groups, discuss and decide on the single image that your small group (or pair) feels best shows life in the Great Depression. Pick out features of the image, for example: faces, background, emotional impact, light and shade, age of featured character, atmosphere or mood (see page 209 for definition of *mood*).

2 In groups, choose three individual characters from the images and try to decide on how each would answer the following interview questions. Using the information you have learned in the introduction to the Great Depression, discuss and then write down some answers they might give.

····⟩ What difficulties do you face at the moment?
····⟩ How do you feel about your immediate situation?
····⟩ How would you like things to be different right now?
····⟩ What is your dream for the future?

3 Look again at the images that show children. Discuss and note some of the similarities and differences between their prospects and yours.

4 Have a class vote. Rank the images from one to seven, on how best they show the effects of the Great Depression on the people of America. Discuss your opinions. Listen to other points of view before you vote.

Exploring character

Who are you?

Before you investigate the characters of George and Lennie, first have a go at describing your own character by completing the character quiz in your Portfolio.

Portfolio 8A

Step 1: Work with a partner. Each of you completes the character quiz on your own. Write yes, no, now and then (Y, N, N & T). Use your **dictionary** to look up words that you are unsure of.

Step 2: Now ask your partner to do the quiz about you. Compare your result with that of your partner and have a chat about differences and similarities. Remember, it is only a quiz – there are no right or wrong answers.

Step 3: Look at the list of **adjectives** below the questions and match them with the questions in the quiz.

Adjectives

- generous
- hard-working
- untidy
- anxious
- reliable
- confident
- impatient
- forgiving
- emotional
- optimistic
- adventurous
- shy
- serious
- competitive
- grumpy
- sociable
- reserved

Contrasting characters – George and Lennie

George and Lennie are very different characters. One is physically strong, but mentally childlike. The other is less physical but is always thinking and planning how to keep the pair out of trouble.

What types of character do you think they are, judging by the photo?

Choose from the following adjectives to describe the character of each man. Use the Contrasting characters sheet in your Portfolio to complete this task.

Portfolio 8B

Adjectives

- grumpy
- emotional
- frustrated
- simple
- complex
- trusting
- intellectually challenged
- impatient
- forgiving
- pessimistic
- optimistic
- gentle

Opening up Chapter 1

George and Lennie

Read Chapter 1. Record in your Portfolio, the main events and characters.

Portfolio 8C

You are now going to explore the **theme of relationships**, that of **George and Lennie** and their **shared dream**.

George and Lennie's relationship

Read the following extract from Chapter 1. Work with a partner. Dip in and out of the text as often as you need to answer the questions.

> ### George won't allow Lennie to keep his pet mouse.
>
> Lennie reluctantly reached into his pocket. His voice broke a little. 'I don't know why I can't keep it. It ain't nobody's mouse. I didn't steal it. I found it lyin' right beside the road.'
>
> George's hand remained outstretched imperiously. Slowly, like a terrier who doesn't want to bring a ball to its master, Lennie approached, drew back, approached again. George snapped his fingers sharply, and at the sound Lennie laid the mouse in his hand.
>
> 'I wasn't doin' nothing bad with it, George. Jus' strokin' it.'
>
> George stood up and threw the mouse as far as he could into the darkening brush, and then he stepped to the pool and washed his hands. 'You crazy fool. Don't you think I could see your feet was wet where you went acrost the river to get it?' He heard Lennie's whimpering cry and wheeled about. 'Blubberin' like a baby! Jesus Christ! A big guy like you.' Lennie's lip quivered and tears started in his eyes. 'Aw, Lennie!' George put his hand on Lennie's shoulder. 'I ain't takin' it away jus' for meanness. That mouse ain't fresh, Lennie; and besides, you've broke it pettin' it. You get another mouse that's fresh and I'll let you keep it a little while.'

Read, write, explore

1 How does this extract show Lennie as a childlike and dependent person? Pick out phrases and sentences to show this.

2 George is the dominant character in this extract. Write out the sentences that show this.

3 George is often cruel to Lennie in Chapter 1. How is he shown to be different in the extract above? What does this tell you about George's attitude to Lennie? How would you describe that attitude?

Investigating theme – The dream

Read the following extract to see how the theme of the dream is introduced in Chapter 1.

George wants to keep Lennie happy so he tells him about a happy place.

Lennie pleaded, 'Come on, George. Tell me. Please, George. Like you done before.'
'You get a kick outta that, don't you? Awright, I'll tell you, and then we'll eat our supper . . . '

George's voice became deeper. He repeated his words rhythmically as though he had said them many times before. 'Guys like us, that work on ranches, are the loneliest guys in the world. They got no family. They don't belong no place. They come to a ranch an' work up a stake and then they go inta town and blow their stake, and the first thing you know they're poundin' their tail on some other ranch. They ain't got nothing to look ahead to.'

Lennie was delighted. 'That's it—that's it. Now tell how it is with us.'

George went on. 'With us it ain't like that. We got a future. We got somebody to talk to that gives a damn about us. We don't have to sit in no bar room blowin' in our jack jus' because we got no place else to go. If them other guys gets in jail they can rot for all anybody gives a damn. But not us.'

Lennie broke in. *'But not us! An' why? Because . . . because I got you to look after me, and you got me to look after you, and that's why.'* He laughed delightedly. 'Go on now, George!'

* * * *

'Why'n't you do it yourself? You know all of it.'

'No . . . you tell it. It ain't the same if I tell it. Go on . . . George. How I get to tend the rabbits.'

'Well,' said George, 'we'll have a big vegetable patch and a rabbit hutch and chickens. And when it rains in the winter, we'll just say the hell with goin' to work, and we'll build up a fire in the stove and set around it an' listen to the rain comin' down on the roof— Nuts!'

Read, write, explore

Discuss each question. Then make a note of your answers.

1 George talks about 'Guys like us'. Using what he says, describe the lonely life that homeless travelling workers usually led.

2 What is your opinion of the life of the homeless workers? How would you feel if you were one?

3 How does George and Lennie's friendship make their situation different? Say what's good about it.

4 'That's it—that's it. Now tell how it is with us.' George tells Lennie about the life they hope to lead. Discuss the details. Is it a realistic life?

5 How do you know that the story about the dream place has been talked about often? What does this tell you about the chances of the dream coming true?

   Hint: Remember the Great Depression.

My dreams and ambitions

Discuss with your partner what you hope life will be like for you at each of the times listed below:

···} When I leave school   ···} In my 20s   ···} In my 30s.

Portfolio 8D

In your Portfolio, write out a short list of ambitions and keep it.

The American Dream

When migrants arrived in the United States from all over the world (many from Ireland), they came to have a new beginning and make a better life. America, 'the land of the free', seemed to offer the promise of 'Life, Liberty and the pursuit of Happiness', as stated in the American Constitution. Although the term 'American Dream' was first invented during the Great Depression, the idea of the dream of freedom, wealth and success was what motivated people to work hard and seek a better life.

In *Of Mice and Men*, we can see the failure of the American Dream, as the men work in poorly paid jobs with no hope of building a future, owning a home or having a family. George tries to keep a dream alive to make Lennie happy.

Let's predict!

Predict the plot of the novel. What are the chances that George and Lennie will achieve their dream? Discuss the clues in Chapter 1 as you try to guess what will happen. Make notes in your Portfolio.

Portfolio 8E

Opening up Chapter 2

The world of the ranch – Big bad attitudes

Read Chapter 2. In your Portfolio record the main events and characters.

Portfolio 8F

You are now going to explore the **setting**, the **character of Curley** and the **theme of women in the novel** (Curley's wife is the only woman in the novel).

Exploring setting – The bunk house

Read these extracts from Chapter 2. Work with a partner. Dip in and out of the text as often as you need to answer the questions.

In these extracts from Chapter 2, George is inspecting his bedding and bunk. He finds a box of powder (insecticide) for shaking on a mattress to kill lice. He is not pleased.

'Say. What the hell's this?'

'I don't know,' said the old man.

'Says "positively kills lice, roaches and other scourges." What the hell kind of bed you giving us, anyways. We don't want no pants rabbits.'[1]

The old swamper shifted his broom and held it between his elbow and his side while he held out his hand for the can. He studied the label carefully. 'Tell you what—' he said finally, 'last guy that had this bed was a blacksmith—hell of a nice fella and as clean a guy as you want to meet. Used to wash his hands even *after* he ate.'

'Then how come he got graybacks?'[2] George was working up a slow anger. Lennie put his bindle[3] on the neighboring bunk and sat down. He watched George with open mouth.

'Tell you what,' said the old swamper. 'This here blacksmith—name of Whitey—was the kind of guy that would put that stuff around even if there wasn't no bugs—just to make sure, see? Tell you what he used to do—At meals he'd peel his boil' potatoes, an' he'd take out ever' little spot, no matter what kind, before he'd eat it. And if there was a red splotch on an egg, he'd scrape it off. Finally quit about the food. That's the kinda guy he was—clean.'

* * * *

George lifted his tick and looked underneath it. He leaned over and inspected the sacking closely. Immediately Lennie got up and did the same with his bed. Finally George seemed satisfied. He unrolled his bindle and put things on the shelf, his razor and bar of soap, his comb and bottle of pills, his liniment and leather wristband. Then he made his bed up neatly with blankets.

¹ **pants rabbits:** lice; ² **graybacks:** lice; ³ **bindle:** clothes/possessions.

Read, write, explore

Discuss each question. Then make a note of your answers.

1 George is suspicious about the cleanliness of his bed in the bunk house. What makes him so suspicious?

2 Do the conditions in the bunk house allow for any privacy? Explain.

3 What objections would you raise about the conditions if you were asked to call the bunk house your home?

4 Would you be satisfied by the old swamper's excuse for the insecticide?

Create

Imagine you are a health and safety inspector coming to vet the living conditions in the bunk house. You will send the report to Curley. Together with your partner, draft a short report under the following headings:

- Beds and hygiene
- Washing facilities (a large trough in the yard)
- Private space
- Food
- Overall cleanliness.

Portfolio 8G

Use the template in your Porfolio to help you to write the report.

Exploring character – Curley's bad attitude

Curley's first meeting with George and Lennie

Read the extract from Chapter 2. Work with a partner. Dip in and out of the text as often as you need to, in order to answer the questions.

Curley enters the bunk house, apparently looking for his father, the boss.

His eyes passed over the new men and he stopped. He glanced coldly at George and then at Lennie. His arms gradually bent at the elbows and his hands closed into fists. He stiffened and went into a slight crouch. His glance was at once calculating and pugnacious.[1] Lennie squirmed under the look and shifted his feet nervously. Curley stepped gingerly close to him. 'You the new guys the old man was waitin' for?'

'We just come in,' said George.

'Let the big guy talk.'

Lennie twisted with embarrassment.

George said, 'S'pose he don't want to talk?'

Curley lashed his body around. 'By Christ, he's gotta talk when he's spoke to. What the hell are you gettin' into it for?'

'We travel together,' said George coldly.

'Oh, so it's that way.'

George was tense, and motionless. 'Yeah, it's that way.'

Lennie was looking helplessly to George for instruction.

'An' you won't let the big guy talk, is that it?'

'He can talk if he wants to tell you anything.' He nodded slightly to Lennie.

'We jus' come in,' said Lennie softly.

Curley stared levelly at him. 'Well, nex' time you answer when you're spoke to.' He turned toward the door and walked out, and his elbows were still bent out a little.

[1] **pugnacious:** looking for a fight.

Read, write, explore

Discuss each question. Then make a note of your answers.

1 Read the first paragraph carefully and talk about Curley's behaviour towards the new men, George and Lennie. How should he have behaved? What general impression of him do you get?

2 Write down a list of words and phrases that help to form your impression of Curley. Compare what you have selected from the extract with what your partner selected.

Portfolio 8H

3 What adjectives would you use to describe Curley's character as he reveals it in the above passage? Make a list of at least five.

Curley's wife – Alone in a man's world

Our first meeting with Curley's wife

Read the extract from Chapter 2. Work with a partner. Dip in and out of the text as often as you need to, in order to answer the questions.

George and Lennie are in the bunk house when Curley's wife enters.

Both men glanced up, for the rectangle of sunshine in the doorway was cut off. A girl was standing there looking in. She had full, rouged lips and wide-spaced eyes, heavily made up. Her fingernails were red. Her hair hung in little rolled clusters, like sausages. She wore a cotton house dress and red mules, on the insteps of which were little bouquets of red ostrich feathers. 'I'm lookin' for Curley,' she said. Her voice had a nasal, brittle quality.

George looked away from her and then back. 'He was in here a minute ago, but he went.'

'Oh!' She put her hands behind her back and leaned against the door frame so that her body was thrown forward. 'You're the new fellas that just come, ain't ya?'

'Yeah.'

Lennie's eyes moved down over her body, and though she did not seem to be looking at Lennie she bridled a little. She looked at her fingernails. 'Sometimes Curley's in here,' she explained.

George said brusquely. 'Well he ain't now.'

'If he ain't, I guess I better look some place else,' she said playfully.

Lennie watched her, fascinated. George said, 'If I see him, I'll pass the word you was looking for him.'

She smiled archly and twitched her body. 'Nobody can't blame a person for lookin',' she said. There were footsteps behind her, going by. She turned her head. 'Hi, Slim,' she said.

Slim's voice came through the door. 'Hi, Good-lookin'.'

'I'm tryin' to find Curley, Slim.'

'Well, you ain't tryin' very hard. I seen him goin' in your house.'

She was suddenly apprehensive. ''Bye, boys,' she called into the bunkhouse, and she hurried away. George looked around at Lennie. 'Jesus, what a tramp,' he said. 'So that's what Curley picks for a wife.'

'She's purty,' said Lennie defensively.

'Yeah, and she's sure hidin' it.'

Oral exploration

1   Look at the description of the girl in paragraph 1. Concentrate on the details and imagine how she looks. Does the photo capture her? Explain.

2   Your teacher or one of the class will place four signs in different places around the room saying *strongly agree/agree/strongly disagree/disagree*. As your teacher reads out the statements you must decide what you feel about each of them, whether you strongly agree, agree, strongly disagree or disagree. Choose carefully as you will have to justify your opinion.

> **Around a ranch she should dress down not dress up.**

> **She is a notice box!**

> **It's obvious that her new husband is neglecting her.**

> **George's saying at the end of the extract, 'Jesus, what a tramp', shows that he fears her femininity.**

> **Lennie does not show her any respect.**

3   We don't see Curley and his wife together in this chapter. Can you pick up any hints that they appear to be an unhappy couple? What are those hints?

4   She is the only female in an all-male world. In what ways might that make life difficult for her?

5   Throughout the whole novel the 'girl' is only ever referred to as 'Curley's wife'. What does this fact tell you about how the men see her?

Let's predict!

Spend a little time with your partner guessing what might happen.

1   George gets increasingly worried about Lennie after encountering Curley and Curley's wife. Do you think he is right to be worried?

2   He frequently reminds Lennie that if he gets into trouble he is to 'hide in the brush by the river'. Does he expect that it will be necessary?

3   Going on the evidence so far, do you think that things are likely to turn out well for George and Lennie? Use the prediction template in the Portfolio to write up your ideas.

Portfolio 81

Opening up Chapter 3

The bunk house – Not a happy place

Read Chapter 3. In your Portfolio record the main events and characters.

Portfolio 8J

You are now going to explore the **themes of cruelty and violence** by looking at **two key moments** – the **killing of Candy's dog** and when **Curley picks a fight with Lennie**.

Key moment 1 – The killing of Candy's dog

Read these extracts from Chapter 3, related to the shooting of Candy's dog. The writer creates a mood. As you read, try to sense the mood as it changes and develops.

> **Mood**
>
> The mood of a key moment is the general experience or feeling that the author creates for the reader as the key moment unfolds. The mood can be funny, scary, exciting, calm, full of tension, dull or any other mood that the author wishes.

Carlson wants to kill Candy's dog.

Candy said, 'Maybe tomorra. Le's wait till tomorra.'

'I don't see no reason for it,' said Carlson. He went to his bunk, pulled his bag from underneath it and took out a Luger pistol. 'Let's get it over with,' he said. 'We can't sleep with him stinkin' around in here. He put the pistol in his hip pocket.

Candy looked a long time at Slim to try to find some reversal. And Slim gave him none. At last Candy said softly and hopelessly, 'Awright— take 'im.' He did not look down at the dog at all. He lay back on his bunk and crossed his arms behind his head and stared at the ceiling.

*   *   *   *

Carlson leads the old dog out of the bunkhouse.

'Take a shovel,' said Slim shortly.

'Oh, sure! I get you.' He led the dog out into the darkness.

George followed to the door and shut the door and set the latch gently in its place. Candy lay rigidly on his bed staring at the ceiling.

*   *   *   *

The men try to keep occupied as they wait for Carlson to do the deed.

George said, 'Anybody like to play a little euchre?'

'I'll play out a few with you,' said Whit.

They took places opposite each other at the table under the light, but George did not shuffle the cards. He rippled the edge of the deck nervously, and the little snapping noise drew the eyes of all the men in the room, so that he stopped doing it. The silence fell on the room again. A minute passed, and another minute. Candy lay still, staring at the ceiling. Slim gazed at him for a moment and then looked down at his hands; he subdued one hand with the other, and held it down. There came a little gnawing sound from under the floor and all the men looked down toward it gratefully. Only Candy continued to stare at the ceiling.

'Sounds like there was a rat under there,' said George. 'We ought to get a trap down there.'

Whit broke out, 'What the hell's takin' him so long? Lay out some cards, why don't you? We ain't going to get no euchre played this way.'

George brought the cards together tightly and studied the backs of them. The silence was in the room again.

A shot sounded in the distance. The men looked quickly at the old man. Every head turned toward him.

For a moment he continued to stare at the ceiling. Then he rolled slowly over and faced the wall and lay silent.

Read, write, explore

1 Read the extract out loud or listen to the recording of it. Try to sense the mood. Think of words to describe the mood. Write them down. Here are some examples – edgy, calm, tense, nervous or painful. Record your thoughts in your Portfolio.

2 Pick out phrases and sentences that capture the mood you have chosen. Write them down and compare them with your partner's choices. Say how they helped to create the mood as you read.

Portfolio 8K

3 How do you think Candy feels as Carlson takes his dog out of the bunk house? Describe his feelings.

4 Read again the paragraph beginning, 'They took places opposite each other at the table . . . ' The scene described is very quiet and no one speaks. Discuss how the writer uses images and onomatopoeic words (sound effects) to create the mood. Write them down.

5 How would you feel if you were in the bunk house as Carlson was out in the dark preparing to shoot Candy's dog? Would you have stopped him? Why? Why not?

6 Soon after his dog is shot, Candy is eager to join George and Lennie in the dream of an independent life on the smallholding. Do you think that the shooting of his dog had any influence on this?

Key moment 2 – Curley picks a fight with Lennie

Language and imagery

Read the extract from Chapter 3. Focus on how the use of **language and imagery**, expresses the **themes of aggression** and **injustice**. Work with a partner. Dip in and out of the text as often as you need to, in order to answer the questions.

Curley is looking for his wife again and gets into a row with Carlson. Curley, however, is afraid of Carlson and on seeing Lennie innocently smiling to himself about the dream, he decides to take it as an insult and attacks Lennie.

Curley attacks Lennie in the bunk house.

Then Curley's rage exploded. 'Come on, ya big bastard. Get up on your feet. No big son-of-a-bitch is gonna laugh at me. I'll show ya who's yella.'

Lennie looked helplessly at George, and then he got up and tried to retreat. Curley was balanced and poised. He slashed at Lennie with his left, and then smashed down his nose with a right. Lennie gave a cry of terror. Blood welled from his nose. 'George,' he cried. 'Make 'um let me alone, George.' He backed until he was against the wall, and Curley followed, slugging him in the face. Lennie's hands remained at his sides; he was too frightened to defend himself.

George was on his feet yelling, 'Get him, Lennie. Don't let him do it.'

Lennie covered his face with his huge paws and bleated with terror. He cried, 'Make 'um stop, George.' Then Curley attacked his stomach and cut off his wind.

Slim jumped up. 'The dirty little rat,' he cried, 'I'll get 'um myself.'

George put out his hand and grabbed Slim. 'Wait a minute,' he shouted. He cupped his hands around his mouth and yelled, 'Get 'im, Lennie!'

Lennie took his hands away from his face and looked about for George, and Curley slashed at his eyes. The big face was covered with blood. George yelled again, 'I said get him.'

Curley's fist was swinging when Lennie reached for it. The next minute Curley was flopping like a fish on a line, and his closed fist was lost in Lennie's big hand. George ran down the room. 'Leggo of him, Lennie. Let go.'

But Lennie watched in terror the flopping little man whom he held. Blood ran down Lennie's face, one of his eyes was cut and closed. George slapped him in the face again and again, and still Lennie held on to the closed fist. Curley was white and shrunken by now, and his struggling had become weak. He stood crying, his fist lost in Lennie's paw.

George shouted over and over. 'Leggo his hand, Lennie. Leggo. Slim, come help me while the guy got any hand left.'

Suddenly Lennie let go his hold. He crouched cowering against the wall. 'You tol' me to, George,' he said miserably.

Curley sat down on the floor, looking in wonder at his crushed hand. Slim and Carlson bent over him. Then Slim straightened up and regarded Lennie with horror. 'We got to get him in to a doctor,' he said. 'Looks to me like ever' bone in his han' is bust.'

'I didn't wanta', Lennie cried. 'I didn't wanta hurt him.'

Get into eight groups of three or four. Within the group elect one person as timekeeper, one as leader, one as researcher, and one as the recorder. If there are only three in your group, the leader could keep an eye on the time.

The leader of each group gives feedback to the class.

Group 1 & 3

Curley is very aggressive in this extract and is unjust to pick on Lennie. However, he does not deserve what happened to him. Do you agree with this estimation of Curley? Say why or why not.

Groups 2 & 4

This is a very violent moment in the novel. Read the extract from 'Lennie looked helplessly at George, and then he got up and tried to retreat'.
Pick out phrases that show the violence of the situation. Write a list of six phrases and rank them in order as to how effective they are in helping you to imagine the fight.

Groups 5 & 7

Strong images make this extract very dramatic. Read the extract with your partner and pick out your five strongest, most dramatic images. Write them down and comment on why they are so strong and so dramatic?

Group 6 & 8

While there is much aggression in the novel in Chapters 1 and 2, the violence between Curley and Lennie is extreme. Discuss how the theme of aggression grows from Curley's first entry in Chapter 2 to the horror of Curley and Lennie's fight.

In your Portfolio record the feedback from the groups.

Portfolio 8L

Let's predict!

What are the chances now that George, Lennie and Candy will make their dream real? How will Curley react to his being shamed by Lennie? Will he look for revenge? Might Lennie need to escape? Predict the plot of the novel. Use the template in your Portfolio.

Portfolio 8M

Opening up Chapter 4

Note to fast readers –
No spoiling! Keep the ending
of the novel a secret!

Saturday night – A gathering of the weak, neglected and lonely

Read Chapter 4. In your Portfolio record the main events and characters.

Portfolio 8N

The main themes explored here are **racism** and **isolation**.

Plight of American black people during the 1930s

Segregation and the Jim Crow laws

The American Constitution declared that every citizen was equal. However, the Southern states got around this by passing the Jim Crow laws which enforced segregation. This resulted in black people being forced to live separately. Black people could not sit with whites at the theatre, cinema or in school. Although declared 'separate but equal', black people were subject to poorer conditions in hospitals, schools and public facilities.

Black people had the worst jobs and the worst standard of education. They also found it difficult to register to vote in elections because of the following:

- Poll tax – In order to be able to vote you had to pay a tax but most black people were too poor to pay.
- Literacy tests (reading) – In order to be able to vote, a citizen had to demonstrate that they could read a difficult text. A large number of black people were illiterate during this period, as a result of poor education.
- Even if a black person managed to pass the test they would be threatened by whites so that they were too frightened to vote.

Racial isolation in the novel

Read the extracts from Chapter 4. Work with a partner.
Dip in and out of the text as often as you need to, in order
to answer the questions.

Here Crooks explains why he has been nasty to Lennie.

Crooks said gently, 'Maybe you can see now. You got George.
You *know* he's goin' to come back. S'pose you didn't have
nobody. S'pose you couldn't go into the bunk house and
play rummy 'cause you was black. How'd you like that?
S'pose you had to sit out here an' read books. Sure you could
play horseshoes till it got dark, but then you got to read books. Books
ain't no good. A guy needs somebody—to be near him.' He whined, 'A guy goes nuts if
he ain't got nobody. Don't make no difference who the guy is, long's he's with you. I tell
ya,' he cried, 'I tell ya a guy gets too lonely an' he gets sick.'

Oral exploration

1 Describe the effect that his segregation has had on Crooks.

2 Do you feel sympathy for his situation?

3 As Crooks describes his situation he uses repetition. How does this use of repetition
express how he feels?

4 Look again at how Steinbeck describes Crooks's tone as he speaks to Lennie:
'Crooks said gently', 'He whined' and 'he cried'. How do these phrases help you to see
the pain that Crooks experiences?

The Ku Klux Klan (KKK)

'Well, you keep your place then, …
I could get you strung up on a tree so easy it
ain't even funny.' (Curley's wife to Crooks)

The Ku Klux Klan

The KKK was a secretive racist
organisation active in the Southern states in
the first half of the twentieth century. Most of its members were
white, anglo-saxon and protestant and they wanted to show that they were better and more
powerful than black people, Jews, Roman Catholics, communists and socialists.

The KKK became known for the following:

- Holding night-time meetings and marching in white clothing with masks over their heads.
- Terrorising black people
- Murdering
- Lynching (mob killings). One hundred and thirty five black people in the state of Georgia
  were lynched from 1924 to 1925.

Members of the KKK were seldom punished because many of the members were policemen, judges and governors. By 1924 there were about five million members.

In this chapter, Curley's wife threatens to have Crooks lynched (hung without trial). The situation of black men in particular was very precarious in 1930s America. If even suspected of a sexual assault against a white woman, a black man could find himself taken by white neighbours or the KKK and hung from a tree without a trial. This was part of the racism in America at that time.

Curley's wife racially threatens Crooks

Read the extract from Chapter 4. Work with a partner. Dip in and out of the text as often as you need to, in order to answer the questions.

Crooks tries to reason with Curley's wife.

Crooks stood up from his bunk and faced her. 'I had enough,' he said coldly. 'You got no rights comin' in a colored man's room. You got no rights messing around in here at all. Now you jus' get out, an' get out quick. If you don't, I'm gonna ast the boss not to ever let you come in the barn no more.'

She turned on him in scorn. 'Listen, […],' she said. 'You know what I can do to you if you open your trap?'

Crooks stared hopelessly at her, and then he sat down on his bunk and drew into himself.

She closed on him. 'You know what I could do?'

Crooks seemed to grow smaller, and he pressed himself against the wall. 'Yes, ma'am.'

'Well, you keep your place then, […]. I could get you strung up on a tree so easy it ain't even funny.'

Crooks had reduced himself to nothing. There was no personality, no ego—nothing to arouse either like or dislike. He said, 'Yes, ma'am,' and his voice was toneless.

Read, write, explore

1. How does Curley's wife show her racist attitude? Examine what she says.

2. She appears to have great power over Crooks. How is this shown in what she says and in his reaction to her?

3. Does what she says change your attitude to her? Why? Why not?

4. What does Crooks's reaction to her tell you about his situation as a black man at the time? Give some details.

5. In your Portfolio, write a paragraph outlining Curley's wife's treatment of Crooks.

Portfolio 8O

Let's predict!

Based on the evidence, what do you think is going to happen? Use the template in your Portfolio.

Portfolio 8P

Opening up Chapter 5

The dream crashes

Read Chapter 5. In your Portfolio record the main events and characters.

Portfolio 8Q

You will focus on two key moments in this chapter, the **terrible accident** and **Curley's response**.

Key moment 1 – The accident

Read the extract from Chapter 5. Work with a partner. Dip in and out of the text as often as you need to, in order to answer the questions.

Lennie doesn't know his own strength.

She struggled violently under his hands. Her feet battered on the hay and she writhed to be free; and from under Lennie's hand came a muffled screaming. Lennie began to cry with fright. 'Oh! Please don't do none of that,' he begged. 'George gonna say I done a bad thing. He ain't gonna let me tend no rabbits.' He moved his hand a little and her hoarse cry came out. Then Lennie grew angry. 'Now don't,' he said. 'I don't want you to yell. You gonna get me in trouble jus' like George says you will. Now don't you do that.' And she continued to struggle, and her eyes were wild with terror. He shook her then, and he was angry with her. 'Don't you go yellin',' he said, and he shook her; and her body flopped like a fish. And then she was still, for Lennie had broken her neck.

Read, write, explore

Discuss each question. Then write down your answers.

1 This violent scene happens quickly but very vivid language makes it memorable. Use the grid in your Portfolio to trace the writer's use of images, simile, strong verbs and adjectives and write brief comments after a discussion with your partner.

2 Look at what Lennie says in this extract. How does it show his innocence?

3 Do you think that George has had too much influence on Lennie? Look again at what Lennie says about him and decide.

Key moment 2 – Curley's response to his wife's death

Read the extract. Work with a partner. Dip in and out of the text as often as you need to, in order to answer the questions.

> ### Curley finds his wife in the barn.
>
> Slim stood looking down at Curley's wife. He said, 'Curley—maybe you better stay here with your wife.'
>
> Curley's face reddened. 'I'm goin', he said. 'I'm gonna shoot the guts outta that big bastard myself, even if I only got one hand. I'm gonna get 'im.'

Read, write, explore

1 What does Curley's response to his wife's death tell you about him and his relationship with her?

2 How did the fight in Chapter 3 affect Curley's intention to get Lennie?

Let's predict!

With a partner, try to imagine a reasonably happy ending to *Of Mice and Men*.

Opening up Chapter 6

The dream ends – The final act of a best friend

Read Chapter 6. In your Portfolio record the main events and characters.

Portfolio 8T

The key moment

Read the extract from Chapter 6. Work with a partner. Dip in and out of the text as often as you need to, in order to answer the questions.

> *George has told Lennie the story about the rabbits for the last time.*
>
> Lennie giggled with happiness. 'An' live on the fatta the lan".
>
> 'Yes.'
>
> Lennie turned his head.
>
> 'No, Lennie. Look down there acrost the river, like you can almost see the place.'
>
> Lennie obeyed him. George looked down at the gun.
>
> There were crashing footsteps in the brush now! George turned and looked toward them.
>
> 'Go on, George. When we gonna do it?'
>
> 'Gonna do it soon.'
>
> 'Me an' you.'
>
> 'You . . . an' me. Ever'body gonna be nice to you. Ain't gonna be no more trouble. Nobody gonna hurt nobody nor steal from 'em.'
>
> Lennie said, 'I thought you was mad at me, George.'
>
> 'No,' said George. 'No, Lennie. I ain't mad. I never been mad, an' I ain't now. That's a thing I want ya to know.'
>
> The voices came close now. George raised the gun and listened to the voices.
>
> Lennie begged, 'Le's do it now. Le's get that place now.'
>
> 'Sure, right now. I gotta. We gotta.'
>
> And George raised the gun and steadied it, and he brought the muzzle of it close to the back of Lennie's head. The hand shook violently, but his face set and his hand steadied. He pulled the trigger. The crash of the shot rolled up the hills and rolled down again. Lennie jarred, and then settled slowly forward to the sand, and he lay without quivering.

Oral exploration

Portfolio 8U

1 How has George changed in his attitude towards Lennie?

2 Were you surprised when you read the scene where Lennie is killed? How did it make you feel? In your Portfolio track your thoughts through key moments.

3 You have found out the surprise ending of the story. What did you think of it? Did you predict it correctly? Now, have a walking debate on the following statements and decide whether as a class you agree, strongly agree, disagree, or strongly disagree with them. Are you surprised by the overall position of the class?

> George did Lennie a favour by killing him.

> Curley has major responsibility for his wife's death and he should stand trial for mistreating her.

> Curley's wife contributed to her own death and bears some responsibility.

> George had no choice but to kill Lennie.

PowerPoint – Jeopardy quiz

Create – Book report

Imagine that you work for a teenage magazine. The editor has asked you to write a book report on a novel that you have read recently. You must also design the page for the magazine. The editor does not want an ordinary, boring book report – it should take a more creative approach and include pictures, speech bubbles and fun graphics. Create a book report based on *Of Mice and Men* using an online program such as Comic Life, then present it to the class. Upload your book report to your e-Portfolio.

Note for Teachers: You will find step-by-step guidelines for this activity in your *How to Create an e-Portfolio* e-book. Log on to www.edcodigital.ie to access the e-book.

Question

Question on *Of Mice and Men*

You have now explored *Of Mice and Men* in detail. It's time to collect your notes and express your thoughts on the novel. Look at the following question. How would you answer it? Look through your notes and plan an answer.

Sample question

Describe a key moment of the novel which you thought was very dramatic and/or moving. Say how the writer made that moment so moving and dramatic.

As you write and redraft your essay, refer to the checklist for writing an essay on page 191, Unit 7.

After you have completed your answer, compare it with the following sample answer.

Sample answer

The key moment that I have chosen is the one at the end of the novel *Of Mice and Men* by John Steinbeck. It is the scene where Lennie kills Curley's wife, which leads to him being shot by George. The death of two important characters is dramatic by anyone's standards.

First we read about Lennie, an intellectually-challenged man, who likes stroking soft things such as mice and rabbit fur. As he was by himself in the barn, crying over his dead puppy, a young woman, the new wife of the boss's son Curley, came in. Curley's wife (we never find out her real name) was a really sad young woman, trapped in a bad marriage, and she talked to Lennie in this scene because there was no other human being who would listen. Curley's wife spoke about her dream of being a star in Hollywood, now lost. Two lonely characters, one unloved in her marriage, the other loved only by his minder and friend. She was innocently looking for company and soon got too close to Lennie when she allowed him to stroke her hair after he admitted that he liked things that were soft to touch. You could just see the horrible action unfolding.

As their conversation went on, she allowed Lennie to stroke her hair. He just wanted to stroke the soft texture of her hair and she got concerned and began to scream when Lennie got rough on her. Lennie did not understand, and fearing a repetition of an event when he stroked a red dress on a girl in Weed, he put his hand around her mouth to stop her. This moment is really dramatic for the reader.

It was really sad to see how things got out of control for him and even sadder for the girl as she struggled and finally had her neck broken. I felt really shocked at this point of the book and my emotions were torn between sorrow for the girl and sadness for Lennie, as he did not know what he had done. It is very dramatic to see what happens to an innocent and harmless man who has done harm.

The final scene is poignant. We see poor Lennie run to the river where George had told him to go in case of trouble. Here he sits waiting innocently and hoping George will sort everything out again. He knows he has done wrong. The scene becomes very dramatic when Lenny imagines his Aunt Clara and a giant rabbit scolding him for his actions. George suddenly arrives and realises that if he lets Lennie live he will be captured by Curley and probably be terrorised, tortured and lynched. Or worse, he will be sent to a jailhouse where he will suffer the loneliness and pain of isolation. So George shoots him as an act of goodness while he recites their dream of living 'off the fatta the land'. I felt very sad as I read this final moment of the novel. It is hard to imagine anything more moving or dramatic than a friend killing another friend as a favour. George has to kill the man who once trusted him so much he said: 'We got a future. We got somebody to talk to that gives a damn about us.' But the only feeling left for the reader is despair.

Use a similar step-by-step guide to answer the following questions on **setting** and the **significance of setting**.

1 **Describe a place *or* setting in a novel you have read.**

2 **How is this place *or* setting important in the novel? Support your answer with reference to the novel.**

Portfolio 8V

Poetry Case Study
Charles Causley

In this unit you will:

····> enjoy poems by the poet Charles Causley

····> carry out a detailed study of his writing style

····> prepare and deliver a short oral presentation on your responses to his poetry.

You will encounter the following poems:

- 'What Has Happened to Lulu?'
- 'My Mother Saw a Dancing Bear'
- 'Timothy Winters'
- 'Who?'

Oral presentation

After you have enjoyed and studied the poems by Causley in this short anthology, you will be asked to make a short **oral presentation** (either alone or with another student) on his poems and say what you think of them. You may, if you wish, focus on one poem, giving a presentation about it and using images to help you.

Your **oral presentation** will be the end result of enjoying, learning about, discussing and noting your responses to the poems.

BIOGRAPHY

Charles Causley

Charles Causley (1917–2003) was brought up in Cornwall, in the south of England, where he lived for most of his life. When he was only seven his father died from wounds he got during World War I. He never forgot the pain his father suffered. His father's death left the family very poor, which resulted in an early end to Causley's formal education.

At sixteen, he got a job in a builder's office. Reluctantly, he left school for work but he felt trapped in his new job; it was, he wrote later, 'the end of the world'. Gloomy years of working in offices followed and all the time he was struggling to be a poet. At 22, he was happy to join the Royal Navy and serve the cause of freedom during World War II. His experiences of war reinforced his belief in peace and non-violence.

After the war he decided to return to education and he trained as a teacher, finally getting a job in his old primary school. As he continued to write he became noted for his ballads about the things he noticed in his day-to-day life. Children feature constantly in his poetry, including the much-praised poem about the neglected child, 'Timothy Winters'. His ability to have a childlike openness in part explains the freshness of his writing. You can see it in his appreciation of the child/narrator's experience in the poems, 'What Has Happened to Lulu?' and 'My Mother Saw a Dancing Bear'.

As an only child, he was the sole witness to his parents' lives and to their traditional goodness. His memory of his mother's moment of awakening in the poem 'My Mother Saw a Dancing Bear' tells how strongly she affected his creative life. He refused to write an autobiography, since he said the truth about his life was available in his poems. He died in 2003 having won much praise for his poems.

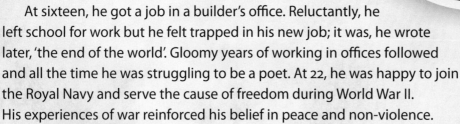

Home of the poet

Before you read

Have you ever been in a situation where someone had information that you madly wanted but they would not tell you? Describe the situation. How did you feel? Describe the emotions.

What Has Happened to Lulu?

What has happened to Lulu, mother?
   What has happened to Lu?
There's nothing in her bed but an old rag doll
   And by its side a shoe.

Why is her window wide, mother,
   The curtain flapping free,
And only a circle on the dusty shelf
   Where her money-box used to be?

Why do you turn your head, mother,
   And why do tear-drops fall?
And why do you crumple that note on the fire
   And say it is nothing at all?

I woke to voices late last night,
   I heard an engine roar.
Why do you tell me the things I heard
   Were a dream and nothing more?

I heard somebody cry, mother,
   In anger or in pain,
But now I ask you why, mother,
   You say it was a gust of rain.

Why do you wander about as though
   You don't know what to do?
What has happened to Lulu, mother?
   What has happened to Lu?

Oral exploration

1 With a partner, figure out the sequence of events in the poem using the timeline in your Portfolio.

Portfolio 9A

2 Read the poem with your partner and take turns to ask each the following questions. Note your answers in your Portfolio.

- What do you think has happened to Lulu?
- What might have caused her to leave?
- Who cried? Why, do you think?
- How did Lulu leave the house? What did she take with her?
- How does the mother feel?
- Who is the narrator of the poem? What age is the narrator?
- What does the mother tell him/her? Why?

Portfolio 9B

3 Discuss with your partner the main emotion the child feels in the poem. Discuss the clues in the poem that help you decide.

4 The child asks lots of questions but does not get honest answers. What is your opinion of the mother's responses?

5 Think about what the child is thinking. How does he/she feel about Lulu? How does the child feel about the mother? What tone does he/she adopt in the questions?

Read, write, explore

1 Read stanza 5 of Causley's poem again. Say it out loud and, as you do so, count the beats in each line. Describe the rhythm to your partner. Tap it out on your desk. Gently!

2 How does the strong rhythm pattern help to create the poem's mood? Say what you think is the general mood of the poem.

3 'Mother' is repeated often. In your opinion, why does the poet use so much repetition?

4 It is a week later and Lulu texts her brother/sister. Write down the text exchange they might have. You can base it on the questions the child asked in the poem itself.

PowerPoint –
Rhythm in poetry

Preparing for my oral presentation

Think about this poem by Causley. Using the worksheet in your Portfolio, collect your thoughts, responses and notes to the following:

Portfolio 9C

- ···➤ An image that represents abandonment
- ···➤ Images that represent youth and innocence
- ···➤ Images/sounds that represent the adult world
- ···➤ Images as metaphors for Lulu's life – past and future
- ···➤ The tone of puzzlement
- ···➤ The mother and her responses.

Think about the following prompts to get you started on preparing your **oral presentation** on the poems of Charles Causley.

1 **The things I learned in discussion with my partner or group.**

   Write the important things you learned and refer to important lines in the poem.

2 **Explore a theme in the poem.**

   Talk about a big theme that struck you in this poem; for example, loneliness, love, secrecy, the difficulty of being little, family break-up or escape. Discuss how the poem brings the theme to life.

Create – Write your own e-book

Have you ever thought of publishing your own book? Well, now you can! This activity invites you to create your own opening chapter or short story using an online writing program. Your opening chapter/short story will be called 'Lulu's story' and will be an entirely fictional account of what happened to Lulu. When you have finished, upload your chapter/story to your e-Portfolio.

Note for Teachers: You will find step-by-step guidelines for this activity in your *How to Create an e-Portfolio* e-book. Log on to www. edcodigital.ie to access the e-book.

Background

The poem 'My Mother Saw a Dancing Bear' recalls a time when animals were abused for public entertainment. The poet's mother is telling him about her experience of a chained bear who was brought to the school gate to entertain the children.

My Mother Saw a Dancing Bear

My mother saw a dancing bear
By the schoolyard, a day in June.
The keeper stood with chain and bar
And whistle-pipe, and played a tune.

And bruin[1] lifted up its head
And lifted up its dusty feet,
And all the children laughed to see
It caper in the summer heat.

They watched as for the Queen it died.
They watched it march. They watched it halt.
They heard the keeper as he cried,
'Now, roly-poly!' 'Somersault!'

And then, my mother said, there came
The keeper with a begging-cup,
The bear with burning coat of fur,
Shaming the laughter to a stop.

They paid a penny for the dance,
But what they saw was not the show;
Only, in bruin's aching eyes,
Far-distant forests, and the snow.

[1] **bruin:** a brown bear.

Oral exploration

1 Discuss the children's attitude to the bear at the start of the poem. Describe it and write down the relevant lines.

2 How did the children's feelings change? Discuss the way that the change came about. Jot down some facts and some lines.

3 How do we know that the bear is suffering? What lines tell us this? Do the lines make you sympathetic to him?

Read, write, explore

1 Try to explain how the children were able to see 'Far-distant forests, and the snow' in the eyes of the suffering bear. What does the line tell you about the bear and its situation?

2 What important theme or issue regarding animals does this poem deal with? Write it down. What opinions do you have about this theme? Is the theme or issue still important in today's world? Say why.

3 Write a similar short poem about another victim of cruelty.

Oral presentation

Preparing for my oral presentation

1 **Explore some of the following:**

···▸ Talk about the lines or stanzas that impress you. Show how the poet uses images to make you imagine the situation the bear finds himself in.

···▸ Be the bear – tell your story from your capture to your appearance in the poem. Describe the things that happened to you.

···▸ Use this poem to talk about the right of animals to be treated humanely in our modern world.

2 **Write down what you consider to be the powerful moments from this poem. Write them in your Portfolio.**

Portfolio 9D

···▸ Briefly say why you chose each moment.

···▸ Mention other moments that contain strong images.

···▸ Mention the feelings that the images create in you.

Before you read

Study these pictures of the lives of the
poorest in Britain taken around 1948.
This was also when the poem 'Timothy
Winters' was written. What things strike
you about the conditions
that the children
live in?

Timothy Winters

Timothy Winters comes to school
With eyes as wide as a football pool,
Ears like bombs and teeth like splinters:
A blitz of a boy is Timothy Winters.

His belly is white, his neck is dark,
And his hair is an exclamation mark.
His clothes are enough to scare a crow
And through his britches the blue winds blow.

When teacher talks he won't hear a word
And he shoots down dead the arithmetic-bird,
He licks the patterns off his plate
And he's not even heard of the Welfare State.[1]

Timothy Winters has bloody feet
And he lives in a house on Suez Street,
He sleeps in a sack on the kitchen floor
And they say there aren't boys like him any more.

Old Man Winters likes his beer
And his missus ran off with a bombardier,
Grandma sits in the grate with a gin
And Timothy's dosed with an aspirin.

The Welfare Worker lies awake
But the law's as tricky as a ten-foot snake,
So Timothy Winters drinks his cup
And slowly goes on growing up.

At Morning Prayers the Master helves[2]
For children less fortunate than ourselves,
And the loudest response in the room is when
Timothy Winters roars 'Amen!'

So come one angel, come on ten
Timothy Winters says 'Amen
Amen amen amen amen.'
Timothy Winters, Lord.

                    Amen.

[1] **Welfare State:** a system in which the government takes
responsibility for the social and economic security of
citizens; [2] **helves:** a dialect word from north Cornwall used
to describe the alarmed lowing of cattle (as when a cow is
separated from her calf); a desperate, pleading note.

Oral exploration

1 Listen to a reading of the poem and try to form a picture of what Timothy Winters looks like.

Now take turns to ask each other the following questions:

- In your own words, describe Timothy Winters' appearance.
- What are his clothes like? How do you know?
- Why would Timothy lick the patterns off his plate?
- How well is Timothy doing in the Maths class?
- Why might Timothy's feet be covered with blood?
- Where does he sleep?
- What is his father like?
- Where is his mother?
- How is Timothy treated at home?

2 Does the boy, Timothy Winters, seem to care much about the fact that he is poor and neglected? What sort of personality has he? Find lines in the poem that show his personality.

3 Does the poem help you to feel sorry for Timothy? Why? Why not? Discuss the feelings that the poem gives you.

4 Do the 'Welfare Worker' (now called Social Worker) or the 'Master' care about Timothy? Look in the poem for evidence.

5 Imagine you met the 'Welfare Worker'; what suggestions would you make to improve Timothy's life? Discuss them and write down three suggestions.

Metaphors and similes

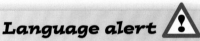
Language alert

Copy this table into your journal and explore the way the poet uses comparisons (metaphors and similes) to give us a vivid picture of Timothy and his life.

Example	Metaphor or simile	Explain the metaphor or simile
Timothy has big eyes	*eyes as wide as a football pool* (simile)	His eyes look so big because…
Timothy's teeth		
Timothy's hair		
Timothy is very hungry		
The law is not fair to Timothy		

Read, write, explore

1 The descriptions of Timothy's appearance and behaviour are somewhat exaggerated. Give a few examples. Try to say why the poet uses exaggeration.

2 Do you think that Causley wrote this poem just to make us laugh or to show that Timothy is neglected and that something should be done about it? Give reasons for your view.

Preparing for my oral presentation

Explore some of the following:

Portfolio 9E

···⟩ Talk about how Causley seems to care about people and about animals in the poems so far. Write down the lines that support this.

···⟩ Talk about the lines or stanzas that impress you. Show how Causley uses images to give a vivid picture of a poor and neglected boy.

···⟩ Be Timothy – tell your story. Explain why you look like you do. Tell the Welfare Worker and the Master what they should do to help.

···⟩ Use this poem to give a talk on children's rights. Write a shortlist to help you. Here are some ideas for the list:

Every child has the right:

● to be fed and clothed   ● to have a parent or guardian

Before you read

Try to recall the child you were at four or five years old. What thing or object did you have that was important to you? What clothes did you like to wear? What place did you most like to go to? Describe the place to your partner.

Who?

Who is that child I see wandering, wandering
Down by the side of the quivering stream?
Why does he seem not to hear, though I call to him?
Where does he come from, and what is his name?

Why do I see him at sunrise and sunset
Taking, in old-fashioned clothes, the same track?
Why, when he walks, does he cast not a shadow
Though the sun rises and falls at his back?

Why does the dust lie so thick on the hedgerow
By the great field where a horse pulls the plough?
Why do I see only meadows, where houses
Stand in a line by the riverside now?

Why does he move like a wraith[1] by the water,
Soft as the thistledown on the breeze blown?
When I draw near him so that I may hear him,
Why does he say that his name is my own?

[1] **wraith:** shadowy ghost-like figure.

Oral exploration

Read the poem with your partner. Then listen to the audio version.

Take turns to ask and answer each of the following questions:

- Mention one thing that is strange about the child in the poem.
- Mention a second strange feature of the child.
- Where is the poem set?
- Is the poet/narrator seeing into the past? How?
- How does the child move in the last stanza?
- Is the child living or dead or has something else happened?
- What does the last line tell you about the child?

Read, write, explore

1 What impression of the child do you get from stanza 1? How has your impression of him changed by the last stanza?

2 The narrator seems to be looking into the past. What clues do you get to show that this is so?

3 Do you think that the experience the poet describes is real or imaginary? Explain your answer.

4 Say how the tone of the questions in the poem is different from the questions asked in 'What Has Happened to Lulu?'

5 Pick out two strong images from the poem and say how they help you to imagine the scene described by the poet.

6 Which word from the following list would you use to describe the atmosphere created by the poet: frightening, mysterious, eerie, calming, sorrowful? Why?

Preparing for my oral presentation

Explore some of the following:

Portfolio 9F

···▶ Talk about the mood of this poem and how Causley uses images and sounds to create it.

···▶ Choose three images to go with a reading of the poem and say why the images work well with the reading.

My oral presentation

A two-minute talk on Charles Causley

Note: If you're doing a joint oral presentation with a partner, take three minutes.

What should I talk about?

You may develop an idea from the exercises you have done so far or you can choose one of the following:

1 My favourite poem – what it means to me. Mention how Causley's use of language appeals.

2 How Causley's poems appeal to young people.

3 Read one poem accompanied by three or four images you select from the Internet. Briefly explain why you chose the images.

4 The effect the poems had on you – things you learned about the world and about yourself.

Checklist

How will I know when I am succeeding in my oral presentation?

Portfolio 9G

My introduction

···▶ Did I state the main purpose of my presentation?

···▶ Did I outline my main argument/opinion?

···▶ Did I mention the poems I intend to discuss?

The main body of my presentation

···▶ Am I clear on the points that I am communicating?

···▶ Am I speaking clearly enough to be heard?

···▶ Am I rushing over parts that I am not sure of?

···▶ Do all my points flow and make sense?

···▶ Have I chosen appropriate supporting material?

···▶ Have I practised maintaining eye-contact?

My conclusion

···▶ Have I summarised the main points that I made?

···▶ Have I referred back to the reasons why I like this poet?

···▶ Am I prepared to take questions?

Get the Message!

Ivory is NOT Art.
#MarchAgainstExtinction

In this unit you will:

- take a series of photographs and create a meaningful album for a class exhibition
- create an informative poster to promote animal welfare
- write a short article about powerful photographs for a website
- write a short opinion column suitable for posting online

- create a poster as part of a campaign
- compose a dialogue in response to an advertisement
- discuss marketing and the consumer
- analyse web page formats
- prepare your own campaign
- analyse a magazine frontpage

You will encounter the following:

- ISPCA web page and article
- Opinion column on animal circuses
- Poster art from a global campaign
- John Lewis Christmas advert 2014

- *Crescents* interview with an Irish journalist
- *Crescents* interview with a magazine editor

Sign systems

Images on pages, posters and screens are a very important part of today's culture. Think about how **sound effects and music** are mixed in with the messages you receive in everyday life and how **language choice** can influence how people react to you.

These **sign systems** operate on television, radio and audio recordings, in performances and online. It's time now to focus on how these elements help the design and shape the meanings and messages you encounter in all sorts of media. Then examine how they affect your experience of media as a speaker, listener, viewer and reader.

Beginning with photographs

The power of photographs

A carefully taken photograph is a message. Look at the following images numbered 1 to 5.

Oral exploration

In the case of each photograph, discuss how the following factors help create its impact.

1. Does the angle at which the photograph was taken affect its impact?
2. Describe the contrast between the subject and the background.
3. Describe the expression on the subject's face.
4. Does any single photograph contrast with the others, in your view? Explain.

Create

Over the next few days, take a series of snaps of family pets or other animals. Your aim is to capture an attitude, an expression, or an interesting position of the subject. Upload them onto a PowerPoint so that you can share them with the class.

Campaigning

The Internet is a powerful tool, not just for entertainment and information but as a means by which you can change the world if you are creative enough. With one flash of inspiration you can go viral! You can promote human and animal welfare, help to save species, bring an end to cruelty or affect any issue you want.

Websites

The ISPCA website is a good example of how to use a website to campaign against cruelty to pets and to promote animal welfare.

Report Cruelty | Tel: 1890 515 515 | Contact Us

ISPCA
Caring for all animals

Visit Our Shop   **Donate**

Home   About Us ▾   Get Involved ▾   News & Media ▾   Give a Pet a Home ▾   Useful Info ▾   ISPCA Inspectorate ▾   Lost & Found ▾

Vhi Women's Mini Marathon

Run the marathon for The ISPCA

About The ISPCA

The Irish Society for the Prevention of Cruelty to Animals is recognised as Ireland's leading animal welfare charity. Our role is to is to prevent cruelty to animals, to promote animal welfare and to proactively relieve animal suffering in Ireland. More

Great **Gift Ideas** at our online shop

Hooded Cat Bed - €30

Rescue Stories
The ISPCA inspectors are at the forefront of animal welfare, they respond to allegations of cruelty, neglect and abuse and also aid sick and injured animals. Read some of the stories by our inspectors of how they rescue animals every day. More

Rehoming
The ISPCA's two rescue and rehabilitation centres were developed in order to support the ISPCA Inspectorate and member societies with the rescue, rehabilitation and responsible re-homing of cruelly treated and neglected animals. More

Lost & Found
This resource allows you to report pets who have been lost or pets that you have found. Knowing what to do when you lose a pet can be unclear, we have compiled guidelines of what to do in case of losing your dog, your cat or another animal. More

Subscribe to our newsletter

Email Address

*

Subscribe

Did you get the message?

Work with a partner to rate this campaigning website. Discuss and rate each feature out of 5, where 5 is the highest score and 1 is the lowest. Fill in the grid in your Portfolio.

Portfolio 10A

- The aim(s) of the page
- Logo
- Use of fonts
- Use of colour
- Percentage of visual and text content
- The use and impact of photos
- How the information is stated
- The weblinks
- The layout
- Does it succeed?

Oral exploration

1 Where is your eye first drawn to on this web page? Why?

2 Does this web page give you a positive or negative feeling? Explain.

3 How does the expression of the puppy in the main image affect you?

4 Find one solution this web page suggests or advises for problems.

5 Which link is presented as the most vital to the welfare of animals? Explain.

Read, write, explore

1 How does the use of scale, the zooming on the puppy's face, affect your response?

2 Do you think this web page is telling you or persuading you what to do? Explain.

3 What audience is this web page aimed at and what are the clues that tell you so?

4 If you were an alien, what conclusions could you draw about Irish society from this web page?

5 If you had the chance to redesign this web page explain one change you would make.

Barbaric act of cruelty on vulnerable puppy

The ISPCA is appealing for information in relation to a terrier puppy found wandering the Dublin Road in Portlaoise on the morning of 17 September 2014.

The dog, now named Missy, was discovered by a good Samaritan who immediately realised that there was something seriously wrong and brought her to a local veterinary surgeon for treatment.

An examination revealed that a tight cord had been tied around her tail as a form of tourniquet and the tail then cut off. The area under the base of the tail had swelled up due to the trauma inflicted.

After initially making her comfortable and administering first aid, the veterinary staff later sedated Missy and cleaned and stitched the wound. The ISPCA is also highlighting the fact that it is now a criminal offence for a lay-person to dock the tail of a pup at any age, and that anybody found to have performed the procedure can and will be prosecuted.

ISPCA Chief Inspector Conor Dowling said: 'This was a barbaric act perpetrated on a vulnerable young pup. We would ask that anybody with any information that might assist us with our enquiries come forward so that those responsible can be held to account.'

Oral exploration

1 What is the main fact in the report?

2 What words evoke an emotion? Explain your answer.

3 List in sequence what the vets did for the injured dog.

4 What role has the ISPCA regarding the incident? Mention some details.

Read, write, explore

1 Would the photograph prompt you to read the report?

2 Is the purpose of this story to get the public to help Missy or to protect dogs? Explain.

3 What other types of photograph would help get the message across?

4 What do you think should happen to the culprits if they are caught? Give reasons.

5 How well do you think publishing this story can help reduce cruelty to animals?

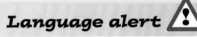

Language alert

Synonyms and antonyms

Synonyms are words that have a similar meaning such as 'bag' and 'satchel'. An **antonym** is a word that means the total opposite, for example 'opened' and 'closed', or 'boring' and 'interesting'.

Work in pairs to match these words from the text with words of similar meaning. Then use a dictionary to find an antonym for each word.

Word	Synonym	Antonym
barbaric	*brought to court*	
vulnerable	*shock*	
good Samaritan	*cruel*	
sedated	*endangered*	
trauma	*performed on*	
inflicted	*action*	
lay-person	*caused*	
procedure	*helpful person*	
prosecuted	*calmed*	
perpetrated on	*unqualified person*	

Create

Create an information poster. Research some information and make a fact sheet in poster format on one of the following issues that relate to animal welfare:

- A list of basic animal rights
- Cruel practices that should be stopped
- General rules for caring for pets.

Opinion columns

Here is an opinion column on treatment of animals from *The Journal*, an Irish online news service. An opinion column usually deals with a topic that stirs people's emotions and has a strong title, for example 'Why Facebook makes life hard for young people'.

Read the following article on animal circuses.

theJOURNAL.ie
READ, SHARE AND SHAPE THE NEWS

Aaron McKenna: Animal circuses are a shameful cruelty that you should avoid funding

Sea lions typically cruise in water at 17kph, and can burst up to 40kph. Three of them stuck in a tank together aren't going anywhere fast. Outside circuses, killer whales swim 120km to 160km per day, a little more than the distance between Dublin and Waterford. A killer whale in Seaworld would have to swim around the tank in a circle 1,600 times to get the same range.

Be it a travelling animal circus you meet on your holiday in the south east or somewhere like Loro Parque in the Canaries, where killer whale shows are popular, you are contributing to an industry of misery by paying to see a show.

Conservation and study

Animals are kept in captivity for a number of reasons. Many zoos and aquariums play an important role in the conservation and study of endangered species. Farms play host to domesticated livestock that feed a good proportion of humanity. Circuses and entertainment venues have no practical function other than to provide a good talking point and a few pictures from a day out.

Unlike a human performer, an animal doesn't head home after a stressful or busy day dancing around the arena. They don't crack open a fizzy drink and watch their favourite programme. They're not even like domesticated pets, such as a dog who has a loving bond with its owner or that plays an important function like aiding a disabled person.

They're wild animals that are sociable and intelligent enough to be trained, locked up in a cage and prodded till they perform meaningless tricks.

Money talks

Ultimately, however, the power to stop animal exploitation like this rests with consumers. Some circuses have dropped animal performances, partly in response to consumer pressure.

If you find a circus setting up near you and it uses animals, please don't go. If you're in the Canaries or Florida or anywhere else a Sea Life Park is found, just don't go. If the animals are forced out to do a show, perform tricks and entertain, then you are furthering animal cruelty by paying to keep it running.

There are lots of other things you can do to pass the time, none of which involve locking wild animals up in cages or putting them in swimming pools.

Did you get the message?

Work with a partner to rate this opinion column. Discuss and rate each feature out of 5, where 5 is the highest score and 1 is the lowest. Fill in the grid in your Portfolio.

Portfolio 10B

- The heading
- How well does it get the message across?
- Facts about the mobility of sea lions and killer whales
- Statistics on killer whales
- How the reader is addressed at the end
- Does it succeed?

Read, write, explore

1 What sentence best states the main argument the writer is making?
2 Does the article display balance?
   Hint: awareness of another side of animal captivity.
3 How does the writer show that there are two sides to animal captivity?
4 Do you agree that the same rules do not apply to dogs and sea lions? Explain.
5 How well do the sub-headings alert you to the main argument?

Joining words such as 'and', 'because', 'after', 'then', 'therefore', 'subsequently', 'but', 'if', 'or' and 'furthermore' **help to persuade and argue**; they are vital for opinion pieces. They link details, show cause and effect and join the various sentences together.

For example:

Five politicians joined the march. *Subsequently* they took selfies for publicity purposes. She turned up *because* I asked her personally. *After* the film, we chatted for ages.

Such **linking words** as these develop an argument: 'subsequently' links politicians' supportive actions to self-interest rather than public interest; 'after' ties 'personally' to 'chatted'.

Find two linking words in the following:

Therefore, if the animals are forced out to do a show, perform tricks and entertain, you are furthering animal cruelty by paying to keep it running.

Typical uses of linking words

- 'briefly' may indicate that a summary is coming up and 'firstly' that a sequence is starting
- 'otherwise', 'instead' and 'though' indicate contrast
- 'namely', 'in other words' and 'for instance' can help to clarify something
- 'therefore', 'as a result' and 'so' can show results
- 'next', 'finally' and 'afterwards' connect and clarify time or time sequence
- 'to begin', 'finally' and 'in conclusion' can indicate a sequence
- 'furthermore', 'along with' and 'likewise' add a sense of a flow

Refer back to this section as you write your essays in order to improve your writing.

Create

Write your own opinion column for a website on the issue of using animal experiments to cure disease in humans. Do some research online. Refer to the checklist for writing opinion columns.

PowerPoint –
History of the media

Checklist for opinion columns

┈┈┤ An opinion column is not a factual report but an expression of your views on a topic in the news.

┈┈┤ An opinion piece needs a catchy heading and a strong opening to gain readers' interest.

┈┈┤ The column will normally begin with a concise summary of particular facts.

┈┈┤ It will then find a relevant news angle or recent event to get the interest of the reader.

┈┈┤ The writer may refer to similar incidents to heighten the concern of the reader.

┈┈┤ An opinion column usually ends in a punchy sentence and offers some sort of verdict.

┈┈┤ Short paragraphs: breaking up your text will make it easier to read on a screen.

┈┈┤ Subheadings: if readers can see your main points clearly, those who want information will find it more easily.

Crescents interview

Listen to the following *Crescents* interview with Irish author and journalist Shane Hegarty. Shane is former opinion columnist and Arts Editor of *The Irish Times*. As you listen, make notes. Then answer the following questions.

Oral exploration

1 Explain Shane's phrase 'seeded from very, very young'.

2 How did Shane develop an interest in journalism while he was at school?

3 List some examples that Shane gives about how young people can gain experience of editing.

4 How are data and words presented differently in modern newspapers?

5 Why is secrecy no longer necessary for newspapers, according to Shane?

6 Does Shane agree or disagree that newspapers need to be entertaining? Explain.

Read, write, explore

1 According to Shane, how can students get involved in writing? Do you feel the same?

2 Do you agree with Shane about how heroes can influence your life? Give an example.

3 How might experience of editing at school help with a career in journalism?

Create

Listen again to what Shane says about changes to newspaper media in the last five years. Then examine a digital version of a newspaper front page and create a pie chart to illustrate what he tells you about how content is presented on a modern newspaper page. Use the following categories: words, video, sound, graphics, data.

Poster art in a global campaign

The Global March for Elephants and Rhinos brought together people in 130 cities worldwide on Saturday, 4 October 2014.

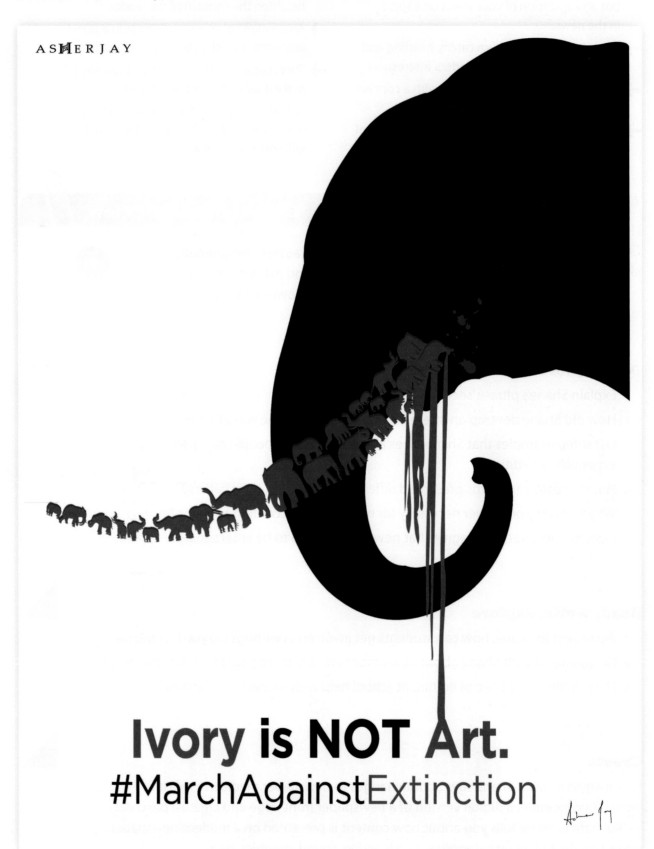

Oral exploration

1 What is the main message of this poster?

2 What is the most striking aspect of this poster?

3 How does colour help to get the message across?

4 What feelings does this poster give you?

5 Are the words in the poster effective?

6 What does the hashtag say about the way in which the campaign is run?

Create

Think of a poster ad you have seen recently. What makes you remember it? Can you remember the message it was trying to put across? Think about its effectiveness and what makes it memorable.

▶ Animation – Pronouns

A website that promotes the living environment

The purpose of the following web page is to engage people on projects that lead to awareness of the natural environment.

> A **tag line** is a catchphrase or slogan, especially used in advertising.

take action on biodiversity loss

> **Logo** is a symbol or other small design adopted by an organisation or company to identify itself and its products.

noticenature

Biodiversity, can we live without it?

NO! Biodiversity supports life on earth and provides us with a significant source of economic, environmental, health and cultural benefits.

Home   Publications   Species of the Month   Learn   Take Action   Notice Nature   Contact   Junior Page

Welcome to Notice Nature

Notice Nature is Ireland's public awareness campaign on biodiversity. The aim of the campaign is to raise awareness of the importance of biodiversity and to encourage everyone to play their part in its protection. This will help halt the damage being done to our plants and animals and the landscape, waters and habitats in which they live.

Junior Page

United Nations Decade on Biodiversity

Local Agenda 21 Environmental Partnership Fund

Do you have a project or initiative that could contribute to increasing local levels of environmental awareness or one which promotes building greener more sustainable communities?

If so, you may qualify for financial assistance from the Local Agenda 21 Environmental Partnership Fund 2013.

The Fund promotes sustainable development by assisting small scale, non-profit environmental projects at local level.

Click here for more information

Irelands Biodiversity at Risk

The IUCN(International Union for Conservation Network) Have recently published Fact Sheets on the state of threatened species in all EU states. Click here to see the Fact Sheet on Ireland.

Irelands Wetlands

The Irish Ramsar Wetlands Committee have published a new leaflet on Irelands Wetlands. Click on the photo below to view the leaflet.

What is Biodiversity?

Put simply, Biodiversity is the variety of life on Earth. It is essential for sustaining the natural living systems or ecosystems that provide us with food, clean water, fuel, health, wealth, and other services we take for granted in our everyday life.

Species of the month

February

Snowdrop

Education Tools for Biodiversity

Green-Schools

With assistance from the National Parks and Wildlife Service, this year sees the introduction of Biodiversity as the latest theme in the An Taisce Green Schools Programme. To assist educators, Notice Nature have introduced a new page on the website especially for teachers to help with introducing the subject of biodiversity into the classroom. Click on the Green Schools Logo to go directly to the page.

NPWS Education Centres

The National Parks and Wildlife Service operates several Education Centres around the country. The centres offer programmes in field studies and nature awareness to

Irish Hen Harrier Winter Survey

Irish Hen Harrier Winter Survey

To find out more about the Hen Harrier just click on the icon above.

Atlas of Mammals in Ireland

> **Reverse psychology** is a way of getting another person to do what one wants by pretending not to want it or to want something else.

> **Font** refers to the typeface chosen, and different sizes of lettering used. For example these words are in Verdana 10 point, or size 10.

Did you get the message?

Work with a partner to fill in the grid regarding this website. Rate each feature out of 5, where 5 is the highest score and 1 is the lowest.

Portfolio 10C

- ⋯⟩ Suitability of logo and website name
- ⋯⟩ The font and biodiversity
- ⋯⟩ Reverse psychology
- ⋯⟩ Number of links
- ⋯⟩ Web page: Visual or informative
- ⋯⟩ Its message: Does it succeed?

Oral exploration

1 What does this website campaign for? How do you know?

2 Where is your eye first drawn to on this web page? Why?

3 Where does the web page use humour to appeal to its audience? Does it work?

4 Find three eye-catching features of this web page.

5 Which elements of the web page appeal most strongly to your emotions? Why?

Read, write, explore

1 Would this web page cause you to get involved or not in a local nature project? Explain.

2 Find at least two arguments for animal conservation on this web page.

3 Based on its design and content, what kinds of people is this web page targeting?

4 How different is this web page from the ISPCA website? List at least two differences.

5 Which web page is more effective and why?

Create – Deodorant advertisement

You have recently been hired as creative director in an advertising agency and your first project is to launch a new deodorant for animals! You have been asked to create the storyboard for a TV commercial using an appropriate software program. When you are happy with your storyboard, present it to the class and then upload it to your e-Portfolio.

Note for Teachers: You will find step-by-step guidelines for this activity in your *How to Create an e-Portfolio* e-book. Log on to www.edcodigital.ie to access the e-book.

Human interaction with animals in ads

Go online and locate the 2014 Christmas advert for John Lewis, 'Monty the penguin'. Did you expect this ad to be for a high street store?

After the first viewing have a short class discussion where the students describe their first reactions. Then view it again with a focus on exploring how it works.

Oral exploration

1 At which moment does the big revelation happen?

   (a) When Monty watches the black-and-white screen
   (b) When Monty fetches the jigsaw pieces
   (c) When Monty plays hide and seek
   (d) When Sam takes his hands off Monty's eyes.

2 At what moment does facial expression best advance the story?

   (a) When Sam smirks to himself on the bus
   (b) When Sam looks confused pointing at the snow
   (c) When Sam is feeding his fish finger to Monty
   (d) When Sam's mother stares at him on Christmas morning.

3 What action of Monty's creates the biggest challenge for Sam?

   (a) Monty pushing him off the sleigh
   (b) Monty ignoring the snowflakes outside the window
   (c) The bulging of Monty's eyes when he observes people in love
   (d) Monty's begging for fish fingers.

4 Predict what flashes through the mind of Sam's mother from the close-up of her face.

    (a) Aw! How cute! I just love my boy

    (b) What's happening?

    (c) Is he that babyish still, at his age?

    (d) Where did that other penguin come from? It's not part of Santa's trove.

5 Which theme does the story suggest overall?

    (a) John Lewis fulfils dreams

    (b) Adults cannot see the hidden, magic world of children

    (c) John Lewis can solve loneliness

    (d) Money can buy you lovely things at John Lewis.

Read, write, explore

1 How well does the video communicate (a) feelings and (b) ideas?

2 Is the ad (a) more visual or (b) more verbal in how it communicates? Explain.

3 Describe the persuasive effect of the sound track, especially 'Just like little girls and boys/playing with their little toys/seems all we really were doing/ was waiting for love.'

4 How does the rest of the world react to Monty and what does that tell you?

5 Does the video suggest any view on how humans interact with animals? Explain.

6 When did you see a John Lewis shop during the video? Why?

Create

Work in groups of four. Using your understanding of what happens in the story, create a script for a conversation between Monty and Sam that takes place in his bedroom. Refer to the secret nature of their world and how weird they find the world of adults. Act out the dialogue in pairs, in turn, with the other pair as audience. Give feedback on the performance.

Portfolio 10D

Or

'Adverts like this that exploit children and animals should not be allowed.' Discuss.

What influences our attitudes?

Oral exploration

Work in pairs and complete the following statements. Discuss your thoughts in the class.

1 When you walk in the door of a newsagent you are bombarded by . . .

2 When you buy a magazine you are attracted by . . .

3 As consumers we don't realise . . .

4 To market magazines, editors use . . .

5 Positioning at eye level is important because . . .

6 The job of marketers is to . . .

Crescents interview

Woman's Way is one of the top Irish weekly magazines for women. A new cover is created every week to attract its many readers. Listen to the following interview with a former editor of *Woman's Way* as she describes how the covers were created.

Make notes on the following:

····▶ the background of the editor

····▶ how to choose a photo

····▶ how to put together a front cover

····▶ the editor's most memorable cover.

©Woman's Way, Issue 11, March 24, 2015

Create

About Us   Contact Us

Safe and healthy eating on the island of Ireland

| Search | | GO |

| Home | Food Safety | Healthy Eating | Education | Professional | Publications | News | Blog |

You are here: Home > Education > Post-primary (ROI) > Take Away My Way

Education

> **Primary (ROI)**

> **Primary (NI)**

> **Post-primary (ROI)**

  Take Away My Way

    ❚ Details

    ❚ Winners

    ❚ Finalists

    ❚ Tips & advice

    ❚ Prizes

    ❚ Information for parents

    ❚ Terms & conditions

  safefood for life

  What's on a label?

> **Post-primary (NI)**

> **Pre-school**

> **Out of school**

> **Additional information**

Take Away My Way

Details

Winners

Finalists

Tips and advice

Home	**Food Safety**	**Healthy Eating**	**Education**	**Professional**
Contact Us	Storing	Recipes	Primary (ROI)	Food Science
News	Cleaning	Food, Diet and Health	Primary (NI)	Events
Blog	Cooking	Weight Loss	Post-primary (ROI)	Nutrition
About Us	Food Poisoning		Post-primary (NI)	Research
	Cross Contamination		Pre-school	**Publications**
	Food Allergies			Research reports

1 Work in groups and explore this food web page. Use the skills you have gained from completing the sets of questions on the other web page in this unit to analyse this website for effectiveness. Write a report on how this web page gets its message across.

Consider the following areas as sub-headings for the report:

- aim
- logo
- fonts
- colours

- layout
- creative word use
- links
- use of graphics/photos

- quality of information
- impact/aim achieved
- helpfulness

Websites, ads, posters and opinion pieces are all ways of broadcasting your message. Imagine that you are working in an advertising agency and you have been asked to create and coordinate a campaign on one of the following:

- Against cruelty to animals
- Against hunting endangered species
- Against/For blood sports
- Against animal testing

You can use any two forms of media to get your message across. You have three minutes to pitch your ideas to the client. As part of your presentation you can include the images you intend to use:

- A mock-up of the website or poster
- Your tag line
- Your logo
- Name of your campaign

Romeo and Juliet

In this unit you will:

- enjoy, explore, experience and reflect as a critical reader on the play
- read, talk and write about key moments in the text
- understand and appreciate Shakespeare's choice of words – use of figurative language, vocabulary, language patterns and imagery
- understand, appreciate, speak and write about character, setting, story and action
- bring the drama alive through acting out the scenes
- focus on the themes such as conflict, family honour, love and freedom
- listen to the *Crescents* interview with a young author
- create a full edition, in digital or hard copy, of *The Verona Voice* for the week of the play's action.

Shakespeare

🖥 PowerPoint –
Shakespeare's time

What do you know about the time in
which Shakespeare lived and wrote his
plays? Watch the PowerPoint presentation and
make notes in your Portfolio on the following:

Portfolio 11A

- Clothing
- Setting
- Roads/transport
- Facts and figures

Would you change anything if you were putting on
a modern version of the play?

William Shakespeare

Timeline for *Romeo and Juliet*

The play is set in Verona and, briefly, Mantua,
40 kilometres away, in the central plains of
northern Italy in the 1300s. Verona grew into
a wealthy city with luxurious gardens, ornate
palaces, great mansions and magnificent
churches during the Renaissance period.

The Prologue – the ultimate spoiler –
predicts doom for the two 'star-crossed lovers'.

ACT 1

1 Sunday morning

In Verona, servants of the Capulets and Montagues trade insults and quarrel.
Benvolio Montague breaks it up. Tybalt Capulet, an upper-class youth, gets it
going again. The Prince proclaims sentences of death on future brawlers.

2 Later that morning

A very lovesick Romeo Montague moans over Rosaline who'll never marry.
Romeo refuses to look at other girls.

3 Sunday evening

Paris is refused a match with Juliet Capulet by her father. Mercutio and Benvolio
drag Romeo to the off-limits Capulet's feast, all masked, to look at other beauties.
There, Romeo spots Juliet and is love-struck. She is shocked that her worshipper is
on her family hate list. Fiery Tybalt, raging at Romeo's 'intrusion', vows revenge.

ACT 2

4 Sunday night

In desperation, Romeo sneaks into Juliet's orchard, overhears her love confession
and accepts her love. Juliet orders Romeo to arrange the wedding.

5 Monday morning

Romeo pushes Friar Laurence to marry them and he agrees, figuring it will help end the feud. In the street, Mercutio mocks Tybalt, who has challenged Romeo by letter. Romeo and Juliet are secretly married, despite the Friar's hunch that 'violent ends' await.

ACT 3

6 Later Monday afternoon

Tybalt and Mercutio taunt each other. Tybalt gets aggressive when Romeo refuses his challenge. Mercutio steps in to fight for Romeo's honour. Tybalt slyly slays Mercutio, who wishes a 'plague' on both families. Romeo fights Tybalt and kills him.

Later

The Prince banishes Romeo. The Friar convinces Romeo not to flee to Mantua till the feud is resolved.

7 Monday, late at night

Capulet agrees to let Paris marry Juliet immediately.

8 Tuesday, dawn

Romeo and Juliet separate sadly. Juliet imagines Romeo dead in a tomb. Her mother informs her of her match to Paris. Juliet refuses. Lord Capulet threatens her.

ACT 4

9 Tuesday morning

Juliet turns to the Friar; he gives her a magic potion so that she can fake her own death, before reuniting with Romeo.

Noon

Juliet pretends to accept Paris's engagement.

10 Tuesday night

Alone in her room, Juliet takes the potion, imagining the horrors of the tomb.

Early Wednesday morning

After a horrible discovery, the Capulets hold Juliet's funeral. The Friar sends a message to Romeo. Plague holds up the messenger.

ACT 5

11 Late Wednesday

Romeo, in Mantua, learns of Juliet's funeral, buys poison and returns to Verona.

12 Thursday, dawn

In Juliet's tomb, Romeo kills Paris, mourns Juliet, and dies from the poison. Juliet wakes up, sees Romeo's body and kills herself. The Friar explains all to the Prince. The feud ends, too late. The families promise to erect memorial statues of the tragic pair.

Teenage issues in *Romeo and Juliet*

The play *Romeo and Juliet* focuses on two teenagers whose love leads to their deaths because of their parents' 'rage' and 'strife'. Throughout the unit there will be writing tasks that revolve around the **issues of teenage freedom**. Your final task, which asks you to create a newspaper aimed at the youth of Verona, will combine some of these themes.

Teenagers and parents

1 Consider the relationship between teenagers and their parents. Key moments of the play focus on different aspects of the teenager—parent relationship. The following statements sum up what is at stake. Read each statement and then rate it. Insert a number from 1–5, where 1 means you least agree and 5 means you strongly agree.

Statement	Rating (1–5)	Code from timeline (1–12)
(a) Parents/guardians have the right to control who teenagers pick as their boyfriend/girlfriend.		
(b) Teenagers do not want adults to manage their love lives.		
(c) Teenagers show more responsibility than adults believe they can.		
(d) Adults are not as good at finding solutions as teenagers are.		
(e) It is natural for teenagers listen to friends and peers more than family.		
(f) If teenagers are aggressive it's likely they learned to be so from adults.		
(g) Teenagers have the right to solve their own problems.		
(h) Parents/guardians often don't understand the needs of teenagers.		

2 Look back at the timeline of the play. Can you match any of the episodes in the play to some of the statements? Write the timeline numbers in the boxes on the right.

3 Collate your results and present your findings. Discuss your findings in the class. Are you surprised at the results? Why? Why not?

4 Take one of the statements and create two lists of arguments, *for* and *against*, the statement. You will need these lists of arguments for an assignment at the end of the unit.

Exploring the Prologue

The **Prologue** in *Romeo and Juliet* reveals to the audience important information about the future of the main characters before the play begins.

Listen to the audio of the prologue. As you listen, follow the text.

Chorus   Two households, both alike in dignity
In fair Verona, where we lay our scene,
From ancient grudge break to new mutiny,
Where civil blood makes civil hands unclean.
From forth the fatal loins of these two foes
A pair of star-crossed lovers take their life;
Whose misadventured piteous overthrows
Doth with their death bury their parents' strife.
The fearful passage of their death-marked love
And the continuance of their parents' rage,
Which, but their children's end, naught could remove,
Is now the two hours' traffic of our stage;
The which if you with patient ears attend,
What here shall miss, our toil shall strive to mend.

Shakespearean language

Find the Shakespearean equivalent for the following words in the Prologue.

enemies, fighting, people's, hatred, cursed, beautiful, locate, families

Predicting the plot

A prologue should give us a taste of what is to come. This one certainly does. Now we know the truth of the plot and the mystery of the ending: two rich families in Verona who hate each other are about to lose their only son and daughter, all because of an ongoing feud between the families!

Oral exploration

Discuss the following briefly in pairs.

1 Do you normally want to know the ending first? Think of a story, film or play that starts at the end, such as *Titanic*, *Forrest Gump* or *The Fault in Our Stars*. Does this early knowledge spoil the story for you?

2 Can you think of any reasons for Shakespeare to begin in such a revealing manner?

3 Does the Prologue suggest one or more themes?

Create – Rewrite the Prologue

In your Portfolio rewrite the first six lines of the Prologue in everyday language. When you are finished, work in pairs. Take turns reading out both the Shakespearean version and your version. Which sounds better? Give two reasons for your answer.

Portfolio 11B

Exploring Act 1

New mutiny – A dramatic scene

Act 1, Scene 1

In an Italian town, a servant called Gregory starts a quarrel by using a gesture to provoke a rival servant called Abram. Abram falls for the bait by replying, 'Do you bite your thumb at us, sir?' A street brawl then takes place.

Describe to a partner one insulting gesture that could provoke street conflict in the twenty-first century. Is it a gesture or the spoken reply, as above, that starts brawls?

Class reading: Read Act 1, Scene 1.

Gregory   I will frown as I pass by, and let them take it as they list.

Sampson   Nay, as they dare. I will bite my thumb at them;
             which is disgrace to them if they bear it.

to

Citizens   Down with the Capulets! Down with the Montagues!

Enter OLD CAPULET in his gown, and LADY CAPULET.

Oral exploration

1 When do each of the following arrive on the scene: Benvolio, Tybalt and First Citizen?

2 Which pair gained courage when they saw Tybalt approaching?

3 Which speaker is the bravest? Give your reason.

4 Which speaker is the most cautious or cowardly? Give your reason.

5 Which of the characters is the most aware of the power of words? Give a reason.

Read, write, explore

1 What word angers Tybalt?

2 Who is Tybalt calling a coward? Is he right?

3 To what extent is Tybalt showing off in front of others?

4 After what word can you imagine adding in the words 'you are' in Tybalt's outburst?

5 What resulted from Tybalt's refusal of the peace offer?

6 Do you think Tybalt added much to the dramatic tension? Explain how.

Conflict role play

This is a conflict role play exercise to experiment with before acting out the brawl scene. Your purpose is to appreciate how good acting enables a drama to come alive. It will help you to feel the atmosphere of conflict on the streets of Verona.

- Divide the class into two groups. One group can have jackets on, the others jackets off, or you can use coloured sport bibs.
- Create a circular space at the centre of the room.
- Imagine two rival sets of supporters or rival gangs, such as the Capulets and Montagues.
- Imagine the space at the centre of the room is in front of a popular chipper or the local football stadium where you have gathered for a league match between rival clubs from the same town.
- In your groups design a few placards with the rival club gang names. Pin them around the room.
- Walk around the space **avoiding eye-contact**.
- Listen very carefully and follow the teacher's instructions.

Your teacher will give the following instructions in thirty-second intervals.

1 'Walk'.

2 'As you walk around, make very brief eye-contact with various other students.'

3 'Stop', 'Start', 'Fast', 'Slow', 'Jump' and 'Walk'.

4 'Now, as you continue to walk, hold eye-contact with someone wearing similar clothing.'

5 'Stop', 'Walk', 'Twist', 'Stop', 'Start and Join'.

6 'Join up with the student you are holding eye-contact with. The pair of you now share the same gang.'

7 'Walk around in gang pairs, using hostile eye-contact and body language to show you are in a gang. Glare at others.'

8 'Stop', 'Start', 'Fast', 'Slow', 'Jump' and 'Walk'.

9 'Break up into your gang groups. Decide on an identity for your gang. Take a label from the table. Write your gang's name on it. Stick on your label.'

10 'Relax briefly'.

Oral exploration

Form groups of six made up of three from each gang. Discuss the following questions in your groups.

1 How did you feel during the eye-contact exercise?

2 What behaviour of your gang partner and rivals did you notice?

3 What changes happened to your own body language and behaviour when you became a gang member?

4 How important was it that others could see you? Did it change how you acted?

Act it out

Act out the lines from the extract. The Capulet trio take on the roles of Sampson, Gregory and Tybalt, while the Montague trio take on the parts of Abram and Benvolio. Balthasar is silent so the sixth student waits until the end to play the role of the first citizen. Read with raised voices, hostile looks and suitable body language and gestures. Your teacher selects one group to perform the scene for the rest of the class. The class stands watching and cheering the action, a little like the **groundlings** in the audience in Shakespeare's Globe theatre.

> **Groundlings** were audience members who couldn't afford to pay for a seat and stood near the stage.

Create

You are a journalist who witnessed the build-up to the brawl and the brawl itself. Write a report (200 words) for *The Verona Voice* about the build-up and the event. Include statements you get personally or overhear from Benvolio and Tybalt. Present it in sensational (exaggerated) or popular style (with puns and catchy expressions) under a big headline.

Portfolio 11C

Prince Escalus's speech

Act 1, Scene 1 (lines 74–96)

Listen to the audio version of Prince Escalus's speech. As you listen, follow the text below.

Prince
Re**bel**lious **subj**ects, **en**emies to **peace**,
Pro**fan**ers of this **neigh**bour-**stain**èd **steel** —
Will they not **hear**? What, **ho** – you **men**, you **beasts**,
That **quench** the **fire** of **your** per**nic**ious **rage**
With **pur**ple **foun**tains **iss**uing from your **veins**!
On pain of torture, from those bloody hands
Throw your mistempered weapons to the ground
And hear the sentence of your movèd Prince.
Three civil brawls, bred of an airy word
By thee, old Capulet, and Montague,
Have thrice disturbed the quiet of our streets
And made Verona's ancient citizens
Cast by their grave-beseeming ornaments
To wield old partisans, in hands as old,
Cankered with peace, to part your cankered hate.
If ever you disturb our streets again,
Your lives shall pay the forfeit of the peace.
For this time all the rest depart away.
You, Capulet, shall go along with me;
And, Montague, come you this afternoon,
To know our farther pleasure in this case,
To old Free-town, our common judgement-place.
Once more, on pain of death, all men depart.

> A **syllable** is a unit of vowel sound, with or without consonants, that makes up a part of a word. For example, **men** is a one-word syllable; the word **fountains** contains two syllables.

> Shakespeare wrote in **iambic pentameter**. In iambic pentameter each line contains five pairs of syllables. The first syllable of each pair is spoken softly, followed by the second syllable which is spoken with emphasis. Continue until you reach the tenth syllable.

Read, write, explore

1 What word does Shakespeare use for 'three times'?
2 What words of the Prince would frighten you if you were Capulet?
3 What colourful image refers to sword wounds?
4 What is your opinion of how the Prince displays his power here?
5 In pairs, read the first five lines. Emphasise the syllables that are in bold.

Create

Imagine that various citizens tweeted about how Tybalt was not punished directly by the Prince. Write a tweet (a message using fewer than 140 characters) on a single page or on a Post-it expressing such a view.

Romeo's love angst and a marriage proposal for Juliet

Act 1, Scene 1
(lines 124–end of scene)

This key moment introduces you to **Romeo, 'the star-crossed lover'**. Montague, his father, can't cope with his son's teenage angst. He describes Romeo's secrecy to Benvolio, whom he asks for help; then Benvolio meets Romeo to check him out.

Class reading: Now read Act 1, Scene 1 (lines 124–end of scene).

Oral exploration

1 Does Montague provide any clues as to why Romeo was not involved in the brawl?

2 Does Montague give us any hints about his relationship with his teenage son?

3 What do we learn from Montague about his son's character?

4 What does Romeo reveal about himself to Benvolio?

5 What does Benvolio mean by 'Be ruled by me'?

6 What words does Benvolio use to try to distract Romeo from his sorrow over Rosaline?

7 Do you think that Romeo accepts Benvolio's advice?

Create

1 Imagine that Benvolio doesn't get a chance to meet up in person with Romeo and instead decides to text him. Having read the type of conversation they had, translate this into a text message conversation in your own (not Shakespearean) language.

2 Can you think of hashtags that describe Romeo's problem? Come up with a list. Choose the top three suggestions in the class and say why they are so relevant. Start your list with #Romeo.

> A **hashtag** is a word or a phrase that is linked to the symbol '#' to label things.

Star-crossed lover – Juliet

Act 1, Scene 2 (lines 1–37)

In this dialogue Paris visits Lord Capulet
to present a 'suit', meaning a request.
It was common for wealthy families to
match their daughters with rich husbands.
Here are the two important short extracts
from the scene. Say the following lines
and discuss the questions below.

Paris   But **now**, my **lord**, what **say** you to my **suit**?…

Capulet   My **child** is **yet** a **stran**ger in the **world**;
                 She **hath** not **seen** the **change** of **four**teen **years**…
                 Earth hath **swa**llowed **all** my **hopes** but **she**…
                 But **woo** her, **gen**tle Paris, get her **heart**.
                 My **will** to **her** con**sent** is **but** a **part**

Oral exploration

1 Capulet has five things to say here to express his feelings. Find a match for each line
    in the text.
    (a) Juliet has to agree; it's not all my decision.
    (b) My young daughter is inexperienced in life.
    (c) My honourable Paris, go ahead and make her fall in love with you.
    (d) Juliet is not yet fourteen or a full woman.
    (e) Juliet is all I've got in life now, so many others I cherish are dead and buried.

2 What do you think of Capulet's attitude to his teenage daughter at this stage?

Capulet invites Paris to a fancy-dress party he organises annually.

Capulet   This night I hold an old accustomed feast…
                 One more, most welcome, makes my number more.
                 At my poor house look to behold this night
                 Earth-treading stars that make dark heaven light.

Read, write, explore

1 Does Capulet sound like a kind man here?

2 Find the phrase Capulet uses for stars that walk on the ground. What does Capulet mean?

3 Write out Capulet's four lines and underline the sounds the actor should stress.

Out and about in Verona

Act 1, Scene 2 (lines 38–101)

Capulet sends out a servant with a guest list to invite people to the feast. Unfortunately the servant must be new as he tells the wrong people, that is, the Montagues, about the party. The language here, because a servant is speaking, does not use the **iambic pentameter**.

Servant	But I am sent to find those persons whose names are here writ and can never find what the writing person hath here writ.

The servant runs in to Romeo:

Servant	God gi' good-e'en. I pray, sir, can you read?
Romeo	Ay, mine own fortune in my misery.

The servant eventually takes a short cut with his checklist and simply invites anyone who is not a Montague to come for a drink at his master Capulet's house:

Servant	My master is the great rich Capulet; and if you be not of the house of Montagues, I pray come and crush a cup of wine. Rest you merry!

Class reading: Act 1, Scene 2 (lines 38–101).

Read, write, explore

1 Is the servant capable of carrying out his duties?

2 In what way does Romeo playfully misunderstand the servant's words?

3 Are you surprised when Romeo reveals his misery to the servant, a stranger?

4 Make a list of five important things you couldn't do if you were unable to read or write.

5 How might this meeting with the servant influence Romeo's immediate future?

Create

Imagine you are one of the citizens of Verona who notices this chance encounter between the Montague youths and a servant of the house of Capulet. Tweet your thoughts and then write another citizen's tweet in reply.

PowerPoint – Review
'Rhythm in poetry' in Unit 9

Read on

Do you remember Capulet's metaphor for young women – 'Earth-treading stars that make dark heaven light'? Benvolio gets a sudden inspiration: these women might provide distraction for Romeo from his love problems.

Benvolio   Tut, man, one fire burns out another's burning.

Later to Romeo:

> At this same ancient feast of Capulet's
> Sups the fair Rosaline whom thou so loves,
> With all the admirèd beauties of Verona.
> Go thither, and with unattainted eye
> Compare her face with some that I shall show,
> And I will make thee think thy swan a crow…

Romeo   The all-seeing sun
> Ne'er saw her match since first the world begun…
> I'll go along, no such sight to be shown,
> But to rejoice in splendour of mine own.

Read, write, explore

1 What does Benvolio actually mean by 'fire' and 'burning'?

2 Do you think that Benvolio is acting as a teenage friend normally would?

3 What does Benvolio suggest about Rosaline?

4 What does Benvolio mean by his bird images?

5 What light image does Romeo use to claim Rosaline is the most beautiful girl?

6 Does Romeo seem determined to keep on loving Rosaline here? Explain.

Create

Based on Capulet's invitation to Paris, create an advertisement for a night club in Verona. Give it your own choice of name and logo. It must aim to get the attention of readers to a website or magazine, provide key information in an interesting way and provide an instant means to book a ticket for an event. It should also use both verbal and visual material.

Shakespearean language

Shakespeare keeps mainly to the standard order of subject, verb and object/complement but varies this in some lines for the sake of rhythm and the sound that language makes on stage.

Shakespearean lines		Standard word order
Benvolio	At this same ancient feast of Capulet's Sups the fair Rosaline…	'The fair Rosaline sups at this same ancient feast of Capulet's.'

An earlier speech in Act 1, Scene 1 (lines 124–125), details Romeo's private grief due to his rejection by Rosaline.

Shakespearean lines		Standard word order
Montague	Many a morning hath he there been seen With tears augmenting the fresh morning's dew	'He hath been seen there many a morning augmenting the fresh morning dew with tears.'

Rewrite these lines in an easier word order and with any other changes you feel like making for clarity:

Shakespearean lines		Standard word order
Montague	Away from the light steals home my heavy son And private in his chamber pens himself	'My heavy son…
Romeo	I'll go along, no such sight to be shown, But to rejoice in splendour of mine own.	

Create – Newspaper article

Imagine you are a reporter for the weekly newspaper, *The Verona Voice*. It is a tabloid aimed at a youthful audience. The servant approached you to read some of the names and you asked him a few questions too. Now you intend to write a front-page article on what Capulet has planned and who he has invited. You heard also that there may be uninvited guests attending. This is your scoop. No other newspaper will have the news! Remember, tabloid newspapers need sensational headlines. Base your article on the information from Capulet's speech in Act 1, Scene 2 and Benvolio's remarks to Romeo page 265.

Note to Teachers: See your *How to Create an e-Portfolio* e-book for guidelines.

Juliet and her mother

Act 1, Scene 3 (lines 65–83)

Just before the feast, Juliet's mother puts her under pressure to marry Paris.

Class reading: Read lines 65–83.

Lady Capulet   Tell me, daughter Juliet,
                    How stands your disposition to be married?

to

Lady Capulet   And find delight writ there with beauty's pen.

Read, write, explore

1 What is the most important line that Lady Capulet speaks?

2 How would you describe Lady Capulet's attitude to her teenage daughter?

3 How does Juliet's answer about marriage show that she is an independent-minded teenager?

4 How does the nurse show that she takes Lady Capulet's side here?

5 Benvolio used a nature image of birds. What image of Paris does Juliet's mother create by using the words 'volume' and 'writ'?

Create

What would this conversation sound like in modern language? Rewrite the dialogue between mother and daugher for a twenty-first-century audience.

Portfolio 11D

Meet Romeo's pal – Mercutio

Act 1, Scene 4 (lines 13–22)

Mercutio attempts to lift Romeo's mood by tempting him to dance with various ladies.

Mercutio	Nay, gentle Romeo, we must have you dance.
Romeo	Not I, believe me…
	I have a soul of lead
	So stakes me to the ground I cannot move.
Mercutio	You are a lover. Borrow Cupid's wings
	And soar with them above a common bound.
Romeo	I am too sore empiercèd with his shaft
	To soar with his light feathers; and so bound
	I cannot bound a pitch above dull woe.
	Under love's heavy burden do I sink.

Read, write, explore

1 When Romeo claims he cannot move, what does that tell us about his mood?

2 What attitude does Mercutio display to his friend here?

3 Find an example of wordplay (pun) used by Romeo.

4 Imagine that Romeo and Mercutio were showing each other images on their phones during this conversation. Based on their words here, describe or download suitable images to capture the contrasting moods of Romeo and Mercutio.

Shakespearean language

Match each of these words with a suitable modern alternative.

Shakespearean

- gentle
- soul of lead
- stakes
- bound
- enpierced
- shaft

Modern

- stabbed
- height
- fixes
- heavy spirit
- arrow
- upper class

▶ **Animation – Most commonly misspelled words**

Romeo meets Juliet – love at first sight

Act 1, Scene 5

Romeo has slipped in to the party with his friends and is taking in the whole scene. Suddenly he sees a girl, not Rosaline, who catches his eye. He tries to check out the girl by asking a servant about her. This servant is not helpful.

Romeo   [to *SERVINGMAN*] What lady's that, which doth enrich the hand
                      Of yonder knight?

Servingman   I know not, sir.

Class reading: Read Act 1, Scene 5 (lines 40–144) from this moment to 'The strangers all are gone.'

Oral exploration

1 In what way does this servant remind you of the servant with the invitations on the street?
2 Who is the unknown lady?
3 Would Romeo's next actions have been different if the servant had identified the lady?

The moment when Romeo falls in love

Act 1, Scene 5 (lines 42–51)

Romeo continues to gaze at the beautiful girl. He utters a speech to himself (soliloquy) in praise of her. This reveals his response to the audience. Romeo uses a lot of interesting comparisons, similes and metaphors to express how beautiful she is.

Romeo   O, she doth teach the torches to burn bright!
                    It seems she hangs upon the cheek of night
                    As a rich jewel in an Ethiop's ear –
                    Beauty too rich for use, for earth too dear!
                    So shows a snowy dove trooping with crows
                    As yonder lady o'er her fellows shows.
                    The measure done, I'll watch her place of stand,
                    And, touching hers, make blessèd my rude hand.
                    Did my heart love till now? Forswear it, sight!
                    For I ne'er saw true beauty till this night.

Read, write, explore

1 Explain the last line in your own words.
2 When Romeo states 'For I ne'er saw true beauty till this night' what is he revealing about his character? (Think of Rosaline as part of your discussion with your partner.)
3 When Romeo imagines an accidental touch from the beautiful girl would leave his hand 'blessèd' does he mean she is like a saint or a goddess? Explain your opinion.
4 Identify three pairs of words that rhyme.

Soaring on Cupid's wings

Act 1, Scene 5 (lines 91–109)

Romeo quickly learns to do as Mercutio has advised; he falls in love and immediately declares it, even though he doesn't do so directly.

Read the following dialogue in pairs. It is the first time the two main characters meet. The dialogue aims to end in a kiss. Romeo uses a description of a pilgrim approaching the statue of a saint to kiss its hands as a polite and disguised way of persuading Juliet to allow him to kiss her. Juliet immediately gets what's happening and joins in.

Romeo	If I profane with my unworthiest hand This holy shrine, the gentle fine is this. My lips, two blushing pilgrims, ready stand To smooth that rough touch with a tender kiss.
Juliet	Good pilgrim, you do wrong your hand too much, Which mannerly devotion shows in this. For saints have hands that pilgrims' hands do touch, And palm to palm is holy palmers' kiss.
Romeo	Have not saints lips, and holy palmers too?
Juliet	Ay, pilgrim, lips that they must use in prayer.
Romeo	O, then, dear saint, let lips do what hands do! They pray; grant thou, lest faith turn to despair.
Juliet	Saints do not move, though grant for prayers' sake.
Romeo	Then move not while my prayer's effect I take. *He kisses her.* Thus from my lips, by thine my sin is purged.
Juliet	Then have my lips the sin that they have took.
Romeo	Sin from thy lips? O trespass sweetly urged! Give me my sin again. *He kisses her.*
Juliet	You kiss by th' book.

Read, write, explore

1 Romeo is impressed by the beautiful girl as she dances. While he watches, he tries to figure out how he will approach her. Which of the following, in your opinion, leads Romeo to refer to the beautiful girl as a saint?
   (a) She is dressed in pilgrim costume as the feast is a fancy-dress event.
   (b) She reminds Romeo of Rosaline, who has sworn to be a nun.
   (c) She looks both beautiful and innocent.

2 Romeo decides he will 'accidentally' brush her hand after she finishes dancing. Write the quote which states this intention.

3 Romeo shows his love in metaphors. By continuing the metaphor of a pilgrim, he is using an **analogy**, a parallel means of expression, as his chat-up line. With a partner, choose three of his religious phrases and rewrite them in ordinary English.

4 What does Juliet first say to show she's playing Romeo's game?

5 What does Juliet say and do in response that encourages him to try to kiss her?

6 Where does Juliet drop her caution and encourage the kissing more?

7 How does Juliet's last comment humorously link to what her mother said about Paris?

The new love is star-crossed

Act 1, Scene 5 (lines 115–144)

Romeo and Juliet receive separate setbacks from the nurse's remarks. She at least is better informed than the male servants. Juliet asks the nurse about the strange boy whom she has just kissed. When Romeo learns that her mother is the lady of the house he realises that he has a difficult problem to overcome.

Romeo	Is she a Capulet?
	O dear account! My life is my foe's debt.

Equally Juliet finds she has a matching dilemma (conflict of loyalties).

Nurse	His name is Romeo, and a Montague,
	The only son of your great enemy.
Juliet	My only love, sprung from my only hate!
	Too early seen unknown, and known too late!

Pick one line from each of Romeo and Juliet that reveals their immediate awareness of a problem.

Create

Write a short letter to an agony aunt as either Romeo or Juliet. Describe your wonderful new feeling and the terrible problem that goes with it. Then pass it to the person beside you to respond as the agony aunt giving you advice.

Portfolio 11E

The villain of the play emerges

Act 1, Scene 5 (lines 52–90)

Every Shakespearean play has a character who deserves a red card. In the following dialogue this character, known as the villain, clearly emerges. He just gets a reprimand, which alerts us as to how dangerous he is. He is the character who declared his hatred of 'peace' in the brawl scene in Act 1, Scene 1. But since there is no referee to issue the red card, he remains in the play to do a lot of damage to the plans of the main characters. It is interesting that he did not come to the notice of the Prince in the same way as he did to the audience in the earlier scene.

> A **villain** is the character whose actions provoke conflict and anger. He brings danger to the main character.

Class reading: Read from:

Tybalt   This, by his voice, should be a Montague.
              Fetch me my rapier, boy. What, dares the slave
              Come hither, covered with an antic face,
              To fleer and scorn at our solemnity?
              Now, by the stock and honour of my kin,
              To strike him dead I hold it not a sin.

to

Tybalt   Patience perforce with wilful choler meeting
              Makes my flesh tremble in their different greeting.
              I will withdraw. But this intrusion shall,
              Now seeming sweet, convert to bitterest gall.

Exit TYBALT.

Read, write, explore

1 What do you learn about Tybalt's character when he orders a servant, 'Fetch me my rapier, boy'?

2 What word does Lord Capulet use to suggest that Tybalt is overreacting to the situation?

3 Is Romeo aware that he has sparked Tybalt's fury?

4 What does Tybalt say that shows pride in his family?

Create

1 Imagine you are Tybalt. Compose a letter to Romeo, a challenge, in about 100 words. Swap letters with another student. The other student is Mercutio, who gets his hands on the letter and decides to reply, leaving Romeo still unaware of the challenge that has been issued to him. As Mercutio, reply to your partner.

2 **Key quotes**
    Work in groups of four and design an illustrated poster for one of the following key quotes from this scene.

···⟩ You kiss by th' book.

···⟩ My life is my foe's debt.

···⟩ My only love, sprung from my only hate!

···⟩ But this intrusion shall,
       Now seeming sweet, convert to bitterest gall.

Checkpoint! End of Act 1

In your Portfolio, fill in the questions on Act 1.

Portfolio 11F

Exploring Act 2

The balcony scene – Lovers' secret wedding plans

At the end of the feast, Romeo and Juliet became aware separately of the dilemma (problem) of falling for a lover who is officially their enemy. Romeo is full of 'unrest'. Romeo acts secretively and doesn't reveal his new love interest to his friends, who think he still pines for Rosaline. Soon after the feast, Romeo, unable to enjoy banter with his friends, impulsively breaks into the Capulet orchard. It is not clear what he hopes to achieve by this, other than escape to a private place to brood on his problems once more. Unexpectedly, Juliet appears at a window above the orchard and this changes everything for Romeo. Juliet surprises Romeo by revealing her feelings to the stars and Romeo comments to the audience about her.

Before you read

1 Do you believe in love at first sight? Why or why not?

2 Do people tend to fall in love the first time they feel attraction for someone?

3 Does Romeo realise a male member of the Capulet family spotted him at the feast?

Class reading: Read Act 2, Scene 2. If possible, listen to an audio recording of the whole scene.

Oral exploration

Share your first impressions of this scene with the rest of the class.

1 Who is most in love?

2 Who is most in danger?

3 Who has their feet on the ground?

4 Are there any plans made before the end of the scene?

5 Do you think that Romeo does a strange thing by jumping over the orchard wall?

6 Does Romeo have a plan or does it just work out for him?

Act 2, Scene 2

Class reading: Read Romeo's soliloquy until Juliet sighs.

Romeo   But, soft! What light through yonder window breaks?

It is the East, and Juliet is the sun!…

It is my lady. O, it is my love!

O that she knew she were!…

I am too bold. 'Tis not to me she speaks.

Two of the fairest stars in all the heaven,

Having some business, do entreat her eyes

To twinkle in their spheres till they return…

See, how she leans her cheek upon her hand!

O that I were a glove upon that hand,

That I might touch that cheek!

Read, write, explore

1 What comparison does Romeo make to express his joy at Juliet's entrance?

2 What image from the feast scene does his comparison remind you of?

3 How do you know Romeo has forgotten Rosaline?

4 Does Romeo know Juliet's feelings before she speaks? What line helps you to answer that?

5 Where in the speech does Romeo imagine that Juliet's eyes have been borrowed to shine in the sky?

6 Explain how Romeo uses the metaphor of the glove.

Create

1 Imagine Romeo writes a quick text message to Juliet in simple English to express how he feels (instead of the soliloquy). Write the message.

2 Draw the beginning of the balcony scene in cartoon frames, using speech bubbles with short key quotes of what they say to each other. Create between four and six frames.

Portfolio 11G

Act 2, Scene 2

Skip to Juliet's first two speeches. One student reads her soliloquy, another reads Romeo's aside.

Class reading: Read from:

Juliet   O Romeo, Romeo, wherefore art thou Romeo?
                Deny thy father and refuse thy name…

to

Juliet   'Tis but thy name that is my enemy…
                                Romeo, doff thy name;
                And for that name, which is no part of thee,
                Take all myself.

Read, write, explore

1 Juliet sees one main problem about the boy who played kiss-the-shrine with her; what is it?

2 What solution does Juliet propose while talking to herself about her tricky new love situation?

3 Is Juliet's first plan likely to work? State your opinion.

Create

Imagine that instead of standing on her balcony talking dreamily to the sky, Juliet is chatting online to a close friend Beatrice about her love troubles. As you write, include some initial chit-chat about the feast and then emphasise some of her concerns that she expresses on her balcony. Each entry should be passed to your desk partner for a reply.

Act 2, Scene 2 (lines 49–70)

Class reading: Work in different pairs and read the conversation in Act 2, Scene 2 (lines 49–70).

Read, write, explore

1 Is Romeo reckless in how he surprises Juliet by shouting out?

2 How do you think Juliet feels the moment Romeo shouts out 'I take thee at thy word'?

3 What sudden promise does he make about his name and why?

4 What is Juliet's main concern about Romeo's presence in the orchard? Use a quote to back up what you write.

5 What does Romeo mean when he says that Juliet's eye contains more danger than twenty of her family's swords?

Read on: Continue to read in pairs from line Act 2, Scene 2 (lines 112–127): 'What shall I swear by?' to 'Th' exchange of thy love's faithful vow for mine.'

Oral exploration

1 What is Juliet's attitude to the traditional habit of lovers swearing their love for each other?

2 Why does she compare their meeting as lovers for the first time to lightning?

3 What other analogy does Juliet use?

4 What does Juliet mean by her statement about 'bud' and 'flower'?

5 What does Romeo request from Juliet as reassurance that their love is real?

Read on: Continue reading from Juliet's speech beginning with 'Three words, dear Romeo' (lines 142–148).

Oral exploration

1 What arrangements does Juliet make with Romeo?

2 Would you say that Juliet is more practical than Romeo? Explain.

Read on: Read from 'What o'clock tomorrow' Act 2, Scene 2 (lines 167–193) to end of scene.

Oral exploration

1 Would you agree that the two new lovers get carried away with happiness in this part of the conversation? Find examples.

2 Is there evidence that Romeo is going to seek help and advice from an adult at the end of the scene? Explain your point.

Create

1 Imagine that you are a director who wants to audition actors for this scene. Select five short key quotes from the balcony scene and record them accurately in bullet-point format.

2 Work in groups of four. Hand your quotes, each in turn, to the others in your group. Each student delivers three of your selected lines. Decide which student wins the first acting role and give them a reason. Write their name and the reason under your list of quotes. Each student in the group takes turns at performing this audition activity.

Romeo and Juliet marry

Act 2, Scenes 3 and 6

In Act 2 Romeo twice meets with a priest, Friar Laurence, who has been his mentor. Romeo persuades the Friar to marry him and Juliet. Here is a **shortened version of the conversation**.

From Act 2, Scene 3:

Romeo
I have been feasting with mine enemy…
But this I pray,
That thou consent to marry us today.

Friar
Is Rosaline, that thou didst love so dear,
So soon forsaken? Young men's love then lies
Not truly in their hearts, but in their eyes…

In one respect I'll thy assistant be.
For this alliance may so happy prove
To turn your households' rancour to pure love.

This conversation links to the following **shortened conversation** *in Act 2, Scene 6:*

Romeo
Do thou but close our hands with holy words,
Then love-devouring death do what he dare –
It is enough I may but call her mine.

Friar
These violent delights have violent ends
And in their triumph die, like fire and powder,
Which as they kiss consume…

Juliet
But my true love is grown to such excess
I cannot sum up some of half my wealth.

Read, write, explore

1 In what line does Romeo convey to the Friar that he was with his enemy, the Capulets?

2 In what lines does the Friar joke about the shallowness of teenage love?

3 What does Friar Laurence hope to achieve by marrying the young lovers?

4 What do you think of Friar Laurence's warning that teenage love can be explosive?

5 How does the Friar's language echo Benvolio's metaphor of 'another's burning' from Act 1, Scene 2 (line 46)?

6 Do you think that Romeo hears Friar Laurence's warning about the danger of sudden marriage?

Checkpoint! End of Act 2

In your Portfolio, note the main events of the act.

Portfolio 11H

Before you read

Before reading the fight scene in Act 3, you have the option of reading Act 2, Scene 4 (lines 1–34) to 'Enter Romeo', for evidence of Tybalt's challenge to Romeo, for a better picture of Mercutio's humorous character and for background on a growing personal rivalry between Mercutio and Tybalt.

Exploring Act 3

Plot update

Romeo has just got married, unknown to his friends. The conflict is developing. Romeo is unaware of a key complication in the plot: Tybalt is on the warpath, seeking revenge for the insult he took at Romeo's presence at the Capulet feast. The anxiety of Benvolio adds to the rising tension as he fears that the Prince's ban on fighting will be ignored by the hot-headed youths of Verona, especially the Capulets: 'For now, these hot days, is the mad blood stirring'. Mercutio, despite his wit, adds to the growing tension. A relative of the Prince and friend of Romeo, he would fight Tybalt if given the chance. Everyone is armed.

Read, write, explore

Before reading Act 3, pretend you are a journalist with a scoop. Rewrite the above summary in the language of a sensational news article using one of these juicy headlines:

'Verona's finest ready to run amok'

'Mad Blood About to Spill'

'Prince of Cats to Scratch his Rivals'

The fight scene – Climax of first half of the play

Act 3, Scene 1

Romeo's friends are gathered in a public space in Verona and Benvolio expects trouble. Benvolio seems to think the hot Italian climate leads to rows. He warns his friends that they speak 'in the public haunt of men'. As you read, think about the following: does the fact that the actions are visible in the street affect how Mercutio and Tybalt behave?

Class reading: Read Act 3, Scene 1 (lines 1–31).

Benvolio	The day is hot, the Capulets abroad. And if we meet we shall not 'scape a brawl, For now, these hot days, is the mad blood stirring… By my head, here come the Capulets.
Mercutio	By my heel, I care not.

Read, write, explore

1 How does Mercutio give the impression he's up for a fight?

2 In this mood, could Mercutio be a dangerous friend for Romeo to have?

3 How does Benvolio remind us that families are raging at each other?

4 How does this key moment remind you of the build-up to the first brawl scene involving the servants? **Hint:** Think 'heel and thumb'.

Act 3, Scene 1 (lines 32–139)

Tybalt arrives and is immediately teased by Mercutio. Tybalt is up for a fight with Mercutio, but Romeo arrives. Tybalt attempts to provoke Romeo into fighting. Mercutio throws himself into the duel to save Romeo's honour. He is fatally wounded and curses both families. Soon Romeo kills Tybalt in revenge. The Prince of Verona banishes Romeo from Verona.

Class reading: Read Act 3, Scene 1 (lines 32–139) from 'By my head, here come the Capulets.' to 'Where are the vile beginners of this fray?'

Read, write, explore

1 What phrase used by Mercutio creates dramatic tension just as Tybalt arrives?

2 What insult does Tybalt use to increase the tension with Mercutio?

3 Mercutio replies with some wordplay that provokes Tybalt. Give one or more examples.

4 What word does Tybalt use to try to provoke a fight with Romeo?

5 How would Romeo's reply to Tybalt's insult surprise bystanders?

6 How does Mercutio show his anger towards Romeo's public response to Tybalt's insult?

7 Who wins the fight between Mercutio and Tybalt and how?

8 Why does Romeo eventually fight and kill Tybalt after at first refusing to fight him?

9 What impression of Verona youths do you get from this scene?

Language of insults

1 In pairs, make a list in your Portfolio of the provocative or insulting words and phrases used by Tybalt and Mercutio. Count them and rate them in order of how insulting they are (1–5), with 1 the most insulting and 5 the least. Now read aloud the dialogue between Tybalt and Mercutio from the arrival of Tybalt until the arrival of Romeo at line 51. Speak the lines of this key moment in a dramatic way, bringing out both the insults and the reaction to them.

Portfolio 11l

2 Two pairs come together, with Mercutio from one pair confronting Tybalt from the other pair. Take turns and say the same lines with anger and menace, throwing the insults at each other.

The death of Mercutio

Act 3, Scene 1 (lines 87–106)

Mercutio turns his death into one of the funniest moments of the play. At the same time, Mercutio curses the two rival families for his death.

Class reading: Read Act 3, Scene 1 (lines 87–106). Consider whether being in the public eye influenced any of the words and phrases Mercutio used as he lay dying on the street.

Read, write, explore

1 What did Mercutio say that caused Romeo to feel very guilty about his death?

2 What curse did Mercutio place on both families?

3 Examine the words of Mercutio's curse and see how they connect to the Prologue.

4 Was Mercutio entitled to curse both families? Explain.

Create

The following five quotes show Mercutio's wit, even in death. Create a cartoon strip or image which captures the humour of Mercutio's words. When you are finished, take a look at some other attempts around you and comment on their differences and similarities.

> 'Ay, ay, a scratch, a scratch.'

> 'No, 'tis not so deep as a well, nor so wide as a church door.'

> 'Ask for me tomorrow, and you shall find me a grave man.'

> 'I am peppered, I warrant, for this world.'

> 'They have made worms' meat of me.'

Act it out

In groups of four explore how the actor playing Mercutio will speak his final lines from when Tybalt wounds him. Mark which lines will be spoken aloud for the benefit of other youths on the street, and which are spoken in a low voice only for Romeo's ears. Then read the dialogue aloud.

Use gestures, facial expression and appropriate tone of voice to bring this key moment alive. If possible choose a floor space as a setting for a dramatic realisation of the events. Your teacher may select one group to act it out, with the rest of the class watching like a street crowd in Verona.

Romeo's fate

Act 3, Scene 1 (lines 174–195)

Lady Capulet   Romeo slew Tybalt. Romeo must not live…

Prince   Immediately we do exile him hence.

Class reading: Read lines 174–195.

Create

Write an editorial for *The Verona Voice*. In your editorial you should condemn violence and feuding in Verona and give a view on what should happen to Romeo. Use Benvolio's summary in Act 3, Scene 1 (lines 150–173) as the basis for the editorial.

Portfolio 11J

Tips on writing an editorial

1 Introduction: explain the issue, such as, youth violence in the streets of Verona.

2 Quick summary of the facts of the issue: for example, fourth brawl with the deaths of two youths and the fashion of wearing rapiers as accessories.

3 A timely news angle, such as the fighting has killed a relative of the ruler of Verona.

4 Give opinions from the opposing viewpoints: for example, the controversy over Romeo's punishment – is it enough or too much?

5 The verdict of the writer, stated without emotion. Deal with issues, not personalities.

6 Urge readers to be good citizens and take a positive approach, for example, to social order.

7 End with a clear and concise conclusion. Write the sentence with a sense of authority.

Read, write, explore

1 In your opinion, was Lady Capulet within her rights to demand a death sentence for Romeo?

2 What does the Prince decide as a punishment for Romeo's crime?

3 Imagine that Romeo's friends decide to hold a student protest against Romeo's banishment. Create a poster for a protest march against the Prince's decision.

4 Write a one-minute speech you would deliver at this protest.

Portfolio 11K

A way out for Romeo

Romeo acts desperately on a visit to Friar Laurence but the Friar offers a solution.
What does the Friar promise for the future?

Friar   Hold thy desperate hand…
         The law, that threatened death, becomes thy friend
         And turns it to exile…
                              pass to Mantua,
         Where thou shalt live till we can find a time
         To blaze your marriage, reconcile your friends,
         Beg pardon of the Prince, and call thee back

Class reading: Now read the full scene.

Family argument

Act 3, Scene 5

Unknown to Juliet, her father has arranged her sudden marriage to Paris. Apart from the nurse, the household is unaware the Friar has married Juliet to the now-banished Romeo.

Class reading: Read from Act 3, Scene 5 (line 107), 'Well, well, thou hast a careful father, child' to (line 168), 'Out on her, hilding!'

Read, write, explore

1 Does Lady Capulet indicate whether she as mother supports the match?

2 Does Juliet show that events are moving too quickly for her? Find a quote that supports this.

3 Imagine you are Juliet's mother here; what is the most shocking thing Juliet says?

4 What does Juliet's father first think is the cause of his daughter's upset?

5 Can you find the line that shows Juliet's mother wishes for Juliet's death?

6 Does Capulet speak to Juliet about the marriage like a good father should? Explain your answer.

7 What was it like to be a teenage girl in Verona at that time?

Create

1 In groups of four, make notes of key incidents in Juliet's life since the feast and how she might have felt at certain moments, for example, hopeful, elated, anxious, thoughtful, impatient and shocked. Fill in the incidents list for Juliet in your Portfolio. Then write two possible questions each to put to Juliet. One question should refer to an incident, one to a feeling. Add to this incidents list after you have read Act 4.

Portfolio 11L

2 In groups of four, 'hot seat' Juliet. One student takes the part of Juliet. The others ask her questions about events of the past two days and how she feels. Repeat the activity with a second student hot-seated as Juliet.

Checkpoint! End of Act 3

In your Portfolio, note the main events of the act.

Portfolio 11M

Exploring Act 4

A desperate solution

Act 4, Scene 1 (lines 89–120)

Friar   And this distilled liquor drink thou off…
        And in this borrowed likeness of shrunk death
        Thou shalt continue for two-and-forty hours…
        Shall Romeo by my letters know our drift.

Class reading: Read Act 4, Scene 1 (lines 89–120).

Read, write, explore

1 What problem is the Friar attempting to resolve?

2 Identify the main steps of the Friar's plan to rescue Juliet from her situation. Make sure to place them in the right sequence.

3 Has the Friar acted responsibly in putting this plan together? Read from 'What if it be a poison which the Friar' to 'For he hath still been tried a holy man', (Act 4, Scene 3 (lines 24–29)).

4 Class poll: take a show of hands on whether the Friar acted responsibly here.

Juliet and the supernatural

Act 4, Scene 3 (lines 55–59)

Juliet   O, look! Methinks I see my cousin's ghost
Seeking out Romeo, that did spit his body
Upon a rapier's point. Stay, Tybalt, stay!
Romeo, Romeo, Romeo. Here's drink.
[*drinks*] I drink to thee.

Oral exploration

1 How does this imagined vision of Juliet add to the theme of revenge in the play?

2 How do Juliet's words add to (a) the atmosphere, and (b) the growing tension of the play?

3 What is your opinion of the ordeal that Juliet, a teenage girl, was facing at this point?

Juliet's fake death

Act 4, Scene 5 (lines 17–40)

Class reading: Read from 'What noise is here?' to 'Life, living, all is death's.'

Oral exploration

1 What evidence is there that Juliet has 'died'?

2 How does the household react to her 'death'?

3 What lines of Capulet suggest that Juliet is married to death?

4 Do you get the impression that events are happening so fast that something could easily go wrong for Juliet? Explain your answer.

Checkpoint! End of Act 4

In your Portfolio, note the main events of the act.

Portfolio 11N

Exploring Act 5

Newsflash

Imagine the following breaking news article in *The Verona Voice*.

On the way from Mantua to Verona, Romeo has stopped by an apothecary (a chemist) and bought some strong poison, 'mortal drugs'. Read the following news article.

The Verona Voice

Police crackdown on illegal pharmacies

An impoverished backstreet apothecary was arrested at midnight last night when agents tracking a prominent Verona exile were led to his door. Apparently he has been supplying poison to members of the feuding cartels for the past three months, the effects of which were wrongly attributed to outbreaks of plague. The mystery of the return of the ancient plague has been resolved, something which should relieve the citizens of Mantua and Verona. It is believed the Verona exile had just departed, having purchased a particularly lethal concoction. The arrested apothecary described a tattoo anchor he imprinted on the youth's right forearm: an anchor entwined with a rose, containing the caption 'Love-Hate'. Members of the public are strongly advised to avoid this dangerous man who now travels under the name of Count Rose.

Class reading: Read Act 5, Scene 1 and compare the article with the actual events.

Act 5, Scene 1

Key quotes

Romeo   Let me have
                 A dram of poison

Apothecary   Such mortal drugs I have.

Act 5, Scene 3 (lines 161–170)

Class reading: Read from lines 161–170, from 'What's here?' to 'Let me die.'

1 Does Juliet's death strengthen our realisation that events move at a very fast pace in this play?

2 Pick an image used by Juliet which makes her death more dramatic for the audience.

3 Perform a mime for your partner of Juliet's final moments after the Friar exits.

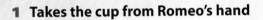

Ten steps for the mime

1 **Takes the cup from Romeo's hand**

2 **Gazes into it**

3 **Puts cup to her lips**

4 **Kisses Romeo's lips**

5 **Reacts with surprise at how warm the lips are**

6 **Hears noise outside**

7 **Reacts to noise by grabbing the dagger from its sheath**

8 **Mouths a final comment silently**

9 **Stabs herself**

10 **Falls**

Act 5, Scene 3
(lines 294–310)

Class reading: Read the following extract from Act 5, Scene 3.

Prince	And I, for winking at your discords too, Have lost a brace of kinsmen. All are punished.
Capulet	O brother Montague, give me thy hand. This is my daughter's jointure, for no more Can I demand.
Montague	But I can give thee more. For I will raise her statue in pure gold, That while Verona by that name is known, There shall no figure at such rate be set As that of true and faithful Juliet.
Capulet	As rich shall Romeo's by his lady's lie; Poor sacrifices of our enmity!
Prince	A glooming peace this morning with it brings. The sun for sorrow will not show his head. Go hence, to have more talk of these sad things. Some shall be pardoned, and some punishèd. For never was a story of more woe Than this of Juliet and her Romeo.

Read, write, explore

Choose a quote from the extract to go with each answer.

1 How has the Prince been punished as a ruler for what has happened? Why?

2 What do Lord Montague and Lord Capulet offer to do to end the feud?

3 Is there any sense of hope for the future to be found in the last moments of the play?

4 What phrase by one of the parents echoes a line in the Prologue?

5 Does the reference to the sun fit in with previous references in the play?

6 What words of the Prince most emphasise the final tragic mood of the play?

Vendetta – a modern story

If you were to write a modern-day *Romeo and Juliet*, where would you set the novel? How would you dress the actors? What themes would be important? What conflicts could arise?

Catherine Doyle is a young author. *Vendetta* is the title of Doyle's first novel, which is the first in a trilogy. There are many similarities between *Vendetta* and *Romeo and Juliet*. In this *Crescents* interview Catherine outlines her plot. As you listen, make notes on the following:

- Similarities in themes
- Similarities in plot
- Similarities in characters

Based on your knowledge of *Vendetta*, what do you think the Prologue could be?

The Verona Voice

The voice of the youth

In groups of six, create a full edition, digital or hard copy, of *The Verona Voice* for the week of the play's action. You need a news editor, an interview writer, a social editor for the gossip columns, an art editor for the cartoon strip and other illustrations, an advertising editor and a sports editor.

Each group will agree on a managing editor who should lead the planning. The group should spend time agreeing on final tasks and then review all the material when it is ready, before putting the final presentation together. Your teacher will review the final editions and may ask for a presenter from each group.

Use the best of the reports already written throughout the unit.

Some ideas:

- Think of a few additional items that will be created to complete the publication, such as an interview with the Friar for a factual account of the main events leading up to the final tragedies.

- Research the Friar's final speech to the Prince in Act 5, Scene 3 from lines 229 to 269.

- Include one detailed report involving the servants in Act 1, Juliet's mother, the Nurse and Benvolio.

- You will need to cover the peace agreement ceremony at the tomb.

- You can include the top citizens' tweets from different days of the week.

- The sports editor might do research on how people entertained themselves in medieval Italy or else make up a few events that she or he summarises in one 'Sports Review of the Week'.

Checklist – Assess your knowledge

Before you move on to the next unit, take a look at the following list and rate how confident you are at discussing the following:

Rate your knowledge out of three – 3 being very confident, 2 confident enough and 1 not confident at all.

	1	2	3
● Main character	☐	☐	☐
● Opening scene/Prologue	☐	☐	☐
● Hero/heroine/villain	☐	☐	☐
● Humour/sadness/dramatic moments	☐	☐	☐
● Tension between characters	☐	☐	☐
● Closing scene	☐	☐	☐
● Monologue/soliloquy	☐	☐	☐
● Important relationships – especially conflict	☐	☐	☐
● Themes: conflict/love/hate	☐	☐	☐
● Winners and losers	☐	☐	☐
● Recommendation/review	☐	☐	☐
● Staging and setting	☐	☐	☐
● World of the text	☐	☐	☐

Go back over the areas that you are still not confident in.

Reaching the Beyond

NASA

In this unit you will:

- ⋯⟫ understand the features of writing a space adventure
- ⋯⟫ engage in purposeful discussion of a variety of texts and ideas on space travel
- ⋯⟫ write articles, reports and letters about the exploration of space
- ⋯⟫ appreciate the creative process involved in writing stories on outer space
- ⋯⟫ research and produce a project based on 'firsts' in space travel history.

You will encounter the following texts:

- 'Irishman Roche keen to explore a new life on Mars' from the *Irish Examiner*
- Amos Ives Root's eyewitness account of the Wright brothers' first flight
- The Greek myth of Icarus

- Timeline of events in space travel
- Lunar Mission One
- *Star Trek*
- *The Jetsons*

Reaching the beyond

Have you ever looked up at the stars and wondered what's out there? Our feet are planted on the ground but our imaginations can travel to where those stars are and beyond.

All human beings have the ability to imagine; to go beyond the limits of our world and create far-flung fantasies of worlds out of reach. Where are the limits of your imagination? Are you Earth-bound, staring up at the stars and wondering what's out there? Or do you launch yourself into outer space to explore and conquer?

At the end of this unit you will be asked to write your own space-age story.

Space facts!

The **sun** is a typical example of a Yellow Dwarf star. It is located at the centre of our solar system and controls the Earth's climate.

Before you launch

Before you initiate your ascent into the cosmos, consider the following question: If you had the chance to go into space, to see what is beyond Earth's atmosphere, would you take it?

Dr Grant, whilst conversing with a young boy, Erik, in *Jurassic Park III*, pondered this question.

Dr Grant I have a theory that there are two kinds of boys. There are those that want to be astronomers, and those that want to be astronauts. The astronomer, or the palaeontologist, gets to study these amazing things from a place of complete safety.

Erik But then you never get to go into space.

Dr Grant Exactly. That's the difference between imagining and seeing: to be able to touch them.

1 What is the difference between an astronomer and an astronaut?

2 Why might an astronomer want to study space and the stars so deeply, but never yearn to go into space?

3 What compels a person to endanger their lives by propelling themselves into the beyond? Would you prefer to be an astronomer or an astronaut?

Space facts!

Did you know? One year on Mars is equal to nearly two years on Earth! Earth Year – 365 days. Mars Year – 687 days.

Irish Examiner

Irishman Roche keen to explore a new life on Mars

In 1971, David Bowie sang: 'Is there life on Mars?' There might be soon, and Irishman Joseph Roche could be one of twenty people to be sent in 2025 to the Red Planet to live, and die, in a space settlement.

'I applied to go to Mars on a one-way trip,' says the 28-year-old. 'The chances of me going are pretty slim, but they improved this week.'

'When they announced this project, 202,500 people applied and, last week, they cut it down to 1,058 potentials. There are three Irish people left in the running.'

The project is Mars One. It is the brainchild of Dutch entrepreneur Bas Lansdrop, and Dutch scientist Arno Wielders. It will establish a human settlement on Mars. The first crew, of four astronauts, will land after a seven-month spin through space.

A new crew of four will be sent every two years thereafter. None will be coming back.

Roche will have to pass a physical before March of this year. That will be followed by a series of interviews to determine his mental strength and suitability. If he passes, he will appear on a reality television show to generate most of the funding for the project.

'I guess a lot of people think it's foregoing a happy life on Earth,' says the astrophysicist. 'But for someone who has given up 12 years of their life to study space and stars, the opportunity to live on another planet, it's not that difficult a decision for me.'

'If they asked me to go in the morning, I'd be gone in a heartbeat.'

Roche grew up on a farm near Dunlavin, on the Kildare side of the Kildare–Wicklow border. It was on his family's small homestead that he developed his appreciation of the night sky and its twinkly delights.

'Because parts of the midlands are more radio-quiet than parts of the Sahara desert, Ireland is great for watching stars,' says Roche. 'On a clear, cloudless night in Kildare you can see everything up there. It's one of the reasons I still love going home.'

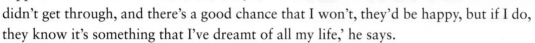

Were he to be successful in his application, Roche would have to rule out ever returning.

His parents, he says, support him.

'My family are very supportive. I'm lucky I've got a very close family that would support me in whatever I do. Of course, if I didn't get through, and there's a good chance that I won't, they'd be happy, but if I do, they know it's something that I've dreamt of all my life,' he says.

Roche attended the Christian Brothers School in Naas, where he had 'great science teachers' who nurtured his love of science. He studied science at Trinity College in Dublin and, after a stint working with NASA in the United States, he returned to Trinity to complete his PhD in astrophysics.

Roche has stayed on in the college, where he works for the Science Gallery.

He says that because of his commitment to work, he is single. He plans to keep it that way for as long as he is a candidate for the mission. If Lynx advertisements are to be believed, his new status as a potential astronaut might make it a bit difficult to fight off potential 'astronettes'.

Assuming he does manage to keep the ladies at bay, there might be a chance of some space-lovin'. After all, each crew will consist of two men and two women and there are only so many boxsets a person can watch.

It sets up the intriguing possibility of humans actually creating, well . . . Martians.

'Actually, that's a huge topic,' says Roche. 'On their guidelines, there's a question about getting pregnant on Mars and their answer is 'please don't'. The human body has evolved to live with gravity on Earth, but on Mars you've got 38% of the gravity you have here and we don't know what that would do to a developing, unborn child.

'So they're asking astronauts not to conceive and that's raising other ethical issues. How far they can enforce that is up for discussion.'

Roche will find out within the next two years whether he is going to Mars. As a scientist, he is, of course, a realist, so he is not pinning everything on getting there.

'I always try to see possible results of situations that are out of my control as wins,' he says. 'If I get to go, then that's the stuff of dreams. If I don't, then I get a chance at a happy life here on Earth and, maybe, convincing some poor woman that I'm husband material and maybe starting a family, or something. That's not such a bad thing either.'

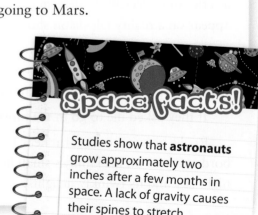

Space facts!

Studies show that **astronauts** grow approximately two inches after a few months in space. A lack of gravity causes their spines to stretch.

Oral exploration

1 How many people should be living on Mars by 2025?

2 Who came up with the plan of Mars One?

3 Why does Roche not find the idea of foregoing 'a happy life on Earth' daunting?

4 Where did Roche grow up and how has that influenced his interest in the cosmos?

5 Do you believe that Roche is well qualified to apply for the Mars One project?

6 Why are the possible candidates encouraged not to produce a family while on Mars?

Read, write, explore

1 What is your impression of Joseph Roche's ambition to live out the rest of his days on Mars? Discuss with your partner the pros and cons of Roche's aspiration, and write down three points for each.

2 If you had the opportunity to travel to one of the solar system's planets and live there, would you? Write the reasons why you would, or would not, want to take this opportunity.

3 If you had the opportunity to ask Joseph Roche any question about his reasons for applying for Mars One, or any question relating to his study of astrophysics, what would it be and why?

4 How has the project progressed since the article? Go online to look up the latest information on the Mars One project. Use the information from all your sources to write an updated version of the article.

Create

Would you apply if you could in the future? Check out the Mars One website to see what the requirements are. Write out your application for consideration to be one of the people chosen to live on Mars.

Portfolio 12A

In addition to your application form, all applicants must include a one-minute video explaining why they should be considered for the mission.

You must include:

···} The traits and qualities you have that you think would be essential for living in close proximity with a limited number of people for the rest of your life

···} The unique skills and abilities that make you an ideal candidate for the job.

Refer to qualities like your resourcefulness, your adaptability, your ability to trust others. Make sure that you give the audience a sense of your personality.

Witnessing man's first flight

Before sending people to establish a permanent settlement on a planet beyond Earth's limits, we first had to discover how to leave the ground and take flight. Let's retrace our steps to when Wilbur and Orville Wright took their first successful flight, which paved the way for the future of aviation and space travel.

In January 1905, the first accurate eyewitness article describing the Wrights' aeroplane in flight was published in an unlikely publication called *Gleanings in Bee Culture*, written by Amos Ives Root. Root was invited by the Wrights to witness and report on an important event in the history of aviation, which was taking place at Huffman Prairie. Here is an adapted version of Amos Ives Root's article.

What hath God wrought? – Num. 23:23.

Dear friends,

I have a wonderful story to tell you—a story that, in some respects, outrivals the *Arabian Nights* fables—a story, too, with a moral that I think many of the younger ones need, and perhaps some of the older ones too if they will heed it. God in his great mercy has permitted me to be, at least somewhat, instrumental in ushering in and introducing to the great wide world an invention that may outrank the electric cars, the automobiles, and all other methods of travel, and one which may fairly take a place beside the telephone and wireless telegraphy. Am I claiming a good deal? Well, I will tell my story, and you shall be the judge . . .

I am now going to tell you something of Orville and Wilbur Wright, from Dayton, Ohio. They began studying the flights of birds and insects. From this they turned their attention to what has been done in the way of enabling men to fly. They not only studied nature, but they procured the best books, and I think I may say all the papers, the world contains on this subject.

These boys, instead of spending their summer vacation with crowds as so many do, went away by themselves to a desert place by the sea coast. With a gliding machine made of sticks and cloth, they learned to glide and soar from the top of a hill to the bottom. I found them in a pasture lot of eighty seven acres, a little over half a mile long and nearly as broad. I recognised at once they were really *scientific explorers* who were serving the world in much the same way that Columbus did when he discovered

America, and just the same way that Edison, Marconi, and a host of others have done all along through the ages.

Nobody living could give them any advice. It was like exploring a new and unknown domain . . . it was my privilege, on the twentieth day of September, 1904, to see the first successful trip of an airship, without a balloon to sustain it, that the world has ever made, that is, to turn the corners and come back to the starting point.

Everybody is ready to say, 'Well, what use is it? What good will it do?' These are questions no man can answer yet. I have suggested before, friends, that the time may be near at hand when we shall not need to fuss with good roads nor railway tracks, bridges, etc., at such an enormous expense. With these machines we can bid adieu to all these things. God's free air, that extends all over the Earth, and perhaps miles above us, is our training field and I confess it is not clear to me, even yet, how that little aluminium engine, with four paddles, does the work.

When it first turned that circle, and came near the starting point, I was right in front of it; and I said then, and I believe still, it was one of the grandest sights, if not the grandest sight, of my life. Imagine a locomotive that has left its track, and is climbing up in the air right toward you—a locomotive without any wheels, we will say, but with white wings instead, we will *further* say—a locomotive made of aluminium. Well, now, imagine this white locomotive, with wings that spread twenty feet each way, coming right toward you with a tremendous flap of its propellers, and you will have something like what I saw. The younger brother bade me move to one side for fear it might come down suddenly; but I tell you, friends, the sensation that one feels in such a crisis is something hard to describe.

When Columbus discovered America he did not know what the outcome would be, and no one at that time knew; and I doubt if the wildest enthusiast caught a glimpse of what really did come from his discovery. In a like manner these two brothers have probably not even a faint glimpse of what their discovery is going to bring to the children of men. No one living can give a guess of what is coming along this line, much better than anyone living could conjecture the final outcome of Columbus' experiment when he pushed off through the trackless waters. Possibly we may be able to fly over the North Pole, even if we should not succeed in tacking the 'stars and stripes' to its uppermost end.

———————————————————————————

A fortnight later, Root published a photograph of one of the Wright brothers flying an early glider and noted:

To me the sight of a machine like the one I have pictured, with its white canvas planes and rudders subject to human control, is one of the grandest and most inspiring sights I have ever seen on earth; and when you see one of these graceful crafts sailing over your head, and possibly over your home, as I expect you will in the near future, see if you don't agree with me that the flying machine is one of God's most gracious and precious gifts.

Oral exploration

1 Why, do you think, does Root compare the Wright brothers to Columbus and Edison?

2 What does Root see as the future purpose of the Wright brothers' invention?

3 How does Root describe the contraption the Wright brothers created?

4 Does the author consider the event as important for the future?

5 Why, do you think, does Root describe the event so positively?

Read, write, explore

1 How important was it for the Wright brothers to have a witness record the details of the experiment?

2 With your partner, discuss the difficulties that the Wright brothers might have encountered trying to set about their first flight. Prepare a 'worry list' which could have been theirs.

3 Imagine the conversation the Wright brothers would have had with Root to persuade him to come to the first flight site. Write a short dialogue.

4 Can you imagine an era when flight wasn't used for transportation? How do you think the Wright brothers would have sold their idea of the future? Make a list of pointers they might have included in their advertising!

Create

1 Has an experience you've shared at a friend's or relative's place ever inspired you to follow a dream? Discuss your inspiration in a detailed written reflection.

2 In the role of a journalist, write a letter of response to the newspaper about the special event as described by Amos Ives Root. It will appear in the editorial section of the newspaper.

Space facts!

Astronauts' footprints on the moon will remain there for millions of years because there is no wind or water to blow or wash them away.

Asking questions

There are different types of question that make for a lively and successful interview.

Animation – Interview tips

Closed questions...

···⟩ establish the facts

···⟩ get a quick and easy answer

···⟩ put the questioner in complete control.

Closed questions start with words like: *do, would, are, will* and *if*. You can force a yes or no answer by adding tag questions, such as *isn't it?, don't you?* or *can't they?* to any statement. This makes it a closed question.

Open questions...

···⟩ ask the listener to think

···⟩ lead to opinions and feelings

···⟩ often hand control over to the other person.

Open questions start with words like: *what, why, how* and *describe*. A good balance is around three closed questions to one open question. The closed questions get conversation points going and summarise progress. Open questions get the other person thinking and continuing to give you useful information about them.

Here are some examples of how to start questions in a successful interview:

- Why are (aren't) you . . . ?
- What about . . . ?
- Could . . . ?
- People have said . . . Do you agree?
- What is the effect . . . ?
- And yet . . .
- Do you wonder . . . ?
- And I know you've . . .
- Are there any instances in which . . . ?
- Refer to a quote and ask: Can a . . . ?
- If I . . . ?
- So is there any chance . . . ?
- That's interesting . . . but do you . . . ?
- How do you regard the fact that . . . ?
- I want to ask you a broader question, about . . .
- You mention the . . .
- Will . . . ever . . . ?
- Is . . . possible?

If you had the opportunity to interview either Wilbur or Orville Wright, what ten questions would you ask them? Use the question-maker information below as a guide.

Portfolio 12B

Snapshot of key information: who, what, when, where, why and how?

Expand the key information with important details and quotes

Background information

Timeline of space travel

Have you ever heard the Greek myth of Icarus, and how he flew too close to the sun?

The king of Crete had imprisoned an inventor named Daedalus, and his son, Icarus, in a castle with high walls so that they could not escape. But Daedalus had an idea.

He made a pair of wings, which he stuck on his shoulders with wax. Then he made another pair for his son. The father and son moved their arms up and down and flapped their wings. Soon they took off and rose above the walls. On reaching Greece, Daedalus landed on the ground and asked Icarus to come down too. But Icarus was enjoying himself up in the air and was very proud that he could fly like a bird.

His father kept calling out to Icarus to come down but Icarus was enjoying himself and kept flying higher and higher until the heat from the sun melted the wax that joined the wings to his shoulders.

The wings broke off and poor Icarus couldn't fly any more and fell down from the sky to his death.

Oral exploration

1 What lesson do you learn from the myth?

2 If we followed the moral of the story, what impact would that have on inventions and space travel progress?

Space facts!

It takes **sunlight** eight minutes to reach Earth travelling at nearly 300,000 km per second.

Space quiz

Humans have dreamed about flight and space travel since ancient times. Centuries ago, the Chinese created rockets for ceremonial and military purposes, but during the twentieth century rockets were developed that were powerful enough to escape Earth's gravity, and such rockets opened up space to human exploration.

In groups, test your knoweldge of twentieth-century space travel. Try to answer these questions. Then scan the space timeline to check your answers. No cheating!

1. In what decade was the first rocket to reach the boundary of space developed? 1930s, 1940s or 1950s? By whom?
2. What was the first animal in space?
3. What was the name of the first satellite to orbit the Earth?
4. What would the result have been if a human had been in the *Luna 2*?
5. Who was the first woman in space? Which country did she fly for?
6. Who is John Glenn and what role did he play in space travel?
7. In July 1969, what iconic event took place?
8. Which planet was the first to be explored in the 1970s?
9. What role did Dennis Tito play in space travel history?

TIMELINE · SPACE TRAVEL

1942   During the Second World War, Nazi Germany saw the possibilities of using long-distance rockets as weapons. In 1942, the German V-2 was the first rocket to reach the boundary of space at 100 kilometres from the Earth's surface. It was designed by Wernher Von Braun, who later went on to work with NASA to create rockets that travelled to the moon.

1949   After fruit flies had been used in 1947 to study the effects of space travel on animals, it was time for the first monkey to journey into space. Albert II was the first monkey in space. He was launched in an adapted American V-2 rocket on 14 June 1949.

1957   On 4 October 1957, the USSR (Union of Soviet Socialist Republics) launched the first satellite into space, *Sputnik 1*. Sputnik translates as 'satellite' in Russian. It was the first satellite to orbit the Earth. Russia then managed to launch the first dog into space. Laika, meaning 'barker' in Russian, became the first animal to orbit the Earth.

1959 By 1959, the US and the USSR were in a tense space race to see which country could get a spacecraft to the moon; the Russians made it first. The space probe *Luna 2* crash-landed into the moon's surface. It was travelling at such high speed that if humans had been travelling in it, they would have been killed. It was going to be another ten years before a human landed on the moon.

1961 On 12 April 1961, the first man in space was the Russian Cosmonaut Yuri Gagarin. His spacecraft, *Vostok 1*, completed one full orbit of the earth before it crash-landed nearly two hours after the launch.

1961 On 25 May 1961, the American President, John F. Kennedy, set the US a goal of 'landing a man on the moon and returning him safely to the earth' by the end of the decade. Kennedy urged Americans to work diligently to progress with space travel because it 'in many ways may hold the key to our future'.

1962 In February 1962, John Glenn made a historic flight into orbit to make him the first American to orbit Earth.

1963 The first woman in space was the Russian Valentina Tereshkova in 1963.

1966 *Surveyor 1* made the second soft landing on the moon on 30 May, a few months after Russian probe *Luna 9* landed successfully. *Surveyor 1* was NASA's robotic spaceship that collected information to ensure human safety in a moon-landing.

1969 On 20 July 1969, Neil Armstrong made his iconic 'giant leap for mankind' onto the moon's surface and became the first man to walk on the moon. Buzz Aldrin and Michael Collins were also on the *Apollo 11* mission. They flew over 250,000 miles to the moon to utter the words 'the Eagle has landed'.

© NASA

1970 A tragedy was averted after *Apollo 13* suffered an explosion two days into its journey to the moon, when NASA scientists guided the astronauts on board to carry out repairs to bring the damaged spaceship and crew home safely.

1971 The fourth planet of the solar system, Mars, was explored by the Russian space probe *Mars 2*. The probe was made of two parts. One part stayed in orbit for a year and the other crash-landed on Mars and never worked as planned.

TIMELINE · SPACE TRAVEL

1981 The *Columbia* Space Shuttle was the first spacecraft to be used more than once in space travel. It was designed to be reused for up to one hundred space visits, in an attempt to make space travel less expensive.

1986 On 28 January 1986, the Space Shuttle *Challenger* disintegrated shortly after launch due to a fuel system failure. All seven astronauts on board were killed in the tragedy, and all shuttles were grounded for the next three years.

1986 Orbital construction of the *Mir* space station started in 1986, with the final piece being fitted ten years later. The station was built in sections, with each piece launched by a rocket and then joined together in orbit. *Mir* was the first consistently inhabited long-term space station, and was destroyed in 2001 when it burned up as it crashed back to earth.

Space Shuttle *Challenger*

1991 In 1989, Helen Sharman entered a competition to become the first British astronaut in space. The spacecraft left Earth on 18 May 1991 and the mission lasted eight days. She spent most of that time at the *Mir* space station.

2000 In 2000 the first permanent crew moved into the International Space Station (ISS), where crews of astronauts have been living ever since. The station's construction is still not complete and is being updated constantly. It is a very important space station for research and space exploration.

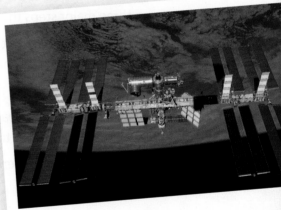

Mir space station

2001 On 28 April 2001, an American millionaire, Dennis Tito, became the first space tourist when he paid approximately $20 million for a journey in the Russian *Soyuz* spacecraft.

2004 *SpaceShipOne* made the first ever privately funded manned space flight. A new airline, Virgin Galactic, was set up to offer private tourist flights into space, using a new version of this space plane.

2014 Virgin Galactic's *SpaceShipTwo* exploded over the Mojave Desert, killing one of the pilots.

Virgin Galactic's *SpaceShipTwo*

2035 In April 2010, American President Barack Obama predicted an asteroid mission by 2025 and an orbital Mars mission by 2035.

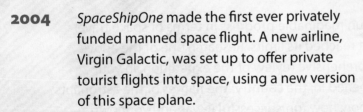

TIMELINE · SPACE TRAVEL

There is no doubt that space travel and systems will continue to develop and become a more integral part of our daily lives and existence. The progress that has been made over the past eighty years is remarkable, and now the future lies before you.

© NASA

Read, write, explore

1 What evidence can you find in the timeline for a space race?

2 What is your impression of the progress that has been made in relation to space travel? Jot down three major steps that have occurred in the timeline of space travel.

3 Discuss with your partner what the next development in space travel should be. Where would you like to see the journey into space take us?

4 Do you think there might be a negative effect of space travel? Discuss with your partner.

5 How did the tragedy of the Space Shuttle *Challenger* bring the dangers of space travel into perspective? Write down three aspects of the danger involved.

6 How important is it to have permanent space stations?

Create

1 The human population has made unimaginable progress in terms of space travel over the last century, but it has not reached its limits. Research one of the above voyages in detail and write a comprehensive review of the expedition. In your review include: the decade it happened in; the country; the names of the astronauts involved; a description of the mission; how (un)successful it was and your own opinion of the expedition.

2 Write a proposal letter to NASA, for you and a specified crew to head up the next mission into space. In your letter you want to outline: **why** you want to go; the **purpose** of the exploratory voyage; **where** your mission is headed in the galaxy; and **what** you need from NASA for your team to succeed.

Preserving 'you' in a time capsule

Before you read

Have you ever heard of Lunar Mission One? Search online for videos on the Lunar Mission One, a private effort aimed at drilling at least twenty metres deep into the moon's south pole.

Lunar Mission One

A key initiative to raise funds to finance the mission is a digital 'memory box' and the opportunity to leave a DNA sample which could last 'a billion years'.

Using innovative technology, Lunar Mission One's aim is to analyse for the first time lunar rock dating back around 4.5 billion years.

To fund the development phase of the project, Lunar Mission One is using the platform *Kickstarter*. Supporters who make pledges to the project via *Kickstarter* will become lifetime members of the Lunar Missions Club. They will have access to a range of information and experiences relating to the project, including the opportunity to have their names inscribed on the lunar landing module.

Kickstarter contributors will also receive rewards including a digital memory box for inclusion in a twenty-first-century time capsule that will be sent to and buried in the moon as part of the mission. A comprehensive record of life on Earth will also be included in the time capsule. This 'public archive' will include a record of human history and civilisation, alongside a species database showing the biodiversity of animals and plants.

Create

1 Imagine that you had the opportunity to include something in Lunar Mission One's time capsule. What would you send and why? Write out the proposal of what you would include and your reasons for it. Include a letter for future generations with five pieces of advice on how to nurture and care for the world around them.

Portfolio 12C

2 Imagine a distant future, some 70,000 years from now, when an extraterrestrial unearths Lunar Mission One's time capsule. Create an 'alien blog' on what you, the extraterrestrial, discover in the time capsule, your opinions on the Earthlings that buried it in the moon's core, and what remains of the planet Earth that is described in the capsule's messages.

Portfolio 12D

Space in fiction

Before you read

Have you ever watched *Star Trek*? With your partner, discuss whether you think *Star Trek* sounds like an appealing TV show and if it is an interesting portrayal of futuristic space travel.

The history of *Star Trek*

Is there anyone out there who has never heard of Mr Spock, the cool half-alien, half-human from *Star Trek*? Or Captain Kirk of the *Starship Enterprise*? They featured as science officer and captain in the long-running series about the *Starship Enterprise* that voyaged in the Milky Way Galaxy around the 2260s.

Gene Roddenberry was the creator of the first *Star Trek* television series. He had the idea of blending TV westerns with science fiction, initially hoping to create a crew of futuristic cowboy types. In the 1960s, TV audiences loved the gunslingers, the independent oddball characters, the wild frontier life and shoot-outs of the imaginary Wild West. Roddenberry put together a unique crew that would voyage in the 'final frontier' left to mankind. He imagined his new science fiction programme as a 'wagon train to the stars'. In the world that Roddenberry created, science would play a huge part. This proved a hit with the early viewers.

The drama of the *Star Trek* series sprang from high-risk adventure and featured an exotic crew of humans, aliens and hybrids. Dark alien antagonists lurked in the universe, backed by sinister uses of science. The first captain, Kirk, exuded charm, took risks and led by example; he was a hero to his crew as he was prepared to break the rules to save the ship. His temper contrasted with the cold logic of Spock, the very practical human-vulcan hybrid. Spock's scientific attitude often led to conflict with the fiery Kirk. However, Spock was trusted for his precision. His characteristic raised eyebrow was his main facial reaction. By contrast, Mc Coy, the ship's doctor, was a very emotional character, quick tempered and stubborn. He was also fiercely loyal and played up his plain approach in a very scientific environment. The show's stars built up a cult of followers, known as trekkies, who would never let *Star Trek* fade from our screens.

From its first episode in 1966, *Star Trek* has survived through six TV series and twelve film versions – for six decades. Every programme of the first series was a complete episode, though just one in a great space odyssey set to last five years. The excitement was upped by the voice-over with the iconic slogan, 'to boldly go where no man has gone before', that preceded each episode.

After 79 episodes the series was cut by television chiefs, but by then it had acquired cult status. Fans in general loved the inventive special effects, while the interplay between the main characters had unexpectedly drawn a large female following. It was campaigning by fans that encouraged *Star Trek: The Motion Picture*, followed by four more 'original series' movies.

Their success let Roddenberry create a new TV series, *Star Trek: The Next Generation*, set eight decades later. The time shift was creative. A huge new starship emerged, inhabited by civilians and scientists, with a bigger star fleet crew. New characters, the blind engineer and the teenage officer, impressed the audience. This series lasted seven years and was followed by the seventh motion picture, *Star Trek Generations*. It provided the back story for how the original *Star Trek* crew handed over to the new crew of the *Next Generation* series. The killing off of Kirk disappointed many trekkies. Three movies followed with a variety of dark forces for the crew to contend with. First was the popular *Star Trek: First Contact* (1996), which featured conflict with the nasty Borg, an alien cyber force that had featured in earlier *Star Trek* history. Its success led to *Star Trek: Insurrection* (1998) and *Star Trek: Nemesis* (2002).

Seven years later, the eleventh film, *Star Trek*, was released (2009). This returned to Kirk and Spock, with new actors, adventuring in an alternative reality due to time travel. Its huge success led to a sequel, *Star Trek Into Darkness* (2013) where the crew returned to deal with terrorism on earth.

The television series continued. *Deep Space Nine* ran from 1993 to 1999. It swapped space voyages for a permanent space station. A parallel series about a lost space ship travelling home through a distance of 70 million light years ran from 1995 to 2001, *Star Trek: Voyager*. This series had a female captain, Katheryn Janeway, and the crew encountered many new alien species. The final TV series in 2001 went back to the pre-Captain Kirk era *Star Trek: Enterprise*. It was the last TV series to be broadcast (from 2001 to 2005). This explored the history of the first space adventures for the *Enterprise*.

Another film is planned – there are simply too many trekkies out there to ignore. More imaginary voyages into new galaxies and time travel await.

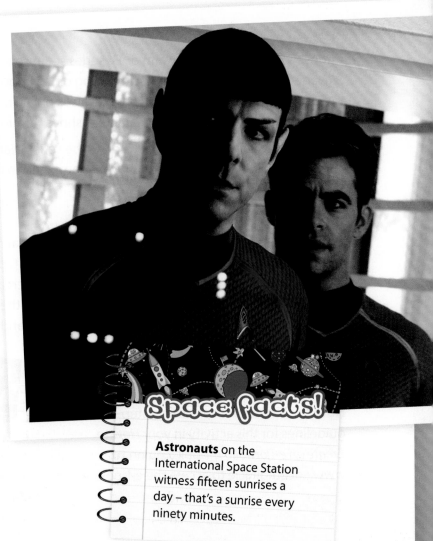

Space facts!

Astronauts on the International Space Station witness fifteen sunrises a day – that's a sunrise every ninety minutes.

Oral exploration

1 What information did you already know?

2 Do you agree that *Star Trek* has an appeal to the general TV audience? Why?

3 Do you think that there is future scope for the *Star Trek* franchise? If so, where could it lead?

Read, write, explore

1 In your own words, what was Gene Roddenberry's aim for the *Star Trek* series?

2 What were the personalities of the three main characters of the original series like?

3 How did Roddenberry come to broadcast the spin-off series, *Star Trek: The New Generation*?

4 What alien race was brought back to the screen in *Star Trek: First Contact*?

5 Using information from the article, construct a timeline for the various television series.

Create

1 Choose a character from any film or TV series set in space and write three entries of a 'Voyage' blog for your character. With a blog on an important voyage, it's essential to include your observations of space, while also conveying your emotions and honest thoughts, so try to walk in your character's shoes through your diary entries.

2 Create your own character for inclusion in the series. Name the character, his/her species and his/her planet of origin. What happened to his/her people and what are the defining traits of his/her people?

3 **Newspaper front page**

Imagine that you are a journalist working for a national newspaper. The 'impossible' has just happened: aliens have made contact with Earth and you have the scoop. The editor-in-chief has asked you to create the front page of the next edition of the newspaper. You must write the main article and an exciting headline, include a sensational photograph and two other minor stories. Use suitable online software to design and create the front page. When you have finished, upload it to your e-Portfolio.

Note for Teachers: You will find step-by-step guidelines for this activity in your *How to Create an e-Portfolio* e-book. Log on to www.edcodigital.ie to access the e-book.

Space facts!

The **sun** is almost perfectly spherical. The diameter of the sun from pole to pole and the diameter of its equator differs by only ten kilometres. A million earths would fit inside the sun.

The Jetsons

Our imagination helps us to reach beyond ourselves. Imagine being alive in 2120. Will modern apps and smart phones be relics of the past? Will people make their own clothes on a 3D printer? After all, our homes are already full of gadgets. An app that lets us see who is ringing our doorbell, even when we're not at home, is no longer far-fetched.

Imagine living in 1962.

It is a time of optimism. Kids play at being astronauts. The moon-landing is another seven years away. Jet packs, rockets, bubble cars, robots and conveyor-belt sidewalks and smart gadgets are all part of the future.

Then Hanna-Barbera creates *The Jetsons*; a futurist animation show of 24 episodes set in 2062 in Orbit City, one of Earth's space cities.

The Jetsons live in Skypad Apartments. The apartments, like the other buildings, rest on adjustable pillars. Both setting and lifestyle seem ultra-modern. The furniture looks space-age. The clothes look cool and informal. Video chat is in use, decades before it is invented for real. The hair-styles are somewhat conventional by contrast.

Daily living is easy, thanks to a vast array of gadgets that save time and effort. It's an exciting material world for the viewer. George Jetson's workday is tedious, but brief. His job at 'Spacely Space Sprockets' is to push a computer button for three hours a day, three days a week. His main complaint is 'push button finger'. Another downside is his boss who is a bit of a tyrant. Many housekeeping chores are seen to by a robot maid, Rosey. Judy Jetson owns a floating electronic diary. People defy gravity in flying bubble cars – thus the American obsession with the family car is carried into the future.

Although it is set in the future, the vision of family is similar to how the family is still portrayed in current TV sitcoms. George Jetson has the job – he is the breadwinner. Jane, his wife, has no job and is the homemaker and leisurely shopper. Their daughter Judy is a typical teenage girl of the time with her mind on boys and how she looks. Their son Elroy is a boy genius who understands the wonders of technology. This suggests that inventing the future is a male-only concern. Typically there is a family dog, Astro. He is futuristic by name, and barks words that begin with R – the dog of the future!

Racial and gender-equality issues that overtake American society in the 1960s soon make the cartoon somewhat dated for that audience. However, after the last episode was aired, *The Jetsons* continued to run on Saturday children's TV for over two decades.

What was the impact of the technology portrayed in *The Jetsons*?

For a TV show created and produced between 1962 and 1987, the technology portrayed in *The Jetsons* had a significant influence on modern twenty-first century society. Many of the technological gadgets used by the futuristic family have since come into modern everyday life, though we may not be flying around in cars which fit into our briefcases like, George Jetson, just yet.

In 1962, it would have been comical to think that the majority of workers would sit behind screens, pushing buttons. Yet, *The Jetsons* predicted the future of micro-technology. They foretold a time when motion sensors, computing power, global networking, communications, advanced military weaponry and other cutting-edge technologies become commonplace. Smart household appliances, a staple in the Jetsons' house, are now part of our everyday lives, allowing people to spend less time on household work.

A couple of examples that appeared in *The Jetsons* are now commonplace technology in our society are:

- **Electronic diary:** Judy used her electronic diary to tell all of her secrets to. Similar devices have now become everyday with smartphones and handheld PCs like iPads.
- **Visaphone:** The visaphone allowed the Jetsons' to communicate via video. In the modern world, this technology is more commonly known as videoconferencing via programmes such as *Skype* and *FaceTime*.

As technologies continue to evolve and change, it is possible that other Jetsons' inventions will be created, and some seemingly absurd inventions will become another technological necessity of our modern lives. Perhaps we will have flying cars some day!

Oral exploration

1 Hanna-Barbera Productions created *The Jetsons* as a futuristic version of what TV programme?

2 Who were the members of the Jetson family?

3 How important is technology in the Jetsons' lives? Give examples from the text.

4 Are you surprised that the TV programme *The Jetsons* was so popular in the 1960s and 1980s?

5 In what ways is the Jetson family similar to a typical modern-day family?

6 *The Jetsons* was initially created for 1962 audiences; in what ways did Hanna-Barbera Productions base their TV programme on stereotypical people's lives?

7 How does the technology featured in the Jetsons' home reflect the domestic technology we are all accustomed to?

8 Could you imagine your life without technology? Discuss five ways in which technology is vital for you.

Read, write, explore

1 Would you have liked to live in Orbit City and been part of the Jetsons' community? Write five points about whether you would like it or not.

2 Do you think it's important that some of the technology imagined for a children's cartoon programme has since come into our daily lives, for example smartphones? Name some TV programmes that can inspire people to invent gadgets for modern life.

Create

Imagine living in Orbit City; list four vital pieces of technology that you think would be necessary for living in space. For each piece of technology, support your reasons for its necessity. You can also imagine new technology that has not been invented yet, but that you could see as an essential for space living.

Space facts!

Jupiter is named after the king of the gods in Roman mythology.

Create a space adventure of your own

How do you create a wild, exciting space adventure? Is it possible to imagine conquering the vastness of the universe without getting lost in space?

The following tips will be of help to you on your tantalising journey into the cosmos:

1 Space is huge

Outer space is unmeasurable! The distances are immense, the radiation outside a solar system is incredibly perilous, and the closer you go to the speed of light, the more your mass increases.

There is limitless potential for your adventure and space exploration in a galaxy of a billion worlds; all you need to do is to put pen to paper and bring them to life.

2 Lightning-quick travel

Vast distances, isolated outposts, undiscovered territories, and alien life-forms are waiting to be explored. Your creative story should recognise the infinite possibilities of where you are headed, and the speed at which your characters will travel.

3 Other civilisations within the galaxy

There are boundless possibilities when it comes to different worlds and civilisations that might exist beyond our planet. So how can you possibly imagine an interstellar civilisation that has not been discovered yet?

It is important to take the following into consideration when imagining the prospects of life-forms and civilisations beyond us earthlings:

···⦚ What do they look like?
···⦚ What language do they speak?
···⦚ How do they travel, especially when it takes centuries to travel from one place to the next?
···⦚ What are they called, and why?
···⦚ Within their galactic empire, do they follow a set of values?
···⦚ How independent or self-sufficient are they?
···⦚ What sort of government do they have?

4 What is your reason for space travel?

If you are willing to risk the dangers that space travel involves, why do you want to go? As an author, you have to incorporate the reasons why your characters are driven to go into the beyond.

Are they naturally curious and belong to NASA or the European Space Agency? Have they dreamt of being an astronaut from an early age? Is Earth in grave danger from other-worldly beings, or has the continuous exploitation of our natural resources put Earth at risk of global flooding, so that we need another planet to exist on if we are to survive?

5 In what year is your story set?

Be aware that you are delving not only into the present, but also the future. Think of the year, century and millennium in which you are space-travelling. Or maybe you want to recreate the space travel that has preceded us.

6 Be bold, but be realistic

As your imagination is in control, you want to create an absorbing story that takes the reader on a journey beyond the page, and beyond our world. Be aware that maintaining a space programme requires a lot of resources, both on Earth and on the space stations in our cosmos, so include the engineers, the astronauts, the educators and the specialists. You are not only writing a story about space travel; you are taking the reader on a journey into space.

You will need to include:

- Mode of transport – how are you travelling into space? And if you are planning on staying up in space to conduct further research and exploration, what is your space station like?
- Time
- Setting
- Characters
- Discoveries – planets, ulterior worlds, extraterrestrial life-forms
- Climax
- Resolution.

Space facts!

Saturn is the sixth planet from the sun. It is the farthest visible planet in our solar system. In 1610, the famous astronomer Galileo Galilei was one of the first to observe Saturn's distinctive rings.

Space facts!

To date, only twelve people have walked on the **moon**.

Your space story

In pairs, plot out your space travel story. Break your story down under the different headings and expand the details of your story. Write your adventure into the beyond using the plotline you developed.

Portfolio 12E

Space facts!

Apart from **Earth**, all the planets in our solar system are named after Greek or Roman mythological figures. Research how other planets got their names.

PowerPoint – Conducting research: a model answer

Poetry Case Study
Seamus Heaney

In this unit you will:

- enjoy reading some poems by Seamus Heaney
- discuss your responses to the poems
- understand the life of the poet through these poems
- prepare and write a response to this collection of poems.

You will encounter the following poems:

- 'Digging'
- from 'Clearances – In Memoriam M.K.H., 1911–1984'
- 'A Kite for Aibhín'
- 'Twice Shy'
- 'Scaffolding'
- 'Who?'

An essay or blog on Seamus Heaney

After you have enjoyed and studied the poems by Heaney in this short anthology, you will be asked to draft and write an essay (two A4 pages) on his poems or write a blog about what you think of his poems. Your aim is to include this writing in your collection of texts for assessment.

Your essay or blog will be the end result of enjoying, thinking about, discussing and noting your responses to the poems.

Before you read

What do you know about the poet Seamus Heaney? Work in groups and collect all your knowledge about the poet, his life and any of his poems you may have read. Then read the following biography.

Portfolio 13A

BIOGRAPHY

Seamus Heaney

Seamus Heaney (1939–2013) was born at his family's farmhouse, Mossbawn in County Derry, in 1939. He was the eldest of nine children. The family later moved to a farm in Bellaghy, a few miles away, and to this day it is still the Heaney family home.

He attended Anahorish Primary School and when he was twelve he won a scholarship to St Columb's College in Derry city. While he was a student there, his brother Christopher, who was four, was killed in a road accident. The poem 'Mid-Term Break' recalls this family tragedy.

During his life as a poet he achieved great fame both in Ireland and throughout the world. His early poetry dealt with the world of his childhood experience in Bellaghy. Later, he addressed the issue of the Troubles in Northern Ireland and produced a body of work that won international acclaim. In 1995 he was awarded the Nobel Prize for Literature.

During his lifetime he was Professor of Poetry at Harvard and at Oxford. In 1996 he was made a 'Commandeur de l'Ordre des Arts et Lettres'. He lived in Sandymount in Dublin until his death in 2013.

His death was mourned by many people in Ireland and across the world. In tribute to him after his death, *The Independent* newspaper described him 'as probably the best-known poet in the world'. On 1 September 2013, two days after his death, a crowd of 80,000 at the All-Ireland football semi-final in Croke Park applauded the late Seamus Heaney for three full minutes. President Michael D. Higgins said: 'what those of us who have had the privilege of his friendship and presence will miss is the extraordinary depth and warmth of his personality.'

Seamus Heaney was brought finally to his home village of Bellaghy and he lies in the same graveyard as his parents, young brother, and other members of the family.

SEAMUS HEANEY *Station Island*

SEAMUS HEANEY *North*

SEAMUS HEANEY *Wintering Out*

SEAMUS HEANEY *Door into the Dark*

SEAMUS HEANEY *Death of a Naturalist*

SEAMUS HEANEY *Seeing Things*

SEAMUS HEANEY *New Selected Poems 1966–1987*

Seamus Heaney *Electric Light*

Seamus Heaney *Human Chain*

Digging

Between my finger and my thumb
The squat pen rests; snug as a gun.

Under my window, a clean rasping sound
When the spade sinks into gravelly ground:
My father, digging. I look down

Till his straining rump among the flowerbeds
Bends low, comes up twenty years away
Stooping in rhythm through potato drills
Where he was digging.

The coarse boot nestled on the lug, the shaft
Against the inside knee was levered firmly.
He rooted out tall tops, buried the bright edge deep
To scatter new potatoes that we picked,
Loving their cool hardness in our hands.

By God, the old man could handle a spade.
Just like his old man.

My grandfather cut more turf in a day
Than any other man on Toner's bog.
Once I carried him milk in a bottle
Corked sloppily with paper. He straightened up
To drink it, then fell to right away
Nicking and slicing neatly, heaving sods
Over his shoulder, going down and down
For the good turf. Digging.

The cold smell of potato mould, the squelch and slap
Of soggy peat, the curt cuts of an edge
Through living roots awaken in my head.
But I've no spade to follow men like them.

Between my finger and my thumb
The squat pen rests.
I'll dig with it.

Oral exploration

1 The poet remembers his father digging potatoes as a younger man twenty years before. Talk about what Heaney admired in the way he worked. Write down words and images that struck you as vivid.

2 What is Heaney's recollection of his grandfather cutting turf? What sort of man was his grandfather? Talk about his qualities as a worker; use information from the poem.

3 How does Heaney feel different from his father and grandfather?

Read, write, explore

1 Read the last three lines again. Heaney's father and grandfather both dug into the earth to gather potatoes or to cut turf. How can Heaney possibly 'dig' with a pen? Recall the meaning of **metaphor** (see page 45, Unit 2) to help you explain how.

   Hint: Think of this question – Into what might Heaney be digging?

2 Heaney compares the pen of the writer to a 'gun' at the beginning of the poem. Can you suggest why he might compare a pen to a gun?

PowerPoint – 'Digging' analysis

Essay or blog

Preparing for my essay or blog

A big theme that struck me in one of the poems – how does the poem bring the theme to life for me?

Portfolio 13B

⋯⟩ Think about the main theme of this poem. Is this an important moment in Heaney's life?

⋯⟩ What is Heaney saying about his life and the direction it will take? Show how he brings the theme to life in the poem. Refer to images.

Make notes in your Portfolio.

Background

This poem recalls the death of Seamus Heaney's mother and the good things he learned during that sad time.

From

Clearances

In Memoriam M.K.H., 1911–1984

In the last minutes he said more to her
Almost than in their whole life together.
'You'll be in New Row on Monday night
And I'll come up for you and you'll be glad
When I walk in the door . . . Isn't that right?'
His head was bent down to her propped-up head.
She could not hear but we were overjoyed.
He called her good and girl. Then she was dead,
The searching for a pulse beat was abandoned
And we all knew one thing by being there.
The space we stood around had been emptied
Into us to keep, it penetrated
Clearances that suddenly stood open.
High cries were felled and a pure change happened.

Oral exploration

1 The poet is remembering the death of his mother whom he loved. What strikes you as sad in the first eight lines of the poem? Does any happy event occur? Discuss how these lines make you feel.

2 Talk about what Heaney has to say about how his father treats his mother at this time. How is it different now that she is dying? Show how, by writing down lines from the poem and discussing them.

3 The poet says 'a pure change happened'. Discuss what he means by this statement.

Read, write, explore

1 Although it is a sad poem, how does the poet find comfort after his mother has gone? Read the last five lines of the poem.

2 Try to explain the idea of 'clearances' as the poet uses it in the final lines of the poem. What can the poet 'keep'?

3 Although the poem is about the death of his mother, the mood at the end is not gloomy. Would you agree with this statement? Why? Why not?

Essay or blog

Preparing for my essay or blog

The effect the poems had on you – things you learned about the world and about yourself.

Portfolio 13C

···⟩ Write down some important things you learned about Seamus Heaney as a poet from reading 'Digging' and 'Clearances'.

···⟩ You may choose to write about any other area if you wish. Be sure to refer to the poems in what you write.

Make notes in your Portfolio.

Background

This poem was written to celebrate the birth of Heaney's second grandchild, Aibhín.

Before you read

What verbs and nouns do you associate with a kite? Give reasons for your choice.

A Kite for Aibhín

After 'L'Aquilone' by Giovanni Pascoli (1855–1912)

Air from another life and time and place,
Pale blue heavenly air is supporting
A white wing beating high against the breeze,

And yes, it is a kite! As when one afternoon
All of us there trooped out
Among the briar hedges and stripped thorn,

I take my stand again, halt opposite
Anahorish Hill to scan the blue,
Back in that field to launch our long-tailed comet.

And now it hovers, tugs, veers, dives askew,
Lifts itself, goes with the wind until
It rises to loud cheers from us below.

Rises, and my hand is like a spindle
Unspooling, the kite a thin-stemmed flower
Climbing and carrying, carrying farther, higher

The longing in the breast and planted feet
And gazing face and heart of the kite flier
Until string breaks and—separate, elate—

The kite takes off, itself alone, a windfall.

Oral exploration

1 Read the poem aloud. Then listen to the audio recording. What do you notice about Heaney's tone when he first catches sight of the kite? Find one other example of joyful feeling in the poem.

2 Check again the meaning of **metaphor**. Do you think the kite could be a metaphor for the newly born child? Say how it might represent the child. Discuss this.

3 Read on from 'As when one afternoon . . .' What is Heaney recalling in the rest of the poem? Pick out verbs that show the kite in flight. Write them down. Try to imagine the movements.

4 Think again about the kite as a metaphor. Now think of the role of the kite flyer. Discuss how Heaney might be talking about the joy of being a parent as the poem comes to its conclusion. What might the breaking string mean?

Read, write, explore

1 Keep the metaphor going! Think about birth and the cutting of the umbilical cord. Write about the final line with this idea in mind.

2 Choose your favourite images from the poem. Write them down. How do they contribute to the poem's mood?

3 There is great emotion shown by Heaney in the poem. Write out one example where this emotion is very obvious. Now name the emotion.

4 In your Portfolio, record all your notes on this poem.

Portfolio 13D

Create – Class blog

You have been working towards writing an essay or a blog. Once you have finished the text for this blog, try setting up your own blog page. When you have finished, upload the blog to your e-Portfolio.

Note for Teachers: You will find step-by-step guidelines for this activity in your *How to Create an e-Portfolio* e-book. Log on to www.edcodigital.ie to access the e-book.

Before you read

In this poem Heaney remembers one of his early walks out with Marie Devlin, a young teacher with whom he was to fall in love and later marry. The title of the poem refers to the proverb, 'Once bitten, twice shy'. Discuss the proverb and try to work out what it means.

Twice Shy

Her scarf *à la* Bardot,[1]
In suede flats for the walk,
She came with me one evening
For air and friendly talk.
We crossed the quiet river,
Took the embankment walk.

Traffic holding its breath,
Sky a tense diaphragm:
Dusk hung like a backcloth
That shook where a swan swam,
Tremulous[2] as a hawk
Hanging deadly, calm.

A vacuum of need
Collapsed each hunting heart
But tremulously we held
As hawk and prey apart,
Preserved classic decorum,
Deployed our talk with art.

Our Juvenilia
Had taught us both to wait,
Not to publish feeling
And regret it all too late –
Mushroom loves already
Had puffed and burst in hate.

So, chary[3] and excited,
As a thrush linked on a hawk,
We thrilled to the March twilight
With nervous childish talk:
Still waters running deep
Along the embankment walk.

[1] **à la Bardot:** wearing a headscarf in the style of Brigitte Bardot, a very beautiful French model and actor;
[2] **tremulous:** nervously excited; [3] **chary:** cautious.

Oral exploration

Talk about the poem using the following prompts and questions.

- Stanza 1 – What two things does he notice about the way she is dressed? Do the young man and the young woman seem to be very close or not?

- Stanza 2 – Do the images suggest that the couple are relaxed? Write down three phrases from the stanza and say what they tell you about how both are feeling.

- Stanza 3 – How do you know that each fancies the other very much? The poet says that they 'held/as hawk and prey apart'. Is this a good metaphor to use in the circumstances? Use a dictionary to find the meanings of 'classic' and 'decorum'. What do the words tell you about how they talked to each other?

- Stanza 4 – What reason is given for both holding back and not rushing into love? Can you work out the meaning of 'Juvenilia' from the rest of the stanza? How does the proverb 'Once bitten, twice shy' fit with this stanza?

- Stanza 5 – What words/phrases in the stanza show their feelings? In your opinion, are they in love yet? Say why. How has the river of stanza 1 become a metaphor in this stanza for their feelings of love for one another?

Read, write, explore

Read the last stanza again. Now imagine that the young couple were planning a future date. Write out a short dialogue that they might have. Include a short description of the setting and a short introduction to the characters.

Portfolio 13E

Before you read

Think about one strong relationship that you have in your life. What makes it strong? Why is it important to you?

Note: This poem was published in the same collection as 'Twice Shy'.

SCAFFOLDING

Masons,[1] when they start upon a building,
Are careful to test out the scaffolding;

Make sure that planks won't slip at busy points,
Secure all ladders, tighten bolted joints.

And yet all this comes down when the job's done
Showing off walls of sure and solid stone.

So if, my dear, there sometimes seems to be
Old bridges breaking between you and me

Never fear. We may let the scaffolds fall
Confident that we have built our wall.

[1] **Masons:** masons build walls and buildings using stone.

Oral exploration

1 Describe the way masons take great care with scaffolding as they prepare to build a wall.

2 Why is the scaffolding taken down in the end? What purpose has it served?

3 In your opinion, who might the person referred to as 'my dear' be?

4 Explain what he means by the metaphor 'old bridges' in the lines:
   '. . . there sometimes seems to be/Old bridges breaking between you and me'.

5 Explain what 'our wall' might mean. Think about the poet's marriage. Have things changed since his first meeting with her in 'Twice Shy'?

6 Can you think of ways we could use other parts of a building as metaphors or similes? For example: roof, window, door, attic or floor.

   Hint: He/she was a roof to shelter me during bad times.

Essay or blog

Writing my essay or blog on Seamus Heaney

Note: Before you write, watch some clips of Heaney reading these poems on the Internet. Combine this experience with what you have learned about the person he is from the poems. Be sure to refer to the poems. Collect your notes on the poems in your Portfolio.

Portfolio 13F

Here are some suggestions as to ways you might choose to write about the poet and the poems:

1 **Seamus Heaney's personality – this is how the poet comes across to me**
   (refer to tone/images)
   Or

2 **Important moments in Heaney's life that I have learned about from his poems**
   Or

3 **My Seamus Heaney blog**

   You may choose to write a personal **blog** on what Seamus Heaney's poems mean to you.

Sample blog

On the next page is a blog written by another Irish writer after he learned that the great poet had passed away. You can model your blog on his but make sure to mention some of the poems you know.

Portfolio 13G

•••⟫ Write your essay or blog in your Portfolio.

•••⟫ Don't forget to check out **The basic steps for writing an essay** on page 192 for more help with writing your piece.

Writing Blog

home   **blog**   work   photos   links   contact   [   ] search

What was it about Seamus Heaney that endeared him to so many?

Tears came instantly to my eyes when I heard about Seamus Heaney's death.

To many Ireland's greatest ever poet – certainly the one who connected most with the ordinary folk who make up the majority of the populace – Heaney died at the age of 74 today following a brief illness.

I learned of it, as so many people learn of so many things these days, on Twitter. Someone posted a link that looked all wrong. 'BBC News: Seamus Heaney Obituary' it read.

It looked all wrong. It felt wrong. I pressed the link, hoping and, if I'm honest, half-expecting it to have been caused by some unexplained kink in technology.

My immediate reaction, when I reflect on it now, a couple of hours later, was clearly one of grief. When the truth became apparent, tears sprang instantly to my eyes.

Since then I've been trying to explain it to myself. Why was Heaney so universally loved and cherished? Here's what I've come up with:

– I never met him, but I felt like I knew him well.

– His smile was always warm; never was there a sign of artifice.

– His humility was always genuine; never, ever, was there a hint of conceit.

– His voice. Oh, we should be glad for the wonders of technology, because his voice can exist forever and a day. What an incredible voice.

– His clarity. Whereas a certain diligence or the aid of footnotes might be required for a spell with Yeats, Heaney seemed to speak to everyone. The potency of 'Mid Term Break', say, was immediately apparent to my eight-year-old self and remains undimmed three decades on. There was no obfuscation.[1] Like Patrick Kavanagh, even more than Kavanagh, Heaney chipped the essence of existence out of the seemingly banal.

Heaney's work touched so many, even those otherwise indifferent to poetry. That, the gift of cerebrally connecting with the masses, is surely one of the hallmarks of the great artist.

Looking at Heaney from afar, he never seemed to be interested in art for art's sake. With him, it felt that art was life, and life was art.

The solace, because in art there is always solace, is that in his death Heaney will find thousands of new readers, and his words will seduce most of them too. Over half a century or so, Heaney has built an altar that will attract worshippers for many more half-centuries to come.

Ar dheis Dé go raibh a anam dílis.

---

[1] **obfuscation:** making the message confusing.

International Short Stories

In this unit you will:

···> read stories from different cultures

···> explore the unique, imaginative worlds of three short stories

···> write your opinion of the truth within each story

···> link to your previous knowledge of plot, use of language, character, dialogue and theme

···> be challenged to produce a variety of creative pieces

···> learn how to carry out a step-by-step comparison analysis of short stories using the table and template in your Portfolio.

You will encounter the following stories:

● 'Oliver Has an Interview' by Mark Yeow

● 'Professor Panini' by Matthew Grigg

● 'The Imperfectionist' by Paul Sohn

Worlds of wonder

Before you start

The stories you will read in this unit have an original approach to the short story form. They have a tight structure and take you on an interesting journey of the imagination. The writers use language in adventurous ways. For example, in 'The Imperfectionist', Paul Sohn, a student writer, uses the language of athletics to trigger a plot that centres on a date.

Neil Gaiman, British novelist

'Short stories are tiny windows into other worlds and other minds and other dreams.'

We get this idea clearly in all stories in this unit, for instance when Oliver 'tumbled into his bathtub in a flurry of feathers and talons' in Mark Yeow's story.

Nam Le, Australian writer

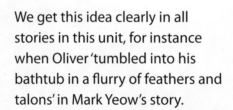

'Art, after all, is – at its best – a lie that tells us the truth.'

The Vietnamese-born Australian writer Nam Le has an interesting view of short stories. He believes that a short story may be created by the imagination, but it reveals the truth about some aspect of life. That's why it is worth **exploring the theme** of each short story.

'A short story must have a single mood and every sentence must build towards it.'

Edgar Allan Poe, American author

Comparing stories

At the end of this unit, you will write a comparison on any two short stories featured in *Crescents*. You will create this by reflecting on how the writers deal with openings, narrator, main characters, crisis, tension, climax and description. You will can also reflect on and explore the **mood and impact of endings** of short stories, as mentioned in Poe's statement.

Magic realism

Mark Yeow

Mark Yeow is from Sydney, Australia. He writes in many genres, such as speeches, feature articles and children's books. He was a *Sydney Morning Herald* young writer of the year regional winner when he was in high school. Mark has played in national youth orchestras and built sixty computers over many hours (but not all at once).

Mark Yeow

Background

The following story is set in Tokyo, Japan. Have a look at these photos. What do they tell you about the city and what it would be like to live in it?

Capsule hotel, Asakusa, Tokyo

Crowd waiting for a subway train on the Yamanote line in Tokyo

Pedestrians stroll across Shibuya crossing. This is one of the world's most well-known examples of a scramble crosswalk

Tokyo skyline

Ueno Park in Tokyo

Oliver Has an Interview

As soon as he had finished his résumé, which was very late, Oliver opened his bathroom window, turned into a hawk, and took off into the depths of Ueno Park. He soared between high-rise towers, their office lights still toiling away to keep each cubicle safe and illuminated. He glided over the train tracks and taxicab-queues made small by distance, the icy coo of the wind flowing past his ears and eyeballs. Flocks of pigeons and the odd crow greeted him as he wafted past, unafraid because they knew that despite his appearance Oliver was entirely amicable and always ate before he went flying. He settled down in the park's enclosure where the Bear was waiting.

'How's things?' asked the Bear, who had lived in the park zoo for almost a decade.

'I've been working on my résumé,' Oliver said as his beak slumped into his chest. 'It's for an administrative position at Tamago Mobile – one of my old classmates does business with them and suggested I apply. My interview is tomorrow morning.'

'What's a résumé?' asked the Bear, cleaning her nails with her teeth. 'It sounds like a fish . . . and a delicious one at that.'

'A résumé is a list of all the important things you've done in your life and what you've learned from them,' Oliver explained. 'But I've never had a job outside of handing out pamphlets at university, and the only thing I learned from that was to hold them far out so that people won't push you out of their way. How do I even have a chance with so little life behind me?'

'It's always hard starting out,' the Bear said. 'You know how I got to be at the zoo? These poachers would put eight cubs in a cage and the last one standing got sold to a trader who then sold them to the municipal council. It sounds like pretty much the same thing here. All you have to do is find a way to show that you are their obvious and only choice.'

'I'd like to think I can,' said Oliver, 'but I can't even kill a pigeon, let alone a bear.'

'It's a metaphor,' the Bear said. 'Trust me – when the time comes, you'll know what to do. And if you don't, then the time's not right just yet.'

Oliver and the Bear talked for a long time about Oliver's career hopes, the food at the zoo (which the Bear opined[1] to have improved in both taste and antibiotic efficacy), and the biologically-unlikely romance between the resident otter and one of the more comely pigeons. Oliver updated the Bear on the latest uproar in the Diet, which had begun when the Parliamentary Secretary lobbed some choice remarks about visiting the Yasukuni Shrine as well as a half-full bottle of Yebisu, at the Shadow Treasurer. They traded critiques of last week's outdoor performance of *Hamlet* (which the Bear had thought somewhat lacklustre but Oliver had rather enjoyed). By the time they parted company, Oliver was so tired that when he got home he curled up in a ball on his windowsill and fell asleep instantly.

*   *   *   *

Oliver woke a few hours later at half past eight.

I'm late! was his first thought, and he tumbled into his bathtub in a flurry of feathers and talons. There was barely any time for him to get to Odaiba by ten o'clock when his interview was scheduled to begin. Oliver changed back into a human and winced as his limbs collided with the sides of the tub. In his university days he had crammed it full of second-hand textbooks, and spent most of his time studying in the bathroom using the sink as a makeshift desk and a repurposed noodle-cup to hold his stationery. His apartment was small even by Tokyo standards – it was the best he could afford with his inheritance. Once, when he'd been a child, Oliver had visited a distant uncle's penthouse in Roppongi which was bigger than his current building's entire floor. He had gawped at the airy spaces and the way he could look down on the cars like so many motes of dust. He dreamt of one day living in such an eyrie[2] of glass and steel, but that had been before he learned to fly. Sometimes, after a day of mailing applications and trawling online job forums, he would transform and waddle around on his talons until he went to bed. Things felt bigger, and happier, when he was a hawk. He swore as he stumbled around looking for his old university blazer and his friend's tie. He grabbed his two copies of his résumé and scampered out the door, the clock tower in Ueno Park clanging in punctual condemnation.

'Ginza Line closed' said the sign. Through the glass, Oliver could see fluorescent officials moving their mouths in silent syncopation. The side-streets were packed with cars and taxis. It was nine o'clock, the peak of peak hour. Oliver waved frantically at the bus that was about to submerge into traffic and flopped through the doors like a salmon in heat just before they shut.

'Ticket,' the bus-driver barked at Oliver who only now realised that his wallet was still on his bedside table where he had left it before flying to the park. He was teetering on the edge of the door, collar starting to smoke with little prickles of shame, when he heard the tinkling of metal and wings rustling like newspapers in the breeze. He turned, looked down, and found exactly ¥320 spinning to a stop on the bitumen.[3] When he looked up, he saw the silhouette of a crow blurring into flight behind him as it rose back out of the neon river and into the sky. Enough cash to get him to Odaiba, but time was less abundant.

Oliver's feet trembled as the interchange came into sight, getting ready to scurry to his connecting ride. The number 16 bus was held up by the sheer weight of people pouring into it. He edged his way through, mumbling *sumimasen* at every suit-shelled back in front of him. The bus was almost within reach when a paunchy salaryman pulled him aside. Oliver spun like a hare bounding gracefully into a glass pane, frantically trying to get his bearing in the ocean of jackets – and the doors had closed. Oliver goggled at the bus as it spat a clump of pachinko-ball smoke in his face and crawled away. His right hand dropped and two gutted résumés drifted up into the sky like feathers cast off from a fledgling's moulting plumage.

Then Oliver began to run. He sprinted past the bus without a glance. His limbs no longer flailed like a stuck carp. There was a sudden fierceness and poise to his movements that made people stare and shirk from his path, as though beholding a dread warlord exhumed from the city's past. He ran faster and faster, cars honking and screeching as he cut between them. His arms and legs and whole body began to blur, as though even the air was having trouble keeping pace. Then in mid-step the boy was gone and the hawk shot into the open sky, catching a scrap of bullet-pointed paper in its beak as it soared away. What might have seemed like the whole of Tokyo craned their necks upwards as the bird rose and rose until it seemed to stop suspended below a cloud. Then it curled around and arrowed away, impossibly fast, toward the South-West of the city.

'Apparently human young suffer from impaired cognitive function in the mornings,' the Bear was telling the crow as they shared a discarded egg muffin. 'Something to do with hormones and their circadian rhythms, I read it in a copy of *Science* which they lined the cage with once. ¥320 should get him to Odaiba, or have they raised the prices since last July?'

'He'll be okay, won't he?' asked the crow. 'You think he'll be okay?'

'I suspect everyone is, in time,' said the Bear, 'but my experience of these matters is admittedly rather limited.'

*   *   *   *

From his office overlooking the water, Mr Junichiro sighed and rested his forehead in his palms. He had been interviewing candidates for the past two days and although it was an unspectacular position, he and his board had hoped to find someone remotely inspiring. The firm was in trouble, despite what the *Wall Street Journal* had written only weeks before – it needed new blood, with the courage to wrest power from his ageing fingers. But every man who walked in wore the same suit, and presented the same grade-points in the same word-processor template with the same crisp solicitude. The overflow of qualifications had only served to make Mr Junichiro nauseous. This stock of youth was weak. He prayed for the company, but even more so that this day would pass quickly.

There was a cry, almost avian[4] in its harshness. Mr Junichiro opened one eye. A moment later, his door was flung open by a young man who was entirely naked except for a piece of paper held extremely immodestly in one hand. Mr Junichiro opened his other eye and sat up slowly. The young man dropped the talon-torn paper on the desk and settled in the chair opposite.

'You are?' Mr Junichiro asked.

The young man pointed at the clock on Mr Junichiro's desk. 'On time,' he said.

[1] **opined:** stated as her opinion; [2] **eyrie:** a large nest of an eagle or other bird of prey, built high in a tree or on a cliff; [3] **bitumen:** a tarred road; [4] **avian:** bird-like.

Oral exploration

1 There are numerous Japanese references in the text. Find the words in the text which mean the following:

- controversial war memorial that commemorated both heroes and war criminals
- a brand of Japanese beer
- a large artificial island in Tokyo Bay, Japan
- Japanese parliament
- 'excuse me' in Japanese
- name for a middle-class businessman in Japan.

2 Discuss these points with a partner:

- List the different locations used for the story.
- Who is the central character and how many forms does he take?
- Why are birds such as the crow not afraid of Oliver as a hawk?
- What do you find surprising when Oliver arrives at the zoo?
- What features of the very modern city of Tokyo are highlighted?
- Mention some moments when Oliver changes form.
- What sudden help does Oliver get with his bus fare?
- Why is Mr Junichiro so dissatisfied with 'the stock of youth'?
- In your view, in which setting does the most important event happen and why? Oliver's room, the zoo, the city or Mr Junichiro's office?
- What word in the opening sentence connects to the final image of 'talon-torn paper'?

3 This story is an example of **magic realism**. Discuss what you think magic realism is.

A note from the author

Mark Yeow sent this email to the readers of *Crescents*.

Email   Send/Receive   Reply   Reply All   Forward

Email

Dear reader,

My writing has been influenced by other authors. I draw a lot on Japanese author Haruki Murakami for magic realism in the suburban setting of Tokyo. Nick Harkaway and Nam Le have inspired my approach to dialogue. It doesn't really sound like stuff people would say in real life, but that makes it all the more powerful.

I guess my biggest influences are the places I've visited and the people I've spoken to: Ueno Park was where I spent my first trip to Japan, for example.

When I wrote 'Oliver Has an Interview', a lot of my friends were graduating or seeking their first jobs at the time, and I was privy to a lot of their struggles – largely because, as someone lucky enough to be in work since a few years before graduating, I was considered some sort of expert on getting a professional job. Job applications, particularly those weird psychometric tests and group interviews, strike me as a rather ingenious mode of torture for young people. I wanted to evoke some of the stresses and doubts that a lot of my friends were feeling as they went through the process – even though, much like Oliver, they often had amazing and entirely unique gifts which the system just didn't recognise.

Tokyo, of course, is well-known for its pressure cooker approach to applying for jobs. I also, I think, wanted to explore how one person can have many different skins, and whether that makes them different people or the same. I wasn't thinking of identity crises at the time, but they are a recurring theme in my work which I've discovered more recently.

To summarise: 'Oliver Has an Interview' was a story to encourage my friends, and myself, to rise above their difficulties, to fly, because I know they can.

Mark Yeow

Read, write, explore

1 The author

Choose one thing that Mark Yeow states in his email that is reflected in his story. Explain.

2 The worlds of the story

···› It is possible to look at the text as having various worlds: human, animal and avian?

···› How does Oliver link those worlds for the reader?

···› Compare what it is like in those three worlds and say which one you'd prefer to live in and why.

···› What views do the bear and the crow express about Oliver?

···› Write one criticism and one positive thing about Oliver as you see him.

Create

1 Write a brief **recommendation** for the story for an imaginary website called 'Storyadvisor'. Focus mainly on the mood created at the end of the story and how well the author built up to it. Write your review in the 'Storyadvisor' template in your Portfolio.

Portfolio 14A

2 Imagine that you are a tour guide in Tokyo. Write the three-minute talk you would give your touring group before you let them off on an unattended walkabout in the city – base it purely on the contents of this story.

3 The author has left the ending up to your imagination. Imagine the final phase of the story takes place next morning as a conversation in Ueno Park. The bear wants to know the details of the interview, and Oliver wants the bear's advice about whether to take the job offer as an administrator.

Portfolio 14B

Create – Comic strip

Mark Yeow stated in his email that the reason he wrote 'Oliver Has an Interview' was to encourage his friends to 'rise above their difficulties, to fly'. Use Toondoo or another suitable online program to create a comic strip based on advice to friends. You must think of at least three of the most helpful pieces of advice you have ever received and include them in the comic strip, which you will create from scratch. When it's complete, share it with your group or with the class, then upload it to your e-Portfolio.

Note for Teachers: You will find step-by-step guidelines for this activity in your *How to Create an e-Portfolio* e-book. Log on to www.edcodigital.ie to access the e-book.

Science fiction

Matthew Grigg

Matthew Grigg comes from North Yorkshire in England. The following story imagines what happens when a high-tech experiment goes wrong. Recently the astrophysicist Professor Stephen Hawking warned that the development of artificial intelligence could spell the end of the human race. Hawking's point is that robots will eventually evolve faster than biological species. He predicts that robots could become self-aware and take over from humanity. Decide for yourself whether the author of the next story is warning us about artificial intelligence or just amusing us with a funny tale.

Before you read

As a class, recall films and stories that feature a mad inventor. List and rank the class's favourite five.

Professor Panini

Before my many years' service in a restaurant, I attended a top science university. The year was 2023 and I was finishing the project that would win me my professorship. In the end, it resulted in my becoming a kitchen employee.

My forty-second birthday had made a lonely visit the week before, and I was once again by myself in the flat. Like countless other mornings, I ordered a bagel from the toaster. 'Yes, sir!' it replied with robotic relish, and I began the day's work on the project. It was a magnificent machine, the thing I was making – capable of transferring the minds of any two beings into each other's bodies.

As the toaster began serving my bagel on to a plate, I realised the project was in fact ready for testing. I retrieved the duck and the cat – which I had bought for this purpose – from their containers, and set about calibrating the machine in their direction. Once ready, I leant against the table, holding the bagel I was too excited to eat, and initiated the transfer sequence. As expected, the machine whirred and hummed into action, my nerves tingling at its synthetic sounds.

The machine hushed, extraction and injection nozzles poised, scrutinizing its targets. The cat, though, was suddenly gripped by terrible alarm. The brute leapt into the air, flinging itself onto the machine. I watched in horror as the nozzles swung towards me; and, with a terrible, psychedelic whirl of colours, felt my mind wrenched from its sockets.

When I awoke, moments later, I noticed first that I was two feet shorter. Then, I realised the lack of my limbs, and finally it occurred to me that I was a toaster. I saw immediately the solution to the situation – the machine could easily reverse the transfer – but was then struck by my utter inability to carry this out.

After some consideration, using what I supposed must be the toaster's onboard computer, I devised a strategy for rescue. I began to familiarise myself with my new body: the grill, the bread bin, the speaker and the spring mechanism. Through the device's rudimentary eye – with which it served its creations – I could see the internal telephone on the wall. Aiming carefully, I began propelling slices of bread at it. The toaster was fed by a large stock of the stuff, yet as more and more bounced lamely off the phone, I began to fear its exhaustion.

*   *   *   *

Toasting the bread before launch proved a wiser tactic. A slice of crusty wholemeal knocked the receiver off its cradle, and the immovable voice of the reception clerk answered. Resisting the urge to exclaim my unlikely predicament, I called from the table: 'I'm having a bit of trouble up here, Room 91. Could you lend a hand?'

'Certainly, sir. There's a burst water pipe on the floor above, I suppose I'll kill two birds with one stone and sort you out on the way.'

The clerk arrived promptly, leaving his 'caution, wet floor' sign in the corridor. He came in, surveying the room in his usual dry, disapproving fashion. I spoke immediately, saying I was on the intercom, and requested that he simply press the large button on the machine before him. 'This one, sir?' he asked, and before I could correct him, the room was filled with a terrible, whirling light, and he fell to the ground.

A minute later he stood up again, uncertainly, and began moving in a manner that can only be described as a waddle. The duck, meanwhile, was scrutinising the flat with an air of wearied distaste. I gazed at the scene with dismay. Suddenly an idea struck the clerk, and with avian glee he tottered towards the window. I spluttered a horrified warning to no avail. He leapt triumphantly from the balcony, spread his 'wings' and disappeared. I would have wept, but managed only to eject a few crumbs.

*   *   *   *

Hours of melancholy calculation and terrible guilt gave no progress, and left me with a woeful regret for the day's events. Determined not to give up hope, I began to burn clumsy messages into slices of bread, and slung these desperate distress calls through the window. I sought not only my own salvation, but also to account for the bizarre demise of the clerk, who must no doubt have been discovered on the street below. I soon found my bread bin to be empty, and sank again into a morose meditation.

A large movement shocked me from my morbid contemplation. Before me, having clambered up from the floor, stood my own body. It regarded me with dim cheer.

'I have been upgraded,' it announced in monotone. The room was silent as I struggled to cope with this information. Then: 'Would you like some toast?'

The truth dawned on me, and I wasted no time in seeing the utility of this revelation. I informed the toaster, which was now in control of my body, that I wished it to fetch help. It regarded me warily, then asked if I would like that buttered. Maintaining patience, I explained the instruction more thoroughly. I watched with surreal anticipation as my body of forty-two years jerked its way out of the flat. It rounded the corner, and there was a hope-dashing crash. It had tripped up on the 'caution, wet floor' sign. To my joyous relief, however, I heard the thing continue on its way down the corridor.

Minutes passed, then hours. I entertained myself flicking wheat-based projectiles at the cat. On the dawn of the third day, I concluded that the toaster had failed in its piloting of my body, and that help was not on its way. Gripped by the despair of one who must solve the puzzle of toaster suicide, I resigned myself to my fate.

Pushed on by a grim fervour, I began igniting the entire stock of bread. As the smoke poured from my casing, and the first hints of deadly flame flickered in my mechanisms, I began the solemn disclosure of my own eulogy.

Suddenly the fire alarm leapt into action, hurling thick jets of water across the flat, desperate to save its occupants. A piercing wail erupted from all sides, and a squabbling mixture of annoyance, relief and curiosity filtered into my mind.

*   *   *   *

Once the firemen had visited and deactivated the alarm, I was identified as the fault, unplugged and hauled away to a repair shop. The staff there, finding nothing to remove but a faulty speech chip, apparently put me up for sale. I only know this because, on being reconnected to the mains, I found myself in a shiny, spacious kitchen. Missing my electronic voice, I could only listen to the conversation of the staff, discussing the odd conduct of their new cook. The end of their hurried discussion heralded his arrival. I gazed at the door in silent surrender, as my body stepped proudly on to the premises, displaying its newly designed menu. At the top of the list I could discern 'Buttered bagel'.

Oral exploration

Here are 20 questions on the story. Divide the class into groups of four, each taking 10 questions, the odd and even ones alternately. Discuss these questions in your group, then share your answers with the class.

1 What different locations are used for the story?

2 Who is the central character and how many forms does he take?

3 What other characters have a role in the story?

4 What was the special capability of the machine the narrator was making? See the second paragraph.

5 Why was the narrator too excited to eat his bagel?

6 Is the cook referred to in the final paragraph a new character? Explain your answer.

7 Mention some moments when characters change form.

8 What was the narrator's cleverest tactic after his transformation?

9 Explain what happens to the clerk.

10 Is there evidence that the toaster becomes self-aware?

11 Do you think that the narrator is satisfied at the end of the story?

12 In your view, what is the most important event that happens and why?

13 Do you think that the narrator remains a scientist at heart despite being a kitchen employee? Explain.

14 Did the narrator ever become a professor? Do you like the title of the story?

15 What are the signs that the narrator's human body was turned into a toaster?

16 What was the main disadvantage for the narrator in being turned into a toaster?

17 Do you think the way the narrator sent out the distress calls was clever?

18 Who do you think took the narrator to the toaster repair shop?

19 Describe how the narrator was reunited with his former body.

20 Does the narrator accept his fate or fight against it? Explain.

Read, write, explore

Work in groups of four. Each group should focus on one of the four headings below. Each group should elect a reporter to share its answers with the class in a class feedback and discussion session. As you listen to each group's feedback, make notes in your 'Professor Panini' summary sheet in your Portfolio.

Portfolio 14C

Group 1: The world of the story

1 Describe the situation of the narrator at different stages of the story.

2 What do you expect from the story when you see the date that is mentioned in the opening?

3 Select at least three phrases or details that show the narrator lives in a futuristic world.

4 The story is about a science experiment that went wrong. Can you name any similar stories?

Group 2: The plot

1 List the main events of the plot structure in a series of boxes linked by arrows. Use one of the following terms as a heading above the event in each box: trigger event, complication, crisis, problem, turning point, climax.

2 Would you agree that the entire story is an explanation of the opening sentence?

3 What unplanned event changed the course the experiment was meant to follow?
Hint: Explore the cat.

4 What sudden help does the narrator get that actually doesn't help him?
Hint: Firemen.

5 Would you agree that the closure contains a twist that rounds off the story well? Explain.

Group 3: Theme(s) of the story

High-tech science has given the narrator a new body, a toaster, to inhabit. The whole story is based on an imaginative lie, but it contains important truths for the reader.

1 To what extent is the story a warning about the dangers of trusting technology too much?

2 Would you agree that the story shows you can plan what should happen but not predict what will happen? Explain, with particular reference to the transfer sequence.

3 Do you know of any other story to which this theme applies? Write a paragraph that links the two.

Group 4: Language and dialogue

One of the many meanings of irony is that human plans do not go according to plan. Irony is a noun, ironic is an adjective and ironically is an adverb. Use one of these words in your answers if you can.

1 Do you regard the title 'Professor Panini' as a good one for this story about a kitchen employee? **Hint:** think of the toaster, the menu and the university project.

2 Is there anything that could be considered humorous in the first two paragraphs?

3 Would you describe the tone of the story as anxious, hopeful or detached at different times? Use one example of each to demonstrate.

4 The dialogue between the toaster and the narrator's previous human self is amusing. Select one example to show this.

Tone and images

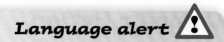

Language alert

1 From the way a narrator expresses himself/herself a reader can detect the emotions they feel towards events. When a narrator doesn't show emotion, even though they may cause a reader to feel emotion, the tone is said to be detached.

Fill in the blanks from the following extract in order to gain a fuller understanding. The missing words have been changed from those in the story. Match up the most appropriate words. Some of the letters in the missing words have been filled in already to help you.

> Hours of **s**_____ ____**ing** and terrible guilt gave no progress, and left me with an _____ **sh**_____ at the day's events. Determined not to give up hope, I began to burn clumsy messages into slices of bread, and _____ these desperate **p**_____ through the window. I sought not only my own _____, but also to account for the **u**_____ **d**_____ of the clerk, who must no doubt have been discovered on the street below. I soon found my bread bin to be empty, and sank again into a **g**_____ **r**_____.
>
> A large movement shocked me from my _____ **t**_____.

gloomy, thinking, thoughts, downfall, moody, threw, reflection, intense, shame, sad, rescue, unusual pleas for help.

2 Rank these images in order (1–4) of how much amusement you got from them, with 1 being the highest score. Write one reason for your ranking in each case.

- the cat attacking the machine ☐
- SOS toast slices ☐
- the waddling clerk full of avian glee ☐
- a human with the mechanical movements of a toaster. ☐

Create

1 Kitchen employee Panini applies for a job as assistant professor to Stephen Hawking. Use all the information available in the story and your imagination to complete his résumé in your Portfolio.

Portfolio 14D

2 Think of the **ending of the story**. Write an alternative ending to the story starting from the point when he sees his body in front of him and realises he's not in it.

Stephen Hawking

Comedic fiction

Paul Sohn

Paul Sohn is a Korean-Canadian/American writer. He wrote this award-winning story when he was a sixteen-year-old secondary level student. The title is 'The Imperfectionist', but it could also be called 'Ready. Set. First date'. What do you think the story is about?

The Imperfectionist

Breakfast at Tiffany's, *Love Story* and *Ghost* aren't just movies I occasionally hear my parents talk about over the dinner table. With a faithful notebook and a limited-edition *Shrek* pen, sitting cross-legged on the lounge-room sofa with a pink marshmallow in my mouth, staring rather intensely at the television screen, I study the films. Scribbling notes I pump up the volume with an extended right leg and big toe gently tapping the positive end of the volume button on my remote control.

Extensive 'love notes' fill up the pages of my notebook.

And as the sound of Audrey Hepburn's sugary voice is replaced by my mother's screaming 'LOWER THE VOLUME', my hope grows for the coming Saturday.

Excitement builds as I look down at my completed notes.

Ready. Set. First date.

Combing my hair, not that it does much, I look at the most truthful object in the world and see my lack of perfection. From head to toe, I'm full of surprises. Size-sixteen feet and brown, tight-curled hair resembling an old fuzzy woollen jumper give me the distinct Australopithecus[1] appearance.

Known at school as quite the nerd, I'm cautious in everything I do. 'Imperfection leads to embarrassment' has been my lifelong motto.

Why?

Because I read in a book once that 'future is fear when it's unknown, but joy when it's clear' so planning has directed my life toward joy.

Zach Mawson, aged seventeen. I am a perfectionist, and proud of it.

A gentle vibration and four loud beeps is all it takes to get my heart rate up and my brain going on vacation to a fantasy dream world. Testosterone levels peak. I almost drown in it.

Hi Zach ~ I'll c u today
in front of the cinemas
at the promised time.
C ya soon! – Zoe

The thing that really drives me crazy, apart from the fact I'm going on my first date, is the squiggle after my name. I can imagine her calling me, with her breathy intonation: 'Oh Zaaaaaach, ah ~ '

While Strathfield Station passes me as a mere blur, my vision transfers from the train window to the kissing couple in front of me. I avoid looking at them, and decide to continue my 'studies'. I revise the notes, taking extra care to pay attention to the highlighted dot points, but for some reason I am constantly distracted by the couple in front.

If only that was me and Zoe . . .

I arrive at the cinemas in a rush, three minutes late. I cry in joy when I discover that my goddess hasn't arrived yet. My good friend Billy told me that the rudest thing a guy could do on his first date with a girl was to be late.

Five minutes later I am Saul on his way to Damascus.[2] Zoe makes certain that I know she has arrived by confronting me like a blinding light that stuns me momentarily. Like Saul, I instantly become a believer, though in a more secular sense.

At once, I put into action note number one.

#1: Don't look like a total idiot when you first see her; best to look as though your attention has been momentarily distracted.

I whip out my phone and pretend to be in the middle of a very important call. When she comes within talking distance, I pretend I haven't seen her, count to three, look up, give her the most stupid, fake surprised look ever and mouth the word 'sorry' to her.

'It's okay,' she replies silently.

When I realise that talking on the phone is also rude, I stop my one-man show with my phone and greet my angel properly.

'Oh I'm so sorry, that was . . .' I look around for something to say. Anything! Luckily, I see a Toyota Camry cruising by. I finish my sentence, 'Toyota.'

'Toyota?' asks my inquisitive little angel, surprised and impressed simultaneously. 'You have a car?'

'Sure do,' I lie, pointing a finger at the sky, giving the most matter-of-fact pose possible. 'They called up about the repairs and when I can pick my car up.'

After a minute or two of pointless conversation, she grabs my left arm. 'Anyway, I'm so sorry. Did you wait long? My train was delayed.'

Study plays its role.

#2: Make her empathise with you.

'Maybe thirty minutes? Not that long.'

I massage my thighs to show I've been waiting for ages. Her grip on my left arm strengthens and her expression becomes sincere.

'Oh I'm so sorry . . . but you know that it's only ten-past three now, don't you? I'm only ten minutes late!'

Darn, she's in control of the situation now.

Fool. Why did I have to say thirty minutes? Ten or fifteen would've sufficed.

I try to regain my optimism. At least I wasn't late.

She tugs on my sleeve and we enter the cinemas together. Surprised that I've come this far, I find myself wearing a delayed smile.

Inside the theatre, we are like an old, comfortable couple.

Eye contact becomes frequent. The double ice cream we share is as chilly as the horror movie we watch, but at the same time, as sweet as Zoe herself. I wait for the right time and place my hand over hers. It doesn't stay there for long, however, as I shield my eyes from watching the next scene. I hate ghosts.

By the end of the horror experience I walk out of the cinema half cursing and half thanking the Japanese for their brilliance in the genre. And for creating horror movies that make girls cuddle up close.

Feeling somewhat more comfortable and in control, we head outside of the cinemas.

#3: Make her feel important by asking about her. However, be careful not to overdo it.

'Do you have any siblings?' I ask on the way to dinner. 'Or is it just you?'

'I have six brothers and eight sisters,' she says. After she observes my jaw dropping in disbelief, she continues, 'Just joking! I have one younger brother.'

A minute of awkward silence follows where I try to identify if this joke was meant to be funny or lame. Note number four is stuck in my head.

#4: If she says something you don't like, something lame or something you don't agree with, don't argue or embarrass her. Just go with the flow.

I decide it was meant to be funny.

'Gosh Zoe, you should do stand-up!' I bellow aloud as if I really, truly mean it.

Fool.

Her expression tells me everything.

She stares at me for a while and smiles a smile that really isn't one. She punches me lightly on my arm. 'I know that wasn't funny, Zach.'

Hostility like a nimbus cloud above us, we walk into the restaurant and take a seat. I quietly excuse myself to go to the bathroom.

Nope, no nose hairs sticking out . . . breath doesn't smell . . . oops, hair's a bit out of place . . .

I check the next points on my list with the sub-heading 'At Dinner'.

#5: Impress her by appearing knowledgeable when ordering your food.

#6: Make her laugh at your clever jokes.

#7: When eating, moderation is the order of the day. Don't eat too fast but don't eat too slowly.

#8: When receiving the bill, don't lose your cool.

With them fresh in my mind, I return to my table. I decide to surprise her from behind to change the atmosphere. The glow from when I first met her hasn't gone and my pupils contract as I near her. As I walk closer I can see that she's holding a menu and, placed inside the menu, a scrap of paper.

I walk closer, and see that it's full of 'love notes' similar to mine.

I try to get even closer but knock her shoulder. Zoe turns and sees me.

'I . . . I . . .' I try to make an excuse but I know that I've made the biggest mistake of the day. With tears welling in her eyes, she pushes me and runs out of the restaurant.

I catch up with her and pull out my notebook to show her.

She refuses to look at me eye to eye. 'What . . . what is it?'

Puffing, I tell her, 'Just read it, I can barely stand up.'

Our breathing slows down as she reads my notebook.

Finally, after many page-flicking minutes, she looks me in the eye.

This gets me smiling, which gradually evolves into a gentle laughter. Zoe joins in and within seconds our laughter becomes hysterical and like two crazies we collapse on the street laughing. Invisible feathers seem to be tickling us – foot, belly, neck, ear – and I realise that she doesn't glow anymore.

[1] **Australopithecus:** an extinct genus of hominids (humans) that resembled apes; [2] **Saul on his way to Damascus:** Saul was on his way from Jerusalem to Damascus to arrest followers of Jesus, with the intention of returning them to Jerusalem as prisoners for questioning and possible execution. The journey was interrupted when he saw a blinding light, and communicated directly with a divine voice. He was then converted.

Oral exploration

1 Did you enjoy reading this story? What parts did you like?

2 Do you think it is a realistic view of a first date?

3 Would you have called the story 'Ready. Set. First date' or 'The Imperfectionist'?
Give reasons for your answer.

Read, write, explore

In groups of four, come up with two questions for each of the following aspects
of the story. Collect the questions created by the various groups and then answer
them in the class or for homework.

1 The world of the story

2 The plot

3 The use of language in the story

4 Characters

5 Dialogue

6 The ending

7 Theme

Create

First dates can be tricky as both parties are trying to make a good impression.
Imagine that you have been asked to contribute to a famous blog. The author is
looking for the five 'dos' and five 'don'ts' of a first date and one top tip! Make the
list in your Portfolio.

Portfolio 14E

PowerPoint – Types
of narrator

Comparing stories

No matter how different short stories may seem, they all have similar aspects in how they are told. Species of birds vary a lot, but they all have beaks, feathers, a pair of claws and that distinctive watchful eye. Similarly, very different stories have similar features.

Every short story has a main character that changes or develops. There is always a plot that contains some sort of conflict; the plot develops towards a **big crisis moment** and ends in a **climax**. Usually there is an **interesting opening** and an **ending** that brings a sense of finality. Many stories have a separate **narrator**, though the narrator is often the main character. Most stories contain dialogue and description. Stories gain a reader's interest, usually through tension, sometimes in the form of suspense, when the reader is impatient to find out what will happen.

The best way to understand the similarities that different stories have is to compare two very different stories like 'Oliver Has an Interview' and 'Professor Panini'. After all, a hawk and a toaster do not seem to have much in common.

Openings

'Oliver Has an Interview' begins strangely: 'Oliver opened his bathroom window, turned into a hawk, and took off into the depths of Ueno Park'. A character reads a résumé and turns into a hawk. This is unusual. 'Professor Panini' has a strange opening too, in the future, looking back on the year 2023: 'Before my many years' service in a restaurant, I attended a top science university'. This interesting set-up make the reader look forward to the story.

Narrator

In 'Oliver Has an Interview' the narrator tells the story in the third person: 'As soon as he had finished his résumé, which was very late, Oliver opened his bathroom window.' The narrator is outside the story and informs us of the facts. In 'Professor Panini' the main character is the narrator and tells the story in the first person: 'My forty-second birthday had made a lonely visit the week before.' This narrator is inside the story and informs us directly of the hopes, dreams and fears of the main character, for example: 'felt my mind wrenched from its sockets'. We learn about Oliver's feelings from the narrator's description and from dialogue: 'Oliver goggled at the bus' and 'How do I even have a chance with so little life behind me?' The reader gets a quicker understanding of the feelings of the main character from the first-person narration.

Main characters

Both of the main characters make plans for their futures. This is what drives the stories: succeeding at an interview and succeeding in an experiment. Each lives alone in a flat where strange things happen.

Both characters rely on animals to help them. Oliver asks a bear for advice; the professor relies on a duck and cat for his experiment. In 'Oliver Has an Interview' the main character, Oliver, turns from a human into a hawk and can talk to animals: 'Oliver and the bear talked for a long time about Oliver's career hopes.' Talking to animals is an interesting skill. In 'Professor Panini' the main character changes into a talking toaster – that too is a strange skill for a toaster. He eventually becomes a kitchen worker. The future for both characters is uncertain or worse at the end.

The big crisis

In 'Oliver Has an Interview' the big crisis comes when Oliver fears being late for an interview. He misses the bus because 'a paunchy salaryman pulled him aside' in the queue. He suddenly changed into his hawk-self and 'shot into the open sky'. In 'Professor Panini' the crisis occurs when the cat messes up the experiment and the professor turns into a toaster, 'with a terrible, psychedelic whirl of colours'. Neither of them is fully in control after the crisis. Each suffers a reversal of his plans.

Tension

In 'Professor Panini', there are several tense moments, most of them funny. When the narrator asks the clerk to help him, an incident occurs. The clerk presses the wrong machine button: "This one, sir?' he asked, and before I could correct him… the disaster occurred.' An example of similar tension is Oliver's sudden arrival at the interview: 'There was a cry, almost avian in its harshness'. Both of these moments cause the reader to wonder what is about to happen. They are both good examples of where the reader feels **suspense**.

Climax

The climax is a disaster for both main characters. They both lose control and find themselves in an awkward situation.

In 'Professor Panini' the climax consists of a fire and the removal of the main character, now a toaster, to a repair shop: 'I was identified as the fault'. He becomes helpless and is trapped in a toaster forever. In 'Oliver Has an Interview' the climax occurs when Oliver arrives suddenly for his interview, wearing neither feathers nor clothes: 'his door was flung open by a young man who was entirely naked except for a piece of paper held extremely immodestly in one hand.' Whereas the toaster has a new chip to calm it down and has all the time in the world, Oliver rushes into the office out of control. He risks missing his chance of getting a job.

Ending

Oliver shocks Mr Junichiro and offers him a very cheeky answer to his first question: 'On time'. The toaster is surprised to find that his human body has been hired as a kitchen worker, displaying a menu with the words 'Buttered bagel'. It is interesting the Oliver hopes to be hired, while the toaster is in shock at who has been hired. Both stories end with a short and sharp pair of words that reveal the final situation: 'On time' and 'Buttered bagel'.

Description

In 'Professor Panini' the events are described in a dramatic manner at times: 'The cat, though, was suddenly gripped by terrible alarm. The brute leapt into the air, flinging itself onto the machine'. The words 'gripped', 'leapt 'and 'flinging' are striking action words. Similarly in 'Oliver Has an Interview' there is an all-action description: 'Then Oliver began to run. He sprinted past the bus without a glance. His limbs no longer flailed like a stuck carp'. The actions words 'run', 'sprinted' and 'flailed' are striking for their energy. These energetic moments help the reader to imagine the story in both cases.

···⟩ Identify five factors that you think make this a very good answer.

···⟩ Could you suggest an area that could be improved?

Keep these in mind as you embark on your own comparison.

Writing a comparison

Write a comparison of any two short stories featured in *Crescents*.
Firstly, in your Portfolio make notes under the following headings
for your chosen stories:

Portfolio 14F

···⟩ Openings
···⟩ Narrator
···⟩ Main characters
···⟩ The Big crisis
···⟩ Tension
···⟩ Climax
···⟩ Ending
···⟩ Description.

Then focus on any four of these headings and write your comparison.
In addition, include references to your favourite moments of the
stories, which story you prefer, and why.

The Novel Experience 2
To Kill a Mockingbird
by Harper Lee

Is fair play marked 'white only' in Alabama?

Mockingbird is key witness to a sin.

In this unit you will:

⟶ read the novel for enjoyment

⟶ study certain extracts in greater detail

⟶ focus on setting, main characters and key moments

⟶ write different journalistic texts in response to events in the novel

⟶ analyse and focus on success criteria in an answer

⟶ prepare a short oral presentation on this novel.

'Shoot all the bluejays you want, if you can hit 'em, but remember it's a sin to kill a mockingbird.'

Harper Lee

Nelle Harper Lee (1926–) was born in Alabama, United States, just before the economic crash of 1929. Like Atticus, Lee's father was a lawyer and representative at the State Legislature. Her mother was mentally unwell and mostly stayed inside the house, perhaps reflected in the lack of a mother in *To Kill a Mockingbird* and in Boo Radley who stayed indoors. Most of her childhood was spent in a small town being a tomboy, somewhat like Scout.

Lee became aware of unjust racial attitudes from an early age. She was close childhood friends with a future author, Truman Capote; and he is possibly reflected in Scout's creative friend Dill. She wrote for a humourous school magazine, *Rammer Jammer*. Though she studied law, Lee realised her career was in writing and published *To Kill a Mockingbird* in 1960.

Harper Lee

···❯ Look at the photos and captions on the PowerPoint that accompanies this unit. What can you learn about racial division and attitudes at that time in 1930s America?

PowerPoint – 1930s America

Before you read

'It's a sin to kill a mockingbird.'

'The one thing that doesn't abide by majority rule is a person's conscience.'

The novel is famous for its wise and witty proverbs about human life such as 'You never really understand a person until you consider things from his point of view . . . until you climb into his skin and walk around in it.' We will read and enjoy this gripping story and appreciate the novelist's skills and talent, which we hope to learn from.

As you study a key chapter, you will explore how and why **characters** develop. You will recognise the importance of narrator and setting and learn about plot. You will become aware of the **writer's skills**, of **pattern** and **structure** in the novel and how they impacted on you.

You will need to have a copy of *To Kill a Mockingbird* with you at all times while working on this unit.

The narrator

When a narrator uses the word 'my' in the opening sentence is this a **first-person narrator** or a **third-person narrator**? Scan the first page. What type of a narrator do we have in *To Kill a Mockingbird*?

The narrator is called Scout Finch and the story of the novel looks back at events during a dangerous period of her childhood in America's Deep South in the Depression era of the 1930s.

Read Chapter 1 for your enjoyment. Then begin your novel experience reflection with the following close study.

Focus on Chapter 1

The exposition

The first chapter of a book is often worth reading twice as it sets up the story. As you read this chapter, make notes in your Portfolio on interesting aspects of setting, character, or how the plot and/or subplot progresses.

Portfolio 15A

The first stage of a story usually precedes the main action. Its purpose is to introduce or expose the readers to the setting and the main characters. The term for this stage is **the exposition**. Now read the opening of the novel.

> When he was nearly thirteen my brother Jem got his arm badly broken at the elbow. When it healed, and Jem's fears of never being able to play football were assuaged, he was seldom self-conscious about his injury. His left arm was somewhat shorter than his right; when he stood or walked, the back of his hand was at right-angles to his body, his thumb parallel to his thigh. He couldn't have cared less, so long as he could pass and punt.
>
> When enough years had gone by to enable us to look back on them, we sometimes discussed the events leading to his accident. I maintain that the Ewells started it all, but Jem, who was four years my senior, said it started long before that. He said it began the summer Dill came to us, when Dill first gave us the idea of making Boo Radley come out.

Oral exploration

1. Do you believe from this opening that the whole story builds up to an 'accident'?
2. Is that detail a spoiler? Why or why not?
3. What detail from the end of the novel is mentioned in the opening sentence?
4. Who are identified here as the characters that started the series of events that the story is built upon?
5. In what way is Jem permanently maimed by the injury he gets in the accident?
6. Have a guess whether Jem or Scout is right about the start of the plot.

Plot

A **plot** is a storyline of incidents or moments concerning the main character and building up to the decisive events. In this novel the main plot starts with the Ewells, the characters mentioned above by Scout.

Subplot

A storyline of less important incidents or moments that run parallel to the main plot is called a **subplot**. In this novel the subplot deals with Scout's childhood in her neighbourhood and kicks off with Dill's attempt to make Boo Radley come out. This is the storyline mentioned by Jem above.

Foreshadowing

Foreshadowing happens when minor details sometimes predict or give a sign of important later events. In this chapter, Jem's arm injury indicates an important character with a maimed arm later in the plot.

Read, write, explore

1 Does the first paragraph gain your interest as a reader? Answer with a comment.

2 Is the story being told as it happens or as a memory of times past?

3 Can you work out how old the narrator is at the time Jem got his injury?

4 Is Scout much older when she narrates the story? Quote a phrase to provide evidence.

Create

Imagine that you were Harper Lee's editor and she sent in the first few paragraphs to you for review. What was your reaction? Did you want to read more? What did you like about it? Write a short note to Harper Lee expressing how you felt when you read it.

Setting

The novel is set in the fictional town of Maycomb. Read the following extract about the town. Do you find anything disturbing in these paragraphs? Discuss with your partner.

Courthouse of *To Kill A Mockingbird* in Monroesville, Alabama

Maycomb was an old town, but it was a tired old town when I first knew it. In rainy weather the streets turned to red slop; grass grew on the sidewalks, the court-house sagged in the square. Somehow, it was hotter then: a black dog suffered on a summer's day; bony mules hitched to Hoover carts flicked flies in the sweltering shade of the live oaks on the square. Men's stiff collars wilted by nine in the morning. Ladies bathed before noon, after their three-o'clock naps, and by nightfall were like soft teacakes with frostings of sweat and sweet talcum.

People moved slowly then. They ambled across the square, shuffled in and out of the stores around it, took their time about everything. A day was twenty-four hours long but seemed longer. There was no hurry, for there was nowhere to go, nothing to buy and no money to buy it with, nothing to see outside the boundaries of Maycomb County. But it was a time of vague optimism for some of the people; Maycomb County had recently been told that it had nothing to fear but fear itself.

Read, write, explore

1   List a detail that reveals:
   - the poverty of Maycomb
   - the quaint lifestyle of Maycomb
   - the climate features of Maycomb
   - a touch of comedy in the description.

2   What words, descriptive verbs and adjectives, capture the atmosphere of Maycomb?

3   What idea about the events of the novel does the last sentence give you?

4   List three synonyms for the verb 'walked' in the second paragraph above.

Later in Chapter 13 it is revealed that Maycomb society has been the same for generations.

It grew inward. New people so rarely settled there, the same families married the same families until the members of the community looked faintly alike. Occasionally someone would return from Montgomery or Mobile with an outsider, but the result caused only a ripple in the quiet stream of family resemblance. Things were more or less the same during my early years.

In your Portfolio keep track of any references which you come across to the setting, Maycomb.

Portfolio 15B

Narrator's situation

An important part of exposition is to give the reader background on the life of the narrator. Listen to the following extract. Find and follow the text in your book as you listen.

> **Read from:**
>
> We lived on the main residential street in town—Atticus, Jem and I, plus Calpurnia our cook. Jem and I found our father satisfactory: he played with us, read to us, and treated us with courteous detachment.
>
> **to:**
>
> We were never tempted to break them. The Radley Place was inhabited by an unknown entity the mere description of whom was enough to make us behave for days on end; Mrs Dubose was plain hell.

Oral exploration

1 What key member of a family is missing from the Finch family? Is it usual in stories that a key family member is absent from the life of the main character?

2 Who appears to be most in control of Scout's daily life? What sentence proves this best?

3 Do you think that the kind of childhood boundaries Scout describes are suitable for a young child today?

Read, write, explore

1 What evidence is there in Chapter 1 to suggest that the narrator's childhood is isolated?

2 Use bullet points to list the details that show Calpurnia was more than just the family cook.

3 How different might Scout's life have been if her mother had not died early in her life?

4 How does the death of Scout's mother enable Harper Lee to make Scout's family situation more interesting for you as a reader?

5 What effect does the phrase 'unknown entity' have on you?

Create

Think about your own neighbourhood and the people around you. A neighbourhood is made up of all kinds of different types of people. In what way is your neighbourhood similar to or different from the one described by Lee in this extract? Create a list of similarities and differences in your Portfolio.

Portfolio 15C

New characters and more aspects of setting

In many stories, good writers use comparison **images** to describe characters and settings. New details of the setting and new characters help to get events moving.

The description below introduces the feeling of an evil presence to the world of the narrator. The evil is found more in suggestion than in details. The Radley place and its mysteries lead to a **subplot** in the novel. It is one of two pillars the story is built on.

Find and read the following extract in your copy of the novel. As you read the extract, note comparison images for a fence, a neighbour and a curious boy.

> **Read from:**
>
> The Radley Place fascinated Dill. In spite of our warnings and explanations it drew him as the moon draws water, but drew him no nearer than the light-pole on the corner.
>
> **to:**
>
> The Radley house had no screen doors. I once asked Atticus if it ever had any; Atticus said yes, but before I was born.

Oral exploration

Discuss these questions with a partner and note your answers. Refer to your copy of the text to answer the questions.

1 Name the two important characters introduced here.
2 Why do you think Dill stared and wondered?
3 Give one detail which proves the Radley house was old.
4 Name one example of a superstition mentioned here.
5 Find one sentence that suggests a stereotype.
6 Find an expression to show that women were not considered as important as men.

Read, write, explore

1 Find these words in the text. Match the words in List (a) with those in List (b). Use a dictionary if necessary. List (a): malevolent, adjoined, predilection, assumed, alien. List (b): very strange, evil, bordered, habit, guessed.
2 Outline, partly in your own words, some of the reasons given for 'The misery of that house . . . '
3 Identify three Gothic details of the Radley place that grip the reader.

Exploring the strange

A character to fear and wonder at.

Gothic stories set in castles and mansions were so popular in Europe that American writers began to use Gothic settings and characters. Originally the Gothic genre consisted of supernatural horrors and an atmosphere of unknown terror. American Gothic stories usually feature disturbed personalities rather than the supernatural. There are usually some negative qualities in the setting that provide a mysterious atmosphere and a dread factor to thrill the reader. Besides providing atmosphere, American Gothic often explores social issues like inequality. Note the atmosphere that builds around the Radleys in these extracts.

According to neighbourhood legend, when the younger Radley boy was in his teens he became acquainted with some of the Cunninghams

* * * *

One night in an excessive spurt of high spirits, the boys backed around the square in a borrowed flivver, resisted arrest by Maycomb's ancient beadle, Mr Conner, and locked him in the courthouse outhouse. The town decided something had to be done;

* * * *

If the judge released Arthur, Mr Radley would see to it that Arthur gave no further trouble. Knowing that Mr Radley's word was his bond, the judge was glad to do so

* * * *

The doors of the Radley house were closed on weekdays as well as Sundays, and Mr Radley's boy was not seen again for fifteen years.

* * * *

Boo was sitting in the living-room cutting some items from *The Maycomb Tribune* to paste in his scrapbook. His father entered the room. As Mr Radley passed by, Boo drove the scissors into his parent's leg, pulled them out, wiped them on his pants, and resumed his activities.

* * * *

Nobody knew what form of intimidation Mr Radley employed to keep Boo out of sight, but Jem figured that Mr Radley kept him chained to the bed most of the time. Atticus said no, it wasn't that sort of thing, that there were other ways of making people into ghosts.

* * * *

But every day Jem and I would see Mr Radley walking to and from town. He was a thin leathery man with colourless eyes, so colourless they did not reflect light. His cheekbones were sharp and his mouth was wide, with a thin upper lip and a full lower lip.

* * * *

Jem said, 'He goes out, all right, when it's pitch dark. Miss Stephanie Crawford said she woke up in the middle of the night one time and saw him looking straight through the window at her... said his head was like a skull lookin' at her. Ain't you ever waked up at night and heard him, Dill? He walks like this—' Jem slid his feet through the gravel. 'Why do you think Miss Rachel locks up so tight at night? I've seen his tracks in our back yard many a mornin', and one night I heard him scratching on the back screen, but he was gone time Atticus got there.'

'Wonder what he looks like?' said Dill.

Jem gave a reasonable description of Boo: Boo was about six-and-a-half feet tall, judging from his tracks; he dined on raw squirrels and any cats he could catch, that's why his hands were blood-stained – if you ate an animal raw, you could never wash the blood off. There was a long jagged scar that ran across his face; what teeth he had were yellow and rotten; his eyes popped, and he drooled most of the time.

'Let's try to make him come out,' said Dill. 'I'd like to see what he looks like.'

Oral exploration

1 What detail do you consider the most frightening?

2 Would you consider that the description of Boo Radley's father helps to create a feeling of horror? Explain.

3 What do you consider to be the wildest rumour in the description above?

4 As a child, would you have tried to make Dracula come out of his castle? Explain.

Read, write, explore

You are a journalist investigating what lies behind the Radley shutters. In your Portfolio, fill in a profile of Boo Radley using information gathered from Maycomb residents.

Portfolio 15D

To interest your readers the profile should highlight his Gothic characteristics or conventions. Use the table on page 64 of Unit 3 to help you.

Create

Can you think of a strange or intriguing character from where you live? Perhaps it is someone that you see but don't know much about. Pretend you are Harper Lee and create a history for the character, saying why they look, act, speak the way they do. This is totally fictional so use your imagination. Write in the same style as Harper Lee.

Portfolio 15E

Chapter recall – The exposition

Oral exploration

1 How does this chapter whet your appetite to read on in the novel?

2 Is Scout just an observer or is she more than that?

Read, write, explore

1 Does the Maycomb legend of Boo Radley make him seem a figure to fear?

2 Does the author succeed in getting you hooked on Boo Radley as a character? Why? Why not?

3 Having read Chapter 1, what key words, phrases and adjectives do you think would have been part of the sketch of the plan for the novel? Make notes on the following: characters, setting, narrator, subplot and emotions which you want to evoke in the reader.

Animation – Connotations

Read on: Chapters 2, 3 and 4

Read each of the following chapters first for enjoyment. Then revisit and answer the related questions for each chapter. As you read each chapter, make notes in your Portfolio on interesting aspects of setting, character, or how the plot and/or subplot progresses.

Portfolio 15A

> **Protagonist**
>
> The reader sees events as Scout sees and experiences them. The character that experiences and feels most of the action in a story or drama is known as the **protagonist**.

Chapter 2

Another setting, more characters and the protagonist's first impression of school.

1. What do you consider unusual about how Walter Cunningham and his family live? Discuss in groups.

2. 'Jean Louise, I've had about enough of you this morning'. Do you have any sympathy for Miss Caroline in her first dealings with Scout? Explain.

3. Calpurnia made Scout pass the time on wet days by copying out passages of the Bible. Compare that with what parents do today when they have a child to entertain on a wet day.

Chapter 3

Through the poverty and ignorance of rural pupils we learn about Maycomb society.

1. Discuss this advice offered by Scout's father, Atticus:

   'You never really understand a person until you consider things from his point of view . . . until you climb into his skin and walk around in it.'

2. How does it apply to Scout's development?

3. Would you consider it helpful advice in your own life?

4. Fill in a Venn diagram to show the similarities and differences between the Cunningham family and the Ewell family.

Portfolio 15F

Chapter 4

Gifts and role play.

1 In what ways does this chapter convey a happy phase of Scout's childhood?

2 Based on the children's game, make some predictions about how the novel will develop.

3 Restate this image in your words: summer 'was a thousand colors in a parched landscape'.

4 Explain why Jem 'went under the front steps and shrieked and howled from time to time'.

5 Does it add a sense of intrigue that Scout, Jem and Dill hide the game they are playing from Atticus?

6 What do you make of the final sentence of the chapter: 'Someone in the house was laughing'?

Create

Imagine Miss Caroline phones her mother in Winston about her first day in her new teaching job in Maycomb. Write the first draft of the script of the phone call, making sure she tells her mother what bothered her. Include her mother's reactions. Use exaggerated language in your dialogue.

Chapter recall

Think about the chapters you have read. How have they progressed the plot? Are there any indications of how the plot or characters will develop?

Focus on Chapter 5

The subplot develops

Wisdom of a neighbour and the obsession with Boo Radley. Dill's obsession with Boo has deeply influenced Jem and as a result the investigation of Boo dominates the story.

As you read this chapter, make notes in your Portfolio on interesting aspects of setting, character, or how the plot and/or subplot progresses.

Portfolio 15A

Oral exploration

1 How would you describe the sibling relationship between Scout and Jem?

2 Has Harper Lee written in a way that is believable?

3 Does the following tell you more about Boo or about Scout: 'I reeled around to face Boo Radley and his bloody fangs'.

4 Do you think that the text of the message in the note to be delivered to Boo is rather innocent? Explain.

Read, write, explore

1 What is Jem's theory about the non-appearance of Boo?

2 What is Miss Maudie's explanation for the non-appearance of Boo?

3 Would the subplot be as interesting if we saw Arthur Radley only as Miss Maudie saw him? Explain.

4 What caused the 'automatic terror rising in me'?

5 What is the most ridiculous claim made about Boo here?

6 Does Atticus believe that Boo is a dark menace to society? Is Atticus too serious? Explain.

Read on: Chapters 6, 7 and 8

Read each of the following chapters first for enjoyment. Then reread and answer the related questions for each chapter. As you read each chapter, make notes in your Portfolio on interesting aspects of setting, character, or how the plot and/or subplot progresses.

Portfolio 15A

Chapter 6

Characters multiply – meet Scout's neighbours. The thriller effect on the reader – spying on a neighbour.

1 Who was lucky to escape gunshot wounds?

2 Miss Maudie announces 'Mr Radley shot a negro in his collard patch.' What does she show by this?

   (a) There's a body in the Radley garden.
   (b) Miss Maudie has night vision.
   (c) Miss Maudie believes that crime tends to be committed by blacks.
   (d) There is a racist attitude towards blacks among white folks in Maycomb.

3 What do we learn in this chapter about Atticus and his relationship with his children?

Chapter 7

Childhood escapades and minor mysteries.

Why was Jem upset at the end of the chapter?

Chapter 8

The novelty of snow; Miss Maudie unites the neighbourhood, philosophical musings. A surprise from the Gothic anti-hero.

What do you learn about Scout's neighbours? In your Portfolio make a list of positive points.

Portfolio 15G

Chapter recall

Think about the chapters you have read. How have they progressed the plot? Are there any indications of how the plot or characters will develop?

Focus on Chapter 9

The main plot begins

Angry racist outbursts against the Finch children trigger the main plot.

Up to now the focus has been on the subplot. Childhood play and episodes with neighbours have centred on Boo Radley as the target of curiosity. Now Scout faces an unhappy complication in her life.

From the moment Scout orders Cecil Jacobs to take back his racist jibe, Harper Lee begins to construct the **second and major pillar of the novel**, the main plot centring on the **trial of Tom Robinson**.

The schoolyard conflict is like the starting gun to the main action of the novel. Atticus has begun to take on a challenge and sees many obstacles ahead. In many adventure-type novels, the plot involves a very difficult challenge that seems almost impossible to overcome.

To remind you of this type of plot, make a list in class of the names of five novels and five films where the hero faces a huge challenge.

As you read this chapter, make notes in your Portfolio on interesting aspects of setting, character, or how the plot and/or subplot progresses.

Portfolio 15A

The following tasks are based on the first two pages of the chapter, beginning from 'You can just take that back, boy!' up to Atticus's declaration, 'Simply because we were licked a hundred years before we started is no reason for us not to try to win.'

Oral exploration

1 How does the opening of this chapter suggest that the story is about to become more complex?

2 How does Scout demonstrate her dislike for school in her dialogue with Atticus?

3 Read the following two statements from the chapter and take a class poll on each related question:

(a) 'every lawyer gets at least one case in his lifetime that affects him personally. This one's mine.'

(b) 'Simply because we were licked a hundred years before we started is no reason for us not to try to win.'

● Which statement, (a) or (b), shows that Atticus believes in destiny?

● Which statement, (a) or (b), shows that Atticus is facing great difficulty?

● Which statement, (a) or (b), most develops Atticus as a character for the reader?

● Which statement, (a) or (b), uses an idiom, a phrase that has a meaning different from its dictionary meaning?

4 Locate one more idiom in the first two pages of Chapter 9.

The black community

The black community lived in a separate part of Maycomb, known as the Quarters.

Slavery was widespread in Alabama and the whole Deep South until the end of the American Civil War in 1865. After the Yankee or Union states in the north had beaten the Confederate south, they destroyed the southern economy and forced them to free their slaves. Generally, this did not mean an improvement in quality of life for black communities. Racial prejudice and inequality persisted.

Members of the black community were not allowed to live in the same streets, attend the same schools, eat in the same restaurants or travel on the same trains or buses as white people. Several local laws were put in place to make sure they remained second-class citizens. This resulted in many black people being forced to take poorly paid jobs which left them as badly off as when they were slaves.

Racism was ingrained and the majority of crimes against black people were ignored. Yet a black person was always presumed guilty, even without a fair trial. During this time there was a rise of racist organisations such as the Ku Klux Klan.

You can find out more about America during this time in Unit 8, page 213.

Read, write, explore

1 Is Atticus's decision to defend Tom Robinson popular with his community?

2 Explain the following: 'There's been some high talk around town to the effect that I shouldn't do much about defending this man.'

3 What does Atticus teach his daughter regarding her use of language?

4 Explain how the new problem is more serious than trying to get Boo to come out.

5 Would you describe Atticus as hopeful of winning the trial? Explain.

6 What do you think Atticus means by 'Maycomb's usual disease'?

7 Which of the following is the reason 'we were licked a hundred years before we started'? Is it (a) fear, (b) prejudice or (c) Tom's guilt?

Focus on Chapter 10

Finch children come through a crisis of confidence.

As you read this chapter, make notes in your Portfolio on interesting aspects of setting, character, or how the plot and/or subplot progresses.

Portfolio 15A

Oral exploration

1 Discuss what the following dialogue means:

"'Shoot all the bluejays you want, if you can hit 'em, but remember it's a sin to kill a mockingbird.'... I asked Miss Maudie about it. "Your father's right," she said. "Mockingbirds don't do one thing but make music for us to enjoy.'"

2 Select an Irish bird to replace the mockingbird and suggest a title for an Irish version of the novel.

3 Is there any connection between Scout's surname and the title?

Read, write, explore

1 Scout compares her father, the lawyer, to other fathers:

'Atticus did not drive a dump-truck for the county, he was not the sheriff, he did not farm, work in a garage, or do anything that could possibly arouse the admiration of anyone.'

Make a list of four careers Scout would prefer for her father.

2 Mention one other criticism Scout makes about her father in Chapter 10.

3 Were you ever in Scout's shoes with regard to the occupation of a parent or guardian?

4 Does Atticus impress you as a character in this chapter? Explain your answer.

5 Why does Scout stop feeling ashamed of Atticus near the end of the chapter?

Create

Write an online advice column that always deals with an urgent problem. The urgent subject is a virus known as 'rabies' that is attacking educational software in your school. A new anti-virus download known as 'marksman' can stop it. Write the article while using as many phrases and words from this chapter as you can.

Download images and present in the form of a Prezi or PowerPoint if possible.

Focus on Chapter 11

Theme of courage and compassion explored.

As you read this chapter, make notes in your Portfolio on interesting aspects of setting, character, or how the plot and/or subplot progresses.

Portfolio 15A

Oral exploration

1 At the end of Chapter 11 what does Atticus mean by the following?

'It's when you know you're licked before you begin but you begin anyway and you see it through no matter what. You rarely win, but sometimes you do.'

2 Do you think that Atticus could be preparing his children for defeat in the trial of Tom Robinson?

Read, write, explore

1 What is the main point Atticus makes to Scout in this chapter?

2 Why do you think it says his face was 'grave'?

3 What is the most important lesson that Atticus teaches Jem after Mrs Dubose has died?

4 What impression of the character of Atticus do you get in this chapter?

Create

Imagine that *The Maycomb Tribune* includes a page devoted to church affairs.

The purpose of the following activity is to develop your speech writing and to reflect on human character. Reverend Sykes delivers a homily in his church remembering Mrs Dubose and praising Atticus for setting a good example as a father. Write the first draft of Sykes's speech (about 150 words), which will be published in the newspaper.

Portfolio 15H

If you like, you can use the following as starting sentences:

Brothers and Sisters! Our neighbour Mrs Dubose has died. People say she was 'wrathful' and 'vicious'…Who are we to judge? Take Atticus Finch . . .

or

You may include facts or quotes from this chapter as part of your speech.

Focus on Chapter 12

Introduces the theme of sibling conflict and explores black communal values.

As you read this chapter, make notes in your Portfolio on interesting aspects of setting, character, or how the plot and/or subplot progresses.

Portfolio 15A

Notice too how Calpurnia acts as a teacher to Scout and Jem about respecting cultures.

> 'Suppose you and Scout talked colored-folks' talk at home – it'd be out of place, wouldn't it? Now what if I talked white-folks' talk at church, and with my neighbors? They'd think I was puttin' on airs to beat Moses.'

Oral exploration

1 What does Calpurnia mean by 'putting on airs to beat Moses'?

2 Do you think Calpurnia is right when she advises Scout to leave Jem to himself: 'He's gonna want to be off to himself a lot now'?

3 Do you get a strong sense of community in Calpurnia's church?

4 What do learn about the crime Tom Robinson is accused of? How is it affecting his wife Helen?

Read, write, explore

Read the following two statements from the chapter:

'Overnight, it seemed, Jem had acquired an alien set of values and was trying to impose them on me.'

'. . . bread lines in the cities grew longer, people in the country grew poorer. But these were events remote from the world of Jem and me.'

1 Pair each quote with one of the following: (a) a changing relationship, and (b) historical setting. Write a short paragraph about each quote.

2 Write a caption for each of the photos on this page.

3 List some films where sibling rivalry is important to the plot. Write about one modern movie that reminds you of the relationship between Scout and Jem and say why.

Focus on Chapter 13

Theme of influence

Aunt Alexandra arrives to drive Scout from her tomboy ways and tries to impose the stereotypes of Deep South feminine dress and behaviour. Calpurnia also offers her view of what is ladylike.

As you read this chapter, make notes in your Portfolio on interesting aspects of setting, character, or how the plot and/or subplot progresses. In this novel, the setting is important for attitudes and values rather than just its physical details.

Portfolio 15A

Oral exploration

1 From the words used in this chapter, to which of the following wars do you think the narrator is referring? American Civil War (1861–65) or First World War (1914–18)?

2 'It would be best for you to have some feminine influence'. Agree on ways in which Scout is not a typical girl and list them in your Portfolio. After a short discussion go back to the novel and find evidence to support your thoughts. Fill in the profile for Scout in your Portfolio. Two facts are already filled in for you.

Portfolio 15I

Read, write, explore

1 Would Scout Finch fit in well in a modern primary school, in your opinion? Explain.

2 Do you agree or disagree with Aunt Alexandra's intention to change Scout?

3 How well does this chapter deal with the topic of the older generation bossing the young?

4 What do you think the sentence 'It grew inward' means?

Focus on Chapter 14

Atticus has mild conflict with Aunt Alexandria and upholds equality by defending Calpurnia. There is a development of Dill's character.

As you read this chapter, make notes in your Portfolio on interesting aspects of setting, character, or how the plot and/or subplot progresses.

Portfolio 15A

Read, write, explore

Place the following sentences from Chapter 14 in the correct box below.

Clue: The correct solution is also the sequence in which they occur in the narrative.

1 'His maddening superiority was unbearable these days.'

2 'There's his chillun."

3 'He could read two books to my one, but he preferred the magic of his own inventions.'

4 'Why do you reckon Boo Radley's never run off?'

5 'Then he rose and broke the remaining code of our childhood.'

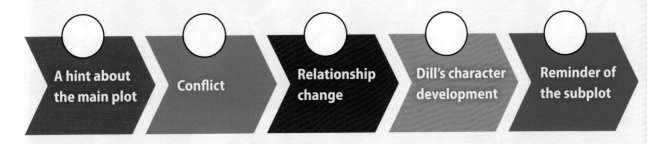

| A hint about the main plot | Conflict | Relationship change | Dill's character development | Reminder of the subplot |

Focus on Chapter 15

Atticus confronts two groups of men before the trial and deals with a crisis at the Maycomb jail.

As you read this chapter, make notes in your Portfolio on interesting aspects of setting, character, or how the plot and/or subplot progresses.

Portfolio 15A

Oral exploration

1 Why does a group of Maycomb citizens meet Atticus in his front yard?

2 What arguments does Atticus use to convince Sheriff Tate not to transfer Tom to another jail?

3 What does this reveal about the character of Atticus: 'that boy might go to the chair, but he's not going till the truth's told'?

4 Where do you think the truth will be told?

5 What does Scout mean near the start of the chapter when she says, 'A nightmare was upon us'?

Read, write, explore

1 Why do you think another group of men turned up at the jailhouse and said to Atticus: 'You know what we want. Get aside from the door Mr Finch'?

Begin a short paragraph with one of the following:

(a) They felt Tom was innocent and wanted to free him.

(b) They were a lynch mob who wanted to hang Tom without a trial.

2 How did Scout's conversation with Walter Cunningham lead to the group of men going home?

Begin with: Scout helped Walter jump into Atticus's skin . . .

Create

Write a radio broadcast

Word has spread about the incident between Tom's attorney and the lynch mob. The media have got word of the story. Imagine that you are a budding journalist who has been given an exclusive interview with Scout. Write out five questions that you intend to ask her.

Portfolio 15J

Now answer the five questions, the way you think Scout would.

Then write the script for a radio broadcast. Write the text of the broadcast in sensational/dramatic style. Think of your listening audience. You have a one-minute slot, so make each word count.

It could begin like this:

'Last night in Maycomb, Alabama, a bunch of over-zealous locals tried to hijack the trial of Tom Robinson . . . '

Focus on Chapter 16

Building to the climax

Setting the scene for the trial.

As you read this chapter, make notes in your Portfolio on interesting aspects of setting, character, or how the plot and/or subplot progresses.

Portfolio 15A

Find and read the following extracts in this chapter where dialogue effectively shows how Aunt Alexandra feels the Finches are superior to black people, in contrast to the views of her brother Atticus.

Read from:

She waited until Calpurnia was in the kitchen, then she said, 'Don't talk like that in front of them.'

'Talk like what in front of whom?' he asked.

'Like that in front of Calpurnia. You said "Braxton Underwood despises Negroes" right in front of her.'

'Well, I'm sure Cal knows it. Everybody in Maycomb knows it.'

I was beginning to notice a subtle change in my father these days, that came out when he talked . . . 'Anything fit to say at the table's fit to say in front of Calpurnia. She knows what she means to this family.'

to:

'I don't think it's a good habit, Atticus. It encourages them. You know how they talk among themselves. Everything that happens in this town's out to the Quarters before sundown.'

My father put down his knife. 'I don't know of any law that says they can't talk. Maybe if we didn't give them so much to talk about they'd be quiet.'

Oral exploration

1 In what ways does this conversation show the theme of prejudice?

2 How well does this show that Atticus is opposed to prejudice?

In another well-written dialogue section, Atticus explains racial tension and the reasons for the jailhouse confrontation. Read the following extract.

'I thought Mr Cunningham was a friend of ours. You told me a long time ago he was.'

'He still is.'

'But last night he wanted to hurt you.'

Atticus placed his fork beside his knife and pushed his plate aside. 'Mr Cunningham's basically a good man,' he said, 'he just has his blind spots along with the rest of us.'

Jem spoke. 'Don't call that a blind spot. He'da killed you last night when he first went there.'

'He might have hurt me a little,' Atticus conceded, 'but son, you'll understand folks a little better when you're older. A mob's always made up of people, no matter what. Mr Cunningham was part of a mob last night, but he was still a man. Every mob in every little Southern town is always made up of people you know – doesn't say much for them, does it?'

'I'll say not,' said Jem.

'So it took an eight-year-old child to bring 'em to their senses, didn't it?' said Atticus. 'That proves something – that a gang of wild animals can be stopped, simply because they're still human . . . '

Read, write, explore

1 What sentence shows that Atticus forgives Mr Cunningham?

2 What does Jem think about what happened outside the jail?

3 Do you agree with Jem or with Scout?

4 Do you agree 'that a gang of wild animals can be stopped, simply because they're still human'?

5 The children arrived late to the courtroom:

'Reverend Sykes came puffing behind us, and steered us gently through the black people in the balcony. Four Negroes rose and gave us their front-row seats.'

What aspect of society is illustrated by the arrangement of the courtroom?

Create – Your student blog

Research the topic of segregation in Alabama before the civil rights campaigns.

Write an opinion article of 200 words for a website set up by a famous civil rights campaigner such as Rosa Parks or Martin Luther King Junior. Then set up a blog site using the step-by-step guide in the e-Portfolio for Unit 13 and include your research as well as your article on this blog.

Note for Teachers: You will find step-by-step guidelines for this activity in your *How to Create an e-Portfolio* e-book (Unit 13). Log on to www.edcodigital.ie to access the e-book.

> *'Each person must live their life as a model for others.'*
> ROSA PARKS

Rosa Parks

Martin Luther King Junior

Focus on Chapter 17

The decisive scene of the novel begins – the trial continues.

As you read this chapter, make notes in your Portfolio on interesting aspects of setting, character, or how the plot and/or subplot progresses.

Oral exploration

Name the character who offers each piece of evidence as follows.

(a) 'It was her right eye, Mr Finch. I remember now, she was banged up on that side of her face . . . '

(b) '. . . as I got to the fence I heard Mayella screamin' like a stuck hog inside the house'

(c) 'I holds with Tate. Her eye was blackened and she was mighty beat up.'

(d) 'I can use one hand good as the other. One hand good as the other'

Read, write, explore

1 What impression does Bob Ewell make on you?

2 Select an example of where his language is revolting.

3 Basing your answer on the quotes above, what is the main strategy of Atticus at the trial?

4 Should Judge Taylor have thrown out the charges after Atticus cross-examined Bob?

Focus on Chapter 18

Drama intensifies as a broken but stealthy character takes the stand.

As you read this chapter, make notes in your Portfolio on interesting aspects of setting, character, or how the plot and/or subplot progresses.

Portfolio 15A

Listen to the extract from the beginning of this chapter to:

The judge leaned back. 'Atticus, let's get on with these proceedings, and let the record show that the witness has not been sassed, her views to the contrary.'

Oral exploration

1. Based on this audio clip, would you say that Mayella was loyal to her father? Explain.
2. Did Atticus succeed in winning over Mayella? Offer evidence in your own words.
3. What does Mayella mean by 'sass', in your view?
4. What other impressions of Mayella Ewell did you form from the rest of Chapter 18?
5. Do you think that Mayella is telling the truth? Give one or more reasons for your answer.

Read, write, explore

1. What does this simile tell you about Mayella: 'like a steady-eyed cat with a twitchy tail'?
2. Explain how the following shows that Mayella has been deprived of an education: 'Long's he keeps on callin' me ma'am an sayin' Miss Mayella. I don't hafta take his sass, I ain't called upon to take it?'
3. List two more aspects of Mayella's court performance that an actress would enjoy performing.
4. What two questions used by Atticus impressed you the most?

Focus on Chapter 19

The drama intensifies as the real victim takes the stand.

As you read this chapter, make notes in your Portfolio on interesting aspects of setting, character, or how the plot and/or subplot progresses.

Portfolio 15A

Oral exploration

1 What does Scout feel about Mayella during Tom's testimony?
2 What similarity does Scout sense between Boo Radley and Mayella?
3 True or false: Tom claims Mayella sought his affection.
4 What does Dill notice about the different styles of cross-examination of Mr Gilmer and Atticus?

Read, write, explore

Think about these questions, then discuss possible answers with a partner. Finally draft your answers.

1 How familiar was Tom Robinson with Mayella?
2 How does Tom Robinson's version of events differ from the Ewells'? You can use bullet points.
3 How surprised are you by Tom's version of events?
4 How does Mr Gilmer make little of Tom?
5 What is Tom's mistake in saying 'I felt sorry for her'?
6 Why is Dill so upset at Mr Gilmer's court style?

Create

How does Scout come to the realisation that Mayella Ewell is the loneliest person in the world? In two paragraphs, respond using relevant quotations from the text.

Portfolio 15K

Focus on Chapter 20

The rising action nears a climax as Atticus tries to persuade the jury.

As you read this chapter, make notes in your Portfolio on interesting aspects of setting, character, or how the plot and/or subplot progresses.

Portfolio 15A

Oral exploration

1 What has Dolphus Raymond got in his paper sack? Why?

2 Why did Dolphus perpetrate 'fraud against himself'?

3 How do Dolphus Raymond's public actions show the real problems in Maycomb society?

In the following extract Atticus delivers a closing speech which identifies Mayella's problem, but also the problem that society faces at that time.

'The state has not produced one iota of medical evidence to the effect that the crime Tom Robinson is charged with ever took place. It has relied instead upon the testimony of two witnesses whose evidence has not only been called into serious question on cross-examination, but has been flatly contradicted by the defendant. The defendant is not guilty, but somebody in this courtroom is.'

* * * * * *

'I say guilt, gentlemen, because it was guilt that motivated her.'

* * * *

'She must destroy the evidence of her offence.'

* * * *

'She was white, and she tempted a Negro. She did something that in our society is unspeakable: she kissed a black man.'

* * * *

'Her father saw it, and the defendant has testified as to his remarks. What did her father do? We don't know, but there is circumstantial evidence to indicate that Mayella Ewell was beaten savagely by someone who led almost exclusively with his left.'

Read, write, explore

1 What statement of Atticus shows that the facts of the case don't matter in court?

2 What, according to Atticus, is the real crime that has been committed?

3 According to Atticus, what did Mayella's father do?

4 Did Atticus perform his work in court like a man who believed he was licked a hundred years before he began? Explain.

Focus on Chapter 21

The climax of the trial; arguably the climax of the main plot.

Portfolio 15A

As you read this chapter, make notes in your Portfolio on interesting aspects of setting, character, or how the plot and/or subplot progresses. Then read the following extract.

Jem was jumping in excitement. 'We've won, haven't we?'

* * * *

'Don't see how any jury could convict on what we heard –'

'Now don't you be so confident, Mr Jem, I ain't ever seen any jury decide in favour of a coloured man over a white man . . .'

. . . it was like watching Atticus walk into the street, raise a rifle to his shoulder and pull the trigger, but watching all the time knowing that the gun was empty.

* * * *

A jury never looks at a defendant it has convicted, and when this jury came in, not one of them looked at Tom Robinson.

Read, write, explore

1 Did you share Jem's optimism here? Explain.

2 How clearly does Reverend Sykes convey the obstacle Atticus was facing all along?

3 How do you as a reader feel after the verdict has been revealed?

Read on: Chapters 22, 23, 24, 25, 26 and 27

As you read each chapter, make notes in your Portfolio on interesting aspects of setting, character, or how the plot and/or subplot progresses.

Portfolio 15A

Chapter 22

Falling action commences, though the subplot has yet to reach its climax.

1 Do you think it is realistic or not that Atticus received gifts from the black community? Explain.

2 How badly is Jem upset? What word would you use: (a) unhappy, (b) disappointed or (c) shattered?

3 What does Miss Maudie mean by 'baby step'?

4 Are you happy with this 'baby step'?

5 Why does Bob Ewell feel the need to get even with Atticus?

Chapter 23

Falling action continues slowly.

1 Discuss whether Aunt Alexandra succeeds in injecting suspense in the following dialogue:

> 'His kind'd do anything to pay off a grudge. You know how those people are.'
>
> 'What on earth could Ewell do to me, sister?'
>
> 'Something furtive,' Aunt Alexandra said. 'You may count on that.'
>
> 'Nobody has much chance to be furtive in Maycomb,' Atticus answered.

2 Do you agree with Atticus' use of the word 'trash' in the following statement?

'whenever a white man does that to a black man, no matter who he is, how rich he is, or how fine a family he comes from, that white man is trash'.

3 Why does Jem agree with Boo Radley's private lifestyle in the final sentence of the chapter? Begin an answer with one of the following:

(a) Jem was so horrified by the verdict that he too felt like staying at home forever.
(b) Jem finally starts to mature and understand the mockingbird idea.

Chapter 24

Focus on setting; the values of Southern society. A shocking late development in the main plot.

1 Explain how the following excerpt reveals that Scout is advancing on her life journey:

'I must soon enter this world, where on its surface fragrant ladies rocked slowly, fanned gently, and drank cool water. But I was more at home in my father's world. People like Mr Heck Tate did not trap you with innocent questions to make fun of you'.

2 How true is the following statement by Aunt Alexandra about the town and Atticus?

'They're perfectly willing to let him do what they're too afraid to do themselves'.

3 Does Tom Robinson's death bring a sense of humility to Atticus?

Hint: 'I guess Tom was tired of white men's chances'.

Chapter 25

Aftermath of Tom's death; an image that echoes the title.

1 What was the typical reaction to the killing of Tom Robinson?

2 What views did Mr Underwood express in his editorial?

3 What comparison image did he use that relates to the title of the novel?

4 How do you think would Atticus react to the editorial?

Chapter 26

The subplot returns; more hypocrisy.

1 Why do you think is Scout still haunted by Boo?

2 Do you think that Boo is still fearsome, like traditional Gothic villains? Refer to the text.

3 Is it hypocritical for Miss Gates to say of Americans 'we don't believe in persecuting anybody'? Explain your view.

4 Why is Jem so upset at the end of the chapter?

Chapter 27

Life appears to be settling back into a normal pattern, but a lurking villain causes unease.

1 Aunt Alexandra fears Bob Ewell's 'permanent running grudge'. List three events in this chapter that remind us of his sinister nature.

2 Describe Scout and Jem's Halloween preparations.

3 What effect does the final sentence of the chapter have on the reader: 'Thus began our longest journey together'?

Chapter recall

Think about the chapters you have read. Have they progressed the plot? If so, how? Are there any indications of how the plot or characters will develop in the final few chapters?

Focus on Chapter 28

A surprise as the main plot provides a final twist; a decisive moment for the protagonist and villain.

As you read this chapter, make notes in your Portfolio on interesting aspects of setting, character, or how the plot and/or subplot progresses.

Portfolio 15A

Read, write, explore

The following statements will help you to evaluate the effectiveness of a key chapter, elements of plot, characters and images. In groups discuss the questions and agree on a single answer.

1. 'Haints, Hot Steams, incantations, secret signs, had vanished with our years as mist with sunrise.'

   (a) Does this show the reader that the subplot, with its focus on childhood, is reaching an end?

   (b) Explain how the simile helps the reader to understand Scout and Jem's progress.

2. 'A circle of light burst in our faces, and Cecil Jacobs jumped in glee behind it. "Ha-a-a, gotcha!" he shrieked. "Thought you'd be comin' along this way!"'
   How does Cecil's prank foreshadow the ending of the chapter?

3. Select one detail from the visit to the house of horrors that lightens the Halloween atmosphere.

4. How did Scout's reaction to her 'mortification' on stage help save her life later?

5. Does the following add comedy or tension? '"Cecil Jacobs is a big wet he-en!" I yelled suddenly.'

6. How effective are sound effect words in the following?
   'what I thought were trees rustling was the soft swish of cotton on cotton, wheek, wheek, with every step.'

7. Which of the following suggests a real crisis? 'He slowly squeezed the breath out of me' or '"Oh Jem. I forgot my money," I sighed.'

8. How does the following echo the opening sentence of the novel?
   'Jem's arm was dangling crazily in front of him.'

9. Does the chapter end on a cliffhanger moment? Explain.

Harper Lee's use of different verbs

The following sentence uses five verbs in various forms: rip, fall, roll, flounder, escape.

> 'Metal ripped on metal and I fell to the ground and rolled as far as I could, floundering to escape my wire prison.'

Focus on Chapter 29

The subplot reaches a climax.

As you read this chapter, make notes in your Portfolio on interesting aspects of setting, character, or how the plot and/or subplot progresses.

Portfolio 15A

Oral exploration

How does the following show the serious nature of the attack in the schoolyard?

'A shiny clean line stood out on the dull wire. "Bob Ewell meant business," Mr Tate muttered.'

Read the following extract from this chapter.

As I pointed he brought his arms down and pressed the palms of his hands against the wall. They were white hands, sickly white hands that had never seen the sun, so white they stood out garishly against the dull cream wall in the dim light of Jem's room.

I looked from his hands to his sand-stained khaki pants; my eyes travelled up his thin frame to his torn shirt. His face was as white as his hands, but for a shadow on his jutting chin. His cheeks were thin to hollowness; his mouth was wide; there were shallow, almost delicate indentations at his temples, and his grey eyes were so colourless I thought he was blind. His hair was dead and thin, almost feathery on top of his head.

When I pointed to him his palms slipped slightly, leaving greasy sweat streaks on the wall, and he hooked his thumbs in his belt. A strange small spasm shook him, as if he heard fingernails scrape slate, but as I gazed at him in wonder the tension slowly drained from his face. His lips parted into a timid smile, and our neighbour's image blurred with my sudden tears.

'Hey, Boo,' I said.

Read, write, explore

1 In groups of four, discuss how this moment brings the main plot and subplot together and then record an answer.

2 How does the colour white help Scout to realise who the strange-looking person in her house is?

3 Does this description remind you of the 'malevolent phantom' of the exposition or do you feel something very different as you read it? Explain with examples of phrases.

Read to the end

As you read each chapter, make notes in your Portfolio on interesting aspects of setting, character, or how the plot and/or subplot progresses.

Portfolio 15A

Chapter 30

Uncertainty over the fate of Boo resolved.

1 What do Sheriff Tate and Atticus disagree over and why?

2 How does Tate convince Atticus to go along with him?

3 Prepare notes for a few minutes and then speak in favour of either the viewpoint of Atticus or the viewpoint of Heck Tate:

(a) 'If this thing's hushed up it'll be a simple denial to Jem of the way I've tried to raise him … I can't live one way in town and another way in my home.' – Atticus

(b) 'Well, it'd be sort of like shootin' a mockingbird, wouldn't it?' – Heck Tate

Chapter 31

Closure and harmony restored.

1 Explain what Scout means: 'I was beginning to learn his body English.'

2 Does Scout realise here that understanding another human being is the most profound (deepest) type of literacy?

3 How do you feel as reader as Scout escorts the rather frail Boo to his door?

4 Are you shocked when she says, 'I never saw him again', closely followed by 'We had given him nothing, and it made me sad'?

5 Is this a happy or unhappy ending to the subplot? Think before you write.

6 What great new understanding did Scout receive when she stood on the Radley porch?

7 Who is the great protector in the last line of the novel?

Chapter recall

You have now reached the end of the novel. Were you prepared for the final chapters? How did you feel when you finished reading the novel? Record your feelings.

Read the following reviews from newspapers. Do you agree? Discuss and then write your own.

> 'No one ever forgets this book.' *Independent*
>
> 'A rich and remarkable novel.' *Daily Express*
>
> 'One of the best first novels I remember . . . uniquely unsentimental.' *Guardian*

The sequel – Go Set a Watchman

Harper Lee had always said: 'I wrote one good book and that was enough.' However, Lee had first written a novel called *Go Set a Watchman* before she published *To Kill a Mockingbird*. *Go Set a Watchman* is also set in Lee's Maycomb, Alabama, but during the mid-1950s rather than the mid-1930s. The civil rights movement was under way by the time Harper Lee wrote *Go Set a Watchman*.

Though written before *To Kill a Mockingbird*, *Go Set a Watchman* is set twenty years after its final moments:

> 'Yes sir, I understand,' I reassured him. 'Mr Tate was right.'
>
> Atticus disengaged himself and looked at me. 'What do you mean?'
>
> 'Well, it'd be sort of like shootin' a mockingbird, wouldn't it?'
>
> Atticus put his face in my hair and rubbed it. When he got up and walked across the porch into the shadows, his youthful step had returned. Before he went inside the house, he stopped in front of Boo Radley. 'Thank you for my children, Arthur,' he said.

Go Set a Watchman narrates how, twenty years later, Scout, now an adult, has returned to Maycomb from New York to visit Atticus. As a grown-up, Scout has to deal with personal and political issues concerning both her father's outlook on society, and how she feels about her home town during the civil rights era. In the new novel, Scout has a series of flashbacks to her childhood. It is from these flashbacks that the novel *To Kill a Mockingbird* was developed. So *Go Set a Watchman* is the parent book of *To Kill a Mockingbird*. It is very unusual to publish a sequel that was actually written prior to the first book, and to do so after half a century is extraordinary!

Speaking about the manuscript of her new novel, Lee said, 'I hadn't realised it had survived, so was surprised and delighted when my dear friend and lawyer Tonja Carter discovered it. After much thought and hesitation I shared it with a handful of people I trust and was pleased to hear that they considered it worthy of publication.'

Read, write, explore

1 Imagine how Maycomb has changed on Scout's return. List some characters that have moved on. Think of some other characters she could bump into and connect with.

2 Work in groups of four and draw up an imaginary report on some of the changes Scout notices in Maycomb on her return. Agree to share online research on Rosa Parks, the Jim Crow laws and 1950s Alabama before writing the report as a group project.

3 Imagine the adult Scout meets the secret hero of *To Kill a Mockingbird*, Boo Radley, on a street corner. In the light of the ending of *To Kill a Mockingbird*, write the dialogue you imagine would take place after twenty years.

How to prepare and deliver a good speech

Success criteria

⋯⟩ Focus on the connection with the experiences of young people today.

⋯⟩ Have interesting content, referring to key moments, ideas, details and quotes from the novel.

⋯⟩ Connect with your audience in a lively manner, using tone, direct address, contact and gesture.

⋯⟩ Use rhetorical questions, repetition and other devices and address the class.

Student speech

The speech below, though it sounds good, needs a few improvements, as suggested in the side boxes.

Friends, I have decided to talk to you about how the novel *To Kill a Mockingbird* by Harper Lee still has relevance.

Please be quiet.

Which one of us has not seen bullying, gossip and racism in action? Harper Lee included all of these in her novel.

As the novel is about growing up and being yourself, I think it has huge relevance for all of us here today.

Early in the novel Jem touches the Boo Radley's house because of a dare. Foolish dares reminds us of our typical Halloween pranks, right?

Why is this simple action a dare though? Because gossip has turned Boo into a sort of monster figure for the children. Gossip has turned Boo Radley into a scapegoat and a fear figure. Has anyone here ever been bullied or slagged on Facebook or known someone who has? Of course you know what I mean now about Boo. Boo wasn't seen for fifteen years because he embarrassed his family. Rumour states that he stabbed his father with a scissors. As a reader can you believe that rumour? What's the latest rumour in your circle? We know that people are harmed inside themselves when others spread lies about them. In Jem's mind Boo used to eat

> Note the direct appeal to the audience and how the speaker asks questions.
>
> But what three words would you leave out?

> Note that this begins with a statement that is too general.
>
> Where would you insert this quote to improve it: 'Tom was a dead man the minute Mayella Ewell opened her mouth and screamed'.

> Boo is one of three well-used examples from the novel. The speech sounds like an argument. It uses facts well, along with quotes. Though it is good, this section could do with better paragraph divisions. Can you suggest two more?

'mockingbirds'. That shows us how far-fetched rumours can be! Eventually we all learned that Boo was as gentle as a 'raw squirrel'. Once he put a blanket over Scout on a cold dark night and he saved Scout at the end of the novel. He's a special person. So what lesson have we to learn from Boo Radley? Yes, in your minds ye know it now. Don't judge people unless you can walk in their shoes, as Atticus would say. So I'm really glad Ms Brophy gave us the chance to read this book.

> Can you find the two quotes that need to be swapped?

And what about Tom Robinson? The people of Maycomb ganged up on him and believed a liar's evidence, all because of racism. We all know the dangers of being racist, how much it hurts. The novel brought it home to us all, especially this statement: 'In our courts, when it's a white man's word against a black man's, the white man always wins. They're ugly but those are facts of life'. Young people today need to feel prejudice. That's the only way we can be sure of preventing angry mobs from taking the law into their own hands like in Maycomb. The media today often shame people, for the sake of selling papers and getting viewers. This book will help us all to fight against the public shaming of innocent victims.

> What sentence would you replace with: 'Young people today need to feel what it is like to be a victim of prejudice'.

Last but not least class, we all learned to admire Atticus for his wisdom and courage. He said 'a jury is only as sound as the men who make it up'. Well, as young people I'm sure you'll agree that the novel has been character-building for us all. The popular thing is not always the right thing, friends. I rest my case with this eloquent quote:

> The main plot about Tom's trial is well used for the argument. Notice the reference to 'young people today'. The focus on 'relevance' is strong again.

'It's a sin to kill a mockingbird.'

Thanks for your attention this morning.

 Now create a short oral presentation for your class, in which you explore the relevance of *To Kill a Mockingbird* to the experiences of young people today. Use the tips in the boxes to improve on this speech and draft your revised version. Then listen to the much-improved verison and compare.

Blood Brothers

In this unit you will:

⋯⋯⟩ **be guided through the play *Blood Brothers* by ten step-by-step lessons**

- Lesson 1: Social context
- Lesson 2: A moral dilemma
- Lesson 3: Weighing up the odds
- Lesson 4: Fate awaits
- Lesson 5: Changes afoot
- Lesson 6: Schooldays
- Lesson 7: Love is in the air
- Lesson 8: Descent into madness
- Lesson 9: 'I'm not saying a word.'
- Lesson 10: A very sad affair

⋯⋯⟩ **understand the plot, themes and characters**

⋯⋯⟩ **read the *Crescents* interview with Rebecca Storm**

Blood Brothers – The musical

Blood Brothers is a play, which is also performed as a musical and enjoyed by an audience. In this unit you will focus on the plot of the play/musical, the characters and how they develop, and the themes which occur throughout. It was originally written as a play in 1981 for a youth theatre group. The songs were added afterwards and *Blood Brothers*, the musical, was first performed in 1983 in Liverpool. Willie Russell is the playwright, songwriter and composer of the musical score for *Blood Brothers*.

The **book** is the official word given to the text which is not sung in a musical. The words of the songs are referred to as the **lyrics**.

If possible, watch the musical and enjoy the performance. As you watch and listen, make notes on the stage, the costumes and the props. Which is the most memorable song or scene in the musical for you? Why?

This unit on *Blood Brothers* is divided into 10 lessons, each of which guides you through the events of the play/musical. Here is a list of the songs and which lesson they appear in.

Blood Brothers – The songs

Overture	Lesson 2
Marilyn Monroe	Lesson 2
My Child	Lesson 2
Easy Terms	Lesson 3
Shoes Upon the Table	Lesson 3
July 18th (not always sung)	Lesson 4
Kids' Game	Lesson 4
Gypsies in the Wood	Lesson 4
Long Sunday Afternoon/My Friend	Lesson 4
Shoes Upon the Table (again)	Lesson 4
Bright New Day	Lesson 4
Marilyn Monroe	Lesson 5
Secrets	Lesson 6
That Guy	Lesson 7
Summer Sequence	Lesson 9
I'm Not Saying a Word	Lesson 9
One Day in October (not always sung)	Lesson 10
Take a Letter to Miss Jones	Lesson 10
The Robbery (not sung)	Lesson 10
Marilyn Monroe	Lesson 10
Light Romance	Lesson 10
The Council Chamber (not always sung)	Lesson 10
Tell Me It's Not True	Lesson 10

Lesson 1: Social context

 PowerPoint – Pre-reading lesson

Learning intentions

In this lesson you will:

···> learn about Willy Russell and the social context of Liverpool in the 1980s

···> have a class discussion about hard work and success

···> conduct research on the city of Liverpool.

Social and cultural context

The author

Willy Russell was born in Liverpool in 1947. He describes himself as working class. At fifteen, he left school and trained as a hairdresser, but by the age of twenty he had decided to change his career choice and he became a teacher. He loved music and wrote many songs and plays for the radio.

Willy Russell

Liverpool in the 1980s

The play was written in 1981. Margaret Thatcher was the Prime Minister of Great Britain. She made some radical changes to the British manufacturing industry believing it to be 'uncompetitive' due to bad management and trade unions that were too powerful. As a result she sold many publicly owned companies. Coal-mine workers were some of the worst affected.

In Liverpool, the Mersey river (once a source of prosperity) became affected by silting, which led to unemployment and strikes.

Unemployment was rife among the industrialised working class. This led to increased crime levels, poor housing conditions, drug abuse and all sorts of social problems. Observe how some of these are depicted in the play.

Thatcher believed that success came from hard work, denying that it had anything to do with social background or wealth. Willy Russell was political in that throughout the play he challenges some of the political beliefs of the time. While the play is set between the 1950s and the 1970s, many of the issues of the 1980s are dealt with.

Oral exploration

Do you agree that it is only by hard work that we become successful?

Read, write, explore

1 Find out three things that Liverpool is famous for.

2 Write a note about each thing.

3 Find out one unusual or surprising fact about the city.

Lesson 2: A moral dilemma

Learning intentions

In this lesson you will:

···> explore the overture or prologue

···> analyse the characters of
Mrs Johnstone and Mrs Lyons

···> design the set for Act 1.

Overture

Class reading: Read the overture.

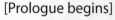

[Prologue begins]
The **Narrator** *steps forward.*

Narrator (*speaking*)	So did y' hear the story of the Johnstone twins?
	As like each other as two new pins,
	Of one womb born, on the self same day,
	How one was kept and one given away?
	An' did you never hear how the Johnstones died,
	Never knowing that they shared one name,
	Till the day they died, when a mother cried
	My own dear sons lie slain?

*The lights come up to show a re-enactment of the final moments of the play – the deaths
of* **Mickey** *and* **Edward**. *The scene fades.*

Narrator	An did y' never hear of the mother, so cruel,
	There's a stone in place of her heart?
	Then bring her on and come judge for yourselves
	How she came to play this part.

The **Narrator** *exits.*

> An **overture** performs
> the same function as a
> **prologue** in a play. It
> often contains the main
> musical theme of the
> work that follows.

Oral exploration

1 Having read this extract, what do you think the musical is about?

2 Why did Mrs Johnstone separate her twins at birth?

3 The play starts with the final moments of the play. Why did the author decide to do
this? Is it a spoiler?

4 How does it compare with the prologue in *Romeo and Juliet*?

5 Make notes of your answers. Write an imaginary summary or synopsis of the
play based on the Prologue.

Portfolio 16A

Before you read

1 Would you walk under a ladder or put shoes on the table? Why? Why not?

2 What does it mean to be superstitious?

3 Can you think of any superstitions?

Class reading: Read up as far as when the Catalogue Man enters.

Oral exploration

1 Having read or listened to Mrs Johnstone's song, does it change our feelings towards her?

2 Why does the milkman refuse to deliver any more milk?

3 What is Mrs Johnstone's job and who does she work for?

4 Who suggests that Mrs Johnstone gives up one of her babies?

Read, write, explore

1 In the section you have read, can you identify any humour? If so, where does it occur and why is it funny?

2 In an attempt to persuade Mrs Johnstone to give up one of the twins, Mrs Lyons identifies several reasons why the child would be better off with her. Name four.

3 Is she taking advantage of Mrs Johnstone? Give reasons for your answer.

4 Why does the narrator say the following? 'There's shoes upon the table and a joker in the pack. The salt's been spilled and a looking glass cracked. There's one lone magpie overhead.'

5 The narrator seems to appear at important moments of the play. Identify two. Why does he appear? What quality does it give him?

6 Why does Mrs Lyons make Mrs Johnstone swear on the Bible?

Create

1 In your Portfolio outline your initial impression of Mrs Johnstone and Mrs Lyons. Consider their personalities, where they live, the way they talk, and how they look.

Portfolio 16B

2 Imagine that you have been asked to design the set for *Blood Brothers*. The director has asked that Mrs Johnstone's house and Mrs Lyons' house are on opposite sides of the stage. Taking this instruction into consideration, draw a rough outline of the set; include props and label your design clearly.

Lesson 3: Weighing up the odds

Learning intentions

In this lesson you will:

···∳ explore colloquialisms in *Blood Brothers*

···∳ think about Mrs Johnstone's decision

···∳ track Mrs Johnstone's thoughts.

Class reading: Read from when the Catalogue Man enters to when Mikey enters, aged seven.

Oral exploration

1 What does 'easy terms' mean?

2 What is meant by 'the never, never'?

3 What do we learn about Mrs Johnstone's spending habits from this extract?

Read, write, explore

1 How does the writer create sympathy for Mrs Johnstone in this extract?

2 Have you changed how you feel about Mrs Lyons?

3 Are Mrs Johnstone's superstitions important in this extract?

4 What do you think is meant when the narrator says, 'the devil's got your number, y' know he's gonna find y''?

5 What is the role of the narrator here?

Create

Thought tracking

In the first person, write four thoughts each that Mrs Johnstone and Mrs Lyons are thinking in this extract. For example:

> **Mrs Johnstone**
> 'I know I am being exploited here but I am so afraid.'

When you are finished, ask the person beside you to read one thought from Mrs Johnstone and then you read one thought from Mrs Lyons. Continue alternating until you have read all their thoughts.
Who do you feel most sympathy for?

> **Mrs Johnstone:**
> *'I know I am being exploited here but I am so afraid.'*

Portfolio 16C

> **Mrs Lyons:**

Lesson 4: Fate awaits

Learning intentions

In this lesson you will:

···⟩ Recap on the events of Act 1
···⟩ Explore how language can reveal character
···⟩ Compare and contrast the characters of Mickey and Edward.

Class reading: Read from Mickey aged seven entering to the end of Act 1.

Revisiting Act 1

Can you remember the sequence of events in Act 1? In which order did the events happen? Below the sequence of events from Act 1 is jumbled up. Put the events into the correct sequence, then write the correct order in your Portfolio.

Portfolio 16D

- The Johnstones move to the country.
- It is seven years since Mrs Johnstone gave Edward away and the twins are reunited; they get on famously.
- Mrs Johnstone starts to work for Mrs Lyons.
- The boys become blood brothers.
- Mrs Lyons suggests that Mrs Johnstone gives her one of her babies as she is unable to have children.
- Mrs Lyons breaks her contract with Mrs Johnstone, gives her some money and asks her to leave the house and never return.

- Mrs Johnstone can't afford to pay the milkman.
- Edward has to move and Mrs Johnstone gives him her locket.
- Mrs Johnstone swears on the Bible that she will never tell anyone about the pact she made with Mrs Lyons.
- The narrator enters and describes the events that are about to unfurl.
- Unable to cope with the boys being friends, Mrs Lyons insists that they must move away.
- Mrs Johnstone agrees to give Mrs Lyons one of her twins when they are born.

Mickey and Edward

Mickey has just referred to the 'f' word.

Edward	What does it mean?
Mickey	I don't know, it sounds good though, doesn't it?
Edward	Fantastic, when I get home I'll look it up in the dictionary.
Mickey	In the what?
Edward	The dictionary. Don't you know what a dictionary is?
Mickey	I do…it's a, it's a thingy, innit?
Edward	A book which explains the meaning of words.
Mickey	The meaning of words, yeh.

 Animation – Homophones

Oral exploration

1 What does this exchange reveal about the boys' education and upbringing?

2 Identify some examples of how Edward's use of language and manner is different from Mickey's and Mrs Johnstone's.

Read, write, explore

Portfolio 16E

1 Think of as many words as you can to describe Mickey and Edward. Before you record them in your Portfolio, explain to the person beside you why you chose that word.

Portfolio 16F

2 In the chart in your Portfolio, outline the differences between Mickey and Edward.

3 Describe how the policeman deals with Mrs Johnstone and Mr and Mrs Lyons. Why does he treat them differently? Is this fair?

Oral exploration

You come home and your mother is sitting at the kitchen table. She asks you to join her as there is something she would like to tell you. You sense that something is wrong. She asks you about your day but you know that she is not really listening to your response. Then she drops a bombshell…'We are moving'.

Discuss your reaction with the person beside you. How do you feel? What will you do? What are your fears? Compare your reaction to Edward's and then to Mickey's reaction.

Create

In your Portfolio, write three paragraphs on one of the following:

Portfolio 16G

● I think Edward is the lucky one because…
● I think Mickey is the lucky one because…
● I'm not sure if either of the boys is lucky…

> **Each paragraph should have 'PEE':**
>
> **P** – a point
> **E** – an example (quotation or reference from the text)
> **E** – an explanation

Lesson 5: Changes afoot

Learning intentions

In this lesson you will:

····⟩ outline the changes to the characters and their personalities

····⟩ examine the change of setting

····⟩ write a police report.

Class reading: Read Act 2 up to the point where Mickey hands his money to the bus conductor, then discuss the questions below.

Oral exploration

1 How many years have passed since Act 1?

2 Mrs Johnstone makes a remark about Mickey being 'that' age. Do teenagers deserve their reputation for being difficult to handle?

3 Mrs Johnstone is using her charm in their new home. Give two examples of this.

4 What type of school does Edward attend?

Read, write, explore

1 List three changes in Mrs Johnstone's life, two changes in Mickey's life and one thing we learn about Sammy.

2 Mrs Jones and Edward seem happy. What indicates this?

3 How is Edward's relationship with Mrs Lyons different from Mickey's relationship with Mrs Johnstone?

4 How has Linda's relationship with Mickey developed?

5 The bus conductor reminds us of the past. What is his message?

Read on: Read as far as where Edward is confronted by a teacher in school.

Create

Imagine that you are the police officer that the bus conductor spoke to after Sammy threatened him with the knife. Write up your report on the incident for your supervisor. Use the police report in your Portfolio.

Portfolio 16H

Lesson 6: Schooldays

Learning intentions

In this lesson you will:

- compare the characters of Mickey and Edward
- discuss the writer's views on society
- identify dramatic irony
- re-examine the role of the narrator.

Class reading: Read as far as Mickey and Linda making their way up the hill.

Dramatic irony

Dramatic irony is a plot device used by playwrights to heighten drama. It results in the audience having greater insights into character and the plot than the characters themselves. A simple way of thinking about dramatic irony is to think of traditional pantomime where the baddie reveals himself to the audience but not to the characters on stage. This frequently leads to the audience attempting to let the characters know by screaming, 'He's behind you!'

Oral exploration

1. What are the similarities between the boys at this stage?
2. What point about society is Russell trying to make in this section?
3. Can you spot the example of dramatic irony in this section?
4. The narrator reappears at the end of the scene. What is his purpose?
5. What do we learn about the two boys in this section?

Create

Imagine that you are Mickey and Edward. Write two diary entries in your Portfolio outlining your day at school. Remember the different registers, word choice and language of the boys; these should be reflected in the diaries.

Portfolio 16I

Checklist

Ensure the following:

- ✓ that the diary entry feels like the character has written it
- ✓ that you use your imagination
- ✓ that the language and tone used sound like the type of language Mickey and Edward would use
- ✓ that it makes sense and reads well
- ✓ that there are no spelling, grammar or punctuation errors.

Lesson 7: Love is in the air

Learning intentions

In this lesson you will:

···▸ examine the role of soliloquies and monologues and create your own
···▸ look at the role of music in the play
···▸ revisit dramatic irony.

Class reading: Read up to the point where Mrs Lyons appears in Mrs Johnstone's kitchen.

Monologues versus soliloquies

Both monologues and soliloquies are solo pieces of dialogue delivered by an actor within a play. A monologue is intended to be heard by **both** the audience and the actors on stage, whereas a soliloquy is a self-reflective piece delivered for the attention of the audience and the actor delivering the lines **only**.

It is for this reason that the contents of the soliloquy are truthful and honest, regardless of the character's nature (this is assuming that the characters wouldn't lie to themselves). It is as if the character were thinking out loud. It gives us a greater insight into what is going on inside the character's head.

Can you think of any soliloquies or monologues you have come across?

Oral exploration

In this scene, Mickey gives us an insight into his true feelings towards Linda. Read how he expresses the things he wants to do and say to her but can't. Read the passage below. Is this a monologue or a soliloquy?

Mickey	What…Linda…Linda…Don't…Linda, I wanna kiss y', an' put me arms around y' and kiss y' and kiss y' and even fornicate with y' but I don't know how to tell y', because I've got pimples an' me feet are too big an' me bum sticks out an'…

Create

1 Imagine that you are Mickey. You are fed up with your inability to show Linda how you feel. You decide to give yourself a pep talk to boost your confidence so that you can talk to her. Think for a few moments.

Portfolio 16J

Record on the board some lines that you might tell yourself. Use your favourite ones to create the perfect pep talk.

2 **Linda's monologue**

Mickey and Linda's relationship has developed somewhat but isn't perfect. They don't seem to be on the same page despite the fact that they really like each other. In your Portfolio create a monologue or soliloquy (the expression of the character's inner thoughts and feelings) for Linda, expressing to the audience how she really feels about Mickey.

Portfolio 16K

Oral exploration

Refer to the explanation of dramatic irony on page 406. What does the song 'That Guy' reveal about being a fourteen-year-old boy? Can you see any trace of dramatic irony in the song?

Read, write, explore

1 Can you remember back to when the boys met when they were seven? How does this meeting, seven years on, resemble that?

2 Why, do you think, does Mrs Johnstone let the boys hang around together?

3 Were you surprised by her reaction to the cinema? What does it tell us about her relationship with Mickey?

Lesson 8: Descent into madness

Learning intentions

In this lesson you will:

- consider where the characters are placed on the stage
- describe and discuss music and sound effects
- examine the language and dialogue
- analyse how Russell presents the relationship between the two women
- track Mrs Lyons' descent into madness.

Class reading: Read up to the point where Mickey and Edward emerge from the cinema.

Oral exploration

1 This is a very dramatic scene between Mrs Johnstone and Mrs Lyons. In order to appreciate fully how the drama was created you must see how Russell achieves it. Form four groups. Each group must make at least two points about their area.

Group One	Look at how he presents the relationship between the two women
Group Two	Look at language and dialogue
Group Three	Look at music and sound effects
Group Four	Look at where the characters are placed on the stage

As the chairperson from each group delivers their feedback, make notes in your Portfolio.

Portfolio 16L

2 From this scene, find three quotations that indicate that Mrs Lyons is descending into madness.

Lesson 9: 'I'm not saying a word.'

Learning intentions

In this lesson you will:

···❯ revisit the characters of Edward and Mickey

···❯ explore their relationship with Linda

···❯ discuss how Russell uses song to develop character and comment on society

···❯ outline the differences between the two boys

···❯ examine the use of the theatrical device of 'dual action'.

Class reading: Read up to the point where Mickey and Linda exit and we are in Mrs Johnstone's house.

Oral exploration

1 Four years pass quickly and we read about the joys of being this age; however, the scene is tainted with hints of doom. Can you identify these?

2 The title of Edward's song is 'I'm Not Saying a Word'. Is this in any way significant in the wider context of the play?

3 In Act 1 we recorded the similarities and difference between Edward and Mickey. Would you add anything in light of recent scenes?

Read, write, explore

1 Edward and Mickey are both attracted to Linda. Outline the similarities and differences in the way they treat her.

2 Find two quotations that reveal how Edward feels about Linda and two quotations that reveal how Mickey feels about her.

Class reading: Read up to the point where Mickey is nervously keeping lookout for Sammy.

Oral exploration

1 Discuss Mrs Johnstone's reaction when Mickey tells her about Linda being pregnant. Is it credible? What does it tell us about Mrs Johnstone?

2 What does the song 'Miss Jones' reveal about Mr Lyons? Is Russell making a wider point about society here?

Read, write, explore

1 Lots of things have changed between Mickey and Edward since Edward has gone to college. Make a list of these changes.

2 How does Russell show the differences between them?

3 Russell uses dual action when Edward asks Linda to marry him and Sammy asks Mickey to do 'a job' for him. What is the effect of this on the audience?

Lesson 10: A very sad affair

Learning intentions

In this lesson you will:

···⟩ track Mickey's character development

···⟩ explore Linda's feelings towards him

···⟩ examine the 'affair' and how it changes everything

···⟩ revisit the prologue/overture.

Class reading: Read to the end of the play.

Oral exploration

1 We are used to a very playful, energetic Mickey. How does the audience react to him when he is depressed?

2 What does the incident of the tablets reveal about Linda's feelings for Mickey?

3 Were you surprised that Linda would have an affair with Edward? Does it change the way you feel about Linda?

4 What was Mrs Lyons' motivation for telling Mickey about the affair?

5 Why did Russell make the play end as it began?

Read, write, explore

1 Create a timeline of what happens in this scene.

2 Think of the games that they played when they were children. How does the narrator link the robbery to these games?

3 Mickey goes to find Edward after he hears about the affair. How is the tension created here?

4 What do Mickey's final words reveal about the important ideas in the play?

The playwright and the play

You have now read the complete play, a play which reflects the life experience of its author. In the light of your full reading, find moments from the play that seem to be influenced by Russell's early life experience.

1 It is said that Willy Russell's childhood memories of growing up in the working-class north of England help to shape the atmosphere and events of the play.

> Find examples of an event and an atmosphere that you found in the play to illustrate this.

2 Russell left school early and worked as a hairdresser but eventually went to work in a factory to raise the extra money to get a college education. Immediately he felt the inequality between managers and workers.

> Can you remember a good moment in the play where the difference between social classes was important to explain **how a character behaved** and as **a cause of conflict**?

3 Russell understood that being well-off allows people the freedom to achieve aims and ambitions.

> Can you remember a moment in the play that demonstrates this point?

4 Russell understood that being poor limits the freedom to achieve aims and ambitions.

> Can you remember a moment in the play that demonstrates this point?

5 Russell loved music and was a member of a band.

> Can you remember a moment in the play that demonstrates this point?

6 'I was brought up as a member of a class whose members were treated like second-class citizens.'

> Does this biographical statement by Russell help you to find a theme in the play? Explain.

Rebecca Storm – Blood Brothers

Over the past thirty years Rebecca Storm has established herself as one of the most popular leading ladies in musical theatre, playing some of the most demanding roles, including Eva Peron in *Evita*, Fantine in *Les Misérables*, Florence in *Chess*, Rose in *Aspects of Love*, Edith Piaf in *Piaf*, Joan of Arc in *Jeanne* and most recently Miss Hannigan in *Annie*.

At twenty-three she auditioned for her first musical *Blood Brothers* and although she was a little young to play Mrs Johnstone – Liverpudlian Catholic mother of seven children – author Willy Russell was so captivated by her voice that he insisted wardrobe and make-up went to work to 'age' the young actress. Her portrayal of Mrs Johnstone has become so popular that she still returns to the role after 27 years.

Crescents interview

Q   What is your favourite song from *Blood Brothers* and why?

A   I love all the songs from *Blood Brothers* and I especially love the way that they are all so different and yet have that wonderful thread of folk song that Willy Russell writes so brilliantly. I'm sure most people would expect me to say the final anthem 'Tell Me It's Not True', but one of my absolute favourite moments in the show is when I reprise the melody of 'Easy Terms' with a new lyric for 'Light Romance' – Linda meets Eddie and pours out her broken heart. Originally Willy wrote the song for Linda to sing but I'm so glad he changed his mind and gave it to Mrs Johnstone!

Q   Who is your favourite character and why?

A   I truly love every character in *Blood Brothers*. Willy Russell introduces them all at the perfect time and gives us the chance to get to know them well. Back in 1984 I learned so much from actors such as Peter Capaldi, Ian Puleston-Davies, Judy Holt, Mark and Joe McGann. I was blessed with a truly amazing cast, but when Willy Russell himself played the Narrator for the Liverpool season he gave that role a resonance that has stayed with me to this day.

Q   What are your feelings towards Mrs Johnstone?

A   Audiences love and admire this funny, realistic character and care for her through the ups and downs of her life. There have been thousands and thousands of real-life Mrs Johnstones and I'm thrilled to have been given the opportunity to tell their story in this amazing show.

Q Has your approach to this role changed as you have grown older?

A I'd like to think that I've improved a little in these last thirty years! Having returned to the role in fourteen different productions, I think I've found something new each time. It may be small and perhaps not that obvious, but life experiences can make you feel differently in your heart and therefore perform a song or a scene in a slightly different way.

Q What is it about *Blood Brothers* that makes it so appealing to the modern audience?

A *Blood Brothers* is a story about real people, real life and real problems such as unemployment, young pregnancy, poverty, crime and all of the consequences that can transpire. It's also about the more well-off who may appear to 'have it all' but actually don't. Through all of this it manages to be extremely funny and touching, whether you're eight or eighty years old. In my opinion every single person in the audience can identify with and understand at least one character in the play. The story begins in the 1950s but is still extraordinarily relevant today.

Q *Blood Brothers* was originally written as a stage play. What do you think the later addition of music brought to the production?

A It's wonderful to know that so much of Willy Russell's writing is now part of the school curriculum. The script stands up as a testament to his genius. I have only been involved with *Blood Brother*s as a musical production and I feel that the songs enhance the storyline, the characters and the depth of the piece.

Read, write, explore

1 What is your favourite song from *Blood Brothers* and why? Refer to page 397 for an outline of the songs.

2 In your opinion, why might Willy Russell have a 'resonance' for Rebecca in the way he plays the narrator?

3 Do you agree with Rebecca Storm's assessment of audiences' response to Mrs Johnstone: 'audiences love and admire this funny, realistic character and care for her through the ups and downs of her life'? Give a reason for your answer.

4 What impression do you get of Rebecca Storm from the interview?

5 What do you think Rebecca Storm means when she says: 'life experiences can make you feel differently in your heart and therefore perform a song or a scene in a slightly different way'?

6 Choose a scene from *Blood Brothers* that you think she may play differently today compared to how she played it for the first time. Give a brief outline of the scene and state how and why she might play it differently.

7 Does *Blood Brothers* appeal to a modern audience? Why? Why not?

8 What question would you have asked Rebecca Storm if you were interviewing her? Refer to Unit 12, page 301 for tips on asking questions.

Create – Human storyboard

In this activity you will be asked to get up on your feet and step into the world of the characters to create a human storyboard. In groups of five, you will create freeze-frames for each of the key moments in *Blood Brothers*. There must be at least six key moments but you can have more. These will form the basis of your own freeze-frame summary of *Blood Brothers*. A member of the group will photograph your freeze-frames and upload the photos to PowerPoint or another program of your choice, then upload the storyboard to your e-Portfolio.

Note for Teachers: You will find step-by-step guidelines for this activity in your *How to Create an e-Portfolio* e-book. Log on to www.edcodigital.ie to access the e-book.

Work in pairs to prepare and deliver a short oral presentation based on your experience of the differences between the worlds of Mickey and Edward and how these differences affected their chances in life. Take turns at presenting.

Portfolio 16M

Title of presentation: Different lifestyles – Different chances

Main points

···> Home life and treatment by parents
···> School and education
···> The way they speak and use language
···> Treatment by the police
···> Where they live

Interview with Mrs Johnstone or Mrs Lyons

The play has ended and the tragedy has happened. You are a reporter sent by your newspaper to interview one of the bereaved mothers. You know the background to the story but want to find out how the mother feels now.

Portfolio 16N

Here are some sample questions you might ask. Remember to base your answers on the words and events of the play. Refer to Unit 12, page 301, for tips on asking questions.

Mrs Johnstone

1 Tell us your fondest memory of your son.
2 Why did you decide to part with one of the twins?
3 How hard was it to make the decision?
4 Do you have any sympathy now for Mrs Lyons? Why?
5 Do you take any blame for the tragedy or do you blame the class system?

Mrs Lyons

1 Tell us your fondest memory of your son.
2 Do you think that you treated Mrs Johnstone fairly in taking one of the twins?
3 You found it impossible to keep Edward away from Mickey. Why was this?
4 Do you think that you made the right decision in taking Edward? Why? Why not?
5 If you could say something to Mrs Johnstone in order to make up with her, what would it be?

Index

Acknowledgements

The authors and publisher would like to thank the following for copyright permission to reproduce the following material:

'Easkey: surf's new role model' reproduced courtesy of the writer, Sophie White, first published in the *Sunday Independent, Living,* 24 December 2012; 'Rescuers save the whales' by Ted Creedon, reproduced by permission of the author and *The Kerryman*; 'Fishermen rescue massive family of 70 dolphins beached in west Kerry' by Nicky Ryan reproduced by permission of *TheJournal.ie*; 'Christmas Charity Appeal 2012: "Let's keep the Paralympic legacy going and change lives"' © Telegraph Media Group Limited 2012; Extract from *Small Wars Permitting: Dispatches from Foreign Lands* by Christina Lamb (HarperPress, 2008); Extract from *Marley and Me* by John Grogan (Hodder & Stoughton, 2007); Extract from THE TEST by Brian O'Driscoll (Penguin Ireland 2014) Copyright © Brian O'Driscoll, 2014; 'Symptom Recital', copyright 1926, renewed (c) 1954 by Dorothy Parker, from THE PORTABLE DOROTHY PARKER by Dorothy Parker, edited by Marion Meade. Used by permission of Viking Penguin, a division of Penguin Group (USA) LLC.; 'The Choosing' by Liz Lochhead from *The Choosing* is reproduced by permission of Polygon, an imprint of Birlinn Ltd (www. Birlinn.co.uk); 'Poem from a Three Year Old' by Brendan Kennelly from *Familiar Strangers: New & Selected Poems 1960–2004* reprinted by permission of Bloodaxe Books; 'A Final Appointment' by Eric Finney reprinted by permission of the author; 'The House at Night' by James Kirkup reprinted by permission of The James Kirkup Collection; 'Hot Food' by Michael Rosen (© Michael Rosen 2014) is printed by permission of United Agents (www.unitedagents.co.uk) on behalf of the Author; 'Exam' by Michael Rosen (© Michael Rosen 2014) is printed by permission of United Agents (www.unitedagents.co.uk) on behalf of the Author; 'Federal Case' by Julie O'Callaghan from *Tell Me This Is Normal: New & Selected Poems* reprinted by permission of Bloodaxe Books; Li-Young Lee, 'From Blossoms' from *Rose*. Copyright © 1986 by Li-Young Lee. Reprinted with the permission of The Permissions Company, Inc., on behalf of BOA Editions, Ltd., www.boaeditions.org; 'Gift' by Czesław Miłosz from *New and Collected Poems: 1931–2001* (Ecco, 2003) ; 'A Summer Morning' from ADVICE TO A PROPHET AND OTHER POEMS by Richard Wilbur. Copyright © 1961, renewed 1989 by Richard Wilbur. Used by permission of Houghton Mifflin Harcourt Publishing Company. All Rights Reserved; Billy Collins, 'Another Reason I Don't Keep a Gun in the House' from *The Apple That Astonished Paris*. Copyright © 1988, 1996 by Billy Collins. Reprinted with the permission of The Permissions Company, Inc., on behalf of the University of Arkansas Press, www.uapress.com; 'In Memory of my Mother' by Patrick Kavanagh is reprinted from *Collected Poems*, edited by Antoinette Quinn (Allen Lane, 2004) by kind permission of the Trustees of the Estate of the Late Katherine B. Kavanagh, through the Jonathan Williams Literary Agency; 'Base Details' by Siegfried Sassoon © Siegfried Sassoon by kind permission of the Estate of George Sassoon; *The Ballad Of Springhill* written by Peggy Seeger, Published by Harmony Music Ltd, reprinted by permission of Bucks Music Group; 'The Listeners' by Walter de la Mare reprinted by permission of The Literary Trustees of Walter de la Mare and The Society of Authors as their representative; 'Escape to Nowhere' written by Kate O'Connor and reprinted by permission; Extracts and images *Son of Rambow* reprinted by permission of Hammer & Tongs; *Odd Socks* by James Butler reprinted with permission of the author; Extract from *The Shadow of a Gunman* by Sean O'Casey reprinted by permission of Faber and Faber Ltd.; Extract from *Noughts & Crosses* by Malorie Blackman adapted by Dominic Cooke (Oxford Playscripts, OUP, 2008), copyright © Dominic Cooke, 2008, reprinted by permission of Oxford University Press; *Heartbreak House* by George Bernard Shaw reprinted by permission of The Society of Authors, on behalf of the Bernard Shaw Estate; 'First Confession' from Collected Stories by Frank O'Connor reprinted by permission of Peters Fraser & Dunlop (www.petersfraserdunlop.com) on behalf of the Estate of Frank O'Connor; 'Christmas Morning' from Collected Stories by Frank O'Connor reprinted by permission of Peters Fraser & Dunlop (www.petersfraserdunlop.com) on behalf of the Estate of Frank O'Connor; 'The Confirmation Suit' by Brendan Behan from *After the Wake* reprinted by permission of The Sayle Literary Agency on behalf of The Estate of Brendan Behan; 'Still I Rise' and AND I STILL RISE by Maya Angelou, copyright © 1978 by Maya Angelou, reprinted by permission of Virago, an imprint of Little, Brown Book Group, digital rights used by permission of Random House, an imprint of and division of Penguin Random House LLC, All rights reserved, additional rights used by permission of Random House Audio Publishing Group, a division of Penguin Random House LLC. All rights reserved. ; 'Touched by an Angel' by Maya Angelou from *A Brave and Startling Truth* (Random House, 1995) reprinted by permission of CMG; 'Caged Bird' from SHAKER, WHY DON'T YOU SING? by Maya Angelou, reprinted by permission of Virago, an imprint of Little, Brown Book Group, additional rights used by permission of Random House, an imprint of Penguin Random House LLC. All rights reserved; 'Brother, Can You Spare a Dime?' Words By E. Y. Harburg, Music By Jay Gorney ©1932 (Renewed) Wb Music Corp. (ASCAP); Extracts from *Blood Brothers* by Willy Russell, Methuen Drama 2001 © Willy Russell 2001, reprinted by permission of Methuen Drama an imprint of Bloomsbury Publishing plc; 'What has happened to Lulu?', 'My Mother Saw a Dancing Bear', 'Timothy Winters', and 'Who?' by Charles Causley from *I Had a Little Cat: Collected Poems for Children* (Macmillan Children's Books) reprinted by permission of David Higham and Associates; 'Barbaric act of cruelty on vulnerable puppy' reprinted by permission of ISPCA; 'Animal Circuses are a shameful cruelty that you should avoid funding' by Aaron McKenna reprinted by permission of *TheJournal.ie*; 'Irishman Roche keen to explore a new life on Mars' by Jonathan deBurca Butler reprinted by permission of *The Irish Examiner*; 'Digging' from *Selected Poems 1965–1975* by Seamus Heaney reprinted by permission of Faber and Faber Ltd; 'In Memoriam M.K.H., 1911–1984' from *Clearances 3* by Seamus Heaney reprinted by permission of Faber and Faber Ltd; 'A Kite for Aibhín' from *Human Chain* by Seamus Heaney reprinted by permission of Faber and Faber Ltd; 'Twice Shy', 'Scaffolding' from *Death of a Naturalist* by Seamus Heaney reprinted by permission of Faber and Faber Ltd; 'What was it about Seamus Heaney that endeared him to so many?' by Shane Breslin reprinted by permission of the author; 'Oliver Has an Interview' by Mark Yeow reprinted by permission of the author; 'Professor Panini' written by Matthew Grigg; 'The Imperfectionist' written by Paul Sohn; Extracts from TO KILL A MOCKINGBIRD by Harper Lee, published by William Heinemann, reprinted by permission of The Random House Group Limited.; Extracts from *Blood Brothers* by Willy Russell, Methuen Drama 2001 © Willy Russell 2001, reprinted by permission of Methuen Drama, an imprint of Bloomsbury Publishing plc

Notes